Disability KEY ISSUES AND FUTURE DIRECTIONS

ETHICS, LAW, AND POLICY

The SAGE Reference Series on Disability: Key Issues and Future Directions

Series Editor: Gary L. Albrecht

Arts and Humanities, by Brenda Jo Brueggemann
Assistive Technology and Science, by Cathy Bodine
Disability Through the Life Course, by Tamar Heller and Sarah Parker Harris
Education, by Cheryl Hanley-Maxwell and Lana Collet-Klingenberg
Employment and Work, by Susanne M. Bruyère and Linda Barrington
Ethics, Law, and Policy, by Jerome E. Bickenbach
Health and Medicine, by Ross M. Mullner
Rehabilitation Interventions, by Margaret A. Turk and Nancy R. Mudrick

Disability KEY ISSUES AND FUTURE DIRECTIONS

ETHICS, LAW, AND POLICY

Jerome E. Bickenbach
Schweizer Paraplegiker-Forschung

SERIES EDITOR
Gary L. Albrecht
University of Illinois at Chicago

Los Angeles | London | New Delhi
Singapore | Washington DC

Los Angeles | London | New Delhi
Singapore | Washington DC

FOR INFORMATION:

SAGE Publications, Inc.
2455 Teller Road
Thousand Oaks, California 91320
E-mail: order@sagepub.com

SAGE Publications Ltd.
1 Oliver's Yard
55 City Road
London EC1Y 1SP
United Kingdom

SAGE Publications India Pvt. Ltd.
B 1/I 1 Mohan Cooperative Industrial Area
Mathura Road, New Delhi 110 044
India

SAGE Publications Asia-Pacific Pte. Ltd.
33 Pekin Street #02-01
Far East Square
Singapore 048763

Publisher: Rolf A. Janke
Acquisitions Editor: Jim Brace-Thompson
Assistant to the Publisher: Michele Thompson
Project Development, Editing, & Management:
    Kevin Hillstrom, Laurie Collier Hillstrom
Production Editor: Jane Haenel
Reference Systems Manager: Leticia Gutierrez
Reference Systems Coordinator: Laura Notton
Typesetter: C&M Digitals (P) Ltd.
Proofreader: Ellen Howard
Indexer: Terri Corry
Cover Designer: Gail Buschman
Marketing Manager: Kristi Ward

Printed in the United States of America.

Library of Congress Cataloging-in-Publication Data

Bickenbach, Jerome Edmund. Ethics, law, and
policy / Jerome E. Bickenbach.

p. cm.—(The SAGE reference series on
disability: key issues and future directions)

Includes bibliographical references and index.

ISBN 978-1-4129-8747-9 (cloth : alk. paper)

1. People with disabilities. 2. People with
disabilities—Legal status, laws, etc. 3. People
with disabilities—Government policy. 4. Ethics.
I. Title.

HV1568.B53 2012
362.4′04561—dc23   2011019186

12 13 14 15 16   10 9 8 7 6 5 4 3 2 1

Contents

I dedicate this book to Alarcos Cieza, colleague and friend.

Series Introduction

T he SAGE Reference Series on Disability appears at a time when global attention is being focused on disability at all levels of society. Researchers, service providers, and policymakers are concerned with the prevalence, experience, meanings, and costs of disability because of the growing impact of disability on individuals and their families and subsequent increased demand for services (Banta & de Wit, 2008; Martin, Freedman, Schoeni, & Andreski, 2010; Mont, 2007; Whitaker, 2010). For their part, disabled people and their families are keenly interested in taking a more proactive stance in recognizing and dealing with disability in their lives (Charlton, 1998; Iezzoni & O'Day, 2006). As a result, there is burgeoning literature, heightened Web activity, myriad Internet information and discussion groups, and new policy proposals and programs designed to produce evidence and disseminate information so that people with disabilities may be informed and live more independently (see, for example, the World Institute of Disability Web site at http://www.wid.org, the Center for International Rehabilitation Research Information and Exchange Web site at http://cirrie.buffalo.edu, and the Web portal to caregiver support groups at http://www.caregiver.com/regionalresources/index.htm).

Disability is recognized as a critical medical and social problem in current society, central to the discussions of health care and social welfare policies taking place around the world. The prominence of these disability issues is highlighted by the attention given to them by the most respected national and international organizations. The *World Report on Disability* (2011), co-sponsored by the World Health Organization (WHO) and the World Bank and based on an analysis of surveys from over 100 countries, estimates that 15% of the world's population (more than 1 billion people) currently experiences disability. This is the best prevalence estimate available today and indicates a marked increase over previous epidemiological calculations. Based on this work, the British medical journal *Lancet* dedicated an entire issue (November 28, 2009) to disability, focusing attention on the salience of the problem for health care systems worldwide. In addition, the WHO has developed community-based rehabilitation principles and strategies which are applicable to communities of diverse cultures and at all levels of development (WHO, 2010). The World Bank is concerned because of the link between disability and poverty (World Bank, 2004). Disability, in their view, could be a major impediment to economic development, particularly in emerging economies.

Efforts to address the problem of disability also have legal and human rights implications. Being disabled has historically led to discrimination, stigma, and dependency, which diminish an individual's full rights to citizenship and equality (European Disability Forum, 2003). In response to these concerns, the United Nations Convention on the Rights of Persons with Disabilities (2008) and the European Union Disability Strategy embodying the Charter of Fundamental Rights (2000) were passed to affirm that disabled people have the right to acquire and change nationalities, cannot be deprived of their ability to exercise liberty, have freedom of movement, are free to leave any country including their own, are not deprived of the right to enter their own country, and have access to the welfare and benefits afforded to any citizen of their country. As of March 31, 2010, 144 nations—including the United States, China, India, and Russia—had signed the U.N. Convention, and the European Disability Strategy had been ratified by all members of the European Community. These international agreements supplement and elaborate disability rights legislation such as the Americans with Disabilities Act of 1990 and its amendments, the U.K. Disability Discrimination Act of 1995, and the Disabled Person's Fundamental Law of Japan, revised in 1993.

In the United States, the Institute of Medicine of the National Academy of Sciences has persistently focused attention on the medical, public health, and social policy aspects of disability in a broad-ranging series of reports: *Disability in America* (1991), *Enabling America* (1997), *The Dynamics of Disability: Measuring and Monitoring Disability for Social Security Programs,* (2002), *The Future of Disability in America* (2007), and *Improving the Presumptive Disability Decision-Making Process for Veterans* (2008). The Centers for Disease Control have a long-standing interest in diabetes and obesity because of their effects on morbidity, mortality, and disability. Current data show that the incidence and prevalence of obesity is rising across all age groups in the United States, that obesity is related to diabetes, which is also on the rise, and that both, taken together, increase the likelihood of experiencing disability (Bleich et al., in press; Gill et al., 2010). People with diabetes also are likely to have comorbid depression, which increases their chances of functional disability (Egede, 2004).

Depression and other types of mental illness—like anxiety disorders, alcohol and drug dependence, and impulse-control disorders—are more prevalent than previously thought and often result in disability (Kessler & Wang, 2008). The prevalence of mental disorders in the United States is high, with about half of the population meeting criteria (as measured by the *Diagnostic and Statistical Manual of Mental Disorders*, or DSM-IV) for one more disorders in their lifetimes, and more than one-quarter of the population meeting criteria for a disorder in any single year. The more severe mental disorders are strongly associated with high comorbidity, resulting in disability.

Major American foundations with significant health portfolios have also turned their attention to disability. The Bill and Melinda Gates Foundation has directed considerable resources to eliminate disability-causing parasitic and communicable diseases such as malaria, elephantiasis, and river blindness. These efforts are designed to prevent and control disability-causing conditions in the developing world that inhibit personal independence and economic development. The Robert Wood Johnson Foundation has a long-standing program on self-determination for people with developmental disabilities in the United States aimed at increasing their ability to participate fully in society, and the Hogg Foundation is dedicated to improving mental health awareness and services. Taken in concert, these activities underscore the recognized importance of disability in the present world.

Disability Concepts, Models, and Theories

There is an immense literature on disability concepts, models, and theories. An in-depth look at these issues and controversies can be found in the *Handbook of Disability Studies* (Albrecht, Seelman, & Bury, 2001), in the *Encyclopedia of Disability* (Albrecht, 2006), and in "The Sociology of Disability: Historical Foundations and Future Directions" (Albrecht, 2010). For the purposes of this reference series, it is useful to know that the World Health Organization, in the International Classification of Functioning, Disability and Health (ICF), defines disability as "an umbrella term for impairments, activity limitations or participation restrictions" (WHO, 2001, p. 3). ICF also lists environmental factors that interact with all these constructs. Further, the WHO defines impairments as "problems in body function or structure such as significant deviation or loss"; activity limitations as "difficulties an individual may have in executing activities"; participation as "involvement in a life situation"; and environmental factors as those components of "the physical, social and attitudinal environment in which people live and conduct their lives" (WHO, 2001, p. 10). The U.N. Convention on the Rights of Persons with Disabilities, in turn, defines disability as including "those who have long-term physical, mental, intellectual or sensory impairments which in interaction with various barriers may hinder their full and effective participation in society on an equal basis with others." In the introduction to the *Lancet* special issue on disability, Officer and Groce (2009) conclude that "both the ICF and the Convention view disability as the outcome of complex interactions between health conditions and features of an individual's physical, social, and attitudinal environment that hinder their full and effective participation in society" (p. 1795). Hence, disability scholars and activists alike are concerned with breaking down physical, environmental, economic, and social barriers so that disabled people can live independently and participate as fully as possible in society.

Types of Disability

Interest in disability by medical practitioners has traditionally been condition specific (such as spinal cord injury or disabilities due to heart disease), reflecting the medical model approach to training and disease taxonomies. Similarly, disabled people and their families are often most concerned about their particular conditions and how best to deal with them. The SAGE Reference Series on Disability recognizes that there are a broad range of disabilities that can be generally conceived of as falling in the categories of physical, mental, intellectual, and sensory disabilities. In practice, disabled persons may have more than one disability and are often difficult to place in one disability category. For instance, a spinal-cord injured individual might experience depression, and a person with multiple sclerosis may simultaneously deal with physical and sensory disabilities. It is also important to note that disabilities are dynamic. People do experience different rates of onset, progression, remission, and even transition from being disabled at one point in time, to not being disabled at another, to being disabled again. Examples of this change in disability status include disability due to bouts of arthritis, Guillain-Barré Syndrome, and postpartum depression.

Disability Language

The symbols and language used to represent disability have sparked contentious debates over the years. In the *Handbook of Disability Studies* (Albrecht, Seelman, & Bury, 2001) and the *Encyclopedia of Disability* (Albrecht, 2006), authors from different countries were encouraged to use the terms and language of their cultures, but to explain them when necessary. In the present volumes, authors may use "people with disabilities" or "disabled people" to refer to individuals experiencing disability. Scholars in the United States have preferred "people with disabilities" (people-first language), while those in the United Kingdom, Canada, and Australia generally use "disabled people." In languages other than English, scholars typically use some form of the "disabled people" idiom. The U.S. version emphasizes American exceptionalism and the individual, whereas "disabled people" highlights the group and their minority status or state of being different. In my own writing, I have chosen "disabled people" because it stresses human diversity and variation.

In a recent discussion of this issue, DePoy and Gilson (2010) "suggest that maintaining debate and argument on what language is most correct derails a larger and more profound needed change, that of equalizing resources, valuation, and respect. Moreover, . . . locating disability 'with a person' reifies its embodiment and flies in the very face of the social model that person-first language is purported to espouse. . . . We have not heard anyone suggest that beauty, kindness, or even unkindness be located after personhood." While the debate is not likely over, we state why we use the language that we do.

Organization of the Series

These issues were important in conceiving of and organizing the SAGE Reference Series on Disability. Instead of developing the series around specific disabilities resulting from Parkinson's disease or bi-polar disorder, or according to the larger categories of physical, mental, intellectual, and sensory disabilities, we decided to concentrate on the major topics that confront anyone interested in or experiencing disability. Thus, the series consists of eight volumes constructed around the following topics:

- Arts and Humanities
- Assistive Technology and Science
- Disability Through the Life Course

- Education
- Employment and Work
- Ethics, Law, and Policy
- Health and Medicine
- Rehabilitation Interventions

To provide structure, we chose to use a similar organization for each volume. Therefore, each volume contains the following elements:

Series Introduction

Preface

About the Editors

Chapter 1. Introduction, Background, and History

Chapter 2. Current Issues, Controversies, and Solutions

Chapter 3. Chronology of Critical Events

Chapter 4. Biographies of Key Contributors in the Field

Chapter 5. Annotated Data, Statistics, Tables, and Graphs

Chapter 6. Annotated List of Organizations and Associations

Chapter 7. Selected Print and Electronic Resources

Glossary of Key Terms

Index

The Audience

The eight-volume SAGE Reference Series on Disability targets an audience of undergraduate students and general readers that uses both academic and public libraries. However, the content and depth of the series will also make it attractive to graduate students, researchers, and policymakers. The series has been edited to have a consistent format and accessible style. The focus in each volume is on providing lay-friendly overviews of broad issues and guideposts for further research and exploration.

The series is innovative in that it will be published and marketed worldwide, with each volume available in electronic format soon after it appears in print. The print version consists of eight bound volumes. The electronic version is available through the SAGE Reference Online platform, which hosts 200 handbooks and encyclopedias across the social sciences, including the *Handbook of Disability Studies* and the *Encyclopedia of Disability*. With access to this platform through college, university, and public libraries, students, the lay public, and scholars can search these interrelated disability and social science sources from their computers or handheld and smart phone devices. The movement to an electronic platform presages the cloud computing revolution coming upon us. Cloud computing "refers to 'everything' a user may reach via the Internet, including services, storage, applications and people" (Hoehl & Sieh, 2010). According to Ray Ozzie (2010), recently Microsoft's chief architect, "We're moving toward a world of (1) cloud-based continuous services that connect us all and do our bidding, and (2) appliance-like connected devices enabling us to interact with those cloud-based services." Literally, information will be available at consumers' fingertips. Given the ample links to other resources in emerging databases, they can pursue any topic of interest in detail. This resource builds on the massive efforts to make information available to decision makers in real time, such as computerizing health and hospital records so that the diagnosis and treatment of chronic diseases and disabilities can be better managed (Celler, Lovell, & Basilakis, 2003). The *SAGE Reference Series on Disability* provides Internet and Web site addresses which lead the user into a world of social networks clustered around disability in general and specific conditions and issues. Entering and engaging with social networks revolving around health and disability promises to help individuals make more informed decisions and provide support in times of need (Smith & Christakis, 2008). The SAGE Reference Online platform will also be configured and updated to make it increasingly accessible to disabled people.

The SAGE Reference Series on Disability provides an extensive index for each volume. Through its placement on the SAGE Reference Online platform, the series will be fully searchable and cross referenced, will allow keyword searching, and will be connected to the *Handbook of Disability Studies* and the *Encyclopedia of Disability*.

The authors of the volumes have taken considerable effort to vet the references, data, and resources for accuracy and credibility. The multiple Web sites for current data, information, government and United Nations documents, research findings, expert recommendations, self-help, discussion groups, and social policy are particularly useful, as they are being continuously updated. Examples of current and forthcoming data are the results and analysis of the findings of the U.S. 2010 Census, the ongoing reports of the Centers for Disease Control on disability, the World Health Organization's *World Report on Disability* and its updates, the World Bank reports on disability, poverty, and development, and reports from major foundations like Robert Wood Johnson, Bill and Melinda Gates, Ford, and Hogg. In terms of clinical outcomes, the evaluation of cost-effective interventions, management of disability, and programs that work, enormous attention is being given to evidence-based outcomes (Brownson, Fielding, & Maylahn, 2009; Marcus et al., 2006; Wolinsky et al., 2007) and comparative effectiveness research (Etheredge, 2010; Inglehart, 2010). Such data force a re-examination of policymakers' arguments. For example, there is mounting evidence that demonstrates the beneficial effects of exercise on preventing disability and enhancing function (Marcus et al., 2006). Recent studies also show that some health care reform initiatives may negatively affect disabled people's access to and costs of health care (Burns, Shaw, & Smith, 2010). Furthermore, the seemingly inexorable rise in health care spending may not be correlated with desirable health outcomes (Rothberg et al., 2010). In this environment, valid data are the currency of the discussion (Andersen, Lollar, & Meyers, 2000). The authors' hopes are that this reference series will encourage students and the lay public to base their discussions and decisions on valid outcome data. Such an approach tempers the influence of ideologies surrounding health care and misconceptions about disabled people, their lives and experiences.

SAGE Publications has made considerable effort to make these volumes accessible to disabled people in the printed book version and in the electronic platform format. In turn, SAGE and other publishers and vendors like Amazon are incorporating greater flexibility in the user interface to improve functionality to a broad range of users, such as disabled people. These efforts are important for disabled people as universities, governments, and health service delivery organizations are moving toward a paperless environment.

In the spirit of informed discussion and transparency, may this reference series encourage people from many different walks of life to become knowledgeable and engaged in the disability world. As a consequence, social policies should become better informed and individuals and families should be able to make better decisions regarding the experience of disability in their lives.

Acknowledgments

I would like to recognize the vision of Rolf Janke in developing SAGE Publications' presence in the disability field, as represented by the *Handbook of Disability Studies* (2001), the five-volume *Encyclopedia of Disability* (2006), and now the eight-volume SAGE Reference Series on Disability. These products have helped advance the field and have made critical work accessible to scholars, students, and the general public through books and now the SAGE Reference Online platform. Jim Brace-Thompson at SAGE handled the signing of contracts and kept this complex project coordinated and moving on time. Kevin Hillstrom and Laurie Collier Hillstrom at Northern Lights Writers Group were intrepid in taking the composite pieces of this project and polishing and editing them into a coherent whole that is approachable, consistent in style and form, and rich in content. The authors of the eight volumes—Linda Barrington, Jerome Bickenbach, Cathy Bodine, Brenda Brueggemann, Susanne Bruyère, Lana Collet-Klingberg, Cheryl Hanley-Maxwell, Sarah Parker Harris, Tamar Heller, Nancy Mudrick, Ross Mullner, and Peggy Turk—are to be commended for their enthusiasm, creativity, and fortitude in delivering high-quality volumes on a tight deadline. I was fortunate to work with such accomplished scholars.

Discussions with Barbara Altman, Colin Barnes, Catherine Barral, Len Barton, Isabelle Baszanger, Peter Blanck, Mary Boulton, David Braddock, Richard Burkhauser, Mike Bury, Ann Caldwell, Lennard Davis, Patrick Devlieger, Ray Fitzpatrick, Lawrence Frey, Carol Gill, Tamar Heller, Gary Kielhofner, Soewarta Kosen, Jo Lebeer, Mitch Loeb, Don Lollar, Paul Longmore, Ros Madden, Maria Martinho, Dennis Mathews, Sophie Mitra, Daniel Mont, Alana Officer, Randall Parker, David Pfeiffer, Jean-François Ravaud, James Rimmer, Ed Roberts, Jean-Marie Robine, Joan Rogers, Richard Scotch, Kate Seelman, Tom Shakespeare, Sandor Sipos, Henri-Jacques Stiker, Edna Szymanski, Jutta Traviranus, Bryan Turner, Greg Vanderheiden, Isabelle Ville, Larry Voss, Ann Waldschmidt, and Irving Kenneth Zola over the years contributed to the content, logic, and structure of the series. They also were a wonderful source of suggestions for authors.

I would also like to acknowledge the hospitality and support of the Belgian Academy of Science and the Arts, the University of Leuven, Nuffield College, the University of Oxford, the Fondation Maison des

Sciences de l'Homme, Paris, and the Department of Disability and Human Development at the University of Illinois at Chicago, who provided the time and environments to conceive of and develop the project. While none of these people or institutions is responsible for any deficiencies in the work, they all helped enormously in making it better.

Gary L. Albrecht
University of Illinois at Chicago
University of Leuven
Belgian Academy of Science and Arts

References

Albrecht, G. L. (Ed.). (2006). *Encyclopedia of disability* (5 vols.). Thousand Oaks, CA: Sage.

Albrecht, G. L. (2010). The sociology of disability: Historical foundations and future directions. In C. Bird, A. Fremont, S. Timmermans, & P. Conrad (Eds.), *Handbook of medical sociology* (6th ed.). Nashville: Vanderbilt University Press.

Albrecht, G. L., Seelman, K. D., & Bury, M. (Eds.). (2001). *Handbook of disability studies.* Thousand Oaks, CA: Sage.

Andersen, E. M., Lollar, D. J., & Meyers, A. R. (2000). Disability outcomes research: Why this supplement, on this topic, at this time? *Archives of Physical Medicine and Rehabilitation, 81,* S1–S4.

Banta, H. D., & de Wit, G. A. (2008). Public health services and cost-effectiveness analysis. *Annual Review of Public Health, 29,* 383–397.

Bleich, S., Cutler, D., Murray, C., & Adams, A. (in press). Why is the developed world obese? *Annual Review of Public Health.*

Brownson, R. C., Fielding, J. E., & Maylahn, C. M. (2009). Evidence-based public health: A fundamental concept for public health practice. *Annual Review of Public Health, 30,* 175–201.

Burns, M., Shah, N., & Smith, M. (2010). Why some disabled adults in Medicaid face large out-of-pocket expenses. *Health Affairs, 29,* 1517–1522.

Celler, B. G., Lovell, N. H., & Basilakis, J. (2003). Using information technology to improve the management of chronic disease. *Medical Journal of Australia, 179,* 242–246.

Charlton, J. I. (1998). *Nothing about us without us: Disability, oppression and empowerment.* Berkeley: University of California Press.

DePoy, E., & Gilson, S. F. (2010) *Studying disability: Multiple theories and responses.* Thousand Oaks, CA: Sage.

Egede, L. E. (2004). Diabetes, major depression, and functional disability among U.S. adults. *Diabetes Care, 27,* 421–428.

Etheredge, L. M. (2010). Creating a high-performance system for comparative effectiveness research. *Health Affairs, 29,* 1761–1767.

European Disability Forum. (2003). *Disability and social exclusion in the European Union: Time for change, tools for change.* Athens: Greek National Confederation of Disabled People.

European Union. (2000). *Charter of fundamental rights.* Retrieved from http://www.europarll.europa.eu/charter

Gill, T. M., Gahbauer, E. A., Han, L., & Allore, H. G. (2010). Trajectories of disability in the last year of life. *The New England Journal of Medicine, 362*(13), 1173–1180.

Hoehl, A. A., & Sieh, K. A. (2010). *Cloud computing and disability communities: How can cloud computing support a more accessible information age and society?* Boulder, CO: Coleman Institute.

Iezzoni, L. I., & O'Day, B. L. (2006). *More than ramps.* Oxford, UK: Oxford University Press.

Inglehart, J. K. (2010). The political fight over comparative effectiveness research. *Health Affairs, 29,* 1757–1760.

Institute of Medicine. (1991). *Disability in America.* Washington, DC: National Academies Press.

Institute of Medicine. (1997). *Enabling disability.* Washington, DC: National Academies Press.

Institute of Medicine. (2001). *Health and behavior: The interplay of biological, behavioral and societal influences.* Washington, DC: National Academies Press.

Institute of Medicine. (2002). *The dynamics of disability: Measuring and monitoring disability for social security programs.* Washington, DC: National Academies Press.

Institute of Medicine. (2007). *The future of disability in America.* Washington, DC: National Academies Press.

Kessler, R. C., & Wang, P. S. (2008). The descriptive epidemiology of commonly occurring mental disorders in the United States. *Annual Review of Public Health, 29,* 115–129.

Marcus, B. H., Williams, D. M., Dubbert, P. M., Sallis, J. F., King, A. C., et al. (2006). Physical activity intervention studies. *Circulation, 114,* 2739–2752.

Martin, L. G., Freedman, V. A., Schoeni, R. F., & Andreski, P. M. (2010). Trends in disability and related chronic conditions among people ages 50 to 64. *Health Affairs, 29*(4), 725–731.

Mont, D. (2007). *Measuring disability prevalence* (World Bank working paper). Washington, DC: The World Bank.

Officer, A., & Groce, N. E. (2009). Key concepts in disability. *The Lancet, 374,* 1795–1796.

Ozzie, R. (2010, October 28). *Dawn of a new day.* Ray Ozzie's Blog. Retrieved from http://ozzie.net/docs/dawn-of-a-new-day

Rothberg, M. B., Cohen, J., Lindenauer, P., Masetti, J., & Auerbach, A. (2010). Little evidence of correlation between growth in health care spending and reduced mortality. *Health Affairs, 29,* 1523–1531.

Shakespeare, T. (2006). *Disability rights and wrongs*. London: Routledge.

Smith, K. P., & Christakis, N. A. (2008). Social networks and health. *Annual Review of Sociology, 34*, 405–429.

United Nations. (2008). *Convention on the rights of persons with disabilities*. New York: United Nations. Retrieved from http://un.org/disabilities/convention

Whitaker, R. T. (2010). *Anatomy of an epidemic: Magic bullets, psychiatric drugs, and the astonishing rise of mental illness in America*. New York: Crown.

Wolinsky, F. D., Miller, D. K., Andresen, E. M., Malmstrom, T. K., Miller, J. P., & Miller, T. R. (2007). Effect of subclinical status in functional limitation and disability on adverse health outcomes 3 years later. *The Journals of Gerontology: Series A, 62*, 101–106.

World Bank Disability and Development Team. (2004). *Poverty reduction strategies: Their importance for disability*. Washington, DC: World Bank.

World Health Organization. (2001). *International classification of functioning, disability and health*. Geneva: Author.

World Health Organization. (2010). *Community-based rehabilitation guidelines*. Geneva and Washington, DC: Author.

World Health Organization, & World Bank. (2011). *World report on disability*. Geneva: World Health Organization.

Preface

Disability ethics, law, and policy covers a vast territory that can only be navigated if the relationships between these three social phenomena are made clear. The best approach is to view ethics as fundamental—both in the sense that it has a direct impact on people's lives and because, conceptually, ethics provides the normative foundations for law and policy. More concretely, controversial and high-profile legal cases have, in often very powerful and personal terms, explored our ethical intuitions about, for example, the moral worth of a life with impairments. Furthermore, all policy is embedded in social values like equality, freedom, and dignity that define who we are as people. Policies and programs for people with disabilities are invariably implemented and enforced by means of laws and regulations, while legal pronouncements by the Supreme Court sometimes require legislators to rethink, or abandon, policies and programs. The interrelationships between ethics, law, and policy, in other words, are complex and often difficult to pin down.

But there is a prior question: What is the difference between *disability* ethics and just plain ethics, and how does *disability* law and policy differ from law and policy? Since people with disabilities are people, all aspects of ethics, law, and policy concern them. Moreover, are we not compounding the injustice of treating people with disabilities as "different" and "non-normal," people who require "special treatment," just by talking this way? On the other hand, unless laws and policies are tailored specifically to the circumstances of persons with disabilities, their important needs and accommodations may well be ignored. After all, we know that treating people the same is not always treating them equally.

This tension between "universal" and "targeted" law and policy is a theme that runs through this volume. As is the question of what the ethical value of equality demands of us in practice: Are protections against discrimination enough, or is the state required to empower people with disabilities with positive programs and entitlements? Another theme is the key political question of whether laws and policies for the benefit of persons with disabilities are best served by state action alone, or whether a partnership between the public and the private sectors would be more effective, and more efficient. But underlying all of these tensions and controversies is perhaps the most unlikely controversy of all: What is disability?

This book will offer a tour of the major tensions, contradictions, and ongoing controversies found in ethics, law, and policy as these domains apply to persons with disabilities, as well as provide a brief history of law and policy that, I hope, will illuminate how these tensions came about. Since this is a book on disability ethics, law, and policy—rather than, say, ethics, law, and policy in the employment sector—the coverage is necessarily selective. The plan is always to move from the general—typically where the underlying ethical questions reside—to the specific and concrete in terms of actual laws and policies. And the aim is to be selective, but representative, of which policies and laws to highlight. It should come as no surprise that the Americans with Disabilities Act of 1990 (ADA), its history, impact, and future prospects, will dominate the landscape. But however important to the disability community the ADA is—as a symbol and triumph of advocacy—most of the law and policy that affects the day-to-day lives of persons with disabilities lies in other domains: education and employment policy, including vocational rehabilitation, access to health care, income maintenance, Social Security and other pensions, assistive technology and personal assistance services, tax policy, housing, and transportation policy. These are the policies and programs of everyday life.

We begin in Chapter 1 by mapping out the territory of ethics, law, and policy, both in general and for persons with disabilities. This leads us to enter the confusing world of conflicting "models of disability" and explore how these models, both historically and conceptually, have been at the heart of many of the tensions in disability ethics, law, and policy. Setting the stage for the next chapter, we outline some of the enduring themes of disability policy and law—the fault lines that have generated, and continue to shape, the debates about the objectives of disability policy and the means available for achieving these objectives. We then turn briefly to disability ethics and review the troubled relationship between bioethics and the disability community, and recent attempts to join forces. We finish the chapter with a history of disability law and policy in the

Anglo-American tradition, from roughly the English Poor Law of 1601 to President Barack Obama's signing of the United Nations Convention on the Rights of Persons with Disabilities in 2009.

Chapter 2 tackles the central debates in disability law and policy, organized in terms of five basic controversies: What is disability? Is the anti-discrimination strategy enough to achieve equality? What is the "human rights approach"? What should be the balance between the public and the private sectors? and Should policy be mainstream or targeted? Each controversy is explained and then made concrete in terms of specific policy areas and laws in which the controversy is particularly troublesome. Then potential solutions in terms of best practices are offered, with a glance at the future and prospects for success. In the case of disability ethics, the controversies are more practical and specific, involving the moral worth of the life with impairments, the importance of autonomy and practical challenges to it, beginning-of-life and end-of-life questions (prenatal testing and abortion, euthanasia and physician-assisted suicide), and questions of distributive justice in the allocation of health care and other scarce resources.

Chapters 3 and 4 supplement the historical background of this book in two ways. First, Chapter 3 provides a short chronology of events relevant to the domains of disability ethics, law, and policy. The chronology for disability ethics is given in terms of the legal cases that raised the profile of ethical issues, and disability law and policy is dated by appropriate events such as passage or signing into effect of laws, implementation of policies, and amendments or other changes in programming. Second, Chapter 4 provides biographies, with suggestions for further reading, of individuals who have contributed greatly to disability ethics, law, and policy. These individuals are often the heroes of the disability rights movement—Frank Bowe, Marca Bristo, Robert Burgdorf Jr., Justin Dart, Gunnar Dybwad, Lex Frieden, Harlan Hahn, Judy Heumann, Ed Roberts, and Irving Zola—but they also include academics, politicians, and others who may be less known but have been noteworthy, and often groundbreaking, leaders in our understanding of disability ethics, law, and policy.

In Chapter 5 Dr. Bruno Trezzini and I present a representative sample of data and statistics relevant to law and policy, as well as both a general discussion of problems with disability data—including the most basic information about prevalence and incidence—and a description of data sources. The United States is blessed with some of the best and most reliable disability data in the world, and anyone wishing to look deeper into the factual basis for the debates and controversies surveyed in this book has the benefit of several electronic and paper sources of pertinent data at her or his fingertips.

Chapters 6 and 7, compiled by my colleagues Nandini Devi, Nicole Emmenegger, and Barbara Phillips, round out the essential tools of a useful resource for further research: a listing and description of the governmental and non-governmental organizations of and for persons with disabilities at the national, state, and international levels (Chapter 6); and an annotated list of print and electronic resources representing historically significant, original and influential, academic and non-academic literature, databases, and other Web-based resources that provide the basis for a thorough, and ongoing, understanding of disability ethics, law, and policy (Chapter 7).

Because of the political activism of the disability rights community, and the realization that at the end of the day all political triumphs are ephemeral unless they are transformed into law and policy, the recent history of people with disabilities, in the United States and around the globe, has been primarily written in the language of laws and policies. Though ethics, by its nature, is perennial and not the product of specific individuals or social movements, the ethical issues relevant to persons with disabilities that are debated both in the public arena and by disability scholars have been raised as the result of the efforts of individual persons with disabilities and their organizations. Disability ethics, law, and policy, in short, owes much to the disability rights movement.

Jerome Bickenbach

About the Author

Jerome E. Bickenbach, Ph.D., LL.B., is a full professor in the Department of Philosophy and Faculties of Law and Medicine at Queen's University. He is the author of *Physical Disability and Social Policy* (1993) and the co-editor of *Introduction to Disability* (1998), *Disability and Culture: Universalism and Diversity* (2000), *A Seat at the Table: Persons With Disabilities and Policy Making* (2001), *Quality of Life and Human Difference* (2003), and numerous articles and chapters in disability studies, focusing on the nature of disability and disability law and policy. He was a content editor of SAGE Publications' five-volume *Encyclopedia of Disability* (2005).

Since 1995 Dr. Bickenbach has been a consultant with the World Health Organization (WHO) working on drafting, testing, and implementation of the International Classification of Functioning, Disability, and Health (ICF), and he continues to consult with WHO on international disability social policy. His research is in disability studies, using qualitative and quantitative research techniques within the paradigm of participatory action research. Most recently his research includes disability quality of life and the disability critique, disability epidemiology, universal design and inclusion, modeling disability statistics for population health surveys, the relationship between disability and well-being, disability and aging issues, and the application of ICF to monitoring the implementation of the UN Convention on the Rights of Persons with Disabilities.

As a lawyer, Dr. Bickenbach was a human rights litigator, specializing in anti-discrimination for persons with intellectual impairments and mental illness. Since 2007 he has headed the Disability Policy Unit at Swiss Paraplegic Research in Nottwil, Switzerland, and he is a professor in the Faculty of Humanities and Social Science at the University of Lucerne.

About the Series Editor

Gary L. Albrecht is a Fellow of the Royal Belgian Academy of Arts and Sciences, Extraordinary Guest Professor of Social Sciences, University of Leuven, Belgium, and Professor Emeritus of Public Health and of Disability and Human Development at the University of Illinois at Chicago. After receiving his Ph.D. from Emory University, he has served on the faculties of Emory University in Sociology and Psychiatry, Northwestern University in Sociology, Rehabilitation Medicine, and the Kellogg School of Management, and the University of Illinois at Chicago (UIC) in the School of Public Health and in the Department of Disability and Human Development. Since retiring from the UIC in 2005, he has divided his time between Europe and the United States, working in Brussels, Belgium, and Boulder, Colorado. He has served as a Scholar in Residence at the Maison des Sciences de l'Homme (MSH) in Paris, a visiting Fellow at Nuffield College, the University of Oxford, and a Fellow in Residence at the Royal Flemish Academy of Science and Arts, Brussels.

His research has focused on how adults acknowledge, interpret, and respond to unanticipated life events, such as disability onset. His work, supported by over $25 million of funding, has resulted in 16 books and over 140 articles and book chapters. He is currently working on a longitudinal study of disabled Iranian, Moroccan, Turkish, Jewish, and Congolese immigrants to Belgium. Another current project involves working with an international team on "Disability: A Global Picture," Chapter 2 of the *World Report on Disability*, co-sponsored by the World Health Organization and the World Bank, to be published in 2011.

He is past Chair of the Medical Sociology Section of the American Sociological Association, a past member of the Executive Committee of the

Disability Forum of the American Public Health Association, an early member of the Society for Disability Studies, and an elected member of the Society for Research in Rehabilitation (UK). He has received the Award for the Promotion of Human Welfare and the Eliot Freidson Award for the book *The Disability Business: Rehabilitation in America*. He also has received a Switzer Distinguished Research Fellowship, Schmidt Fellowship, New York State Supreme Court Fellowship, Kellogg Fellowship, National Library of Medicine Fellowship, World Health Organization Fellowship, the Lee Founders Award from the Society for the Study of Social Problems, the Licht Award from the American Congress of Rehabilitation Medicine, the University of Illinois at Chicago Award for Excellence in Teaching, and has been elected Fellow of the American Association for the Advancement of Science (AAAS). He has led scientific delegations in rehabilitation medicine to the Soviet Union and the People's Republic of China and served on study sections, grant review panels, and strategic planning committees on disability in Australia, Canada, the European Community, France, Ireland, Japan, Poland, Sweden, South Africa, the United Kingdom, the United States, and the World Health Organization, Geneva. His most recent books are *The Handbook of Social Studies in Health and Medicine*, edited with Ray Fitzpatrick and Susan Scrimshaw (SAGE, 2000), the *Handbook of Disability Studies*, edited with Katherine D. Seelman and Michael Bury (SAGE, 2001), and the five-volume *Encyclopedia of Disability* (SAGE, 2006)

One

Introduction, Background, and History

Ethics, Law, and Policy: How Are They Different, How Are They Linked?

This volume is about disability law, policy, and ethics, so the first question that needs to be addressed is, how are these three things related, what is the link between them? This is not an easy question—it is far easier to describe, as we will below, how ethics, law, and policy differ—but it is an important question. Are law, policy, and ethics on separate, but parallel tracks? Are they just different things with no reliable connection between them? Or does one of them, say ethics, inform or even determine the content of the other two? Since law, policy, and ethics are all complex social phenomena, any answer is bound to be too simplistic. But we need some guidance on it, nonetheless.

This is our proposal: Ethics is fundamental, not because it has more impact on people's day-to-day lives, or certainly not because it is simpler and univocal; rather, ethics is fundamental because it deals with underlying human issues in basic, normative terms—terms like good and bad, right and wrong. It is controversial whether law embodies a public consensus on ethical questions, or whether it should. But certainly in the case

1

of the issues that come up in this and the next chapter under the heading of "disability ethics," the law—both in the form of legislation and judicial decision—most certainly tackles the same issues in more or less the same terms. Policy is complex because it is created and governed in part by law, in part by practice, in part by convention. But it too reflects and is implicitly shaped by ethics.

Saying that ethics is fundamental, and constitutes the foundations of law and policy, is dangerous because there are persistent myths about ethics that would turn this proposition into nonsense. We will address these myths below, but for the moment, all that needs to be said is that ethics is a collection of social and individual beliefs, constitutive of religious, cultural, and other forms of socialization, often unorganized and inconsistent, that form around specific practical issues and controversies that each of us faces, or will face, sometime in our lives. We may, as individuals, be able to postpone thinking about ethical questions—Should I lie to my spouse about my affair, or just hope she never finds out?—but as citizens we participate, whether we choose to or not, in social debates about very practical issues that, evidence suggests, will not go away—Should abortion be illegal? Should people be able to seek physician-assisted suicide? The intriguing thing about social ethics (as this area of ethics is called) is that *not deciding* to resolve an issue *is itself a decision* that has ethical consequences.

The plan in this chapter is therefore to assume that ethics, and so disability ethics, is foundational and always in the background, and that law and policy are in the foreground. The tough question of how ethics, law, and policy are connected or linked will not be answered, except indirectly: If we carefully describe each domain, what should be revealed is how these domains differ and how they interact. We begin then with the foreground—disability policy and law—and then go to the background—disability ethics. In each case, we briefly describe policy, law, and ethics in general, before turning to the case of disability policy, law, and ethics. With this background completed, we turn to a review of the history of disability policy and law.

Background

Policy and Law

What Is Policy?

"Policy," "public policy," or "social policy" is broadly defined as all of the actions (and inactions) of the state addressed to governance, regulation, and organization for the public good. More concretely, policy refers to the creation and implementation of laws, regulations, entitlements and prohibitions, income generation programs, taxation strategies and spending priorities, and, finally, state actions (all of which are called "policy tools") that respond to issues that arise in all areas of human social life, including how we interact with each other, whom we associate with, where we live, how we become educated, how we work, travel, communicate, come together in groups, or be alone.

In short, policies govern, regulate, and sometimes even define—whether successfully or not—everything done within a political organization and social structure. It is extremely difficult to describe all of the distinct areas of public and social policy for the simple reason that it is hard to know what to leave out. Moreover, it is a fundamental question of political philosophy what the proper scope of "public policy" should be, where to draw the line between the utterly personal and the social. For our purposes, and without any claim to being exhaustive, it is enough to list in no particular order the uncontroversial areas of public policy and set aside for later special, temporary, ad hoc, or borderline cases of policy. So, the clear areas of policy are:

Health and public health

Social or income security

Social insurance (welfare)

Public security and crime control

Economic affairs

Commerce and trade

Communications

Housing

Immigration

Transportation

Employment (unemployment)

Workers' compensation

Taxation

Education

Political participation

Civil and human rights

Science and technology

These areas of policy (and the myriad of specific policy issues that fall under each heading) constitute the subject matter or domains of governmental departments and agencies—federal, state and local. For complex reasons, some constitutional and others political, some areas of policy are within the exclusive jurisdiction of the federal government, others exclusively state, and others both federal and state. For the most part, which level of government has jurisdiction over an area of policy mirrors the legal jurisdiction of each level of government, so that a federal court or a state court has initial jurisdiction to hear cases involving the subject matter of that policy area. But legal jurisdictional questions are hugely complicated and political and need not detain us.

Some areas of policy are highly specific and concern sub-populations (policies on aging, youth in trouble with the law, and so on), and some policies are designed to address specific needs or events, such as natural emergency relief or epidemic response programs. Generally, the overall subject matter of public policy addresses basic human needs and concerns, deals with activities and life projects that people generally engage in, responds to problems people face, or want to avoid if possible, in their daily social life, and finally proposes ways of facilitating, or enhancing, the small and large plans that each of us has, day to day, and across a life span. In a word, there are no hard and fast boundaries to what can or cannot be the subject matter of public policy, other than the obvious one: Policy is about human needs, wants, desires, and plans.

Making and Analyzing Policy

Policy scientists agree that there are four stages in the life of any policy, big or small. First, there is a recognition—by some combination of the public at large, bureaucrats, or politicians—that some social or human *goal* is worth achieving (and can be feasibly achieved or at least furthered in some manner), and that there is a mandate for trying to achieve the goal. Next, in light of this goal and an understanding of actual social conditions, *specific objectives* for planning policy are identified. Then, *mechanisms* for reaching these objectives, subject to specified milestones, are proposed and existing *policy tools* are used, or new ones created, to implement the mechanisms. Finally, *implementation is monitored* for effectiveness and, if necessary, the objectives are refined, the mechanisms modified, and the tools recrafted accordingly. (Usually, though, the underlying social goals are so fundamental that they are never wholly abandoned except in emergencies or other rare circumstances.)

Of course, this sequence of steps—social goals, objectives, mechanisms and tools, and monitoring—is an idealized scheme, rarely followed so logically. Many policies are proposed without much thought or planning, and without a clear idea of what they should achieve. Sometimes policy solutions are so effective that they are implemented without a clear understanding of whether there is a genuine problem that needs solving. And sometimes goals are subtly shifted when bureaucrats or politicians realize that the public is not at all happy with how their lives are directly affected when the policy tools are implemented.

Nonetheless, although unrealistically logical and abstract, the scheme does underscore the fact that policy is the outcome of a political, social, and organizational process that depends entirely on the existence, and operation, of basic social institutions. When societies and governments break down, policy slowly disappears. We might even say that the existence of public policy is one indication of the existence of a viable government. Since policy is both a matter of content (what the policy is about, i.e., security, employment, taxation) and process (how the policy is created, developed, and implemented), the institutions that make policy possible have to directly address the ways and the means of policy.

Lastly, this idealized scheme defines the scope of what is usually called "policy analysis." Hence, policy analysis is a matter of (a) *interpreting and clarifying* policy goals in light of basic social values such as liberty, equality, and dignity; (b) *exploring the relationship or connection* between these goals and proposed objectives; (c) *evaluating the effectiveness* of the policy mechanisms—regulation, entitlement, guidance, prohibition, coercion, public education, or whatever; (d) *describing* the policy tools that are involved—laws, regulations, guidelines, programs, or other state actions; and (e) *monitoring the outcomes* once all of these are implemented. This will be our framework for scrutinizing disability policy in what follows.

Law as a Toolbox for Policy; Ethics as Its Foundation

It should be noticed that the law of the land, on this broad understanding of policy, is merely a collection of tools that facilitate or implement public policy. Lawyers might object (as they tend do) that the law is far more than this, but it is enough to say that the law is at least this much: a toolbox for policy implementation. Legal policy tools range from the punitive and coercive to the merely persuasive and recommendatory. Since policies are the products of either executive or legislative branches of government, legal tools tend to be the most common. But they are not the only tools available, nor are they always the most effective ones. As a rule, people like to be free to do the right thing rather than to be forced, and people like to know the reasons for following social rules rather than to be treated like children and told what to do, on threat of punishment. So, information and public education campaigns are common techniques that can have a substantial impact on changing attitudes and behaviors in pursuit of policy objectives. Finally, the state and its bureaucratic agencies—federal, state, and local—have at their disposal a bewilderingly wide range of inducements, tax incentives, and other forms of persuasion that can directly or indirectly affect public behavior.

These tools implement policy even when it seems as if no explicit policy is in evidence. For example, there is no explicit policy for the law that prohibits murder, rape, or theft and empowers the state to enforce criminal law and punish offenders. In criminal law, the goals are so obvious that the law and legal organizations are a social expression of fundamental moral values that are no longer up for political discussion. There will always be debate and movement around the edges, of course, since social values are themselves dynamic. But although it is popular to say that social values are always changing, in fact the fundamentals of these values are really not all that dynamic. The moral evil of being cruel or intentionally causing harm or death is not a matter of debate, and so laws against assault, rape, and homicide are unlikely to become controversial (although, needless to say, whether abortion constitutes murder, or whether racial slurs constitute harm, will remain so).

At the other extreme from criminal law is the law regulating and enabling commercial activities, including the operation of corporations, and the law relating to taxation. Here laws and regulations are highly dynamic, technical, and subject to unceasing fine-tuning in light of changing economic circumstances and shifts in political will and ideology. This kind of law is nothing more than a regulatory toolbox for putting into effect, or implementing, commercial, business, and trade policies, or state revenue-generating policies.

At the same time, even this technical law reflects implicit social values that are ultimately moral in nature, as well as goals and explicitly chosen policy objectives.

Underlying the Uniform Commercial Code, for example, are the values of freedom and reasonable expectation of security of contract, both ultimately moral values. The law that is generated from this and related codes will be closely monitored and evaluated for its effectiveness in achieving the stated objectives. Laws protecting freedom of contract express a social consensus that, generally speaking, people should be free to arrange their lives and financial interactions with others as they wish. Laws prohibiting predatory business strategies, monopolization, and unfair practices (including laws regulating the safety of drugs, foods, and other potentially dangerous products) reflect the social concern that people should not be taken advantage of, especially when they have no way to protect themselves.

As a general matter, policies always point in the direction of underlying social values and goals (even when they are actually results of shameless political expediency and the expressed values are more image than reality). The reason for this is very simple: Without some linkage to fundamental social values such as liberty, equality, security, dignity, and so on, policies would be (and would quickly be seen to be) mere exercises of arbitrary power and would be very unpopular. It is important not to be naïve about this—the history of policy in the United States, like everywhere else, is replete with mischief and calumny, deceit and treachery. But, even the worse offenses were effective only as long as the image of ethical justifiability in light of agreement with social values could be plausibly maintained.

Disability Policy and Law

It might not seem controversial to say that disability policy and law is just policy and law that addresses the needs and issues of a person with disabilities. After all, some laws explicitly use the word (the most obvious example being the Americans with Disabilities Act, 1990), and there is much policy and law that is, in the jargon, "targeted" to this population, such as the disability benefit programs of Social Security Disability Insurance (SSDI) and Supplemental Security Income (SSI). There is also education policy for children with learning problems, workers' compensation for people injured on the job, and policies encouraging the development, marketing, and accessibility of assistive technologies, such as wheelchairs, orthotics, or Kurzweil readers. All of these would be called "disability policy."

So understood, disability policy, from the beginning of the 20th century onward, has been a permanent feature of the U.S. policy landscape, as it has been around the world. It is difficult to estimate the overall cost of disability programming—even if we set aside general or mainstream health care, which people with disabilities need like everyone else—but one estimate of cash and in-kind programming at the federal level suggests that disability policy constituted in 2002 somewhere in the area of 12% of all federal outlays (roughly 2.2% of gross domestic product), and that states contributed an additional $50 billion under federal–state disability programs. Most of this money is spent on income support and the specific health care needs of working-age people with disabilities who are either unemployed or underemployed (Goodman & Stapleton, 2007).

It would not be difficult to defend targeted disability policy since, however a "person with a severe disability" is defined (which is not a simple matter, as we shall see), there is no lack of evidence that this population falls behind the nondisabled U.S. population in nearly every social and economic indicator standardly used in policy: The unemployment rate for people with severe disabilities is roughly three times that of the nondisabled population; salaries for those who are employed are roughly 60% of the nondisabled average; education rates are far lower; the poverty rate is far higher; and only one in ten people with a severe disability own their own home (see Chapter 5 for further details). Disability policy is thus policy for a sub-population that clearly needs targeted and programmatic relief.

What's Wrong With Calling It "Disability Law and Policy"?

Yet, there are two problems with approaching disability policy and law in this way. The first problem is obvious: People with disabilities are people, so arguably all policy and law applies to them. Conversely, anyone can become a person with disabilities, so disability policy and law applies, potentially, to everyone. In this sense, criminal law is disability law, and environmental protection policy is disability policy. Similarly, all foreseen or unforeseen phenomena that affect public policy—from demographic changes in aging patterns to wars, climate change, and economic downturns—affect people with disabilities as well (though often in different ways).

The second problem is more subtle and rooted in history. As we shall see below, much of what we now understand to be targeted disability law and policy arose as ad hoc, "special" add-ons to "normal" law and policy. From the early Middle Ages onward, disability was conceptualized either as a personal misfortune of no concern to the community, or a "special problem" that needed to be dealt with, often by making people with disabilities invisible or objects of charity. Given this history, even to use the label "disability" for a species of policy and law is to perpetuate an ancient injustice, namely the view that society first must devise policy for normal people, and then, if it absolutely must, it can turn to policy for special populations with special needs.

This aspect of the historical emergence of disability law and policy remains the source of ongoing controversies to this day. Sociologists and political theorists have puzzled over the strange dynamics of disability policy in which people with disabilities, because of the best of intentions, are sometimes included and sometimes excluded from policy on the basis of being "different," sometimes equal and sometimes not. At its most generic, this phenomena is called the "dilemma of difference" (Minow, 1990): In order to seek and achieve social equality, people are tempted to deny their differences ("we are just like you"); but sometimes doing that creates barriers, even insurmountable ones, to actually achieving meaningful equality, because the differences are genuine and may require adjustments, modifications, and additional resources. As we will explore in detail in the next chapter, the dilemma of difference is reflected in policy terms as the debate between universal and targeted policy options. In legal terms, the dilemma is expressed as the difference between conceptions of legal equality: formal equality versus substantive equality that includes reasonable accommodation.

Although we will continue to speak of disability law and policy, it is important to appreciate that the historical roots of this policy and law are significant for another reason. It is impossible to describe, let alone understand, the nature of disability policy and law without seeing the role that conceptions or models of disability have played in its evolution, and continue to play in current debates. These models not only affect how disability is defined for programs and laws, but also the fundamental epidemiological questions of prevalence (how many people with disabilities are there?) and incidence (now that the population is aging more rapidly, how many new persons of disability are there?). Knowing these numbers is essential for resource allocation decisions for present policy and planning for future policy needs. But beyond statistics, models of disability are influential in all aspects of policy and law. The historical details of these models we will canvass below, but first we need to look briefly at the broad contours of the central models of disability that have shaped, and continue to shape, disability law and policy.

Disability Policy and the Models of Disability

First a word about models. No topic in disability studies has been more extensively discussed than "models of disability," and it is easy to become lost in the terminological and ideological tangle. A model of disability is a general theory that tells us what a disability is, what it means to have a disability, who a person with a disability is, and what it means to be a person with a disability (Altman, 2001). There are many models, variants of models, and sub-models, but in the history of public policy there have only been four dominant conceptions of disability that have left their marks on disability policy and law.

In the late Middle Ages, disability policy took the form of state charity. This first model arose primarily as an enlightened and compassionate response to the perception of disability as punishment from God, a personal misfortune or tragedy, or some combination. Though for individuals charity is a moral virtue, once institutionalized it shows a darker side by reinforcing a stark division between normality and deviancy, between the virtuous alms giver and the pitiable and wholly dependent alms receiver. In the model of charity, moreover, policy for those with disability is inherently exceptional, not mainstreamed, and always vulnerable to changing social circumstances—charity is a luxury.

The second dominant approach to disability, and in some ways the original theme of disability policy, was economic in nature. The explicitly legislated distinction between the unworthy and the worthy poor in 15th century English Poor Laws was the first indication of the division between those who were not expected to work or be part of the economy because they were physically incapable of doing so, and therefore were proper objects of pity and charity, and those who were essentially criminals or outcasts. It was certainly an advantage to be in the first group, but there was a catch. To qualify as worthy poor, one had to be a victim of an incapacity, not a willing participant in it. If incapacity was voluntary, then it was blameworthy laziness, malingering, or immorality. Being without talent or trade was one's own fault; being injured, diseased, or born with a defect was not. For not dissimilar reasons, as we shall see, much of the disability policy of the last two centuries has resulted from the felt need to compensate injured veterans for their service. Not only were they not to blame for their incapacities, they became incapacitated in the service of their country and deserve compensation and tribute for this service. On the other hand, being an alcoholic, drug abuser, or pedophile is voluntary and immoral, so not worthy of being classified as having a disability.

Sometime around the late 19th century, however, an abrupt change in the public conception of disability arose, clearly in response to the growing influence of physical sciences and the emergence of the economic and policy sciences. This was the creation of the medical model of disability, the no-nonsense, scientific view that disability was not a matter of guilt or innocence, possession by demons or god's wrath, or the object of pity and charity, but a perfectly understandable biological or psychological defect, infirmity, or injury. Disability was a medical problem calling for a medical solution. More or less at the same time, scientific public policy depicted disability—along with disease, poverty, crime, and other social ills—as a matter for social engineering, a problem of redistribution of public resources so that, to the greatest extent possible, those with physical or psychological defects were to be treated humanely, outside of the economy, and protected by the largess of the community. The social policies that were created in response to this view built and reinforced what has been called the welfare conception of disability.

Although the medical and the welfare models of disability diverged in their implications for policy—one insisting on access to appropriate medical care and rehabilitation, the other on income support from public coffers—they shared the view that disability was a problem that, so to speak, resided exclusively in the body and mind of the inflected individual (Drake, 2001). Sharing this premise, however, the two approaches went off in different directions, and were sometimes in conflict. Medical sociologists have argued that the policy grounded in the medical model served to colonize people with disabilities by insisting that medical expertise alone was the solution to their "problem," and then abandoned and stigmatized them when they were incurable and beyond fixing (Hahn, 1985; Zola, 1989). The medical ghettoization of disability left a distinct stamp on disability policy. On the other hand, political theorists have argued that the welfare approach, at least in some cultures, was the antithesis of the charity approach, as it was rooted in a sense of community solidarity in which disability was not at all a personal misfortune but a universal risk to which everyone was vulnerable (Hahn, 1986). This view, too, left its distinctive stamp on disability policy: Welfare or social assistance was not a matter of charity but of entitlement.

The Social Model of Disability

In the 1960s and 1970s, the conceptualization of disability went through a profound, revolutionary change, leading to what is now known as the social model of disability. The historical development of the social model—which we will outline below—was a complex product of academic social theorizing across disciplines, insights from the practice of rehabilitation therapeutics, and grassroots political movements. Like all powerful ideas, at the heart of the social model was a clear and simple insight: The actual impact on a person's life of a problem of physical or mental functioning is as much a matter of his or her physical, social, political, and attitudinal environment as it is a matter of the functional problem itself. Indeed, as early as 1917 an English physician, arranging rehabilitation services for soldiers returning from World War I, remarked that it was foolish to plan therapy in terms of the nature of the injury, since two soldiers with the same injury would require different therapies depending on what job they wanted to go back to (Fox, 1917). A disability does not reside in a person's body; it is a relationship between the person's body and the world in which he or she lives and acts.

The insight found its expression in many ways. At one extreme, disability was said to have nothing at all to do with the body but was purely a "socially constructed disadvantage" (Oliver, 1990). Society disables, people are "just different." Although good political rhetoric, this view dangerously underestimated the impact that the underlying functional problem had on a person's life. The limitations that a person who is blind since birth will face may be greatly influenced by the absence of supports and the presence of fear, stigma, and stereotypes; but the impact of a spinal cord injury on a person's life has much less to do with the social environment. The radical version of the social model was roundly criticized, by both the disability community and the feminist community, for "making the body disappear" and ignoring the lived experience of most people with disabilities (Hughes & Paterson, 1997; Shakespeare & Watson, 1997; Swain & French, 2000). To do justice to disability, especially for policy purposes, they argued, it makes good sense to acknowledge the realities both of the person's environment and the underlying functional condition.

Although terminological debates continue to rage, for our purposes it will be helpful to follow the well-established practice of using the term "disability" for the complex, multidimensional phenomenon that results from interactions between features of human bodies and minds and features of the physical, human-built, social environment in which people live, while using the term "impairment" to name the essentially biomedical, underlying functional condition that is intrinsic to the person. Impairment constitutes the essential health component of disability; but disability itself is more complex and variable across environments.

There are further refinements of the social model that have been suggested and argued for, most notably those found in models proposed by Saad Z. Nagi (1969) and, much later, the model in the World Health Organization's *International Classification of Functioning, Disability, and Health* (ICF) (World Health Organization, 2001). We will return to these models later, but for now the simplistic disability–impairment distinction will serve us well enough.

Stripped to its essentials, then, the social model views disability as the overall lived experience of a person with disabilities, shaped both by external features of the person's environment—physical and social—and by internal or intrinsic features of a person. Calling these intrinsic features "medical," though common, is not entirely adequate since they are problems in functioning—moving across the room, seeing trees, driving cars, and so on. It is better we call these health problems in functioning (the sort of problems that rehabilitation therapists of various sorts work on, for example). That said, whether, and the degree to which, disability is disadvantageous to the person depends not merely on the extent and severity of these functional problems—impairment and its consequences—but also on features of the external world the person lives in.

Impairments may be sensory (difficulty in hearing or visual impairment) or physical (difficulties in moving or standing up) or psychological (difficulty in coping with stress, depression, or memory loss); but, in any case, they are best described in biological or psychological terms. Impairments may be congenital or caused later in life by diseases, injuries, or disorders. They may be trivial differences or major disruptions, temporary or permanent. Importantly, impairments enter into the discussion—and are distinguishable from mere differences, like hair color—because they may create specific needs that if not responded to, will undermine independence and participation in major life areas. These basic facts about impairments are essential to keep in mind since disability policy must, at the very least, address the realities of impairments. (Needless to say, mere differences, such as most racial or sexual characteristics, though obviously not impairments, have historically been the basis for discriminatory treatment as well.)

Environmental factors, on the other hand, can be barriers for people when they deny them access to needed resources or opportunities, discriminate against them, or otherwise undermine their dignity, equality, or autonomy. Alternatively, environmental factors may be facilitators, by responding to impairment needs, providing people with disabilities with support and assistance required to participate in all areas of life, or empowering them to be independent and in charge of their own fates. As barriers, these factors may be overt and obvious: curbs or other roadblocks that prevent wheelchair use, inaccessible rooms or public buildings, or people's attitudes and discriminatory behaviors. And barriers may be hidden or systematic: bureaucratic decisions about how scarce health resources are to be distributed, economic policies that directly or indirectly prevent people with disabilities from entering the work force, or cultural assumptions about the social value of people with mental health problems. Facilitators in the environment cover a similarly extensive realm, from wheelchairs and other assistive technology to personal assistants, accessible public buildings, antidiscriminatory employment policies, and positive cultural representations. Knowing the range of what hinders or helps in a person's environment is equally essential for policy purposes.

Although we normally think of disabilities as permanent or chronic, and usually serious, it is important not to be stuck in the stereotypical examples of mobility problems, blindness, deafness, and cognitive impairment or mental disorder. Many disabilities have natural histories or trajectories, changing as we age, sometimes getting more severe as the underlying health condition or impairment gets worse, sometimes becoming less severe. And many of us will move in and out of disabled states, either as the health condition changes (e.g., postpartum depression, arthritis, episodic schizophrenia) or as our environment changes (e.g., climate change, job change, policy or legal change). Although some people with disabilities are hesitant to acknowledge this, there is no reason why a disability cannot be temporary or curable: If one is fired from one's job because of the flu or a broken arm, there is no reason to deny that this is discrimination on the basis of a disability.

In summary, the social model of disability that stands the best chance of being workable, realistic, and true to the lived experience of disability—and so a good basis for understanding and evaluating disability policy and law—has the following characteristics:

1. Disability is a *multidimensional phenomenon* that includes: intrinsic features of the human body and mind (impairments described in biological, physiological, psychological language); the impact of impairments on the way people perform or execute actions as whole persons (sometimes called "functional limitations" or "activity limitations"); and finally the overall lived experience in the person's actual physical, social, attitudinal, and political environment ("participation restrictions"). As a global concept, disability is all of these things.

2. Disability is the outcome of an interaction—the complex nature of which we are only beginning to understand empirically—between features of the person (impairments and functional limitations) and features of the overall physical, human-built, social, attitudinal, and political environment. The same impairment in different environments will affect the person's life in different ways, so it is invalid to infer from impairment anything at all about how disability is actually experienced. People who are blind are blind everywhere on earth; but what blindness means to their life, what their opportunities, challenges, benefits, or ways of living will be, depend on environmental factors (Fougeyrollas & Beauregard, 2001).

3. Disability is a continuous, not dichotomous phenomenon. All dimensions of disability are matters of "more or less," not "yes or no." For policy purposes—the distribution of resources, the allocation of opportunities, and the eligibility for programming—we must draw a line between those who are disabled for the purposes of the policy or law, and those who are not. But, importantly, this line is negotiable: It is not a scientific fact where the cutoff along the continuum should be drawn; it is a political decision that depends, among other things, on available resources.

4. Disability is a universal human condition, a feature of what it means to be a human being and vulnerable to impairments and other limitations of functioning; it is not a mark of a distinct and insular, permanent minority group. Anyone can become a person with disabilities though diseases, disorders, accidents, or even just living long enough (Shakespeare, 2006; World Health Organization, 2001).

The social model, so construed, helps us ask the questions that set the stage for the entire policy agenda: Should policy be designed to respond to impairments—by preventing them, when possible, or ensuring that their impact on a person's life is limited or accommodated—or should policy be designed to remove environmental barriers and make provision for environmental facilitators? Since the disability policy agenda undoubtedly requires both kinds of responses, the challenging issue is choosing where the focus should be, or in social model terms, what policy produces an environment that is the most facilitative and constitutes the least barrier for persons with disabilities?

The Social Model and the Rights Approach

The impact of the social model of disability on disability policy has been profound, mostly because the disability movement expressed its demands in social terms, specifically in terms of civil and human rights. These two varieties of basic rights are similar, but also importantly different.

The standard distinction between civil and human rights is that the former, but not necessarily the latter, are inextricably bound to the role of the citizen. It is sometimes said that the civil rights approach extends the social model of disability by adding that persons with disabilities are a minority group who are entitled to equal citizenship—a view usually credited to the political scientist Harlan Hahn (see Hahn, 1985, 1986). Hahn was greatly impressed by the parallels he saw between the civil rights movement, and in particular the political dynamics of an oppressed "insular and discrete" minority group, and the disability rights movement. Others, however, remarked that as people with disabilities are an amazingly diverse group, it is difficult both in theory and in practice to view them as a minority group (Zola, 1989).

Still, the demand for equal citizenship was politically strategic and effective as the rallying cry of the disability movement during the 1970s in its fight for substantial legal change (Anspach, 1979; Driedger, 1989; Scotch, 1984). Somewhat later, and influenced by European voices, U.S. disability rights activists made the case for human rights—rights owed to all human beings, regardless of national affiliation and independent of cultural or political context. Rights such as those enumerated in the 1948 United Nations Universal Declaration of Human Rights, it was argued, were so utterly basic that their denial amounted to a travesty of justice. This approach has continued and culminated in the 2006 United Nations Convention on the Rights of Persons with Disabilities, which the United States signed in 2009.

In the United States and many other high-resource, industrialized countries, the disability rights movement—grounded upon one or another version of the social model of disability—has played itself out against a background of civil or human rights and has strived to incorporate these rights into specific policies, primarily in the areas of health, rehabilitation, transportation, education, and employment. As we shall see below, moreover, nearly all disability policy in the United States can be traced to the demands of disabled veterans: The very first attempt to shape disability policy at the federal level was the 1918 Veterans Rehabilitation Act. This has left its mark. Disability policy and law, despite the rights revolution, tends to be reactive and piecemeal (Bickenbach, 1993; Leichowitz 1988; Stone 1984). Often, too, disability policies have seemed to be more responsive to the professional needs of service providers and bureaucrats than to people with disabilities themselves (Albrecht, 1992).

Disability policy has always been incoherent and highly vulnerable to shifts in political attention. Programs for disabled veterans have been created and financed, it is true, but once they were put in place, it was assumed that "the disability problem" had been solved, and policy makers turned to other issues. The disability rights movement, being essentially a consumer protest, has long been aware of the inherent inadequacies of disability policy, its incoherence, its reactive and ad hoc nature. As we shall see, one of the central and ongoing challenges of disability policy is discovering how to mainstream it so that it is fully integrated with public policy, rather than added on after other policy decisions have been made.

The Anti-Discrimination Strategy in Disability Law

How have the social model and human rights approach shaped disability law? In some ways that is an easy question since law is the primary vehicle for human rights. Philosophically, the civil and human rights approach rests on a demand for equality for persons with disabilities. But translating that abstract political demand into specific laws has always been challenging (and not just for people with disabilities; the same has been true for African Americans and women). The most natural approach, as mentioned, was to follow the pattern of the civil rights movement and secure enforceable protections against discrimination on the grounds of disability.

In retrospect, the social model and rights approach can be credited with nearly every change in attitude and treatment of people with disabilities in the last three decades, from the provision of curb cuts and accessible bathrooms, to the creation of programs to integrate developmentally disabled children into the public schools, to the implementation of anti-discriminatory employment policies. As it has matured, the social model and rights approach has adopted some of the theoretical developments introduced by feminists and Black theorists, including identity politics. Yet, through it all, faith has been retained in the legal representation of disability rights in anti-discrimination legislation in general and the Americans with Disabilities Act of 1990 (ADA) in particular.

Reading through the academic and popular literature of the disability rights movement in the United States from the 1960s through to the 1990s, one theme that keeps recurring is that while the "equality agenda" is first and foremost, the "cultural agenda" is not far behind. The U.S. disability movement has always reacted strongly against the cultural view of disability expressed in stereotypes of people with disabilities as infirm, inferior, and childlike in their dependency on the good will (or charity) of the majority, "normal" population. Although some disabled feminists argued that dependency is universal and part of the human condition (Morris, 1992) while fully sharing the goal of equal opportunity, the disability movement often aligned itself with the very different goals of independence, unfettered autonomy, and self-sufficiency.

Few disability theorists have more clearly expressed the prominent role that anti-discrimination protection must play in disability policy and law than Harlan Hahn:

> All facets of the environment are moulded by public policy and . . . government policies reflect widespread social attitudes or values; as a result, existing features of architectural design, job requirements, and daily life that have a discriminatory impact on disabled citizens cannot be viewed merely as happenstance or coincidence. On the contrary, they seem to signify conscious or unconscious sentiments supporting a hierarchy of dominance and subordination between nondisabled and disabled segments of the population that is fundamentally incompatible with legal principles of freedom and equality. (Hahn, 1993, pp. 46–47)

Here Hahn ably identifies the core rationale for putting anti-discrimination at the heart of disability law and policy. Because of their minority group status, people with disabilities are denied the full enjoyment of their rights, principally through entrenched discrimination created by prevailing attitudes that are part of the very fabric of our culture and suffuse all social institutions. For Hahn, "the primary problems confronting citizens with disabilities are bias, prejudice, segregation, and discrimination that can be eradicated thorough policies designed to guarantee them equal rights" (Hahn, 1987, p. 182). Although Hahn was well aware that courts and judges are not immune from prevailing "disabling images" and attitudes, he argued that legally enforceable prohibitions against discrimination based on disability stand the best chance of guaranteeing civil and human rights to all people with disabilities.

In its pure form, anti-discrimination, either as a policy or as an explicit legal tool, has an internal logic that requires us to, first, identify a *group characteristic* that defines the oppressed minority group; second, identify an action or behavior that is *discriminatory* against a person or group identified by that characteristic; and finally, provide a compensatory *remedy* for the discriminatory action or behavior. Each of these three requirements has created problems of judicial interpretation for the ADA. Saving the details for later, these problems focus on (a) disability as a group characteristic, (b) discrimination as an action or behavior, and (c) the appropriateness of the remedy in light of the background objective of full participation and equality.

Enduring Themes of Disability Policy and Law

As we shall see in Chapter 2, controversies that hearken back to the question of whether the anti-discrimination strategy, however extended or modified, is sufficient for the rights approach and the equality aims of persons with disabilities are an enduring theme of disability policy and law. Although no commentator has argued that discrimination against people with disabilities does not exist—indeed, recognition of discrimination is a consensus that crosses the U.S. political spectrum—there are certainly those who argue that the ADA is either counterproductive to the interests of persons with disabilities (e.g., Epstein, 1992), or essential to their interests but not sufficient to the task of protecting rights, achieving meaningful equality, or fulfilling the policy aspirations of persons with disabilities (e.g., Bagenstos, 2009; Bickenbach, 1993; Schriner, 2001). Moreover, the responsibilities incurred once the United States ratifies the UN Convention on the Rights of Persons with Disabilities have the potential to profoundly affect how the rights agenda is developed in the United States.

Suffused through these debates is a classic controversy about the proper role of the law, or more precisely of the rule of judges, in policy development. Legislatures at all levels of government pass laws and regulations that implement policy; but in common-law countries like the United States, lawyers and judges interpret these laws and policy is affected by these interpretations. It is an open question whether it is appropriate, beneficial, or indeed unavoidable that judges contribute to the shaping of policy though their decisions. Most scholars argue that this interplay is potentially beneficial to secure clarity and general applicability of laws as policy tools. In part as a response to this interplay between legislatures and the judiciary, agencies of the executive branch of government may be established to provide guidance in the interpretation of laws in the hope that courts will abide by interpretations that preserve the spirit of the policy. The Equal Employment Opportunity Commission (EEOC) is such an agency, responsible for enforcing and interpreting several pieces of anti-discrimination legislation in the employment sector, including the ADA (see further discussion of the EEOC's role in Chapter 5).

The following sections introduce other enduring themes or debates, some of which have already been hinted at, that will also set the agenda for Chapter 2.

What Is Disability?

A report prepared for the Interagency Committee on Disability Research (2003) found 67 different legal and policy definitions of "disability" (or "handicap") in federal statutes, from civil rights, education, and internal revenue to Social Security.

And this is only the tip of the iceberg. In the hundreds of distinct programs for persons with disabilities administrated by the federal government, there are many other definitions of who is disabled and qualifies for the program; across state programs, there are countless more. With effort, one might be able to reduce this number to a handful of model definitions, but one thing is clear: At all levels of government, disability policy is governed by many different definitions of disability that identify different groups of people.

The enduring debate is whether this is a sign of incoherence that should be remedied, inevitable and something we just have to live with, or, finally, appropriate and perfectly acceptable. Would anything be gained by having a single definition of disability that would be used across policy sectors and for all objectives? Would a single definition undermine the effectiveness of different kinds of disability policy that aim to achieve very different goals? We return to this complex issue in Chapter 2.

Universal or Targeted

Another pervasive concern is whether policy should be universal, in the sense of being designed to fulfill policy objectives for everyone, or specifically targeted to people with disabilities. Universal policy, while not singling out sub-populations by name or description, when properly designed can accommodate differences between and among sub-populations, so that the overall policy objectives are achieved fairly and equally by all. Targeted policies focus on the needs and objectives of a defined population, often in response to historical inequalities of treatment or abuse. Targeted policies require "eligibility determination" that qualifies an individual to benefit from the targeted program.

Universal policies also need a characterization of sub-populations, but only in order to identify the differences that need to be accommodated in order to universally achieve the overall policy objectives.

In part, the contrast between targeted and universal policies reflects another contrast already mentioned: that between Harlan Hahn's minority group approach and Irving Zola's universal approach. The impact of this contrast on policy is quite far-reaching, as it affects how the political and economic argument for the need for disability policy is constructed. All policy is driven by demographic information, and in particular prevalence statistics (Stone, 2002): The greater the number of people affected, the bigger the social problem and the more likely policy will have a higher political profile and economic impact. Hahn's call to focus on a minority group status, created as a deviation from culturally defined standards of the normal and operationalized in terms of explicit indicators of social visibility (wheelchair use, blindness, aberrant behavior, difficulty communicating), suggests that the prevalence of disability should be relatively low, since to be socially noticeable as an "insular and discrete" minority group, the disability will tend to be severe. Zola's universalism, which clearly reflects a longitudinal and continuous understanding of disability, points to far higher prevalence—potentially everyone may be covered. (In Chapter 5 we look in more detail at the issue of prevalence.)

Inclusive or Separate

A similar theme has a greater application to areas of life, such as education, in which differences impact centrally on how the program is constructed and delivered. The issue is whether the program should aim for separate but equal services, for inclusion, or for full integration. Each option has its consequences, both positive and negative, and debates continue about both the effectiveness and the fairness of different policy strategies. Is mainstreaming always the best solution, or is more good than harm done by retaining "special" services tailored to specific, and potentially unique, needs (Scotch, 2000)?

Impairment Focus or Environment Focus

A theme with many manifestations across policy areas is whether our objective should be to address, prevent, or mitigate the impairment aspect of disability—to change the person, so to speak—or to invest our resources in accommodations and other modifications to the physical, human-built, and social world so that the impairment does not unduly or unfairly affect a fair range of opportunities. If, as seems sensible, the answer is that both approaches should be adopted, the issue then becomes, given limitations of social resources, how should the balance be achieved?

Underlying the previous three themes, and to some degree cutting across them, is a partly empirical, partly political controversy that takes us back to competing models of disabilities. The issue is whether impairments matter, and if they do, how and how much do they matter (Wasserman, 1998)? Advocates of the medical model insist that impairments and functional limitations are the entire story: If we deal with those, then disability will disappear. On the other side, radical social model advocates insist that impairments, functional limitations, and other "differences" are not relevant to disability at all, as this is purely a matter of socially constructed disadvantage (Oliver, 1990; Roth, 1983). One underlying challenge for disability policy, therefore, is to find a way between these extremes, or in the words of the U.S. Commission on Civil Rights report in 1983, "The goal is neither to exaggerate and stereotype nor to ignore . . . functional limitations" (USCCR, 1983).

Sword or Shield

Another theme in disability law involves a common legal metaphor: Should disability law be a sword or a shield? That is, should the law enable and empower an individual or a group of persons with disabilities to take on barriers, whether physical or social, and where successful alter social, cultural, economic, or political institutions to dismantle these barriers? Or should the legal tools we create function primarily to protect the interests of people with disabilities that might otherwise not be taken into account in the pursuit of other policy objectives? Again, if we adopt a balanced approach using the law in both ways, how can we identify the proper and most effective balance?

Reactive, Piecemeal Policy or Unified and Coherent Policy

Although not unique in this regard, disability policy has long been reactive and ad hoc rather than unified and coherent. Ed Berkowitz (1987) notoriously described employment policy for people with disabilities as consisting of "layers of outdated programs" piled one on the other in an incoherent attempt at reform or response to new political pressures or economic conditions. The hundreds of federal and state programs that come and go, relying on an equal number of definitions of disability for eligibility, often have different, if not conflicting, objectives and use policy tools that create an administrative nightmare for those who could benefit from them. On the other hand, it might be argued that this incoherence is not only unavoidable, it has the virtue of being flexible and individualized, and a "one size fits all" disability policy might be coherent, but unfair and ineffectual.

Equality of Opportunities or Results

A theme that calls forth more fundamental political values is whether the desired outcome of all of our policy and law for people with disabilities should be to achieve a "level playing field" of equal opportunities (acknowledging the fact that some people with disabilities will not be able to translate opportunity into a successful, or even viable, life), or whether we should adopt the far more radical approach of seeking equality of results (acknowledging that, in the face of unavoidable human differences in talent and ability, our policy and law must be tailored to make continual adjustments and responses to unequal results over time)?

Intersectionality

Another theme that needs to be dealt with in legal and policy terms involves the recently labeled notion of "intersectionality," which recognizes that people may hold more than one social identity at a time—people are disabled and women, disabled and aging, disabled and African American (Silvers, 1999). This is a challenge for targeted policy and anti-discrimination law, or indeed for any response to disability that ignores other, potentially influential affiliations with other groups who have an equality agenda that may or may not align with that of disability.

Public or Private

A debate that rages across all areas of policy is whether the state and its agencies—the public sphere—is the best, or the only, institutional structure for responding to the needs and interests of persons with disabilities, or whether it would be more effective and efficient to allow the private sector, in particular the free market, to deal with these concerns. Although disability policy of the past century rejected the private, charity approach in favor of some form of public response, it remains a policy question whether the best policy tools might be private, either for the delivery of services or remedial response to discriminatory practices. Although often a technical economic question beyond the scope of this volume, the public–private debate is indeed an enduring theme of disability policy.

A related issue of great importance to persons in need of personal assistance services for the basic activities of daily life is whether these services should to any degree be within the scope of public regulation (for example, by means of a state-funded and monitored service brokerage arrangement), or whether they should be left entirely to the open market in a consumer-run and directly funded approach following the so-called "independent living" model. Similarly, the assistive technology market might arguably be best created and managed by the state, regulating the development, production, and safety of wheelchairs and other mobility aids; transportation, communication, and other impairment-related aids; and durable medical equipment such as orthotics and prosthetics. Alternatively, it might be suggested that the free market is best for both development and distribution of these technologies and aids.

Finally, there is one remaining public–private issue that arises most clearly in disability ethics. The question is whether there are some aspects of life that are unquestionably outside the proper purview of public policy and law, some areas of privacy in which nothing is achieved, and much potentially sacrificed, by bringing them into public scrutiny. Are there, for example, areas of life that are so private—involving the decision to have or keep a child, to continue living or seek a painless end of life, or to maintain the life of another where there is no prospect of recovery and only continued pain—that our policy and our law should not interfere with them, even if decisions made are potentially detrimental to the interests of persons with disabilities?

All nine of these enduring policy debates have consequences on the lives of people with disabilities: They are neither abstract nor academic concerns. It would impossible in a single volume to deal adequately with all of them, so in Chapter 2 we will return in more detail only to the issue of definition, the public–private balance, and the debate between universal and targeted policy. At this point, however, and before we turn to the history of disability policy, we need to complete our introduction by looking at disability ethics.

What Is Disability Ethics?

Ethics in General

Ethics is a branch of philosophy concerned with issues of right and wrong, good and bad, virtue and vice. Although often used interchangeably, the term "ethics" is occasionally used for specific moral codes of professions and other groups, while the term "morality" (or mores) is restricted to the actual ethical beliefs and customs of particular cultures. But this is mostly a verbal distinction. The important difference is between morality as a matter of personal beliefs or cultural customs that can be empirically discovered, and the systemic and analytic treatment of moral issues, which is called ethics.

There are common misconceptions about morality which, were they true, would make ethics of little relevance to policy and law, of no interest to disability studies, and indeed of little interest to anyone. The first is that morality is purely subjective or just a matter of taste or opinion. The evidence for this is supposed to be that ethical controversies seem unending and that people sometimes get very emotional about the positions they hold. But this is compatible with moral issues being very difficult to resolve (which they often are) and people caring about them (which they often do). If moral issues were really subjective, no one would waste time arguing over them. (Truly subjective topics, like preferences in flavor of ice cream or other likes and dislikes, are neither debated—no one can show that you are wrong about your preferences — nor of much lasting interest to others.)

The other misconception is that morality is so completely culturally determined that there is no scope for reasoning or theorizing about it. But this view as well is inconsistent with the facts. People from vastly different cultures share many basic moral beliefs (that it is generally better to live a full and active life than not, that people matter, that one should take care of one's children, and so on), and we debate moral issues both earnestly and rationally. A related misconception is that morality may be all well and good, but sometimes it is too expensive to be moral, or other considerations are more important. But this too mistakes moral beliefs for mere preferences: Moral problems require practical solutions, not impossibly impractical and idealistic solutions. Moral solutions are "all things considered" solutions that take into account everything relevant to the situation. If an option to solve a problem is too expensive in time, resources, or human energy, then it is impractical and ethically unsound since it unduly sacrifices other important interests.

Usually when these or other skeptical views about morality are expressed, the speaker is not thinking of real, concrete moral dilemmas that she or he has had to face, or could face, in his or her life. If your parent is dying but has not yet been told, should you tell him or her? If your spouse wants children but you do not, should you change your mind to make your spouse happy? Should you risk your life to save a stranger from drowning? Should you to save someone else's child from drowning? To save your own child? If four people need a liver transplant to live and there is only one available liver, do you give it to a young child who has cognitive impairments, to someone who is very old, but rich, to someone who is an alcoholic, but a marvelous musician, or to your good friend who will spend the next 20 years in prison for murder? These are not easy questions. But they are neither trivial, unimportant, nor just a matter of irrational personal preference. These are the kinds of questions that ethics in general, and disability ethics in particular, is about.

There is some point, however, in distinguishing between personal morality (the basis for how one lives one's life and the decisions one makes about oneself) and social ethics (the basic moral principles, values, or ethical theories about which there is sufficient agreement to form an important input into our public policies and laws). Social ethical values inform and underwrite our civil and human rights, and, at least for viable and relatively stable cultures, there is not much dispute or controversy about what those principles and values are. The disputes that make the newspapers and academic journals typically involve more concrete and particular questions where values conflict, or when the issue is just too complicated or novel for an easy answer. Social ethics (or "practical ethics") is the ethics of real, concrete, practical social issues, and typically these are dilemmas in the true sense of that word: problems about which reasonable people, in good faith, and sharing common values, can disagree, since there is no perfect answer and more than one solution seems ethically justifiable.

Bioethics and Disability

Bioethics, or health care ethics, is a particularly volatile and high profile example of practical ethics. There are others, such as business ethics, the ethics of legal and other professions, or journalistic ethics, and these too raise troubling issues. But since bioethics deals with life and death issues, involving basic values like autonomy, dignity, and respect for persons, it is an ethical domain of considerable interest and controversy. It is also the primary source of moral issues that involve the concept of disability, as well as the lives, rights, and interests of persons with disabilities. As with disability policy and law, since people with disabilities are people, all areas of practical ethics concern them. But there have been highly sensitive and troubling moral issues requiring ethical analysis that have engaged the disability community, and these have tended to overlap with the domain of bioethics.

The relationship between bioethics and disability, however, has not been an easy one, and disability scholars have vigorously condemned much of the work of "mainstream bioethicists." On the face of it, as Adrienne Asch (2001) has remarked, this seems peculiar since bioethics and disability studies converge at many points. Both appeared only in the last 50 years, both grew out of responses to the actions and paternalistic assumptions of the biomedical clinical and research communities, and both expressed themselves ethically in terms of basic human values of autonomy, self-determination, and respect for persons.

Even their early histories converged. Bioethics arose in the United States in reaction to the abuses in World War II Germany, and carried on in the postwar United States in response to medical scientists who performed harmful research on vulnerable people—prisoners and cognitively impaired and institutionalized people. Prompted by a whistleblowing researcher at Harvard Medical School (Beecher, 1966) and publicity surrounding the egregious case of the Tuskegee Syphilis Study (1932–1972), the National Commission for the Protection of Human Subjects of Biomedical and Behavioral Research in the Department of Health, Education, and Welfare revised and expanded its regulations for the protection of human research subjects. In 1978, it released the Belmont Report, formally titled "Ethical Principles and Guidelines for the Protection of Human Subjects of Research" (U.S. Department of Health, Education, and Welfare, 1978). The report listed three ethical principles that governed research on human subjects: respect for persons and their autonomy; beneficence, in the sense of maximizing benefit and minimizing risk; and justice, ensuring non-exploitative research and fairly distributing costs and benefits to all research participants. But these values were also part of the ethical foundations of the independent living and disability rights movement that was in ascendency at more or less the same time.

Yet when disability researchers first investigated the bioethical literature, they were appalled (Parens & Asch, 2001). Mainstream bioethics seemed to be built on the assumption that impairments necessarily and catastrophically diminish the person's quality of life, so that living with a disability, almost by definition, meant living a life of less value. The concern was made concrete in the early 1970s with very public legal cases involving people with brain injuries in a "persistent vegetative state"

(PVS). The 1976 Karen Ann Quinlan case brought the quality of life argument to the forefront (as did the Terri Schiavo legal battle three decades later). Public opinion was split on whether it was morally acceptable to end the lives of people with such injuries because their impairments so dramatically and permanently undercut the value of their lives that death was preferable, not just for their families, but for them as well.

Following the release of the influential President's Commission Report in 1982, hospital guidelines for withholding lifesaving therapies also reflected an increasing social tolerance for ending the life of newborns with impairments. Although they were not of one mind on these issues, mainstream bioethicists tended to agree that euthanasia of those in PVS, or selective abortion based on prenatal screening, were justifiable social practices because they prevented the continuing life, or the birth, of individuals whose lives had diminished value. Disability scholars, for their part, insist that the quality of life for persons with disabilities, if lessened at all, is lessened far more by discrimination than by the underlying impairment, and that "a truly objective and demographic study of low QOL [Quality of Life] among disabled people would show that it is caused by the same factors that cause low QOL among nondisabled people" (Amundson, 2005, p. 120).

The disability community was particularly offended by the position held by Australian philosopher Peter Singer, who argued on utilitarian greatest-good-for-greatest-number grounds that abortion and infanticide on the basis of disability is not only morally correct, but should be made public policy. The 1985 book by Helga Kuhse and Peter Singer provocatively titled *Should the Baby Live? The Problem of Handicapped Infants* set the stage for a vigorous political and academic response from the disability community. Although initially somewhat modest in his views, Singer later remarked that "the killing of a defective infant is not morally equivalent to the killing of a person; very often it is not morally wrong at all" (Singer, 1993, p. 184)—a claim that the disability community likened to Nazi campaigns to "purify the race," eugenics, and other historical examples of abuse directed at vulnerable people, including persons with disabilities (Duster, 1990; Gallagher, 1990).

Mainstream bioethics, in short, failed "to question the traditional understandings of impairment, illness, or disability" (Asch, 2001, p. 299). From the disability perspective, bioethicists seemed more concerned about preventing people with disabilities from being born, than about ensuring that they had equal access to health care and the right to make their own decisions. These days, mainstream bioethics has changed its focus, and a more productive relationship between disability and bioethics may be possible (see Daniels, 2008; McLean & Williamson, 2007).

The Future Scope of Disability Ethics

Although disability ethics arose primarily as a critique of mainstream bioethics, and will continue to contribute to these debates, it is likely that the scope of disability ethics will broaden in the future. As we shall see in the next chapter, from the outset the principal controversies in disability ethics centered around high profile legal cases involving individuals. Increasing issues of justice in allocation have moved disability ethics from the sphere of practical or applied ethics to the deeper and richer territory of political philosophy, where concerns of distributive justice and the implications of equality predominate. Disability studies scholars have remarked that the disability focus is now clearly linked to the intersection between bioethics and political philosophy (Silvers, Wasserman, & Mahowald, 1998), and theorizing about the nature of disability has merged with the current and developing ethical and political theoretical frameworks, such as in the application of Nobel Prize–winning economist Amartya Sen's theory of capability in the work of Martha Nussbaum and others (Nussbaum, 2007). Without doubt, there are many exciting developments awaiting disability ethics in the future.

History

The Early History of Disability Policy and Law

Although one could argue that religious laws and charitable institutions from the classical ancient world, the Middle Ages, and up to the early modern period were all precursors of disability law and policy, it was not until early 17th century that law and policy existed in forms recognizable today. There are two exceptions to this broad claim. The first is that most legal of the ancient cultures, namely Rome, which singled out people with sensory, mobility, and mental impairments for various social purposes. The second is the beginning of recorded English common law (roughly the 13th century on), when the Crown was assigned legal responsibility for protecting those with intellectual impairments ("natural fools") and those with mental illness ("lunatics") (Berkson, 2006).

The first clear example of a law about disability in the English-speaking world is the English Poor Law of 1601 (technically known as *Reginae Elizabethae Anno* 43), enacted as a direct response to the increasing numbers of beggars along the roads and city streets, a result of the Reformation and the closing down of hospices, almshouses, and other refuges run by the Catholic Church. The law shifted the responsibility for poor people to the Parishes, giving them the power to raise taxes for this purpose.

Notoriously, the Poor Law created three categories of the poor: the "lame, impotent, old, blind" poor who could not work and were provided for in almshouses; the able-bodied poor who were sent to work in workhouses; and the idle poor (and vagrants) who were sent to houses of correction. There is some evidence that while people with intellectual impairments were able to benefit from this distinction, stigma and fear associated with the aberrant behavior of people with mental illness led to their being classified as idle or dangerous and so imprisoned (Rushton, 1988; Stiker, 1999). The distinction between the "worthy" and the "unworthy" poor—with people with impairments being the paradigm of the first group—was fundamental to the English social policy on poverty for the next 300 years.

The Poor Law traveled directly to the English colonies, and the first almshouse in what would become the United States was established in Boston in 1662, although public institutions explicitly for persons with disabilities did not come on the scene until the 1820s. Mental hospitals sprung up on the European continent; and in particular the famous Bethlem Royal Hospital (from which the word "bedlam" is derived) for "poor distracted people" was established in London in 1620. This became the model for other such hospitals in England, with legislation in 1714 authorizing confinement for the "furiously mad." Throughout the early part of the 18th century in England and Europe, madhouses and mental hospitals proliferated without explicit legal regulation. England, reacting to horror stories from private mental facilities, began to regulate them in 1774, passing what became essentially the first mental health legislation in Europe.

The Pennsylvania Provincial Assembly had authorized the establishment of the first such mental hospital in the American colonies (for "Lunaticks or Persons distempered in Mind and deprived of their rational Faculties") in 1751, which was built the following year under the leadership of Benjamin Franklin and physician Thomas Bond. In 1793, the state of Kentucky passed legislation authorizing payment to families who were too poor to take care of relatives with mental illness or intellectual impairment.

Anticipating a pattern that characterized later U.S. developments in disability policy, veterans of the Revolutionary War were the first individuals to receive a "disability" or "invalid" pension for war-related impairments. The Continental Congress decided, in 1776, that the new country should not permit "him, who, in the pride and vigor of youth, wasted his health and shed his blood in freedom's cause, with desponding heart and palsied limbs to totter from door to door" (Liachowitz, 1988; Teipe, 2002). Unfortunately, by 1783, Congress realized it could not afford to pay the pension annuities, and General George Washington himself had to step in to negotiate with a group of officers who, in protest, had refused to disband (Teipe, 2002).

A hundred years later, after the Civil War, the federal government created a pension program for disabled Union veterans that, at the time, was the world's largest and most generous social insurance scheme, although veterans with mental disorders and infectious diseases benefited far less than those with more traditional war injuries. Over time, the program was plagued by corruption and political patronage. As the press exposed alleged frauds and bogus claims, the definition of disability came into question. Disabled veterans were portrayed as scamming the system and taking advantage of the public trust (Blanck, 2007). It has been argued that this portrayal set the stage for the reliance on medical determinants of disability and on doctors as "gatekeepers" of disability policy, which characterized the U.S. experience for the next 100 years (Blanck, 2001, 2007; Blanck & Millender, 2000).

Nineteenth Century: The Rise of the Institution

Nineteenth-century Europe was noted for the development of educational programs for deaf and blind children, with innovators such as Louis Braille and Jean Itard, as well as the beginnings of what would become physical and speech therapies. In the United States, in response to a major influx of immigrants, urbanization, and rapidly changing demographics, the 1820s saw the growth in a variety of institutions—from mental institutions to residential schools for children who were deaf and blind. The first treatise on the education of children with disabilities was published in the United States in 1846—Edouard Seguin's *The Moral Treatment, Hygiene, and Education of Idiots and Other Backward Children*—pointing the direction toward what would later be called "special education" (Jaeger & Bowman, 2005).

Also in 1840s, the efforts of Dorothea Dix helped to improve conditions in U.S. mental hospitals and to persuade state legislatures to step up the construction of new institutions. The rationale for institutions was that mental illness (by means of so-called "moral treatment") could be cured. As populations in prisons grew, inmates who were dangerous or disturbed were shifted to the mental asylums, which in turn became overcrowded, leading to the construction of even more institutions (Rothman, 1990). Nineteen state mental facilities that housed 5,000 or so persons in 1850 were augmented by 55 new institutions with a combined population of 41,000 by 1880. The total number of mental institutions doubled by 1890, and again by 1910 (Braddock & Parish, 2001).

Spurred on by the eugenics movement in the latter decades of the 19th century, most states passed laws either authorizing sterilization of the "feebleminded" or prohibiting them from marrying (Snyder & Mitchell, 2003). Although there was a shift in policy toward children with intellectual impairments that sought to train them to be productive workers, rather than wards of the state, this proved difficult given the unemployment and recession that followed the Civil War, and training schools shifted back into custodial asylums (Wolfensberger, 1976).

By the turn of the 20th century, custodial care, for both those with mental illness and those with intellectual impairments, was a firmly entrenched social policy. With the eugenic view that intellectual impairment was not only inheritable but linked to criminality and poverty, these institutions soon took on the appearance, if not the overt behavior, of prisons. Justified by the immigration policy of 1882 that excluded "defective" individuals, the practice of intellectual testing to identify mentally deficient immigrants was instituted at all ports of entry (Gould, 1981).

Twentieth Century: The Era of Rehabilitation

The combination of institutional and warehousing "solutions" to the problem of intellectual impairments and mental illness, and the growing strength of the eugenics movement, set the stage for the emblematic legal case of the early 20th century. The U.S. Supreme Court's 1927 decision in *Buck v. Bell* affirmed the right of states to sterilize people on grounds of "feeblemindedness." Chief Justice Oliver Wendell Holmes Jr. argued that "it is better for all the world, if instead of waiting to execute degenerate offspring for crime, or to let them starve for their imbecility, society can prevent those who are manifestly unfit from continuing their kind."

In California alone, relying on legislation that was to be the model for Nazi Germany's eugenic sterilization law in 1933, between 300,000 and 400,000 persons were sterilized for feeblemindedness (Reilly, 1991). For persons with mental illness the situation was equally frightening, as this was the era in which electroshock therapy and lobotomization were developed and heavily relied on.

For people with physical impairments in the United States, the 20th century saw the creation or entrenchment of nearly all major forms of disability policy. In Europe these programs, which in time would be the social security components of the "welfare state," arose much earlier with German Chancellor Otto von Bismarck's social security legislation, dating from 1881, first with health and accident insurance for workers and then, by 1889, invalidity and old age insurance for workers. England was one of the last industrialized European countries to follow Germany's lead, in 1908, with an old age pension system and, in 1911, with a National Insurance Act providing sickness and unemployment insurance benefits for some workers on a contributory basis.

In the United States, as mentioned, most early programs were aimed at veterans with war-related impairments, with secular charitable organizations, such as the Red Cross's Institute for Crippled and Disabled Men, created in 1917, joining in. The other beneficiaries were injured workers. As early as 1898, a workmen's compensation bill was introduced in the New York legislature, but it failed to pass. The first state to succeed in passing such legislation was Maryland in 1902, but it was only when the Federal Compensation Act, covering federal employees, was passed in 1908 that other states followed. By 1920, workers' compensation laws were in place in all states of the union (Obermann, 1968).

But the central message of disability policy for most of the 20th century was *rehabilitation*, the view that returning veterans, injured workers, and those with physical impairments yet to enter into the workforce could and should be trained, or otherwise prepared to become gainfully employed. The rise of workers' compensation contributed to the increased prominence of the rehabilitative response, since states were motivated to reduce the cost of compensation by getting workers back to work (Scotch, 1984). Because of the inadequacies of the states' response to rehabilitation, however, and the increasing need for a productive workforce after World War I, the first federal civilian vocational rehabilitation act (the Smith-Fess Act) was signed into law in 1920 by President Woodrow Wilson. The Vocational Rehabilitation Act of 1920 merely extended the coverage of the Smith-Sears Act of 1918, which had been designed to provide vocational rehabilitation and return to employment of disabled individuals discharged from the armed forces, and which itself was a variant of the Smith-Hughes Act of 1917 for vocational education and the Soldier Rehabilitation Act of 1918 (Obermann, 1968).

As several commentators have remarked, the turn to vocational rehabilitation as the primary response to disability in the United States left a permanent mark on disability policy, and as we shall see, on the legal interpretation of the ADA as well (Drimmer, 1993; Hahn, 1986; Obermann, 1968; Scotch, 1984). The effect was threefold. First, as the motivation for disability policy was overwhelmingly economic, the only justification for providing vocational rehabilitation, first to injured veterans and then to others, was the expected economic return. The result was a policy grounded in the category of "employability" (Stone, 1984). Those who had the potential for gainful employment after vocational training, job placement, and counseling were the beneficiaries of rehabilitation services. Those who lacked this potential, however, were left without assistance until the post-Depression Social Security and assistance programs were put into place. The services one received were not a matter of civil rights but—since many existing vocational programs were private or charitable—a matter of federal charity. Second, disability policy was exclusively "supply side" and directed at making the disabled individual—whose defect or infirmity made him or her unable to do the job—employable, rather than making the job more accessible. Finally, disability policy was under the auspices of professional experts who were financed by the government, federal or state, to change the person to fit the demands of the workplace. The disabled individual played no active role in designing the rehabilitation program; that was left to the experts.

World War II and the Great Depression

The next stage in the development of disability policy in the United States began with the Great Depression, starting in 1929. Wages throughout the 1920s had remained fairly stable, although the economy relied entirely on continuing investment by the very wealthy. After World War I, the United States was a creditor nation, exporting more than it was importing; but the edifice was crumbling, and when the stock market crashed and the wholly unregulated banking system unraveled, unemployment soared, GNP and other economic indicators suffered, and soup

kitchens, bread lines, and shantytowns known as Hoovervilles proliferated across the country. Franklin D. Roosevelt easily won the 1932 presidential election and almost immediately created the Committee on
Economic Security to make recommendations on a comprehensive program concerning old age security, unemployment, sickness, and health
insurance. Prior to the 1930s, support for poor individuals, disabled or
not, involved an incoherent patchwork of state, local, and private, charity-
based services that offered more moral admonition than benefits (Bowe,
1978; Scotch & Berkowitz, 1990). Roosevelt's committee responded with a
proposal for a program, new to the United States, that had been introduced across Europe some 50 years earlier: Social Security.

The first welfare legislation in America was the Social Security Act of
1935, but for persons with disabilities, it was disappointing. The act's
eleven titles covered old-age benefits, "dependent and crippled children," maternal and child welfare, public health, unemployment compensation, and blind persons. In each instance the act either provided
federal monies to be transferred to states for various programs (as in
the extensive programming for children and unemployment compensation), or created a new federal program (as in the case of the federal
old-age benefits), based on a contributory system in which workers
contributed to their future retirement—the sort of social insurance program we normally think of as Social Security. Although there was a limited program of supplementing state aid to blind persons (in effect the
only federal public assistance program for persons with disabilities
until 1956), as Harlan Hahn has observed, the legislation that was more
reflective of American attitudes toward disability during this period
was probably the Randolph-Sheppard Act of 1936, which allowed persons who were blind to be licensed to operate vending stands in federal
buildings (Hahn, 1986).

Nonetheless, the Social Security Act of 1935 was the predecessor of what
were to become the largest and most expensive programs designed to benefit persons with disabilities, namely, in 1956 Social Security Disability
Insurance (SSDI), and in 1970 Supplemental Security Income (SSI).

The Vocational Rehabilitation Act of 1920 reached relatively few people
with physical disabilities. Although some 250,000 people acquired impairments per year, from 1920 until the passage of important amendments to
the act in 1943, only 12,000 people per year benefited (O'Brien, 2001). The
New Deal changed little about how the program was run, although by
1938 its administration was shifted to the Federal Security Agency (FSA),

under the Social Security Administration that administered the Social Security Act. Vocational rehabilitation stayed with the FSA until 1949, when the FSA was abolished and its functions transferred to the newly formed Department of Health, Education, and Welfare (HEW). At FSA, vocational rehabilitation found a champion in Mary Switzer. As head of the Office of Vocational Rehabilitation, Switzer took the lead during World War II in expanding the conception of vocational rehabilitation from job education and counseling, to the medical and other rehabilitation interventions intended to restore "the whole man" to employability.

The Vocational Rehabilitation Act of 1943 was the first step in a new approach to rehabilitation promoted by Mary Switzer and physicians Howard Rusk and Henry Keeler, all of whom were unapologetic advocates of the medical approach to disability. The act expanded coverage to include rehabilitation for people with mental illness and intellectual impairments, and provided funding to increase rehabilitation and medical services and, for the first time, to support research to reduce, prevent, and eliminate disabilities. The Vocational Rehabilitation Act Amendments of 1954, enthusiastically supported by the Eisenhower administration, allocated more funds for state vocational rehabilitation programs and provided grants for special demonstration projects, research, and training to showcase rehabilitation as the primary response to the needs of America's disabled population.

The 1954 amendments reflected the view that if a disabled person could be made fit for employment by means of rehabilitation, then he or she could become a tax producer rather than a tax consumer, making it just a matter of common sense to provide these necessary services. Federal funds could and should be used to "prime the pumps" for private initiatives and to fund state vocational rehabilitation programs, the argument went, as long as the program did not unduly interfere with how the states used the funding. The act made it clear that it was definitely not the job of the federal government to guarantee rights for persons with disabilities or to remove external barriers in the labor market, but only to provide extra assistance to disabled people to develop their potential (O'Brien, 2001).

In the case of Social Security, the original 1935 act was amended in 1939—to extend benefits to the spouse and minor children of a retired worker and survivor benefits in the case of premature death of a covered worker—but continued without change until 1950, when cost of living increases, pegged to inflation rates, were instituted. As early as 1936, however, plans had been made for a disability insurance that would distinguish the temporarily unemployed individual from the person who, because of severe impairments, was unemployable for his or her entire life. Given this aim, the proposed definition of "disability" was very strict: "an impairment of mind or body which continuously renders it impossible for the disabled person to follow any substantial gainful occupation . . . for the rest of a person's life." Progress on this component of Social Security was delayed during the war years, but by 1949 the view began to circulate throughout the Social Security Administration that perhaps the science of rehabilitation had reached a state where lifetime unemployability was no longer inevitable and these payments could end. It took six years of debate on this utopian possibility before the Congressional Committee on Ways and Means was convinced that cash benefits will always be necessary for some individuals (Berkowitz, 1987).

SSDI and SSI

In 1956, by a bare majority, the Senate Finance Committee finally abandoned its opposition to the House bill, which had passed without difficulty, and after a last-minute compromise limiting benefits to those age 50 or over, the Social Security Disability Insurance program (SSDI) was passed. Ironically, because of the age restriction, the linkage that the Eisenhower administration wanted between application for disability benefits and vocational rehabilitation never made sense, as this age group had a very low rate of success in rehabilitation. Also because of the age restriction, the applicants tended to have age-related impairments such as heart disease and arthritis rather than mental disorders more prevalent with younger populations. In effect, as Berkowitz argues, SSDI became a retirement program rather than a true disability benefit (Berkowitz, 1987).

Much later, during Richard Nixon's first term in office in 1969, it was believed that the existing programs (such as Aid to the Blind, Aid to the Permanently and Totally Disabled, and Aid to the Elderly), which were administered by state and local governments with federal funding, could be brought together under the Social Security Administration. The state programs were administrated by more than a thousand agencies, with huge differences in payment amounts from state to state. It was assumed that the new program, called Supplemental Security Income (SSI), would only apply to the elderly who needed extra income on top of Social Security benefits to bring them out of poverty. But Congress increased Social Security benefits in 1972 and indexed them to the rate of inflation, with the result that the elderly were less likely to need the supplement, and the SSI caseload shifted to adults and children who were blind or had substantial impairments.

The Time of Change: 1960s and 1970s

The period from the late 1950s through to the 1970s in the United States and around the globe was one of fundamental change, not so much in the bureaucratic approach to people with disabilities or other marginalized groups, but socially and culturally. Academically, this was a period in which the social model of disability sprung from various sources, including those captured in the titles of two highly influential texts of the period: Beatrice A. Wright's *Physical Disability: A Psychosocial Approach* (1960) and Constantina Safilios-Rothschild's *The Sociology and Social Psychology of Disability and Rehabilitation* (1970). More importantly, though, this was also a period of widespread and highly visible conflicts over civil rights for African Americans, as well as the re-emergence of the feminist movement and student antiwar activism. The first major result of the social protest was legislation that was to become the model and rallying cry of the emerging disability rights movement a decade later (Scotch, 1984), namely the Civil Rights Act of 1964.

Introduced by President John F. Kennedy, and after his assassination carried to passage by President Lyndon B. Johnson, the six titles of the Civil Rights Act barred unequal application of voter registration, encouraged the desegregation of public schools, outlawed discrimination in public accommodation and facilities on grounds of race, religion, gender, or ethnicity, and banned discrimination on these grounds by any government agencies that received federal funding. In rapid succession, the Civil Rights Act was supplemented by the Voting Rights Act of 1965, guaranteeing access to political participation, and the Civil Rights Act of 1968, guaranteeing access to housing. These acts not only addressed discrimination against African Americans, they also established the crucial constitutional doctrine that the federal government had the power to legislate and enforce protections of civil rights across the country. A closely related triumph for persons with disabilities—often cited as the first step in legislation that led to the ADA itself—was the Architectural Barriers Act of 1968. This act was the first federal law mandating equal physical access to public buildings, and it established what is now know as the Access Board, which remains the primary source of U.S. accessibility standards.

Despite the growing power of social movements in the United States, political activism did not come easily to people with disabilities. Sociologist Rene Anspach in 1979 argued that activism only became a possible strategy for the physically disabled and former mental patients when, using the tools of social protest, they created a political identity for themselves as independent and capable of political action. This required them to address and combat the rehabilitation image of passive victims with broken bodies and minds (Anspach, 1979). The isolated social protests by persons with disabilities that occurred before the 1960s—such as the actions of the League of the Physically Handicapped in Depression-era New York City or those of the National Federation of the Blind in the 1940s—tended to copy the arguments and political actions of European leftist and labor movements (Longmore, 2000). Besides the social agitation that produced the Architectural Barriers Act, in the 1960s people with disabilities closely watched the politics of activism around them and learned its lessons.

The first trans-disability movement did not arise in the United States until the early 1970s, led in part by a truly home-grown social movement: the independent living (IL) movement. The first Center for Independent Living was created in Berkeley, California, in 1972 to assist students with disabilities at the University of California (for histories of the movement see Charlton, 1998; DeJong, 1979; Roberts, 1989; Scotch, 1989). Ed Roberts, a post-polio quadriplegic, entered the university in 1962 (but only after bringing a successful admissions lawsuit against the university) to discover that the only place he could reside was the university health facility with other students with severe disabilities. Roberts immediately got involved in the Berkeley-based radical politics of the 1960s—the free speech movement, Black Power, and the women's movement—and eventually organized a disability group called the Rolling Quads. With a grant from the federal Office of Education, Roberts created the Physically Disabled Students' Program in 1970, primarily to deal with the practical problems facing students in wheelchairs who wanted to live on their own.

In 1971, a Pennsylvania court declared in *PARC v. Commonwealth of Pennsylvania* that segregated education for disabled children was unconstitutional. This and other successes motivated Roberts, Lex Frieden in Texas, and others to move out of the university hospital into the community and organize the Center for Independent Living to provide services that people with disabilities could control on their own, independent of professionals and institutions.

Centers for independent living began to sprout up across the country, catering to local needs of persons with disabilities. The intellectual roots of the IL movement can be linked to civil rights—from the political agenda of deinstitutionalization and demedicalization sought by organizations advocating for those with psychiatric impairments to the self-advocacy group People First for individuals with intellectual impairments—and the emerging consumerism and self-help movements. A central tenet of the movement was a critique of the usually nondisabled professionals who worked on disability issues and whose very careers depended on the "business of disability" (Albrecht, 1992)—the doctors, physiotherapists, rehabilitation counselors, and vocational rehabilitation specialists. These professionals wanted domination and dependence, or as Justin Dart (a prominent player in the passage of the ADA) put it, they were fond of the socialist, "welfare mentality" that saw people with disabilities as broken and needy (Bagenstos, 2006). No less of a scholar than blind lawyer Jacobus tenBrock argued in 1966 that social welfare programs perpetuate dependence and discourage independence, undermining the very "right to live in the world" (tenBroek, 1966).

Rehabilitation Act Title V

Many of the political themes that characterized the U.S. disability rights movement from that time on grew out of this experience. The leaders of the growing disability rights groups transferred the political lessons they had learned from other political movements to a disability context (Scotch, 1989). Building in particular on the African American civil rights movement (Barnartt & Scotch, 2001), the disability movement consciously added the element of independence to the political rhetoric: "Nothing about us without us," the powerful political slogan that animated disability groups around the world (Charlton, 1998), captured the rejection of the professionalism and enforced dependency of the rehabilitation approach that had dominated U.S. policy from the 1920s onward. Although some critics have argued that the movement may have too quickly rejected all aspects of social welfare in favor of individualist market solutions to the discrimination people with disabilities faced (Williams, 1983), clearly the message resonated. Soon after Judy Heumann, a disability rights organizer from New York, moved to Berkeley to attend graduate school, the political focus of this ever-growing movement shifted to anti-discrimination law.

Although in the early 1970s there were nearly 30 federal laws that prohibited discrimination against "handicapped people," the act that was to be the catalyst for change was an old act with a new title, the Rehabilitation Act of 1973. The reason that President Nixon vetoed the act when it was first proposed in 1972 was not the usual vocational rehabilitation provisions, which were unchanged since 1920, but because of Title V, and in particular Sections 503 and 504, often called the first civil rights legislation for individuals with disabilities. Disability rights advocates had no direct hand in writing these sections, which were modified versions of Title VI of the Civil Rights Act of 1964 (among the many histories of this period, see Fleischer & Zames, 2001; O'Brien, 2001; Scotch, 1984; Shapiro, 1993; and from a European perspective, Driedger, 1989).

Still the law of the land, Section 503 requires federal contractors to adopt affirmative action programs to hire people with disabilities. Section 504 stated: "No otherwise qualified handicapped individual in the United States . . . shall, solely by reason of his handicap, be excluded from the participation in, be denied the benefits of, or be subjected to discrimination under any program or activity receiving Federal financial assistance." Earlier Title V provisions required any program receiving federal funding to make reasonable accommodation for individuals with disabilities so that they may participate fully.

Although Nixon eventually signed the bill into law—after Judy Heumann and 80 activists organized a sit-in on Madison Avenue in New York—there was a catch: To be fully implemented, the law required federal agencies to adopt regulations governing the implementation process, and these were not part of the act. What was needed, it turned out, was for disabled student James Cherry's request for a parking place to be turned down by his university (Fleischer & Zames, 2001). Cherry's lawyers, after exhausting the administrative route to getting the Section 504 regulations drafted, began a lawsuit that resulted, four years later, in a decision by the U.S. District Court for the District of Columbia to issue an order requiring the Department of Health, Education, and Welfare (HEW) to issue Section 504 regulations. Although this order was stayed by the Court of Appeals, the next day President Jimmy Carter took office and directed the new Secretary of HEW, Joseph Califano, to implement Section 504.

It came as a shock to the disability community, including Frank Bowe, the head of the American Coalition of Citizens with Disabilities, Inc., when Califano demanded time to "study" the regulations and proceeded to drastically water down their effectiveness (Bowe, 1978). Bowe and a coalition of other rights advocates called for public protest at the vocational rehabilitation offices in 11 cities. Most of the protests were defused, but in San Francisco the occupation of the HEW offices led by Judy Heumann lasted 25 days before, finally, on April 28, 1977, Califano announced that he would sign the regulations without amendment. This was the first clear victory for a united and organized disability rights movement in the United States. As other anti-discrimination acts came into force—first the Education for All Handicapped Children Act in 1975 (which guaranteed children with disabilities the right to public education, and was later renamed the Individuals with Disabilities Education Act), then the Developmental Disabilities Assistance and Bill of Rights Act in 1976, and the amended version of the 1968 Architectural Barriers Act, as well as several positive results in public transport accessibility cases—the future looked bright for disability rights.

But the first case interpreting Section 504, which reached the Supreme Court in 1979, *Southeastern Community College v. Davis,* was disappointing. The case involved a severely hearing impaired nurse, Frances Davis, who used Section 504 as the basis for her claim that the Community College should change its requirement of functional hearing for acceptance into the nursing program. Although several issues were explored in this case and there were many encouraging comments made by the court, still Davis lost on the grounds that the accommodation requested constituted affirmative action, not anti-discrimination protection, which was all that Section 504 offered. Moreover, the court insisted that Davis needed to prove that the college designed its nursing program explicitly to exclude people with disabilities. The failure to acknowledge reasonable accommodation as intrinsically related to the protection against discrimination, and the implication that discrimination needed to be intentional, suggested that the courts were still uncomfortable with disability rights. The *Davis* decision was to be modified five years later in the *Alexander v. Choate* decision, in which reasonable accommodation was distinguished from affirmative action: Reasonable accommodation is designed to remove present barriers, not to compensate for past unfairness, as is the case with affirmative action.

Paralleling these developments, from 1982 to 1984 an unlikely coalition formed in response to the Baby Doe cases, in which medical treatment was withheld from disabled infants. Advocates representing groups such as the Disability Rights Center out of California and the National Association for Retarded Citizens joined with the predominantly religious and politically conservative right-to-life groups to seek federal protection for newborns with disabilities for whom lifesaving treatment was denied, apparently as a matter of standard medical procedure (Paige & Karnofsky, 1986; Scotch, 1984).

Since many disability rights organizations were pro-choice and politically liberal, the alliance was fraught with tensions, many of which had to be addressed by feminist disability advocates (see the debates in Fine & Asch, 1988). Yet, as political action often requires otherwise untenable alliances, the two groups issued joint statements and filed court briefs in support of the policies of the Reagan administration to protect newborns. Other than an amendment to the Child Abuse and Neglect Act of 1984 that required states to report and investigate instances where treatment for a newborn appeared to be denied on the basis of disability, the coalition had limited success, primarily because Congress was reluctant to create a role for the federal government in medical decisions. From the 1980s, the disability rights–religious conservative alliance has from time to time regrouped to address common bioethical concerns.

The Road to the ADA

During the 1980s, disability lawyers and advocates began to suspect that the resources of Section 504 were simply not good enough to ensure full protection against discrimination. The Berkeley Independent Living Center helped to found the Disability Rights Education and Defense Fund (DREDF) in 1979 to make it clear that disability rights were just as important as civil rights based on race or gender. DREDF went on to become one of the primary sources of legal expertise that went into the drafting and passage of the ADA at the end of the 1980s. Attempts to expand the coverage of the Civil Rights Act of 1964 to more fully protect people with disabilities met with legislative resistance, and an unsympathetic HEW continued to interpret Section 504 restrictively, insisting, for example, that individuals needed to use the courts, rather than a cheaper, faster, and generally more convenient administrative process, to have their complaints addressed. And with few exceptions, the courts were generally unsympathetic, or simply misunderstood the point of disability rights, and their overly legalistic decisions made Section 504 an increasingly unattractive remedy (Wegner, 1983–1984).

In 1982, President Ronald Reagan replaced President Carter's appointees to the National Council on the Handicapped—created in 1978 as an advisory body under the Department of Education, and later called the National Council on Disability (NCD)—with Republican disability leaders Justin Dart, Sandra Parrino, and later Lex Frieden. Legal academics, especially Bob Burgdorf, argued that a stand-alone anti-discrimination act for disability was essential (Burgdorf & Bell, 1984; for a detailed account of this period, see Burgdorf, 1991). In 1983, the U.S. Commission on Civil Rights prepared a far-reaching, and often neglected, document called *Accommodating the Spectrum of Individual Abilities* that addressed the issue of whether the social phenomenon of disability discrimination differs sufficiently from race and gender discrimination to require separate legislation. Historically, this might be called the beginning point of the complex political and social process that created the Americans with Disabilities Act of 1990. (There are several histories of this period; one of the most complete, although somewhat self-serving, is that of the National Council of Disability itself [NCD, 1997]; see also Burgdorf, 1991.)

The Commission Report carefully analyzed the Section 504 cases, especially *Davis*, and came to the conclusion that merely adding the "handicap" category to the Civil Rights Act would be unacceptable, for three reasons: (1) The category of "handicap" was very unlike that of gender and race because it is grounded in actual functional differences that may impede performance, and because the category defines an extremely heterogeneous population that is non-exclusive, in the sense that anyone can become a member; (2) the concept of neutrality (or as it is put in the language of race-based anti-discrimination law, "color-blindness") is only partially applicable to handicap discrimination because being indifferent to functional difficulties is itself discriminatory; and (3) affirmative action may be essential to remedy discrimination against persons with disabilities, because "efforts beyond nondiscrimination requirements are required to achieve an equitable level of participation" (USCCR, 1983). In the end, Burgdorf and Christopher Bell, while accepting the findings of the report, rejected these three conclusions, a fact that shaped how the Americans with Disabilities Act ended up being drafted, defended, and eventually sold to Congress and President George Bush.

The legal and social case for a stand-alone disability anti-discrimination law was described in a 500-page, closely and carefully argued NCH report released in 1986 called *Toward Independence: An Assessment of Federal Laws and Programs Affecting Persons With Disabilities—With Legislative Recommendations*. The report carefully argued for an effective anti-discrimination law as an essential component of an overall strategy for persons with disabilities, a strategy framed in terms of how federal dollars can be spent "more prudently and productively." Only the first part of the report (written by Burgdorf) deals directly with anti-discrimination as an "equal opportunity law," recommending the enactment "of a comprehensive law requiring equal opportunity for individuals with disabilities, with broad coverage and setting clear, consistent, and enforceable standards prohibiting discrimination on the basis of handicap." The rest of the document speaks to employment and disincentives to work in Social Security law, transportation, housing, independent living, personal assistance services, and education for children with disabilities, but also in terms of the need to secure equality of opportunity.

Burgdorf summarizes all of the problems with the Rehabilitation Act, Title V—problems with scope of coverage, an unclear mandate for reasonable accommodation, and problems in terminology and judicial interpretation. He recommends a law with a clear definition of "disability," standards for applying a prohibition of discrimination, and enforcement standards that are administrative, giving a complainant a wide variety of remedies, with a private right of action in federal court should administrative relief be unsatisfactory or slow in coming. He argues for an enforceable Bill of Rights for persons with disabilities, viewed as a "discrete and insular minority" that has suffered a history of unequal treatment, and the creation of a system in each state to protect, and fund, legal advocacy for disability rights. Burgdorf suggests that the statute might perhaps be called the Americans with Disabilities Act of 1986.

A first attempt at a bill in 1988 concentrated on regulating the "disabling environment," but this was thought to be unfeasible and unrealistic. Also in 1988, Congress passed the Fair Housing Amendments Act, which prohibits discrimination against people with disabilities. This was the most significant housing discrimination measure since the Civil Rights Act of 1968, and it created a broad protection against discrimination in housing. A revised and extended version of the ADA, based on a draft proposed by Bob Burgdorf in another NCD report in 1988, was introduced by Senator Tom Harkin (Democrat from Iowa) and Representative Tony Coelho (Democrat from California) in April of that year. This version emphasized the need to empower persons with disabilities with the ability to bring legal actions against discriminators, as well as to use the power of the federal government in areas of transportation and telecommunication to mandate accessibility.

Fortuitously, a hotly disputed presidential and congressional election was underway and Republican presidential candidate George Bush was eager to demonstrate his support for disability rights. During his campaign, Bush expressed support for the students at Gallaudet University—a federally chartered university in Washington, D.C., serving deaf and hearing-impaired students—who demanded that school administrators appoint a deaf president. In the end, after a series of compromises and concessions, both houses of Congress passed the bill by significant margins. On July 26, 1990, President Bush signed the Americans with Disabilities Act of 1990 into law (for a step-by-step chronology of the passage of the ADA, see Chapter 3).

There is no doubt that the ADA was a bold step. Its drafters wanted not merely a shield against discrimination that could be used by individuals, but also a proactive sword requiring businesses and governments to make the world more accessible to people with disabilities. Although one can trace the origin of each provision of the ADA to prior legislation and judicial judgment, the drafters did more than cobble together previous law: The ADA has a wholeness and integrity that makes it unique. The NCD document *Equality of Opportunity* summarized the process of producing the ADA in this way:

> A whole host of circumstances worked in its favor: effective leadership; advocates in key government positions; the rightness of the cause; the mobilization of the grassroots disability community; a string of legislative successes offering momentum; legal and lobbying expertise in the disability community; the willingness of persons with disabilities to unite for a common cause; the cautious support of the business community; and ideological justifications from both the right and the left. The time was right and the cause was just. (NCD, 1997)

The ADA and Its Aftermath: "Backlash"

The ADA set the standard for anti-discrimination law, not only for the United States but around the world, although many countries sought also to supplement anti-discrimination law with affirmative action programming (Bickenbach, 2001). At the international level, the United Nations World Program of Action that began in 1982 led, after several disability-focused human rights declarations, to the 1994 Standard Rules on the Equalization of Opportunities for Persons with Disabilities (UN, 1994). These bold attempts at international action met with disappointing results, however, which arguably helped to make the case for the Convention on the Rights of Persons with Disabilities (CRPD) a decade later.

The ADA has five titles: (I) Employment, (II) Public Services, (III) Public Accommodations and Services Operated by Private Entities, (IV) Telecommunications Relay Services, and (V) Miscellaneous. As mentioned, the meaning of all of key legal terms in the ADA—"otherwise qualified," "reasonable accommodation," "undue burden"—were products of legal debates and judicial decisions of the Supreme Court in Section 504 cases in the previous decade. In particular, the governing definition of "disability" for the ADA followed the lead of both academic and judicial comments by moving away from the Rehabilitation Act of 1973 definition, which focused on employability, to a controversial three-pronged definition:

The term "disability" means, with respect to an individual,
    (A) a physical or mental impairment that substantially limits one or more of the major life activities of such individual;
    (B) a record of such an impairment; or
    (C) being regarded as having such an impairment.

And Title I, which set out the general rule prohibiting discrimination "against a qualified individual with a disability because of the disability of such individual" in any aspect or dimension of employment, required an additional definition:

The term "qualified individual with a disability" means an individual with a disability who, with or without reasonable accommodation, can perform the essential functions of the employment position that such individual holds or desires.

One of the compromises that arose during Senate debate in 1989 involved the creation of exclusions from the class of protected individuals with disabilities. The focus of conservative "oratorical diatribes" (Burgdorf, 1991), most coming from the Republican senator from North Carolina, Jessie Helms, were psychiatric and psychological conditions that were considered immoralities—pedophilia, schizophrenia, kleptomania, transvestitism, and homosexuality (then defined as a psychiatric disorder)—as well as sinful behaviors, such as voyeurism, alcoholism, and compulsive gambling. Bizarrely, certain physical diseases, in particular HIV-AIDS, were also excluded, perhaps on the theory current at the time that these were closely linked to sexual misconduct. The result was a modification of the definition of "an individual with a disability" to exclude people with these psychiatric conditions and anyone who was "a current user of illegal drugs." Somewhat offsetting this retrograde result, the disability community scored a significant victory in employment protection. The ADA contained a provision recognizing that the failure to provide reasonable accommodation for a physical or mental limitation of a qualified person with a disability, unless doing so would impose an undue hardship on the operation of the business, was itself a form of discrimination.

The other titles of the ADA were equally important. Title II focused on discrimination by "public entities" (all levels of government, and all components, including those providing public transportation). This title greatly extended what Section 504 had previously covered and included an explicit mandate to remove architectural, communication, and transportation barriers, and to provide auxiliary aids and services as required for accessibility. Title III turns to public accommodations, defined to include most types of privately owned businesses providing services to the public. This title also creates a mandate for accessibility and the removal of barriers. Title IV, finally, covers telecommunications services, including both telephone and television. Companies offering these services are required to provide accommodations such as telecommunications devices for the deaf (TDDs) and closed captioning for the deaf and hard-of-hearing.

The Equal Employment Opportunity Commission (EEOC)—established in 1965 under the Civil Rights Act of 1964—was directed to issue regulations for implementing ADA Title I (and related areas of the federal government were similarly directed for the other titles). The relationship between the EEOC and the Supreme Court became more and more adversarial as the Supreme Court began in the mid-1990s to severely restrict the scope of the Title I protection. Indeed, surveying the Title I employment discrimination cases in the decade of the 1990s reveals an extraordinarily dismal picture. Although the first Supreme Court case to consider the ADA—the 1998 case of *Bragdon v. Abbott*, involving a complaint by a person with asymptomatic HIV infection—hinted at an inclusive and flexible approach, a study done by legal scholar Ruth Colker in 1999 revealed the astonishing result that employers won ADA cases 93% of the time at trial, and 84% of the time on appeal, results far worse than in any comparable area of law (except prisoner rights cases) (Colker,

1999, 2001; and see the ADA statistics in Chapter 5). In 2008, the American Bar Association did a follow-up study that found that employers prevailed in nearly 98% of cases (compare Chapter 5, Table 13). Explanations for this poor record point to larger questions we shall return to about the effectiveness of the anti-discrimination approach. When an unprecedented decline in the employment rate of working-aged people with disabilities was reported during the first decade of the ADA, it ignited a further debate among economists about whether the ADA may indeed be in part responsible (see Acemoglu & Angrist, 2001; Epstein, 1992; Stapleton & Burkhauser, 2003).

Although the ADA is the anti-discrimination act with the highest profile, individual states also developed or enhanced their civil rights protections of persons with disabilities during and after the passage of the ADA. Indeed, some states passed legislation with anti-discrimination provisions that were in some respects more powerful than the ADA protection. The civil rights provisions of New York and California provide a broader range of protections for a broader range of persons with disabilities, and other states have provisions for damages, which the ADA lacks. Strategically as well, the involvement of a state attorney general or state office of human rights enhanced the effectiveness of the legal address of rights violations (Hill & Blanck, 2009).

In the first decade of the ADA, however, except for a small number of favorable results, the judicial reception was very discouraging. The most welcome outcome was undoubtedly the 1999 *Olmstead v. L. C.* case, in which the Supreme Court upheld the integration presumption of Title II of the ADA. This provision required states, where appropriate, to place individuals with mental health problems in community facilities rather than isolating institutions. This result, which was taken up by the George W. Bush administration in its New Freedom Initiative in 2001, has potentially wide-ranging consequences for all public health agencies as well as for the Medicaid program, which had a provision requiring Medicaid services in institutions but not in communities, which in light of *Olmstead* likely violates the ADA.

But a group of Supreme Court cases that have been called the "backlash against the ADA" (Krieger, 2003) far more accurately captured the reception of the ADA in the highest court of the land. In 1999, a trio of cases represented by *Sutton v. United Air Lines* dramatically restricted the class of persons who could bring complaints under Title I for employment discrimination. In the *Sutton* case, two pilots were turned down for employment because they failed the visual acuity tests, but they were denied redress under Title I because their visual impairment was correctable with glasses. Other cases involving medication and other "mitigating measures" soon followed, leading to the illogical result that individuals could be denied employment or fired from a job on the basis of a disability, but still not meet the ADA definition of a disability in order to challenge that treatment. In the 2002 case of *Toyota Motor Manufacturing, Kentucky, Inc. v. Williams,* the Supreme Court narrowed the definition of a "major life activity," ruling that the activity must be of "central importance" to most people's daily lives or else the impairment does not qualify as an ADA disability. The complainant was removed from her assembly-line job for not being able to lift because of bilateral carpal tunnel syndrome, but the Court held that lifting was not of central importance to most people's lives and that the ADA definition requires that the individual be fundamentally or seriously disabled, not disabled only with respect to the demands of a particular job. By raising the threshold of what constitutes a disability to the point that no one meeting this threshold would likely be able to find a job of any sort, the Court effectively undermined the point of the ADA's anti-discrimination protection for employment.

In other words, the Supreme Court took the wording of the ADA that people with disabilities are a "discrete and insular minority" seriously, and insisted that the ADA only covers people who have severe, immitigable impairments that substantially limit life's most basic day-to-day activities. The message was clear, and what the Rehnquist Court began the Roberts Court would complete: a narrowing down of the application of ADA Title I to the most extreme cases in order to prevent a "flood of litigation" that, as Ruth Colker has demonstrated, almost invariably is unsuccessful for the complainant.

In 2000, the National Council on Disability published a detailed, 500-page report significantly titled "Promises to Keep" that argued that the federal government, and all relevant agencies, needed to step up its ADA implementation activities to keep its promises. Four years later, it launched the "Righting the ADA" report, which went through the Supreme Court decisions point by point, arguing that the "judicial resistance" contradicted the intentions of Congress, the executive branch in the form of the EEOC, and the American people. The report included a proposed "ADA Restoration Act" directly addressing the recent Supreme Court decisions (NCD, 2004). In a further attempt to reverse the judicial trend, the EEOC passed new regulations, but as the Court is not obliged to follow regulations from an executive branch agency, the attempt was mostly symbolic.

The New Century: 2000–2010

A notable feature of the last 20 years of the 20th century in Social Security for persons with disabilities was the steady increase in SSI and SSDI expenditures; but after 2000, the growth rate dramatically accelerated (see Table 15 and Figures 10 and 11 in Chapter 5). The Contract with America Advancement Act and the Personal Responsibility and Work Opportunity Reconciliation Act, both passed in 1996, tried to bring the numbers down by requiring more stringent medical examinations, preventing people with drug addiction from applying, and terminating benefits for non-citizens (while, more positively, increasing the earnings limit exemption for retired Social Security beneficiaries). But the expenditures continued to increase into the new century.

The final step in the reform process was the Ticket to Work and Work Incentives Improvement Act of 1999, signed into law during the last days of the Clinton administration, which made a radical shift in the underlying philosophy of disability policy. The act created the Ticket to Work and Self-Sufficiency Program, which, when it was phased in across the states under the George W. Bush administration in 2002, aimed to provide SSI and SSDI beneficiaries with resources to purchase vocational rehabilitation, employment preparation, and other support services with the goal of reducing their dependence on public funds and helping them enter the workforce.

Among the incentives for Social Security beneficiaries to use this voluntary program was a deferral of the medical disability review, an expedited return to benefits if the person became unable to continue working, and, most importantly, the option to purchase Medicaid coverage and to keep it while working, up to a set income level. Preliminary studies of the program indicated that it worked—at least in the sense that those who opted for the program were less disabled, in better health, and more likely to be employed than those who did not, although the absolute number of those who found employment, or used the voucher for vocational rehabilitation, was very low (Kennedy & Schiro-Geist, 2004). As part of his American Recovery and Reinvestment Act of 2009, President Barack Obama sought reauthorization and added more money to the program. But the underlying concern and the source of many of the problems in programming administered by the Social Security Administration was the complexity, expense, and fairness of the process for determining disability status and adjudicating disability claims (DRI, 2005). Both the Office of Inspector General and the General Accountability Office (GAO), the watchdogs over federal public expenditures, had for decades issued a stream of reports critical of the SSA's adjudication procedures. The statutory definition of "disability" SSA used had not substantially changed since 1939, when the point of the definition was to ensure that only the very severely disabled would be able to claim benefits. The definition was thought to be entirely medical, relying on a listing of serious impairments and disease conditions that, it was believed, would make determination of eligibility both scientifically precise and final. Unfortunately, that was not to be, and a complex, multi-layered system of second opinions, tribunals, and appeals developed that was both indeterminate and costly.

By the time the SSA decided to hand over the problem to the highly respected Institute of Medicine (IOM) in 2001 (SSAB, 2001), the situation was dire. Although the IOM 2007 report reluctantly maintained the medical focus of determination, it made it clear that in 2007 the purely medical approach was unjustifiable, although there was likely no option but to rely on it: "[The SSA definition] is complex, and it has medical, functional, and vocational components. . . . [But] SSA does not have the resources to perform such an extensive assessment for every one of the 2.6 million disability applicants who will come through its doors in 2007." President Obama's reauthorization of the Social Security Act added half a billion dollars to its budget, earmarked for increased information technology and further research into the eligibility determination process and its persistent problems.

The much-applauded "integration mandate" of the *Olmstead* decision had been promoted in 2003 by changes in Housing and Urban Development (HUD) regulations under the Fair Housing Act that offered vouchers for public housing for those leaving institutions, although concerns remained 10 years after the *Olmstead* decision as to whether the states have the capacity to provide community living services to those who required them. Since 2005, HUD has expanded its regulations and guidelines for accessible housing, including "visitable" housing to ensure that homes can be visited by people with disabilities. Immigration policy, which since the 18th century had imposed bans or stiff quotas on people with disabilities, eased somewhat in 2004 with the removal of quotas, at least for persons with physical disabilities (Weber, 2004).

In education, the Individuals with Disabilities Act was amended in 2004 to provide more extensive support for early education and to ensure mainstreaming of children with disabilities, except in cases where the nature or severity of the disability makes that impossible. Very soon after entering office in 2001, President George W. Bush proposed the No Child Left Behind Act, which received bipartisan support in Congress. The act set into place an educational standards-based reform package, aimed at ensuring educational quality improvement and accountability, and required states to develop assessment procedures for basic skills for students at different stages during their education. Although the act led to substantial increases in educational funding, including funding for "special needs," the reaction of the disability community was and continues to be mixed, and independent assessment has not convincingly shown that children with disabilities have been, overall, beneficiaries of the program (GAO, 2005).

It had long been noticed that persons with disabilities benefited disproportionately from advances in computer technology and telecommunications, both in employment and everyday living (Ritchie & Blanck, 2003). In 1998, Congress amended the Rehabilitation Act, adding Section 508 requiring federal agencies to make their electronic and information technology accessible to people with disabilities. The legislation also required federal agencies to create for the Access Board country-wide standards of accessibility for all electronic and information technology, including computer menus and controls that do not require vision, software with text-to-speech capability, and so on. Over the decade following its passage, Section 508 has been used to match information technological developments with accessibility standards, for the Internet and Web-based technology, as well as telecommunication products. The impact of Section 508 is bolstered by the Assistive Technology Act of 1998 (which provides federal funds to states to address assistive technology needs of individuals) and the Telecommunications Act of 1996 (especially Section 255, which requires manufacturers to ensure that equipment and services are accessible).

ADAAA and CRPD

In 2006, a group called Consortium for Citizens with Disabilities (CCD) began to lobby for concrete steps toward, as the NCD had put it in 2004, "righting the ADA." On the last working day of the 109th Congress, the Americans with Disabilities Act Restoration Act was introduced in order to "restore the intent of the Americans with Disabilities Act of 1990 to more fully remove the barriers that confront disabled Americans." The bill died in committee, but in 2007 Senators Tom Harkin and Arlen Specter introduced a similar bill with House co-sponsors. The business community lobby opposed the bill, and the next year a negotiating group met regularly to iron out the differences. A renamed ADA Amendments Act of 2008 (ADAAA) easily made its way through House committees and the House itself by June 2008. In the Senate, however, a dispute arose about the possibility of simply dropping the phrase "substantially limits," one of the major definitional roadblocks created by the Supreme Court's strict and unrealistic reading of the phrase. A compromise was reached, the House passed the bill, and President George W. Bush signed it into law on September 25, 2008.

Although the ADAAA retains the three-pronged definition of disability in the ADA, it explicitly states as one of its purposes to overturn the *Sutton* and the *Toyota Motor* cases by clarifying and expanding the definition and its intended application. The act does this in a variety of ways (see Rozalski et al., 2010). First, the finding that persons with disabilities are a "discrete and insular minority" is deleted, as this had led the Supreme Court to assume that disabilities must be severe and restricted to a small, and easily identifiable, group of Americans. Second, the act provides that the definition of disability "shall be construed in favor of broad coverage . . . to the maximum extent permitted by the terms of this Act" and that the troubling phrase "substantially limits" must not be construed to create a demanding standard. Third, the act prohibits courts from considering the so-called "mitigating measures" (medication, assistive technology, accommodations, or other modifications) when determining whether an impairment substantially limits a major life activity. Finally, the act expands the list of major life activities and major bodily functions to overcome the trend created by the *Toyota Motor* case of making it unlikely that anyone other than the very severely disabled would qualify:

> Major life activities include, but are not limited to, caring for oneself, performing manual tasks, seeing, hearing, eating, sleeping, walking, standing, lifting, bending, speaking, breathing, learning, reading, concentrating, thinking, communicating, and working. . . .
>
> A major life activity also includes the operation of a major bodily function, including but not limited to, functions of the immune system, normal

cell growth, digestive, bowel, bladder, neurological, brain, respiratory, circulatory, endocrine, and reproductive functions.

The open question, of course, is whether the changes will accomplish the goal, as the act states, of "reinstating a broad scope of protection to be available under the ADA."

During the 1990s, an international effort slowly built up momentum for a United Nations convention that would set out in clear and enforceable terms the rights of persons with disabilities. Building on the Standard Rules of 1993, this endeavor was founded on the understanding that the human rights perspective on disability is transcultural and transnational—in a word, universal—and must be more than a mere expression of aspiration or voluntary adherence. It was also realized that the issue was not one of "special rights" for persons with disabilities, but the same rights that everyone enjoys—but which, for various reasons, people with disabilities have been denied. After a proposal in late 2001 by the Mexican government to the UN General Assembly to establish an Ad Hoc Committee to consider proposals for "a comprehensive and integral international convention to promote and protect the rights and dignity of persons with disabilities," the committee was created and spent the next four years discussing and drafting. Disability rights organizations and individuals with disabilities, from across the globe, were strongly represented in the committee's membership. On December 13, 2006, the Convention on the Rights of Persons with Disabilities (CRPD) was adopted by consensus at the UN General Assembly.

The CRPD represents the shift in attitudes and approach to persons with disabilities that is embodied in the ADA and has defined the disability rights approach to policy and law in the United States for the past 30 years. At the same time, it avoids the definitional trap of the ADA by not formally defining the notion but instead characterizing disability in broad and open-ended terms in the Preamble ("Recognizing that disability is an evolving concept and that disability results from the interaction between persons with impairments and attitudinal and environmental barriers that hinders their full and effective participation in society on an equal basis with others . . ."). The CRPD enumerates, both broadly and in detail, a wide variety of rights: accessibility, right to life, legal capacity, access to justice, liberty and security of the person, freedom from torture and exploitation, independent living, mobility, freedom of expression, privacy, home and family, education, health, rehabilitation, employment, standard of living, and participation in political, public, cultural life.

Finally, and uniquely for a UN treaty, the CRPD explicitly requires those countries that have signed and ratified the Convention (some 150 signatories and 100 ratifications as of early 2011) to establish a mechanism for monitoring the implementation of the Convention and to create a "focal point" in government that is required to work in concert with organizations of persons with disabilities to prepare reports on implementation progress to be considered on a regular basis by a Committee on the Rights of Persons with Disabilities (UN, 2006). Finally, an additional Optional Protocol (which 60 countries have ratified as of 2011) grants individuals or groups within countries the right to present to the committee claims that their rights have been violated by their own country.

Although the CRPD is firmly in the tradition of the disability rights movement represented by the ADA, U.S. disability law and policy remains a model for other countries in the world, and some of the principal contributors to the drafting and lobbying effort behind the CRPD were American disability advocates. Still, the CRPD embodies a feature of disability rights that is quite at odds with the mainstream U.S. political and ideological framework. In the U.S. political tradition, with some historical exceptions, civil rights are primarily negative rights (rights to be free from interference, discrimination, or other unfair disadvantage) rather than positive rights (rights to resources that actively remove barriers and realistically enable an individual or group to achieve equal enjoyment of rights). In the U.S. context, there are indeed many instances of programs and policies that reflect the positive side of rights, but the clearest example of explicit reliance on positive rights are cases of affirmative action, which have always been fraught with political controversy.

On July 30, 2009, President Obama directed Susan Rice, his ambassador to the United Nations, to sign the UN Convention on the Rights of Persons with Disabilities, making the United States the 142th country to do so. In his speech to announce his decision, President Obama said that "disability rights aren't just civil rights to be enforced here at home; they're universal rights to be recognized and promoted around the world. And that's why I'm proud to announce that next week, the United States of America will join 140 other nations in signing the United Nations Convention on the Rights of Persons with Disabilities—the first new human rights convention of the 21st century." He concluded with a poignant reference to an earlier time and an earlier president:

Every morning, I walk along the Colonnade that connects this house to the Oval Office. And there's something you might not notice unless you're really paying attention. But there's a gentle slope at the end of that Colonnade, a ramp that was installed during a renovation of the West Wing 75 years ago, making it much easier for one of my predecessors to get to work. Back then, fear and prejudice towards Americans with disabilities was the norm, but most Americans didn't even know that President Roosevelt had a disability. That means that what most Americans also didn't know was that President Roosevelt's disability made absolutely no difference to his ability to renew our confidence, or rescue our economy, and mobilize our greatest generation to save our way of life. (White House, 2009)

References

Acemoglu, D., & Angrist, J. D. (2001). Consequences of employment protection? The case of the Americans with Disabilities Act. *Journal of Political Economy, 10*(5), 915–957.

Albrecht, G. L. (1992). *The disability business: Rehabilitation in America.* Newbury Park, CA: Sage.

Altman, B. (2001). Disability definitions, models, classification schemes, and application. In G. L. Albrecht, K. D. Seelman, & M. Bury (Eds.), *Handbook of disability studies* (pp. 97–122). Thousand Oaks, CA: Sage.

American Bar Association, Commission on Mental and Physical Disability Law. (2008). *Employment decisions under ADA Title1—Survey update.* Retrieved from http://www.abanet.org/disability/docs/2009TitleISurvey.pdf

Amundson, R. (1992). Disability, handicap, and the environment. *Journal of Social Philosophy, 9,* 105–119.

Amundson, R. (2005). Disability, ideology, and quality of life: A bias in biomedical ethics. In D. Wasserman, J. Bickenbach, & R. Wachbroit (Eds.), *Quality of life and human difference* (pp. 101–124). New York, NY: Cambridge University Press.

Amundson, R., & Tresky, S. (2007). On a bioethical challenge to disability rights. *Journal of Medicine and Philosophy, 32,* 541–561.

Anspach, R. (1979). From stigma to identity politics: Political activism among the physically disabled and former mental patients. *Social Science and Medicine, 13,* 765–773.

Asch, A. (2001). Disability, bioethics, and human rights. In G. L. Albrecht, K. D. Seelman, & M. Bury (Eds.), *Handbook of disability studies* (pp. 297–326). Thousand Oaks, CA: Sage.

Bagenstos, S. (2006). Disability, life, death and choice. *Harvard Journal of Law and Gender, 29,* 425–463.

Bagenstos, S. (2009). *Law and the contradictions of the disability rights movement.* New Haven, CT: Yale University Press.

Barnartt, S., & Scotch, R. (2001). *Disability protests: Contentious politics 1970–1999.* Washington, DC: Gallaudet University Press.

Beauchamp, T., & Childress, J. (2001). *Principles of biomedical ethics* (5th ed.). New York, NY: Oxford University Press.

Beecher, H. (1966). Ethics and clinical research. *New England Journal of Medicine, 74,* 1354–1360.

Berkowitz, E. D. (1987). *Disabled policy: America's programs for the handicapped.* New York, NY: Cambridge University Press.

Berkson, G. (2006). Mental disabilities in western civilization from Ancient Rome to the Prerogativa Regis. *Mental Retardation, 44*(1), 28–40.

Bickenbach, J. (1993). *Physical disability and social policy.* Toronto, ON: University of Toronto Press.

Bickenbach, J. (2001). Disability human rights, law and policy. In G. L. Albrecht, K. D. Seelman, & M. Bury (Eds.), *Handbook of disability studies* (pp. 565–584). Thousand Oaks, CA: Sage.

Blanck, P. (2001). Civil war pensions and disability. *Ohio State Law Review, 62*(1), 109–238.

Blanck, P. (2007). "The right to live in the world": Disability yesterday, today, and tomorrow. *Texas Journal on Civil Liberties and Civil Rights, 13*(2), 367–402.

Blanck, P., & Millender, M. (2000). Before disability civil rights: Civil War pensions and the politics of disability in America. *Alabama Law Review, 52*(1), 1–50.

Botsford, A. L., & King, A. (2005). End-of-life care policies for people with an intellectual disability. *Issues and Strategies Journal of Disability Policy Studies, 16,* 22–30.

Bowe, F. (1978). *Handicapping America: Barriers to disabled people.* New York, NY: Harper and Row.

Braddock, D., & Parish, S. (2001). An institutional history of disability. In G. L. Albrecht, K. D. Seelman, & M. Bury (Eds.), *Handbook of disability studies* (pp. 11–68). Thousand Oaks, CA: Sage.

Brock, D. M. (1995). Justice and the ADA: Does prioritizing and rationing health care discriminate against the disabled? *Social Philosophy & Policy, 12,* 159–184.

Brock, D. M. (2000). Health care resource prioritization and discrimination against persons with disabilities. In L. Francis & A. Silvers (Eds.), *Americans with disabilities: Exploring implications for individuals and institutions* (pp. 223–235). New York, NY: Routledge.

Brown, S. (2000). *Freedom of movement: Independent living history and philosophy.* Berkeley, CA, & Houston, TX: Independent Living Research Utilization Project.

Buchanan, A., Brock, D. W., Daniels, N., & Wikler, D. (2000). *From chance to choice: Genetics and justice.* New York, NY: Cambridge University Press.

Burgdorf, R. (1991). The Americans with Disabilities Act: Analysis and implications of a second-generation civil rights statute. *Harvard Civil Rights–Civil Liberties Law Review, 26,* 413–512.

Burgdorf, R., & Bell, C. (1984). Eliminating discrimination against physically and mentally handicapped persons: A statutory blueprint. *Mental and Physical Disability Law Reporter, 8*, 64–71.

Charlton, J. (1998). *Nothing about us without us: Disability oppression and empowerment.* Berkeley, CA: University of California Press.

Coleman, D. (2010). Assisted suicide laws create discriminatory double standard for who gets suicide prevention and who gets suicide assistance: Not Dead Yet responds to Autonomy, Inc. *Disability and Health Journal, 3*, 39–50.

Colker, R. (1999). The Americans with Disabilities Act: A windfall for defendants. *Harvard Civil Rights-Civil Liberties Law Review, 34*, 99–162.

Colker, R. (2001). Winning and losing under the Americans with Disabilities Act. *Ohio State Law Journal, 62*(1), 239–284.

Daniels, N. (1993). Rationing fairly: Programmatic considerations. *Bioethics, 7*, 224–233.

Daniels, N. (1998). Distributive justice and the use of summary measures of population health status. In M. Field & M. Gold (Eds.), *Summarizing population health: Directions for the development and application of population metrics* (pp. 58–71). Washington, DC: National Academies Press.

Daniels, N. (2008). *Just health: Meeting health needs fairly.* New York, NY: Cambridge University Press.

DeJong, G. (1979). Independent living: From social movement to analytic paradigm. *Archives of Physical Medicine and Rehabilitation, 60*(10), 435–436.

Dhanda, A. (2007). Legal capacity in the disability rights convention. Stranglehold of the past or lodestar for the future? *Syracuse Journal of International Law and Commerce, 34*, 429–462.

Diamond, M., & Glenn Beh, H. (2006). The right to be wrong: Sex and gender decisions. In S. Sytsma (Ed.), *Ethics and Intersex.* Dordrecht, Netherlands: Springer.

Disability Research Institute (DRI). (2005). *Disability claims, review, hearings and appeals procedures: An analysis of administrative best practices.* Retrieved from http://www.dri.illinois.edu/research/p04-03c/default.htm

Drake, R. F. (2001). *The principles of social policy.* Basingstoke, UK: Palgrave.

Driedger, D. (1989). *The last civil rights movement.* London, UK: Hurst.

Drimmer, J. C. (1993). Cripples, overcomers, and civil rights: Tracing the evolution of federal legislation and social policy for people with disabilities. *UCLA Law Review, 40*(5), 1341–1410.

Duster, T. (1990). *Backdoor to eugenics.* New York, NY: Routledge.

Epstein, R. A. (1992). *Forbidden grounds: The case against employment discrimination laws.* Cambridge, MA: Harvard University Press.

Equal Opportunity Employment Commission (EEOC). (2009). Regulations to implement the equal employment provisions of the Americans with Disabilities Act, as amended. 74 Fed. Reg. 48431. Washington, DC: Author.

Fine, M., & Asch, A. (Eds.). (1988). *Women with disabilities: Essays in psychology, culture, and politics.* Philadelphia, PA: Temple University Press.

Fleischer, D., & Zames, F. (2001). *The disability rights movement: From charity to confrontation.* Philadelphia, PA: Temple University Press.

Fougeyrollas, P., & Beauregard, L. (2001). Disability: An interactive person-environment social creation. In G. L. Albrecht, K. D. Seelman, & M. Bury (Eds.), *Handbook of disability studies* (pp. 171–194). Thousand Oaks, CA: Sage.

Fox, F. F. (1917). *Physical remedies for disabled soldiers.* London, UK: Bailière, Tindal, & Cox.

Gallagher, H. G. (1990). *By trust betrayed: Patients, physicians, and the license to kill in the Third Reich.* Arlington, VA: Vandamere.

Gill, C., & Voss, L. A. (2005). Views of disabled people regarding legalized assisted suicide before and after a balanced informational presentation. *Journal of Disability Policy Studies, 16,* 6–15.

Golden, M., & Zoanni, T. (2010). Killing us softly: The dangers of legalizing assisted suicide. *Disability and Health Journal, 3,* 16–30.

Goodman, N., & Stapleton, D. (2007). Federal program expenditures for working-age people with disabilities. *Journal of Disability Policy Studies, 18*(2), 66–78.

Goodman, N., & Waidmann, T. (2003). Social Security Disability Insurance and the recent decline in the employment rate of people with disabilities. In D. C. Stapleton & R. V. Burkhauser (Eds.), *The decline in employment of people with disabilities: A policy puzzle* (pp. 339–368). Kalamazoo, MI: W. E. Upjohn Institute for Employment Research.

Gould, S. J. (1981). *The mismeasure of man.* New York, NY: Norton.

Government Accountability Office (GAO). (2005). *No Child Left Behind Act: Most students with disabilities participated in statewide assessments, but inclusion options could be improved* (GAO-OF-616). Washington, DC: Author.

Hahn, H. (1985). Towards a politics of disability: Definitions, disciplines, and policies. *Social Science Journal, 22*(4), 87–105.

Hahn, H. (1986). Public support for rehabilitation programs: The analysis of U.S. disability policy. *Disability and Society, 1,* 121–137.

Hahn, H. (1987). Civil rights for disabled Americans: The foundation of a political agenda. In A. Gartner & J. Tom (Eds.), *Images of the disabled, disabling images* (pp. 181–200). New York, NY: Praeger.

Hahn, H. (1993). The political implications of disability definitions and data. *Disability Policy Studies, 4*(3), 41–52.

Hill, E., & Blanck, P. (2009). Future of disability rights advocacy and "The right to live in the world." *Texas Journal on Civil Liberties and Civil Rights, 15*(1), 1–31.

Hughes, B., & Paterson, K. (1997). The social model of disability and the disappearing body: Towards a sociology of impairment. *Disability and society, 12*(3), 325–340.

Institute of Medicine (IOM). (2007). *Improving the Social Security disability decision process.* Washington, DC: National Academic Publishers.

Interagency Committee on Disability Research (ICDR). (2003). *Federal statutory definitions of disability*. Retrieved from http://www.icdr.us/documents/definitions.htm

Jaeger, P. T., &. Bowan, C. A. (2005). *Understanding disability: Inclusion, access, diversity, and civil rights*. Westport, CT: Praeger.

Kennedy, J., & Schiro-Geist, C. (2004). A national profile of SSDI recipients and applicants: Implications for early intervention. *Journal of Disability Policy Studies, 15*(3), 178–185.

Koch, T. (2006). Bioethics as ideology: Conditional and unconditional values. *Journal of Medicine and Philosophy, 31,* 251–267.

Krieger, L. I1. (Ed.). (2003). *Backlash against the ADA: Reinterpreting disability rights*. Ann Arbor, MI: University of Michigan Press.

Kuhse, H., & Singer, P. (1985). *Should the baby live? The problem of handicapped infants*. Oxford, UK: Oxford University Press.

Lane, H., & Grodin, M. (1997) Ethical issues in cochlear implant surgery: An exploration into disease, disability, and the best interests of the child. *Kennedy Institute for Ethics Journal, 7*(3), 231–251.

Liachowitz, C. I I. (1988). *Disability as a social construct: Legislative roots*. Philadelphia, PA: University of Pennsylvania Press.

Longmore, P. K. (2000). Disability policy and politics: Considering consumer influences. *Journal of Disability Policy Studies, 11*(1), 36–44.

McLean, S., & Williamson, L. (2007). *Impairment and disability: Law and ethics at the beginning and end of life*. Oxford, UK: Routledge-Cavendish.

Minow, M. (1990). *Making all the difference: Inclusion, exclusion, and American law*. Ithaca, NY: Cornell University Press

Morris, J. (1992). Personal and political: A feminist perspective on researching physical disability. *Disability, Handicap, and Society, 7*(2), 157–166.

Nagi, S. Z. (1969). *Disability and rehabilitation: Legal, clinical and self-concepts and measurement*. Columbus, OH: Ohio State University Press.

Nanette, J. G., & Stapleton, D. C. (2007). Federal program expenditures for working-age people with disabilities. *Journal of Disability Policy Studies, 18* (2), 66–78.

National Council on Disability (NCD). (1997). *Equality of opportunity: The making of the Americans with Disabilities Act*. Retrieved from http://www.ncd.gov/newsroom/publications/1997/equality.htm

National Council on Disability (NCD). (2000). *Promises to keep: A decade of federal enforcement of the Americans with Disabilities Act*. Washington, DC: Author.

National Council on Disability (NCD). (2004). *Righting the ADA. Implementation of the Americans with Disabilities Act: Challenges, best practices and new opportunities for success*. Washington, DC: Author.

National Council on the Handicapped (NCH). (1986). *Toward independence: An assessment of federal laws and programs affecting persons with disabilities—with legislative recommendations*. Retrieved from http://www.ncd.gov/newsroom/ publications/s1986/toward.htm

Nussbaum, M. (2007) *Frontiers of justice: Disability, nationality, species membership.* Cambridge, MA: Harvard University Press.

Obermann, C. E. (1968). *A history of vocational rehabilitation in America* (5th ed.). Minneapolis, MN: Dennison.

O'Brien, R. (2001). *Crippled justice: The history of modern disability policy in the workplace.* Chicago, IL: University of Chicago Press.

Oliver, M. (1990). *The politics of disablement.* New York, NY: St. Martin's Press.

Orentlicher, D. (1996). Destructuring disability: Rationing of health care and unfair discrimination against the sick. *Harvard Civil Rights–Civil Liberties Law Review, 31*(1), 49–87.

Paige, C., & Karnofsky, E. (1986). The antiabortion movement and Baby Jane Doe. *Journal of Health Politics, Policy, and Law, 11*(2), 255–269.

Parens, E., & Asch, A. (Eds.). (2001). *Prenatal testing and disability.* Washington, DC: Georgetown University Press.

President's Commission for the Study of Ethical Problems in Medicine and Biomedical and Behavioral Research. (1982). *Making health care decisions.* Washington, DC: Government Printing Office.

President's Commission for the Study of Ethical Problems in Medicine and Biomedical and Behavioral Research. (1983). *Deciding to forego life-sustaining treatment: A report on the ethical, medical, and legal issues in treatment decisions.* Washington, DC: Government Printing Office.

Reilly, P. R. (1991). *The surgical solution: A history of involuntary sterilization in the United States.* Baltimore, MD: Johns Hopkins University Press.

Ritchie, H., & Blanck, P. (2003). Promise of the Internet for disability: Study of online services and accessibility of centers for independent living Web sites. *Behavioral Sciences and the Law, 21*(1), 5–26.

Roberts, E. V. (1989). A history of the independent living movement: A founder's perspective. In B. Heller et al. (Eds.), *Psychosocial interventions with physically disabled persons* (pp. 231–252). New Brunswick, NJ: Rutgers University Press.

Rock, M. (2000). Discounted lives? Weighing disability when measuring health and ruling on "compassionate" murder. *Social Science and Medicine, 51*, 407–417.

Roth, W. (1983). Handicap as a social construct. *Society, 20*, 56–61.

Rothman, D. J. (1990). *The discovery of the asylum: Social order and disorder in the new republic.* Boston, MA: Little, Brown.

Rozalski, M., Katsiyannis, A., Ryan, J., Collins, T., & Stewart, A. (2010). Americans with Disabilities Act Amendments of 2008. *Journal of Disability Policy Studies, 21*(1), 22–28.

Rushton, P. (1988). Lunatics and idiots: Mental disability, the community, and the Poor Law in north-east England, 1600–1800. *Medical History, 32*, 34–50.

Safilios-Rothschild, C. (1970). *The sociology and social psychology of disability and rehabilitation*. New York, NY: Random House.

Schriner, K. (2001). Disability and institutional change: A human variation perspective on overcoming oppression. *Journal of Disability Policy Studies, 12*(2), 100–106.

Scotch, R. K. (1984). *From good will to civil rights: Transforming federal disability policy* (2nd ed. 2001). Philadelphia, PA: Temple University Press.

Scotch, R. K. (1989). Politics and policy in the history of the disability rights movement. *Milbank Quarterly, 67* (Suppl. 2, Pt. 2) [Disability Policy: Restoring Socioeconomic Independence], 380–400.

Scotch, R. K. (2000). Disability policy: An eclectic overview. *Journal of Disability Policy Studies, 11*(1), 6–11.

Scotch, R. K., & Berkowitz, E. D. (1990). One comprehensive system? A historical perspective on federal disability policy. *Journal of Disability Policy Studies, 1*(1), 1–19.

Shakespeare, T. (2005). Disability, genetics, and global justice. *Social Policy and Society, 4*(1), 87–95.

Shakespeare, T. (2006). *Disability rights and wrongs*. New York, NY: Routledge.

Shakespeare, T., & Watson, N. (1997). Defending the social model of disability. *Disability and Society, 12*(2), 293–300.

Shapiro, J. P. (1993). *No pity: People with disabilities forging a new civil rights movement*. New York, NY: Times Books.

Silvers, A. (1999). Double consciousness, triple difference: Disability, race, gender and the politics of recognition. In M. Jones & L. A. Marks (Eds.), *Disability, divers ability, and legal change* (pp. 75–100). Dordrecht, Netherlands: Kluwer.

Silvers, A., Wasserman, D., & Mahowald, M. (1998). *Disability, difference, discrimination: Perspectives on justice in bioethics and public policy*. New York: Rowman and Littlefield.

Singer, P. (1993). *Practical ethics*. New York, NY: Cambridge University Press.

Snyder, S., & Mitchell, D. (2003). *Eugenics in America, 1848–1935: A primary sourcebook in disability studies*. Ann Arbor, MI: University of Michigan Press.

Social Security Advisory Board (SSAB). (2001). *Charting the future of Social Security's disability programs: The need for fundamental change*. Washington, DC: Author. Retrieved from http://www.ssab.gov/Publications/Disability/disability whitepap.pdf

Stapleton, D. C., & Burkhauser, R. V. (Eds.). (2003). *The decline in employment of people with disabilities: A policy puzzle*. Kalamazoo, MI: W. E. Upjohn Institute for Employment Research.

Stein, M. S. (2006). *Distributive justice and disability*. New Haven, CT: Yale University Press.

Stiker, H.-J. (1999). *A history of disability* (W. Sayers, Trans.). Ann Arbor, MI: University of Michigan Press.

Stineman, M., & Musick, D. (2001). Protection of human subjects with disability: Guidelines for research. *Archives of Physical Medicine and Rehabilitation, 82* (Suppl. 2), S9–S14.

Stone, D. (1984). *The disabled state.* Philadelphia, PA: Temple University Press.

Stone, D. (2002). *Policy paradox: The art of political decision making.* New York, NY: Norton.

Swain, J., & French, S. (2000). Towards an affirmative model of disability. *Disability and Society, 15*(4), 569–582.

Teipe, E. (2002). *America's first veterans and the revolutionary war pensions.* Lewiston, NY: Edwin Mellon Press.

tenBroek, J. (1966). The right to live in the world: The disabled in the law of torts. *California Law Review, 54,* 841–919.

Union of the Physically Impaired Against Segregation (UPIAS). (1976). *Fundamental principles of disability.* London, UK: Author.

United Nations. (1994). *Standard rules on the equalization of opportunities for persons with disabilities,* A/RES/48/96. Retrieved from http://www.un.org/disabilities

United Nations. (2006). *Convention on the Rights of Persons with Disabilities,* A/RES/ 61/106. Retrieved from http://www.un.org/disabilities

U.S. Commission on Civil Rights (USCCR). (1983). *Accommodating the spectrum of individual abilities.* Washington, DC: Author.

U.S. Department of Health, Education, and Welfare (HEW). (1978). *Belmont Report: Ethical principles and guidelines for the protection of human subjects of research.* Washington, DC: Author.

Wasserman, D. (1998). Distributive justice. In A. Silvers, D. Wasserman, & M. Mahowald (Eds.), *Disability, difference, discrimination* (pp. 147–207). New York, NY: Rowman & Littlefield.

Weber, M. (2004). Opening the golden door: Disability and the law of immigration. *Journal of Gender, Race and Justice, 8,* 153–175.

Wegner, J. (1983–1984). The antidiscrimination model reconsidered: Ensuring equal opportunity without respect to handicap under Section 504 of the Rehabilitation Act of 1973. *Cornell Law Review, 69*(3), 401–516.

White House. (2009). *Remarks by President Obama on signing of the UN Convention on the Rights of Persons with Disabilities Proclamation.* Retrieved from http://www .whitehouse.gov/the_press_office/Remarks-by-the-President-on-Rights-of -Persons-with-Disabilities-Proclamation-Signing

Williams, G. (1983). The movement for independent living: An evaluation and critique. *Social Science and Medicine, 17*(15), 1003–1010.

Wolfensberger, W. (1972). *The principle of normalization in human services.* Toronto, ON: National Institute on Mental Retardation.

Wolfensberger, W. (1976). On the origin of our institutional models. In R. Kugel & A. Shearer (Eds.), *Changing patterns in residential services for the mentally retarded* (pp. 35–82). Washington, DC: President's Committee on Mental Retardation.

World Health Organization (WHO). (2001). *The International Classification of Functioning, Disability and Health.* Geneva, Switzerland: Author.

Wright, B. (1960). *Physical disability: A psychosocial approach.* New York, NY: Harper and Row.

Zola, I. (1989). Toward the necessary universalizing of a disability policy. *Milbank Quarterly, 67,* 401–428.

Court Cases

Alexander v. Choate, 469 U.S. 287 (1985).

Bowen v. American Hospital Association, 54 LW 4579 (USSC, 1986).

Bragdon v. Abbott, 118 S.Ct. 2196 (1998).

Buck v. Bell, 274 U.S. 200 (1927).

Olmstead v. L. C., 527 U.S. 581 (1999).

PARC v. Commonwealth of Pennsylvania, 334 F. Supp. 1257 (E.D. Pa. 1971).

School Board of Nassau County v. Arline, 480 U.S. 273 (1987).

Southeastern Community College v. Davis, 442 U.S. 397 (1979).

Sutton v. United Air Lines, Inc., 527 U.S. 471 (1999).

Toyota Motor Manufacturing, Kentucky, Inc. v. Williams, 534 U.S. 184 (2002).

Legislation

Americans with Disabilities Act, Pub. L. No. 101-336, 104 Stat. 328 (1990).

Americans with Disabilities Act Amendments Act, Pub. L. No. 110-325 (2008).

Architectural Barriers Act, 42 U.S.C. § 4151 (1968).

Assistive Technology Act, Pub. L. No. 105-394 (1998).

Civil Rights Act, Pub. L. No. 88-352 (1964).

Developmental Disabilities Assistance and Bill of Rights Act, 42 U.S.C. § 6000 (1986).

Education for All Handicapped Children Act, 20 U.S.C. § 1232 (1975).

No Child Left Behind Act, Pub. L. No. 107-110 (2002).

Rehabilitation Act, Pub. L. No. 93-112 (1973).

Telecommunications Act, Pub. L. No. 104-104, 110 Stat. 56 (1996).

Ticket to Work and Work Incentives Improvement Act, Pub. L. No. 106-170 (1999).

TWO

Current Issues, Controversies, and Solutions

As we saw in Chapter 1, policy analysis has five components: clarifying policy goals in terms of social values such as liberty, equality, and dignity; exploring the connections between these goals and policy objectives; evaluating the effectiveness of mechanisms for implementing objectives; describing the policy tools used in these implementation mechanisms; and finally, monitoring the outcomes of implementation in light of the policy goals, the objectives, and ultimately the social values. In this chapter, all of these components of policy analysis need to be called upon as we seek to understand the persistent controversies in disability policy, the concrete policy problems these controversies have created, and the possible solutions to these problems.

Describing the controversies will require us to be clear about how the social values everyone agrees upon connect to policy goals and policy objectives. Being clear about what problems arise in policy programming will require using policy-analytical skills to identify the mechanisms and tools of policy implementation and evaluate the results of attempts to monitor their effectiveness. Finally, solutions proposed by policy analysts and academics bring all five components of analysis together: Should we revise the way we monitor policy, or should we change the tools and mechanisms we employ, or should we think again about our policy goals and objectives?

But we have to be realistic. Currently, there are hundreds of disability policy initiatives and programs, so that, even ignoring policy that impacts people with disabilities but was not specifically addressed to them, trying to grasp the entire picture would be next to impossible. This complex programming is also constantly changing, either because of mechanisms built into the structure of the policy or through explicit legislative action—creating new programming, abandoning other efforts, or making subtle changes in the design of programming. So, we have to be selective.

Our strategy in this chapter, therefore, will be to focus on the major controversies in disability policy—those that have persisted and in many cases continue to have an impact on people's lives, as well as those that affect the broadest range of disability policy. This is not hard to do, because some of these controversies—the best example being that of defining "disability"—are both perennial and well-known, and have an impact on all disability policy. Given that we are focusing on the big controversies, we need to ensure that the problems that these controversies have created cover a fairly representative sample of areas of policy. It would be perfectly possible to write a chapter on controversies, problems, and solutions in disability employment policy alone; but doing so would not paint a realistic picture of the depth of a controversy, or of the different ways it affects the structure of policy. Also, to be consistent with our approach in Chapter 1, the law will be primarily understood as a source of policy tools that facilitate or implement public policy.

So much for disability policy and law. In the case of disability ethics, which we save for last, our strategy is more straightforward. The ethical controversies and concrete ethical problems in disability have been clearly delineated in legal cases over the past four decades, and we can do no better than to focus on these legal cases. Doing so may cramp our focus somewhat—new technological developments, as well as shifts in public attitudes or political ideologies, will undoubtedly create new controversies in the future—but as will become apparent, all disability ethical controversies raise, although in very different forms, the same underlying values of equality, dignity, and respect.

Controversies We Have to Set Aside

It goes without saying that disability policy shares with all social policy the unavoidable fact that it is subject to external forces that push policy objectives in different directions, sometimes very quickly and drastically. These forces are, as one might expect, primarily economic and ideological.

The overall economic health of any country, or its regions and states, directly affects how social policy is shaped and implemented. If economic health is robust, then the voices of all stakeholders, including interest and lobbying groups and other policy-shapers—especially the print and electronic media—will be heard. Existing programs will be well-funded and more innovative, or experimental, and policy programming will be created. By contrast, when economic health is poor, these voices will less readily be heard, the competition for resources will be fierce, and only the very basic and traditional programs may survive.

Economic forces may be real or merely manipulated for other reasons: Special interest groups may influence politicians to favor some constituencies over others, to favor one region over another, or generally to plead economic necessity in favor of, or against, a social policy program or initiative. "We cannot afford increases in welfare expenditures" or "Increasing support for vocational rehabilitation will require reductions in education funding" are familiar political claims that inevitably impact all areas of social policy. Finally, emergencies such as wars, climatic catastrophes, or public protests will create economic conditions that can directly, and often very quickly, affect policy proposals, their transformation and implementation.

Ideological forces—sometimes framed in economic terms or supported by economic arguments—are both more familiar and less predictable in their impact. No political party or philosophy in American social history has had a monopoly on ideological arguments, nor has any political party eschewed the ideological approach of standing firm against all practical objections. Our problem is that it is nearly impossible to describe ideological associations and arguments in neutral terms. A goal that one ideological camp describes as "creating an atmosphere in which the rigors of the free market can be unleashed" will be described by another as "giving tax breaks and other benefits to the wealthy for direct political gain." In the past decade or two, "personal responsibility" has become an ideological code phrase from the political right that is used to limit resource redistribution to the disadvantaged, while "social justice" has become a slogan from the political left used to increase resources. Obviously, the ideological terrain is filled with landmines.

Although many ideological forces have shaped disability policy in the United States, in some respects, and ironically, disability policy has been privileged by its origins in charity and pity. No politician, of any party or ideology, would be comfortable publicly opposing social programs for veterans (although it happens from time to time). Similarly, few politicians would go on record as rejecting programs for the "blind, crippled, and dumb." The disability movement began in the 1960s and later felt it had to fight long and hard against the charity approach in favor of equal citizenship and human rights. In doing so, it incurred the risk that its arguments against dependency and for equality could undermine what had been the most dependable ideological support for disability programming, namely, charity and pity. People with disabilities who were relatively well-off and self-sufficient were willing to take that risk; others who were more vulnerable were less willing.

Although economic and ideological forces have power over policy development and implementation, it is far beyond the scope of this chapter to discuss these controversies and problems—let alone propose solutions. From time to time, however, their impact will be clearly in the background of our discussions. It is, for example, a policy problem of considerable proportions—one that affects everyone with limited resources, not merely people with disabilities—to come up with a way to smooth out the support and programming available to people who require it as the economy goes through its periodic ups and downs. Other relevant issues that are too big to discuss include those of basic political theory: for example, the fundamental problem of the limits of social policy in a representative democracy, or the proper role of the judiciary with respect to policy. And for constitutional reasons, the question of whether the federal or state governments should determine and implement policy looms large in American politics. Although all of these issues, and others besides, are in the background of disability policy, they are too much for us to handle here.

We also have to set aside the fascinating area of what might be called "the psychology of policy tools." Reduced to their essentials, there are four basic tools for implementing a policy or law: creating an entitlement (an enforceable legal right to a benefit), an incentive (a benefit given in exchange for participation or cooperation), an enforceable requirement (where failure to participate brings a punishment or other disincentive), or an unenforced or voluntary recommendation. The choice of tool is governed in part by political expediency or compromise, but also by efficacy and cost-effectiveness, both of which are governed in turn by psychological considerations (Gilbert, 1992). For example, an incentive that encourages and enables people to behave in the policy-desirable manner (for example, the free provision of day-care services for women to encourage them to enter into job-training programs) increases program costs and may fail if people react against the manipulation. An enforceable requirement (for example, requiring people to participate in public work projects in order to qualify for job training) not only increases costs, but creates the motivation to cheat the system. Finally, "no-strings-attached" entitlements (say, free health care) may create the moral hazard of over- or unnecessary utilization. Although choosing the most effective policy tool is crucial, since it can make or break a policy initiative, we have to set this controversy aside.

Our Controversies

With these caveats, the plan for this chapter is as follows. For disability policy and law, we will look at five broad controversies:

- What is disability?
- Is the anti-discrimination strategy enough to achieve equality?
- What is the "human rights approach"?
- What should be the balance between the public and the private sectors?
- Should policy be mainstream or targeted?

Each fundamental policy controversy, once described, will be made concrete in terms of specific policy problems that the controversy has created in selected areas of disability policy. We begin with (and spend the most time on) the definitional controversy, as there is no question that it is the most far-reaching controversy in disability law and policy. But, once again, we have to be selective in which concrete policy problems to consider, since all of these controversies have a wide impact on policy. Finally, potential solutions that have been suggested will be briefly reviewed.

In the case of disability ethics (and related law), the controversies will be represented by the following ethical and legal debates:

- Nature and value of health: normality, impairment, and quality of life
- Autonomy: informed consent, compromised capacity, and substitute decision making
- Beginning-of-life issues: prenatal testing and newborns with impairments
- End-of-life issues: euthanasia and physician-assisted suicide
- Justice: health care allocation and access to health care

The Policy Controversies

The "What Is Disability?" Controversy

We begin with the most influential, and in many ways the most mysterious, controversy that affects nearly every area of disability law and policy: What is disability? In Chapter 1 we looked at the impact that debates over models of disability have had on the history of American disability policy. These debates were not academic alone; they reflected deep social, cultural, and ideological disagreements with profound legal and economic consequences. To appreciate the impact of these debates, it need only be remarked that the so-called medical model has been argued to be responsible for the "gatekeeping" role of medical and, later, rehabilitation professionals that profoundly shaped federal Social Security policy from its beginnings (Drimmer, 1993; Stone, 1984). Even more important, although more technical, is the impact that these models have had on the demographics of disability, and in particular on the issue of prevalence, or "how many" people with disabilities there are (see Kirchner, 1993, and see Chapter 5 for a discussion of the current, best story on disability prevalence in the United States). Policy analysts are well aware that models of disability directly affect who is counted as disabled, and that "the numbers" matter a great deal when making the case for the urgency and scope of public policy. The importance of statistics is concretely reflected in the sheer number, and influence, of federal statistical agencies: the Bureau of Labor Statistics, the Bureau of Economic Analysis, the National Center for Health Statistics, and many others.

Despite the academic literature on disability models, it is not always clear how, or even whether, a particular conceptualization of disability affects concrete policy. The gap between abstract theory and the concrete language of policy is usually too great to be confident that the one directly affects the other. For this reason, most practically minded policy analysts eschew the abstract world of models and focus on the more concrete domain of the definition of disability. Here, the controversy takes on another form: the imposing number of different definitions of disability that are in effect in policy and law. Although, amazingly, the precise number of definitions in federal and state law and policy is not known, a study commissioned by the Interagency Committee on Disability Research in 2003 found 67 definitions of disability, disabled person, individual with a disability, and other variations just in the United States Code (ICDR, 2003).

To be sure, many of these legal definitions overlap or can be plausibly grouped together; but since there are substantial differences between these definitions, it is nearly impossible to derive basic prevalence information that can be usefully fed into policy development and planning. More simply, we have no idea how many people with disabilities there are.

This plethora of definitions came about because disability policy, as its history makes clear, was neither planned nor coherent but arose in a piecemeal and reactive manner, responding to political pressures and perceived needs—frequently those of returning veterans. As each new program or entitlement was created, it became necessary to define who was eligible for it, and a definition was created that was fit for that purpose. There was nothing inherently wrong with this approach, since if the objective of a policy is to respond to the needs of a group of people, then it made sense to restrict the program to people with those needs. But it is at this point that conflicting models of disability came back into the picture, since the definitions that were created were influenced by preconceptions of what disability, so to speak, really is, and this judgment depended entirely on the dominant or favored model of disability. Because of its dominance, the culprit was usually the medical model; but in recent years, some versions of the social model have also led to problems.

The controversy about what disability is has persisted because, unlike policy for people who are poor or unemployed or need housing or transportation, disability policy has historically been tailored for those who are poor *and* disabled, unemployed *and* disabled, or need housing or transportation *and* have a disability. As a result, being disabled has always been a separate eligibility criteria for receipt of benefits. The lack of consensus about the nature of disability impacts different policy areas differently. For some policy challenges, such as access to medical services, the definitional issue causes few problems and can be safely ignored. But in other areas of policy, the definitional problem cannot be ignored. In particular, there are two very important areas of disability policy in which the definition of disability causes major difficulties—anti-discrimination and Social Security.

Anti-Discrimination Policy and the Definition of Disability

Both the Rehabilitation Act of 1973 and the Americans with Disabilities Act of 1990 provided protection against discrimination for "persons with a disability," or in the case of the ADA's Title 1 employment protection, for "a qualified individual with a disability." But, as described in Chapter 1, the ADA came under a judicial "backlash" in the form of U.S. Supreme Court decisions like *Sutton v. United Airlines* (1999), *Toyota Motor v. Williams* (2002), and others that focused on the definition of disability. In all these cases, the result was that the scope of anti-discrimination protection was drastically reduced, so much so that disability leaders believed that new legislation was required to repair the damage the Court had done (eventually leading to the ADA Amendments Act of 2008). Predictably, some commentators insisted that the problem was that the Court was looking at the ADA through the distorting filter of the medical model of disability (Smith, 2007), or that the ideologically unsympathetic Court simply used definition as an excuse to undermine the spirit of the ADA. But others argued that this was too simplistic an analysis and that the real culprit was the minority group approach, which seemed to imply that only a few individuals—those with very severe impairments that cannot be ameliorated by medication or assistive devices—are truly disabled (Bagenstos, 2009).

Whatever the explanation, it is clear that the definition of disability has been the weakest link in anti-discrimination policy and may well be a contributing factor in the very dismal rate of successful claims of employment discrimination over the life of the ADA (Colker, 1999, 2001). What is particularly frustrating for the disability advocate is that the ADA definition very clearly relies on the social model, inasmuch as it applies the term "disability" to individuals who are merely "regarded as" having a substantially limiting impairment, thus acknowledging the socially constructed nature of the disability label.

The problems created for the ADA by the definition of disability go well beyond the need to "get the definition right." The real question is why, for the purposes of anti-discrimination law, does there need to be a definition of disability at all? The aim of anti-discrimination law, and the reason it is so important to people with disabilities, is not that it opens the door to eligibility for services, but that it provides a remedy for socially unfair treatment. Anti-discrimination law and policy, in other words, is categorically different from policy that provides special license plates for parking or wheelchairs and other assistive devices for those who need them. There are good reasons to carefully circumscribe who gets these goods and services, since to be fit for this purpose the person must have the impairments that make these goods and services needed. But there is no good reason to exclude people from the protections of anti-discrimination law because they are not "truly needy," in the sense that they actually possess a medically determined impairment. It should be enough that they are unfairly treated (Bickenbach, 2000).

Social Security and the Disability Determination Process

As described in Chapter 1, Social Security Disability Insurance (SSDI) and Supplemental Security Income (SSI) are the two major federal programs of cash and medical benefits for persons with disabilities (for the statistics related to these two programs, see Chapter 5, especially Table 15). SSDI provides payments for those already covered by the Social Security program, and SSI is a means-tested income assistance program for disabled, blind, and aged persons who have limited income, whether or not they were previously employed. Given the aim of income replacement for those unable to work because of disability, eligibility for both programs requires a definition of disability that focuses on the appropriate population in need—the so-called "target population." The definition should neither exclude those actually in need nor include those not in need. The problem with the definitions used for these programs is simple enough: The cost in financial and human terms of the administrative procedures for determining whether an individual qualifies as disabled threatens to make the entire system not only unfair, but utterly unworkable. What has been called the "largest system of administrative adjudication in the world" (Mashaw, 1983, p. 18) cannot be sustained.

Since the earliest versions of the Social Security Act in the mid-1930s, with some minor amendments in the late 1970s, an individual is considered disabled if he or she is unable "to engage in any substantial gainful activity by reason of any medically determinable physical or mental impairment which can be expected to result in death or which has lasted or can be expected to last for a continuous period of not less than 12 months." By the late 1970s, the Social Security Administration (SSA) added the requirement that an applicant will be deemed to have a disability "only if his physical or mental impairment or impairments are of such severity that he is not only unable to do his previous work but cannot, considering his age, education, and work experience, engage in any other kind of substantial gainful work which exists in the national economy." This provision is still in place (see 42 U.S.C. § 410).

In the case of SSDI, which is contributory and requires the recipient to have worked before disability prevented it, successfully qualifying not only entitles one to a monthly amount (with spousal and children's benefits, when applicable) but also to Medicare, which, for a person with impairments, can be a substantial advantage indeed. For SSI, the recipient need not have worked before, but must have limited income; the successful applicant also receives a monthly amount, and in most states also can get Medicaid, unless already eligible for Medicare.

Following a steep rise in the number of people receiving benefits from both programs in the early 1990s, the Department of Health and Human Services (DHHS) noticed a growing backlog in processing claims, the result of the fact that processing a claim could take up to 155 days, and as long as 550 days if there were appeals (Social Security Administration, 1994). In response, the DHHS instituted the Disability Evaluation Study, later renamed by SSA the National Study of Health and Activity (NSHA), thought to be the cornerstone of a long-term disability research agenda to understand the growth of the disability programs. The aim of the research was not only to predict future use of the two programs, but also to find ways of overhauling the determination process. Although DIIHS initially invested in an ambitious redesign of the entire process, by 1996 it abandoned that effort in favor of funding basic research on disability data collection and, in light of that research, making small changes to the existing determination process.

It was clear to everyone, however, that the reason the process was not working had entirely to do with the complexity of the legislative definition of disability, with its medical, functional, and vocational components. Trying to use this definition had led to an administrative process that the Government Accountability Office (GAO) in 1994 called "a bureaucratic nightmare." To describe it in its basics, the SSDI and SSI determination process consists of four steps, including a detailed clinical evaluation of the underlying medical causes and prognosis of the impairment; a comprehensive assessment of the work-related functional limitations attributable to the impairment and of the individual's remaining functional capacity; a detailed vocational analysis of the individual's work history and acquired work skills, educational background, and age; and, last, an analysis of the individual's current vocational prospects. Since SSA has never had the resources to perform such an extensive assessment for each of the nearly three million new or returning applicants per year, and since negative decisions are reversed on appeal at an exceptionally high rate, the result is a high level of successful applications. Though it may seem cynical, it is fair to say that if an applicant has the fortitude to use every avenue of appeal and reassessment available, then the chances of success are nearly guaranteed (Institute of Medicine, 2007b; see Figure 12 in Chapter 5).

In 1996, SSA came to the conclusion that the determination process needed to be refurbished and put out a tender for this immense project. At the same time it approached the highly reputable and independent Institute of Medicine (IOM), the health arm of the National Academy of Sciences, to do the basic research to redesign the system. IOM issued three reports in the 1990s, culminating in its *Dynamics of Disability* report in 2002. The expert IOM committee agreed that though there are many factors that contribute to the upsurge in applicants—demographic changes, shifts in labor-market dynamics, economic conditions, legislative and regulatory changes, and court decisions—the underlying reason for this phenomenon was also the explanation for the cost and complexity of the determination process—namely, that there was no agreement on what "work disability" means because "there is no agreement on the definition and measurement of disability."

Since the mid-1950s, the SSA had hoped to work around this lack of agreement by relying upon medical professionals, and their high level of social prestige, to act as gatekeepers and disability screeners. The so-called "listings of impairments" used for the third, medical step in the determination process consisted of categories of impairments defined by medical signs, symptoms, and laboratory findings that described the level of severity required for each impairment to meet the administrative threshold for "work disability." But, because of the increased use of appeal processes, the listings in practice became less and less useful as a screening tool to limit successful applicants. Originally the listings accounted for more than 90% of the initial disallowances, but by 2001 that number had fallen to 52% (Social Security Advisory Board, 2001).

At the end of the day, however, the core of the problem is that, in the absence of agreement about what disability is, there is simply no "gold standard" for determining how many Americans *should* qualify for SSDI or SSI benefits, and so it is impossible to know what the "correct" number of valid claims should be. The problem here was much more pressing, and difficult to resolve, for mental health problems leading to work disability (Kennedy, 2002). Although there are best practices for making the disability determination process more administratively fair (Disability Research Institute, 2005), and implementing these practices is a considerable achievement, without agreement about what the outcome of the process should be in each case, there can be no valid guidelines for making the process more reliable and accurate.

What Is Disability? Possible Solutions

Whenever the definitional controversy comes up, disability scholars insist that the solution is to recognize the domination of, and reject, the traditional medical model in favor of the social model. In many respects, this reaction is surely justified; we need only consider the so-called "meat-chart" or Baremas system for work capacity assessment, in which parts of the body are assigned percentage values of work incapacity (for an international survey of this approach in action, see OECD, 2004; compare Stiker, 1999). Equating body parts with a person's ability to work is the crudest form of the medical model, since it purports to make its determination independently of the person's actual capacities or workplace requirements, let alone the possibilities for changing the workplace to make it more accessible. Nor is the Baremas approach ancient history, long abandoned. Quite the contrary, it remains dominant and is embodied in the American Medical Association's *Guides to the Evaluation of Permanent Impairment* (2007), the standard that continues to be used in most state workers' compensation systems in the United States and around the globe.

But does this mean that the solution lies in embracing the opposite approach, namely, the social model? Unfortunately, the social model, with its insistence that a person's social environment creates his or her disability, can lead us in the direction of making another, opposite mistake of ignoring the importance of medical determinations of disability. After all, eligibility criteria for health or rehabilitative services—for example, criteria that help determine what assistive device a person with a mobility problem requires—must rely on the actual and measurable physical needs that medically describable impairments have created. To do justice to this kind of policy, we need to know both facts about the person's impairments and information about the person's physical, human-built, and social environment.

The solution depends on the obvious insight that legal or policy definitions of disability must at the end of the day be "fit for purpose," in the sense of being directly relevant to the objectives of the policy. Knowing what the point of a policy is—its objectives—is a vital step in policy analysis, since it determines which policy tools will be relevant and which outcomes will need to be monitored. In other words, the fact that U.S. disability policy uses different definitions of disability should not be a concern to us, as long as these definitions are relevant to and fit for purpose for the objectives of the specific policy to which the definitions are attached. But definitions do not float in the air, they depend on how we understand the underlying concept of disability. Definitions of disability are policy tools that need to do specific jobs well; but we only recognize them as alternative definitions of disability if they reflect a single conception of disability.

As was argued in Chapter 1, there is growing recognition that a conception of disability that is workable and realistic for the full range of diverse areas of disability policy is one in which disability (a) is a multidimensional phenomenon that includes intrinsic features of both the human body and mind; (b) is the outcome of an interaction between features of the person (impairments and functional limitations) and features of the overall physical, human-built, social, attitudinal, and political environment; (c) is a continuous rather than dichotomous phenomenon; and finally, (d) is a universal human condition, rather than the distinguishing mark of a discrete minority.

Currently, there are at least two models of disability that view disability in this way, one associated with the work of American epidemiologist Saad Z. Nagi (1964; 1969; 1976; 1979; 1991), the other the World Health Organization's International Classification of Functioning, Disability, and Health (ICF) (World Health Organization, 2001). The Nagi model has been the most influential in research and policy in the United States, providing the conceptual foundations for the influential IOM reports on disability (IOM, 1991; 1997; 2007a). Both the Nagi model and the ICF identify dimensions of the overall phenomenon (which Nagi calls "disablement" and the ICF calls "disability") that are roughly the same, namely: a biomedical dimension (impairment); a functional dimension, in which impairment causes decrements in a person's capacity to perform actions; and a social and interactive dimension, in which these dimensions interact with the person's complete environment to produce an outcome.

There are many differences between the Nagi model and the ICF (see Bickenbach et al., 1999; Jette & Badley, 2000), but they are also importantly similar. Neither model is exclusively medical or exclusively social: They are combinations of both, which avoid the extremes of either. The ICF calls its model "biopsychosocial" to underscore the fact that it incorporates both the biological, or health, component of disability, and the psychosocial component, for which the person's environment is an essential determinant.

As the ICF also provides complete classifications of these dimensions of disability, as well as environmental factors, it has had far more international and cross-professional uptake, and we can continue to use its terminology in what follows. In the ICF, the three dimensions of disability are called impairments, activity limitations, and participation restrictions. These dimensions are derived from their positive correlates, which are called body functions (and structures), activities, and participation (which, taken together, are called dimensions of functioning). Disabilities, therefore, are problems or difficulties at the level of the body (impairments), at the level of the person (activity limitations), and in interaction with environmental factors (participation restrictions).

How does the ICF help us to solve the What Is Disability controversy? First, the ICF incorporates in a single model the three dimensions of disability. This means that as long as the policy definitions in use are individually consistent with the ICF model, then disability policy as a whole will to that extent have a conceptual unity and coherence. (As an aside, this also means that, for data collection, as long as survey questions are clear about which of the three dimensions they are addressed to, the survey as a whole will be able to paint an overall picture of disability in the population that can be used for policy purposes.) Second, the fact that there are three distinct dimensions of disability shows how it is possible to use the same model of disability while sometimes defining disability in impairment language (for access to assistive devices) and other times in the language of participation restriction (for anti-discrimination). Third, viewing all three dimensions of disability as matters of "more or less" (continuous) rather than "yes or no" (dichotomous) more clearly represents the policy need to include thresholds of the severity of the problem in the definition. Thresholds demark what is socially viewed as disabled from what is viewed as non-disabled and, given that there is no gold standard that can scientifically establish this cut, should be the result of transparent and open political debate, taking into account both needs and available resources.

Solving the Anti-Discrimination Definitional Problem

Is this approach to the conceptualization of disability—one which is consistent with different definitions of disability, and fit for different policy purposes—the solution to the controversy? It is impossible to say for sure, but at least with respect to anti-discrimination law and Social Security determination, there are grounds for thinking that this approach might help.

Consider the ADA definition of disability (104 Stat. 328 § 12102):

The term "disability" means, with respect to an individual
- (A) a physical or mental impairment that substantially limits one or more of the major life activities of such individual;
- (B) a record of such an impairment; or
- (C) being regarded as having such impairment.

Although there is a mountain of academic literature on this legal definition, all we need to ask is whether it is fit for purpose, given that the objective of the ADA is to protect people with disabilities against discrimination in employment and other areas. Discrimination, and unfair treatment generally, is a social phenomenon, a feature of the person's environment. That would suggest, at a minimum, that a fit-for-purpose definition would focus on the environment, not on the person. Clauses B and C do just that, by directing our attention to people's attitudes and perceptions. But Clause A does not. This clause requires that a person with a disability be someone who has a biomedical problem (an impairment) and experiences this impairment at a certain level of severity ("substantially limits . . ."). Expressed bluntly, Clause A states that unfair social treatment of individuals is possible only if the unfairly treated individuals can prove that they have a sufficiently severe, biological problem that affects their functional status. If a person cannot do this, then it appears that other people in society are perfectly within their rights to treat the person in unfair, irrational, and hurtful ways as much as they like, since the person has no redress. How could this be a fit-for-purpose definition of disability?

Many legal authors have noted this peculiarity and have explained it by pointing out that, historically, the ADA was derived from the Rehabilitation Act, which had as its primary objective to provide rehabilitation services to those who need them and, given this objective, would need to rely on a definition of disability grounded in the impairments these services addressed (see, for example, Bagenstos, 2004, 2009). Whether this is true or not, it is rare for an American lawyer to question why a definition is needed for the ADA's purposes, although some argue that evidence of any impairment or any degree of severity should be enough (Satz, 2006).

But the question remains why, given its objective, should the ADA put up a hurdle in the form of an eligibility requirement for those who have been discriminated against? Setting aside this hurdle does not make the task of proving discrimination any easier; indeed, it requires courts to scrutinize the putatively discriminatory behavior even more carefully. There are some jurisdictions with anti-discrimination protections—for example, Canada and Australia—that do just that and focus on the discrimination, and not on whether the person is truly, or severely enough, disabled (Bickenbach, 2000; Jones & Marks, 2000).

Will the ADA Amendments Act fix this problem? If the judicial backlash that made the amendments necessary is purely ideological, then perhaps nothing would make a difference. But even if the Supreme Court faithfully follows the spirit of the ADAAA, the underlying problem will remain, since the impairment-based definition is still in place in that act. Already legal strategists are arguing that it is essential for courts to feel free to "filter at least marginal cases of disability" by means of an impairment-based test in order to avoid a more dramatic, and devastating, judicial backlash (Anderson, 2009, p. 1). One legal scholar, looking with alarm at the first cases decided under the ADAAA, which appear to be repeating the judicial backlash, argues that the only way to avoid this is to make the definition of disability as inclusive as possible (Goodwin, 2009). This is a first step but, even if successful, it may not avoid the problem.

Solving the Social Security Definitional Problem

Social Security policy has very different social objectives than anti-discrimination policy: Its aim is to provide a "safety net" against abject poverty for people who, because of their impairments, are not able to work. Since there are many explanations for why a person cannot get and keep a job, not all of which involve functional limitations, the SSI and SSDI programs, to serve their intended population, must determine eligibility on the basis of impairments. Moreover, since whether or not a person *can* work is a matter of both the individual's work capacities and the vocational requirements of the job, determining eligibility will always require a complex determination of the match between person and job. In short, as long as Social Security is maintained as a needs-adjusted, targeted policy, complexity in the determination process is unavoidable.

As mentioned, the SSA has been using the impairment listings as a screening tool since the 1950s. There are many reasons of efficiency and certainty for this. In theory, and ideally, the decision process should be both *sensitive* (identify and include those who really qualify) and *specific* (identify and exclude those who do not). The political costs of denying benefits to those who actually qualify is high, but so are the political and economic costs of awarding benefits to those who actually do not qualify. In the late 1970s, the decision was made in favor of increased specificity with a stricter definition (moving from "engage in substantial gainful activity" to "engage in *any* substantial gainful activity"). The stricter definition reduced false positives (those who should not qualify), but at the cost of creating false negatives (those who should). The rationale was that this was the first screening step in the five-step process, and so as long as the applicant could appeal and move on to the other steps, which are less strict, the rate of false negatives would be reduced. But, as already remarked, by increasing the number of appeals of which applicants took advantage, the listings soon lost their effectiveness as a screening tool.

The question is not whether work disability determination should rely on an impairment test, but whether that test should be validly related to employment capacity, or just be an arbitrary tool for lowering the number of eligible applicants. In either case, the background worry is that impairments become equated with disabilities. As noted above, this is the problem with the American Medical Association's *Guides to the Evaluation of Permanent Impairment*, which indeed infer disability directly from impairment, independently of the effect of the person's environment. Even the most recent sixth edition continues this approach, despite purporting to be based on the methodology of the ICF (American Medical Association, 2007).

After a decade of study and several reports, the IOM expert committee in 2007 made several recommendations that reflect both the persistence of the What Is Disability? controversy, and the dilemmas that targeted disability programming invariably faces (IOM, 2007b). The report focused all of its attention on improving the sensitivity of the impairment listings, having conceded at the outset that it could find no compelling reason for SSA to abandon the listings process. The IOM expert committee in effect viewed the cost of false positives to be worth the benefit of increasing accuracy in screening, hoping that in the process awards for true positives would be expedited. As an attempt to move some distance away from a purely medical approach, the committee recommended research that would link the qualifying impairments in the listings to actual decreases in a person's functional capacity to perform standard or basic employment tasks, in the hope of making the listings a more relevant and realistic guide to the inability to work.

One feature of the disability determination process slipped by without comment, although it reflects a very ancient assumption about the motivations of persons with disabilities. It is the assumption that, without safeguards, malingerers and other unworthy applicants will "game the system." This assumption is most obvious in the listings for the musculoskeletal system, in particular their treatment of pain symptoms. Although pain is an obvious factor contributing to functional loss relevant to work capacity, pain is subjective and so a possible source of fraudulent claims. The current listings guard against this by insisting that pain will only be taken into account when "medical signs or laboratory findings show the existence of a medically determinable impairment(s) that could reasonably be expected to produce the pain" (Social Security Administration, 2008, Sec. 1.00). Since people lie about their pain, the theory goes, it is necessary to look for objective verification, although this is at best an indirect indicator of pain.

Lessons Learned and a New Approach

The ADA and the new ADA Amendments Act retain an impairment test that, on the face of it, is inconsistent with their anti-discrimination objectives. The SSA determination process retains its impairment test, but without reducing costs. Abandoning the eligibility hurdle of the ADA, while strengthening the requirement to show discrimination, would be sensible, but is unlikely to happen. A cynic might argue that it would cheaper in the long run to award SSDI benefits to anyone who asks for them, since the cost of the determination process approaches one-third of the SSA's budget, and eliminating the lengthy determination process would incur massive cost savings that could then be used to cover the anticipated false positives. On the other hand, a realist would point out that neither approach would be politically possible, since the prevalent view is that anti-discrimination protection, and Social Security benefits, must only be available to those who qualify as truly disabled.

But is it really necessary that a person can only be called truly disabled in terms of a medical determination? Apparently so, since from the dawn of disability policy the consensus has been that disability protection and benefits must only be available to the morally innocent and "worthy" person with a disability. Thus, the ADA excludes from protection people with socially unacceptable impairments, such as pedophilia, kleptomania, and alcohol and substance abuse, and the SSA protects itself against malingerers and frauds. The primary lesson we can learn from the What Is Disability? controversy, therefore, is that the controversy is not really about what disability *is*, but what disability *must be*, politically and ideologically.

Recently, in reaction to the problems with all available models of disability, there has been academic interest in another form of the interactive approach of Nagi and the ICF. This model is based on the capability theory of Nobel Prize–winning economist Amartya Sen, which has been applied to disability by philosopher Martha Nussbaum (2007) and others (Mitra, 2006; Ruger, 2010; Satz, 2008b; Silvers & Stein, 2007). The future of the What Is Disability? controversy may well lie in this direction.

Although capability theory is a general account of freedom and human well-being, it is straightforwardly adaptable to disability social policy and law, because it identifies barriers to overall social participation as defects in one's capabilities to achieve one's life goals. Capabilities are complex interactions between inherent human capacities—including, but not restricted to, health conditions and impairments—and all aspects of the person's world that either contribute to, or interfere with, these goals. Capability theory avoids the reductionism of the medical model (in which disability turns into impairments) and the oversimplification of the social model (in which disability becomes nothing more than a designator for a disadvantaged minority group); it does so, as does the ICF model, by building on the interaction between person and environment.

As developed by Nussbaum and others, the capability approach shares all of the features of the ideal model of disability that we have suggested best serves the interests of disability law and policy: It views disability as multidimensional and person-environment interactive, as well as both continuous and a universal feature of all human beings. The advantages of the capability approach include the great sophistication of the underlying interaction between its components, as well as the prospect it offers of merging disability into a broader understanding of human capability, thereby avoiding the age-old trap of making disability a matter of "special" needs or separate treatment. Whether the capability approach becomes the next-generation conceptualization of disability, suitable as a basis for disability law and policy, that finally resolves the What Is Disability? controversy remains to be seen.

Is the Anti-Discrimination Strategy Enough to Achieve Equality?

The shape of present-day disability law and policy, although in part determined by old and persistent assumptions and ideologies, is undoubtedly the result of the reliance on the anti-discrimination strategy that underwrote the development and passage of the Americans with Disabilities Act in 1990. This strategy has had a profound impact on disability law and policy ever since. This much is clear from the history summarized in Chapter 1. What is less clear is how we might assess the overall impact of this political and legal strategy. Has law and policy benefited from the anti-discrimination strategy? Is the strategy enough to secure the ultimate prize of equality for persons with disabilities?

As we saw in Chapter 1, the anti-discrimination strategy was motivated in part by a very powerful cultural reaction against the prevalent image of the disabled individual as dependent, even infantile, and in need of "special" treatment (Charlton, 1998; Scotch, 1984; Shapiro, 1993). This image was undoubtedly generated by the medical model, which focused on the person and his or her biological problems and failures. But the reaction was also strongly influenced by the perceived successes of the civil rights movement of the 1950s and 1960s, as well as by the academic development of the social model of disability and its subsequent political use.

As a result of these complex, but relatively well-known, cultural and political forces, interlocking assumptions were woven into the anti-discrimination strategy that were politically very useful at the time, both for the passage of the ADA and for critiques of disability policy across the board. These assumptions were that

- people with disabilities are a disadvantaged minority group;
- all that is holding people with disabilities back are social attitudes; and
- disability is a civil rights issue, a denial of equality of opportunity.

In each case, however, these assumptions have been shown to be either factually dubious or politically counterproductive. As early as 1983, legal academic Judith Wegner observed that the denial of equality on the basis disability is very different from the denial of equality on the basis of race, so that the civil rights approach is not particularly useful for disability. She argued that denials of equality in the case of disability are generally not matters of malevolence or ill will, but of ignorance and misconceived benevolence. Moreover, people with disabilities actually have physical and mental problems that need to be addressed and accommodated; indeed, in many cases they are vulnerable and dependent individuals (Morris, 1992; Wegner, 1983; and compare Fineman, 2008). This situation is very much unlike other historically disadvantaged groups, such as African Americans and women, for whom it is plausible to insist that stigma, fear, or prejudice alone kept them marginalized.

After ten years of the application of the ADA, disability lawyer Bonnie Tucker similarly remarked that the civil rights model that focuses on anti-discrimination was not the best approach to disability, since the remedy to the denial of equality was not to put into effect "distinction-neutral" (as, for example, "color-blind") law and policy. People with disabilities need accommodations to compete in employment and other life areas, and that cannot be achieved by ignoring their real differences (Tucker, 2001).

The political rhetoric of the independent living movement, though both admirable and effective, was similarly factually dubious. A person with complete lower-limb paralysis is dependent on a wheelchair. This is not discrimination; it is a fact. Finally, despite the political impact of adopting the language of the Civil Rights Act to the effect that people with disabilities are a "distinct and insular minority," the insistence on minority group status was more political myth than reality given the enormous range of impairments, their overall relatively high prevalence, and the fact that many of these impairments are linked to the universal experience of aging (Bagenstos, 2009; Williams, 1983).

The impact of this controversy in the law has centered on the uneasy role that reasonable accommodation plays in the anti-discrimination strategy. In policy, it has taken the form of the controversy between mainstreaming and targeted programming, which we will come to later. Nothing symbolizes this controversy better than the seemingly unavoidable "dilemma of difference" mentioned in Chapter 1 (see Minow, 1990): In order to achieve equality, individuals or groups feel pressure to de-emphasize features of themselves that mark them as different; yet, in the case of disability, ignoring the real differences created by impairments can stand in the way of practically achieving equality, since without accommodations and assistive technology, full participation in society is impossible. The anti-discrimination strategy, perhaps only as a rhetorical flourish, insisted that only irrational social stigma kept people with disabilities from living independently "like everyone else"; but the legal and political demand for "reasonable accommodation" is only achievable—and only makes logical sense—if accommodations are necessary because of the real differences that impairments make.

Lawyer and political theorist Mark Kelman (2000–2001) has contributed to our understanding of the issues by offering a distinction between simple discrimination and accommodation. Simple discrimination, he argues, is a direct violation of a person's right to be treated with dignity and respect, and as such is the sort of violation that cannot be easily justified. Accommodation, on the other hand, is a claim grounded in distributive justice, and as such is always susceptible to "reasonable" social balancing in light of scarce resources. Thus, while considerations of cost and economic efficiency would not justify an assault on someone's basic dignity as a human being, they are relevant to reallocation of resources. The moral source of reasonable accommodation is simply not the same as that of simple anti-discrimination.

Another way of putting Kelman's distinction is this: While the right to be protected against discrimination is a necessary condition for the achievement of equality for persons with disabilities, it is not a sufficient condition. Anti-discrimination is not sufficient because allocations of resources that disadvantage some groups of people, although they may be unjust, are not necessarily violations of basic human dignity. In short, for the purposes of achieving equality, the anti-discrimination strategy may not be enough. It must be supplemented with entitlements to the redistribution of scarce social resources to achieve justice—that is, entitlements to positive state action to secure reasonable accommodation.

So much for the theory. Has this controversy had any impact on the practice of the ADA or other disability policy that purports to follow the mandate of the anti-discrimination strategy so well represented in the ADA? There are at least two areas of policy—one that has been a problem area for disability for decades, and the other relatively new—in which the sufficiency of the anti-discrimination strategy is a concrete policy issue.

The Anti-Discrimination Strategy and Employment

Writing a "personal postscript" in 1992, economist Edward Berkowitz argued that in his view, the ADA continues a long tradition of "using the policy process to soften the conflict between the rhetoric of rights and the realities of economies" (Berkowitz, 1992, p. 2). A decade later, it seemed that, in the area of employment, economic realities had won and rights had lost. In a disturbing study published in 1999, Ruth Colker raised the spectre of the ADA being, as she put it in the title of her paper, "a windfall for defendants." Her analysis of ADA employment-discrimination cases indicated that complainants lost an astonishing 93% of their cases at trial (Colker, 1999; updated in Colker, 2001 and 2005b; and see the statistics on ADA cases in Chapter 5). She searched in vain for some distinctive feature of these legal actions that could explain these results.

Other researchers insisted not only that the courts were acting reasonably, but that it should have been anticipated that the ADA would lead to a decrease in the employment rate among people with disabilities. In this vein, conservative economist Richard Epstein argued that, given economic realities and the understandable behavior of employers, the ADA merely encouraged employers to avoid hiring people with disabilities to eliminate the possibility of legal action, even if charges of discrimination had a high rate of failure (Epstein, 1992). Ten years later, as the employment rate among people with disabilities continued to fall, Epstein's claim was repeated (Acemoglu & Angrist, 2001) and the so-called "judicial backlash" phenomenon began in earnest.

Even those who were generally sympathetic to the disability cause pointed out that the ADA mistakenly assumed that people with disabilities were a homogenous minority group facing only irrational stigma and prejudice. Employers did not think of themselves as bigots, but instead thought they were protecting their business against what they assumed were high accommodation costs, and avoided hiring people with disabilities as a matter of good business practice (Baldwin, 1997; Russell, 2000). Although several academic symposia were held to debate these questions in the early 2000s (e.g., Hotchkiss, 2003; Krieger, 2003; Stapleton & Burkhauser, 2003), no consensus was reached about the causes of the fall in employment rates. Some academics raised concerns about the absence of good data and the lack of knowledge about why people with disabilities choose not to enter the labor force (Blanck et al., 2007; Blanck & Schwochau, 2003); others refused to believe that empirical research studies actually showed conclusively that the problem was, as the conservative economists insisted, that the ADA distorted the open labor market (Blanck et al., 2003). As for persons with disabilities themselves, it appears that a large majority believe that the ADA made no difference to their lives (see Chapter 5).

To the extent that empirical research on this thorny policy question reached any conclusion, it was probably that the employment results were caused by a bewilderingly complex combination of social factors: an increase in the severity of impairments among those who were working or hoped to work (caused in part by the aging population); the relaxing of the impairment listings as a screening tool for SSDI and SSI (and the modest increase in the level of benefits of those programs); and the fact that taking up a job usually meant giving up Medicare health care coverage (a problem repaired by the Ticket to Work and Work Incentives Improvement Act of 1999). These factors also included, possibly, the implementation of the ADA, especially the potential impact of the reasonable accommodation provision on employer decisions to hire persons with disabilities (Issacharoff & Nelson, 2001; Stapleton & Burkhauser, 2003).

Given the lack of reliable data, caused in part by shifting and inconsistent definitions of disability in the employment sector, we will probably never know for sure whether the ADA was responsible for the downturn in employment rates or, as seems more likely, only partially responsible. But the controversy over the anti-discrimination strategy's effectiveness remains. Of more concern in some ways is the failure to clearly distinguish the impact of anti-discrimination protection—in Kelman's "simple discrimination" sense—from the impact of the reasonable accommodation provision. It would be far more troubling if a prohibition against simple discrimination was responsible for the lower rate of employment, rather than employers' real fears about the potential for accommodation costs. The latter at least reflects rational (if purely self-interested) concerns rather than irrational stigma and stereotyping.

But, one conclusion seems unavoidable: Whether it was or was not the cause of slowly decreasing employment rates among persons with disabilities, the anti-discrimination approach to employment was clearly not sufficient to remedy a situation that has plagued disability policy for decade—persistent unemployment, both in good and bad economic times.

The Anti-Discrimination Strategy and the UN Convention on the Rights of Persons with Disabilities

In Chapter 1, it was mentioned that although leaders of the American disability rights movement have been strongly supportive of, and contributed directly to the drafting of, the United Nations Convention on the Rights of Persons with Disabilities (CRPD), there is a sense in which the underlying philosophy of this innovative UN treaty is in conflict with the historic U.S. approach to disability rights, with its focus on negative rather than positive rights. We are now in a position to expand on that conflict, since the anti-discrimination strategy principally involves creating a legal shield against discriminatory treatment, which is a classic example of the negative right *not to be harmed*.

Although one of the main pillars of the CRPD, as expressed in its Article 3, is non-discrimination, the bulk of the document speaks of rights to the implementation of access to opportunities, and in some instances to public resources, all of which are classic examples of positive rights *to be benefited*, or in the policy jargon, entitlements of one sort or another. In the U.S. context, moreover, these rights are often labeled "affirmative action" rights, reflecting the sense in which they are rights to have certain positive actions done by the state in order to enhance opportunities and provide needed resources.

As an example, CRPD Article 8 on accessibility requires states that have ratified the treaty to "take appropriate measures to ensure to persons with disabilities access, on an equal basis with others, to the physical environment, to transportation, to information and communications, including information and communications technologies and systems"—a complex right that, the Article goes on, includes "the identification and elimination of obstacles and barriers to accessibility." These are not anti-discrimination obligations, strictly speaking, since they are not reactions to, or compensation for, a proven complaint that some individual has been harmed by lack of accessibility (calling upon the logic of a negative right); they are obligations that the state has to *positively and proactively* benefit persons with disabilities.

To be clear, the anti-discrimination strategy is not opposed to these positive rights, but the strategy does not mandate them either. This in part was the reason why—prior to the shift in policy in 2009 by the Obama administration—the CRPD was not signed by the United States (although nearly 150 countries of the world had signed it). In 2003, Assistant Secretary of State for International Organization Affairs Kim R. Holmes wrote to National Council of Disability Chairman Lex Frieden informing him that there was no expectation that the United States would become a party to the CRPD because "the United States has an outstanding record with regard to the promotion and protection of basic human rights and fundamental freedoms. The message that we preach abroad, we also practice at home. . . . As you are well aware, the Americans with Disabilities Act is among the most comprehensive civil rights laws protecting the rights of people with disabilities in the world" (see Chaffin, 2005, p. 129). The message was clear: We do not need a human rights document because we have anti-discrimination law.

There is, as might be imagined, considerable interest in the U.S. disability advocacy community, especially among lawyers, for the United States to actively participate in the "paradigm shift" represented by the CRPD (see, for example, Lord & Brown, 2010; Stein, 2008; Stein & Lord, 2010a and 2010b; Stein & Stein, 2006–2007). Many of these scholars recognize that this fundamental shift goes beyond the familiar shift from the medical to the social model; it also embodies a rather different shift from an agenda for equality based exclusively on anti-discrimination to one enunciated in the CRPD that unequivocally speaks of the need to secure economic, social, and cultural rights through direct, substantive action by the state. Creating an obligation for the state to make the social and economic environment more supportive of equality for persons with disabilities is an ideological shift that is, to say the least, highly contentious.

No advocate for disability rights would ever doubt the essential need for an anti-discrimination strategy, but not all advocates are as eager to take the additional step and admit that a more activist state may be required to secure the full and meaningful enjoyment of human rights for all persons with disabilities (Bagenstos, 2009). Those that do, however, are implicitly arguing that the anti-discrimination strategy may need to be augmented with a more positive rights agenda that, unavoidably, cedes authority to the state to proactively remedy the social and economic determinants of disability inequality.

The Sufficiency of the Anti-Discrimination Strategy—Possible Solutions

Unlike the definition of disability controversy, which may be resolvable in different ways for different legal and policy purposes, this controversy is fundamentally political and ideological and can only be addressed directly and generally. Recently, the legal analyst Samuel Bagenstos (2009) has offered an innovative solution. Provocatively, Bagenstos argues that the judicial backlash, both in the treatment of employment discrimination cases and in the infamous trio of cases (*Sutton v. United Air Lines, Murphy v. United Parcel Service,* and *Toyota Motor v. Williams*) that led to the ADA Amendments Act, was not only an expected development, but that these decisions were perfectly in line with the underlying ideology of the ADA. Blaming the Supreme Court, or seeking complex sociological explanations for the downturn in employment rates, misses the point, Bagenstos argues. The ADA reflects the triumph of the "independence" and minority group approaches to disability rights—the view that people with disabilities neither need nor want charity, pity, or government handouts, since once the impact of ignorance, stigma, and discrimination are removed, people with disabilities are perfectly able to be self-sufficient and independent. The Supreme Court's decisions merely reflect this view, since they underscore the position that only those with very severe impairments—health problems that are incurable and cannot be ameliorated—and who, in addition, have been intentionally abused, can seek the assistance of the ADA; all other persons with disabilities are independent and self-sufficient individuals who do not require, and are unjustified in asking for, the Court's help.

As we saw in the history of the American disability rights movement, anti-charity and independence were undoubtedly dominant views that fed directly into the movement from the 1960s onward. Whether this was a savvy political move to gain the support of political conservatives—for whom anti-welfarism and individual freedom certainly resonated—or a naïve political miscalculation, Bagenstos argues that the anti-welfarist position is at the core of the anti-discrimination strategy. The movement held as an article of faith that removing discrimination would empower people with disabilities to enjoy their human rights and achieve full participation in all areas of society by dint of their own individual effort.

Although the ideology of independence and self-sufficiency well-served the interests of solidarity that made the lobbying effort for the ADA and other civil rights legislation possible, the ideology was, in the end, entirely mythical—not because people with disabilities are dependent and childlike, but because *everyone* is dependent on others, and that is more or less what it means to be human. Highlighting this salient truth of the human condition was at the center of the feminist reaction to much of the rhetoric of the disability rights movement (Morris, 1992), and it has recently resurfaced as the basis for a powerful new approach intended to "anchor equality in the human condition" (Fineman, 2008).

By mapping out the inherent limitations of the anti-discrimination strategy, Bagenstos and others are not arguing for the abandonment of the ADA. Since discrimination is a continuing social problem, anti-discrimination redress is, and will likely continue to be, an essential component of human rights protection. At the same time, though, these scholars argue that the utility of the legal notion of reasonable accommodation has been limited by the rhetoric of independence and self-sufficiency, since it focuses on the unfair behavior of individuals and burdens them with the costs of making accommodations, while ignoring the far more damaging systemic barriers that can only be addressed by proactive and systematic state action. The sheer social and economic complexity of applying reasonable accommodation systematically—as is explicitly mandated by provisions of the CRPD—makes it clear that the distributive consequences of this legal doctrine are not reconcilable with the narrowly defined notion of accommodation that has developed in the jurisprudence of ADA cases (Stein, 2003).

Theory aside, the practical problem is that the most significant barriers to employment, transportation, communications, or other major areas of life for persons with disabilities are systemic rather than personal. Individual employers may fire employees with disabilities unfairly, but most barriers to participation are enmeshed in large and complex institutional structures that produce, for example, the lack of accessible transportation, the failure to develop and distribute new assistive technology, or the inability to provide smooth administrative transitions from vocational rehabilitation to employment. Given the complexities of modern life in general, and of the education and employment sectors in particular, it is unlikely that accommodations to increase opportunities for persons with disabilities can be affected, or afforded, by the private sector, let alone private individuals.

For this reason, some policy experts and advocates argue that the future of disability law and policy must be nudged toward a more creative blending of anti-discrimination and basic social welfare policies that are both effective and affordable (Bagenstos, 2004; Satz, 2008a). The fact that people with disabilities are poor and unemployed needs to be addressed, not by individual lawsuits, but by innovations in social insurance that provide more flexible, partial, and focused protections against impairment costs without an individual being totally excluded from the workplace (Weber, 2008). As the National Council on Disability has argued, federally mandated and state-enforced changes in health insurance would more positively affect the employment situation of persons with disabilities and chronic conditions than nearly any other legal or policy change (NCD, 2009; Satz, 2008b). Extending Medicaid coverage to include personal assistance services would also have a major impact on the employability of those who cannot leave their homes without such services (Bagenstos, 2004). These and other social welfare reforms address unemployment and poverty systematically, rather than in the reactive and ad hoc fashion required by a complaint-driven anti-discrimination law.

The UN Convention on the Rights of Persons with Disabilities mandates a blended human rights agenda combining anti-discrimination and positive action through reforms in social welfare policy and law. Should the United States ratify the CRPD, which is the next step after signing the document, it will be answerable to a yearly audit showing, in terms of hard evidence and sound statistics, that it has taken steps to implement not merely the anti-discrimination features of the CRPD, but the substantive articles that require positive state action, invariably involving economic and resource redistribution. Needless to say, this is a politically sensitive action agenda that will require genuine and sustained cross-party agreement.

Data showing the number of successful complaints brought under the ADAAA will be one kind of information the UN monitoring agency will be interested in seeing; as will figures showing a reduction in per capita poverty among persons with disabilities, or a real increase in the employment rate for persons with disabilities, or the measurable availability of financial support for personal assistance services (see some of these sociodemographic data in Chapter 5). Such is the potential future of disability policy and law in the United States, but it is unclear how, in light of the strong tradition in the American psyche in favor of equality of opportunity, but not equality of results, the United States will fare in meeting these international requirements.

What Is the Human Rights Approach?

For anyone familiar with the disability rights movement, in the United States and around the globe, it might seem peculiar to suggest that the question of what the human rights approach amounts to is controversial. The slogan that "Disability is not a health issue, it is a human rights issue" is almost as well known as "Nothing about us, without us." There is no doubt that the human rights approach is central to disability politics and is readily called, especially when characterizing the basic thrust of the CRPD, the "paradigm shift" in our understanding of disability. Yet, ironically, although there is consensus about what the human rights approach is *not*, and what it is a *reaction against*—the medical model to be sure, but also the service approach, the professional approach, and the charity approach—there is little clarity about what the human rights approach *is* and *requires*. We know what the human rights approach is *against*, but not so much what it is *for*.

By contrast, in the broader international rights literature, what is called "the rights approach" is an established doctrine with a clear substantive and procedural characterization (Jonsson, 2003). Across the United Nations system, the human rights and development agenda characterizes the human rights approach as a strategy grounded in internationally recognized human rights, and the political and administrative processes required for implementing these rights. As understood by international experts, the rights approach refers to a legal, policy, and administrative strategy that is governed by the following principles (UNAIDS, 2004; United Nations, 2003):

- The primary responsibility for the legal imperative to respect, protect, and fulfill human rights rests on government officials, and this is not a matter of charity but of legal obligation.
- The government must discharge its obligation to secure rights both transparently and with the full participation and collaboration of people with disabilities.
- Governments are responsible and accountable not only for the realization of rights but also for the manner or process in which decisions are made.
- Government responsibility is systemic across all areas of policy subject to human rights.

The human rights approach to disability law and policy, in short, creates governmental accountabilities not merely to protect specific rights, but to support all areas of policy that need to be taken into account to successfully implement these rights, including mechanisms for monitoring the effectiveness of the implementation of rights. Finally, the human rights approach mandates basic principles of good governance, including transparency and the full participation of people with disability in the efforts to secure their rights. These aspects of the human rights approach are explicitly identified in the Preamble of the CRPD.

On this reading, the human rights approach demands a great deal from states and their governments. Indeed, this is precisely the source of the policy controversy that surrounds the human rights approach. Although the phrase is a political slogan and core message of the disability rights movement, it is not clear whether these advocates fully subscribe to what is required, politically and legally, to turn the slogan into policy and legal practice. There is at least one political ramification of the human rights approach as it applies to disability policy that is particularly controversial, namely, that governments, both federal and state, are the central players in implementing the human rights approach.

In the American political landscape, the assumption that the human rights agenda is entirely a public-sector issue firmly places the human rights approach into a left-of-center or liberal framework. This is both ironic—since Bagenstos (2009) and others have made the point that the primary political resources drawn upon for the ADA and other innovations were right-of-center or conservative—and troubling as a matter of political strategy. Historically, the disability rights movement in the United States has been particularly adept in avoiding partisan politics and making its case acceptable to a wide spectrum of political viewpoints (a point forcefully made early on by Anspach, 1979; and Driedger, 1989).

Thus, when the human rights approach is made concrete in terms of policy principles that have international currency, another controversy looms, namely, what is the role, if any, of the private sector in disability policy, and how does it relate to the role of the public sector? It is to this controversy that we now turn.

What Should Be the Balance Between the Public and the Private Sectors?

Like many of the controversies and problems already raised, the question of the respective roles of the public and private sectors in enforcing or implementing policy and programming is not at all restricted to the domain of disability policy. The role of the private sector is ubiquitous in all areas of public policy, so the issue is not *whether* the private sector should be involved, but *how much* it should, and whether there should be government regulation (and to what extent), oversight, or governance. This is a matter of balance, and so subject to many considerations, some political, some cultural, but given the underlying nature of public policy, mostly economic. The two areas of disability policy that are used as examples of this controversial balancing exercise have direct impact on the lives of many persons with disabilities, namely, health care, and personal assistance services and assistive technology.

The Problem of Balance in Health Care

For people with disabilities, health care is a major issue: According to a recent Centers for Disease Control and Prevention report (Altman &

Bernstein, 2008), about one-half of adults with a movement, sensory, emotional, or cognitive impairment assess their overall health as fair or poor, as compared to 3% of adults without these impairments. In addition, the disabled population has far higher rates of the three standard risk factors for serious, chronic health problems—namely, obesity, smoking, and limited exercise. At the same time, in the population of non-institutionalized adults with moderate to severe impairments, an average of 20% were uninsured (and those with emotional difficulties had the highest rate of uninsured, at 28%). Although disparities in access to health care are not as great among people with severe disabilities as they are among the poor, people with severe disabilities, given their consistently high need for care, generally have worse health outcomes as a result (Agency for Healthcare Research and Quality, 2010). There are also hidden costs: Being unable to afford needed health care will directly impact a person's ability to work in order to pull out of the poverty cycle (Batavia & Beaulaurier, 2001). In surveys of people with disabilities, the perceived problem here is not the health problems as such, but the cost-related barriers to care that would improve work capacity (Hanson et al., 2003; Meyer & Zeller, 1999).

The U.S. health care delivery and financing system is not only the most expensive in the world, it is the most unequal (WHO, 2000), owing in part to the complexity and transaction costs of the private approach to insurance and care provision. The two massive public-sector programs, Medicare and Medicaid, are by contrast relatively cost effective (Franks et al., 2005; Moon, 2006). All of this adds up to the result that there is no better example of the problem, in all of disability policy, of balancing private and public sectors than that of health policy.

The 906 pages of the Obama administration's health care plan, the Patient Protection and Affordable Care Act (PPAC), with a myriad of provisions that phase in from passage in March 2010 to late 2018, represent, among other things, an attempt to balance the roles of the public and private sectors in the payment and delivery of health care services. Despite its complexity, on this issue the approach of the PPAC is very simple: Keep the two public health care programs in place, maintain the essentially private health care financing and delivery system, but increase the role of the public sector by instituting substantial regulatory oversight of the insurance industry, expanding Medicaid eligibility, subsidizing insurance premiums for those who cannot afford them, providing incentives for businesses to provide health care benefits, and making health care coverage mandatory for all Americans.

This last provision is the most controversial, and has been the subject of court challenges, with inconsistent rulings (the far more controversial "public option" was withdrawn during negotiations). Requiring everyone to have health insurance is a way of redistributing income from the young and healthy (who are less likely to want health insurance) to the under-65 and less healthy, since increasing the overall number of enrollees in insurance increases the percentage of less-risky people in the risk pool, which in turns lowers the health insurance premiums for the riskier members. Universal health insurance, it is argued, will increase the overall health of the population, thereby increasing productivity across the board, increasing tax revenues, and lowering the federal deficit. This is all to be accomplished by the PPAC in a manner that greatly upsets private-sector defenders, since, in effect, the government will increase its control over the country's productive resources (estimated at nearly a trillion dollars in ten years), thereby causing a decrease in the private sector's control of these finite resources. The consequences of this public-sector control depend on one's political and economic theory: Either the economy's long-term rate of growth will slow because of the increase in government spending, or a healthier workforce will increase overall productivity and the rate of growth will not slow, or will increase. At least, that is what the theories tell us.

Theory aside, it is clear that the short-term benefits that the plan offers for people with disabilities are real and entirely the result of increased regulation. Immediately in 2010 for children with disabilities, and considerably later in 2014 for adults, the law prevents private health-insurance plans from excluding coverage for people with pre-existing conditions or a medical history of ill-health (including a genetic history). The PPAC also prohibits rescissions of existing policies when the insured individual becomes sick or disabled, as well as annual or lifetime limits on benefits for new group or individual health insurance plans. In addition, it requires premium rate reviews to track increases in premiums and puts a cap on how much insurance companies can charge in administrative costs. Again, all of these features of the plan tend to benefit people with disabilities more than other Americans. Although these regulatory provisions seem technical, in practice they can mean the difference between having or not having health care coverage for persons with disabilities.

Yet the question is open, and only time will tell, whether this mix of public and private sectors will help to resolve the major problem with the U.S. health care system—that it is far too expensive (now nearly $2.5 trillion per year) and unsustainable given its present trajectory of cost escalation. Whether it will better serve the health care needs of persons with disabilities is yet another open question. The absence of the public option, and the fact that the system retains its essentially private-sector, for-profit dominance (a dominance that exists in no other developed country), suggests that the "balance" continues to favor the private over the public sector. Although some of the more troubling abuses of private health insurance are regulated in the PPAC, it imposes no controls on the price private insurers can charge for premiums, which makes it somewhat unlikely that the enormous costs of the health care system will decrease rapidly, if they decrease at all.

The Problem of Balance in Personal Assistance Services and Long-Term Care

As we saw, the need for personal assistance services (PAS) was the lightning rod in the independent living movement of the early 1970s, and PAS and other long-term care issues remain important for people with severe mobility problems and impairments that affect capacity to perform activities of daily living. The Patient Protection and Affordable Care Act created a voluntary self-insurance program called Community Living Assistance Services and Supports (CLASS) for the purchase of long-term services, including PAS, and in 2011 the PPAC put into place a scheme of long-term care insurance based on payroll deductions for people who become disabled after having paid premiums for at least five years. Neither program, however, covers assistive technology—wheelchairs, canes, splints, or durable medical equipment—which is left to programs at the state level.

Perhaps because of its close association with the early disability rights movement, it has long be argued that the best approach to PAS is to leave it to the free market but empower, usually though financial supplements, the individual to exert consumer control over these services (Batavia, DeJong, & McKnew, 1991). Absent a comprehensive and nationwide long-term care policy for home-based PAS, people with these requirements are either dependant on their families, or on Medicare and Medicaid programs, if they qualify, or, in the worst cases, have to resort to some form of institutionalization. For those with PAS needs who have always enjoyed a full and active life in the community and wish to enter or stay in the workforce, the independent living model was the only viable option (DeJong,

1979, 1981). Ideologically, the independent living model transformed "patients" into "consumers" and structured service provision according to a straightforward market model, in which services are offered and accepted on mutually agreed terms, with the consumer making all the major decisions relevant to his or her life and situation. In its original version, created to meet the actual needs of its founder, Ed Roberts, PAS was the focus; but it was clear that consumer- or person-directed service models were easily transferable across all impairment groups where long-term needs are a concern, with the possible exception of mental health problems (Powers, Sowers, & Singer, 2006).

The case for person-directed service models for long-term care was strengthened by the 1999 Supreme Court decision in *Olmstead v. L. C.* The case involved two individuals with intellectual impairments who fought under the ADA to receive care in the community rather than the institutions in which they had been placed. Somewhat surprisingly, given the Court's general reaction to ADA litigation, the majority held that unjustified institutionalization was discrimination and ordered that, as long as treatment professionals agreed, treatment should take place in the least restrictive environment, which usually means in the community, subject only to the resources available to the individual state. The federal government immediately stepped in and provided both guidelines for transition out of institutions and some funding, and in 2001 President George W. Bush issued a presidential executive order requiring the immediate implementation of the *Olmstead* decision federally. Several states followed suit (see Batavia, 2002).

The right to person-directed care, however, depends on access to the necessary funds. Starting in the mid-1970s, states had the option to offer personal care services under their Medicaid plans, but these were highly focused programs and required medical supervision. This approach was modified so that the individual could lure relatives to perform basic personal care services. In 1981, the Social Security Act was further modified to allow the waiver of federal requirements should states wish to provide home and community-based services explicitly to enable persons with disabilities to avoid institutionalization. The so-called Home and Community-Based Services (HCBS) waivers created by the act soon dominated the scene at the state level. These waivers provided the individual with a measure of control, but since they were designed to serve state needs, both the services financed and the populations targeted were narrowly defined. In addition, states offered little or no training or guidance about the basic skills of person-directed services: how to hire, train, supervise, evaluate, and fire assistants. Waiver programs had to resolve the dilemma of respecting the autonomy and independence of their "customers" while providing them with the essential tools they needed to be successful employers.

Two other financing models have been tried in various states (see Powers, Sowers, & Singer, 2006). A brokered support approach originated with people with developmental disabilities who required a considerable amount of assistance coping with the life skills required to manage their own affairs. A broker or personal agent was assigned to each client to provide ongoing support, often with the broker or other intermediary maintaining a measure of control over the funds allocated. Another approach, which avoids the worry about client autonomy, is called "cash and counseling." This approach has been used to support a larger range of people with long-term personal care needs, including the elderly and people with severe physical disabilities who are nonetheless working. On this plan, customers cash out their Medicaid payments to pay for services, and fiscal management, employment assistance, and other forms of counseling are provided, when needed, by case managers, providers' agencies, or self-help organizations. Since the person's capacity to self-manage is still the determination of a professional, even this approach risks compromising autonomy, although it remains an attractive alternative.

In the end, despite several decades of experimentation, the question remains of how to balance two irreconcilable approaches—a free-market and autonomous customer approach versus a public-sector financing and (to one degree or another) paternalistic monitoring approach. Given that the funding for long-term personal care and other services comes ultimately from tax dollars, the state has an obligation to ensure that these funds are successfully used, and that requires some degree of monitoring. On the other hand, since the point of these programs is to foster and support independence and self-management as much as possible, the intrusion of the state in what are highly personal decisions may seem objectionable. The problem of balance remains for what, given aging trends, will be the central long-term policy problem in the coming decades.

How to Balance Private and Public Sectors—Possible Solutions

The balancing conundrum highlights some of the more difficult political and economic issues of the post–World War II period in America. Given that neither a wholly private-sector, free-market approach to disability policy, nor a completely public-sector approach, appears to be acceptable, the challenge is to come up with some form of "mixed" approach that is feasible, affordable, publicly and politically acceptable and, finally, effective. Abstractly, this means determining what both sectors tend to do well, and what they tend to do badly, and then finding a mixture in which the strengths of each are utilized and the weaknesses avoided. Easy to say, but hard to do.

As is often the case in policy debates, the solution is to look for examples of best practices in a variety of policy areas and see if the lessons learned can be exportable to other areas. Here are a three such examples.

Assistive Technology

The Assistive Technology for Individuals with Disabilities Act of 2004 (originally passed in 1988) concerns a policy area that is of essential importance to persons with mobility and other impairments and that is not particularly well-served by the private sector. Assistive technology (AT) can be low-, medium-, or high-tech and range from very costly items, such as power and manual wheelchairs and scooters, to augmentative communication devices, orthotics, prosthetics, and other durable medical equipment and supplies, to work, study, and recreation-relevant equipment and modifications. People who require AT often are unable to participate in work or education, or even handle more basic day-to-day activities, without AT; but with it, they can be fully active and lead productive lives.

There are three essential components to this complex policy area that are well-served by the 2004 Assistive Technology Act: (1) the collection and provision of basic information about available AT products; (2) the provision of low-cost loans and other financial support to purchase or lease the equipment that is required, as well as pay for training and technical support, demonstration of the proper use of the equipment, and referrals for repairs and servicing; and (3) the availability of substantial funding for research and development projects for universities, commercial businesses, and nonprofit organizations. The funding process is similar to that of Medicare, in which the federal government provides each state with a grant to fund an Assistive Technology Act Project (ATAP) that provides the services and distributes the funding.

The AT development and distribution policy created by the act has been described as a workable "public and private partnership" (Sauer et al., 2000;

Wallace, 2003) because it builds on the strengths of each sector. Because the market for AT tends to be small, and sometimes very small, potential suppliers avoid it since the development costs will not easily be recovered from sales, especially to a population that tends to be poor. Federal funding, distributed by state-level ATAP, helps to fund seed projects and development research to alleviate this problem by reducing the risks of not recouping investments in development costs. By funding information about AT, the federal government also helps to reduce the transaction costs of what is otherwise an open market for products. Finally, by assisting in the financing, ATAP secures and stabilizes demand for AT in a way that helps to guarantee supply, as well as provides an essential support for people who otherwise might not be able to work (and so pay taxes that can offset the federal funding).

Workers' Compensation

Although there are many problems with workers' compensation programs—not the least of which is the general reliance on unreliable "meat-chart" or impairment-rating schemes for the determination of benefits—the underlying theory is an example of how private-sector failures can be remedied without resorting to a wholly public-sector approach. Workers' compensation pays for medical care, rehabilitation, and cash benefits for workers who are injured on the job or who contract work-related illnesses. It also pays benefits to families of workers who die of work-related causes. Each state has its own program that has no federal involvement in financing or administration; the federal government too has a program for its workers.

According to the most recent review of state programs by the National Academy of Social Insurance (Sengupta et al., 2009), more than 130 million American workers are covered by workers' compensation, with a total of $55.4 billion in benefits paid out in 2007 (roughly half in medical care and half in cash benefits). Between 2006 and 2007, the benefits to injured workers increased by an average of 3.3%, but the costs to employers for this mandatory benefit to their employees dropped by an average of 2.7%. Although programs differ state to state, from the longevity and relative stability of these programs, it is apparent that they well serve their objective of providing medical and income replacement for workers who are injured at work, without unduly burdening either the private-sector employees or the public-sector administrators.

Workers' compensation was, and remains, a compromise solution to a problem created by the inadequacy of a private-sector, free-market approach to workplace perils. In the 19th century, if a worker was injured at work, his or her only remedy was a (public sector) negligence action against the employer. This solution was quite inadequate for all sides: The employee had to incur the cost of bringing the action, assuming that medical or other expenses made it possible to afford the time to do so; and the employer had to incur the expense of defending against it, the burden of being unable to plan in light of potential liability, and the cost of compensating the employee if the defense was unsuccessful (although, given the slant of negligence law, defenses were more often than not successful).

In the end, both sides saw the logic of workers' compensation legislation, which would ensure that the worker who sustained an occupational injury or disease in the course of employment would receive predictable compensation without delay and irrespective of fault, and that the employer would benefit by the predictable and considerably lower costs of participating in the program, which required the worker to give up the right to sue. Perhaps most importantly, the state's involvement is restricted to enforcement and secondarily to administration and information concerning the rights on all sides. Because all of this made good sense, workers' compensation was the first form of social insurance in the United States. After appearing first in Maryland in 1902, it quickly spread.

It is difficult to imagine a more mutually satisfactory balance, of not only private- and public-sector interests, but also those of the injured worker. There remain difficulties on the public side of guaranteeing horizontal equity by reconciling state workers' compensation plans, and on the private side of the increased burden of mandatory premiums that try to keep pace with soaring medical expenses. There are also issues on the side of the injured worker concerning the adequacy of compensation and the perplexing problem of seeking assistance in returning to work. All of these issues granted, workers' compensation programming still represents a best-practice solution to the problem of balancing individual and social interests as well as private- and public-sector needs. The open question is whether it would be feasible to transfer this approach to other areas of disability policy.

Supported Employment

For people with intellectual impairments or other challenges to mental capacity, or for those with stable or episodic mental illness or neurological disorders—from depression, anxiety disorders, or schizo-phrenia, to Parkinson's disease, traumatic brain injuries, or dementias, to alcohol and substance abuse—employment is an enormous policy and personal challenge. This is especially so for those with early onset impairments and diseases who have been excluded from the workforce from the beginning. The traditional solution for those with intellectual difficulties, or very severe physical or emotional problems, has been sheltered employment, in which individuals are effectively removed from the labor force and put into "protective environments" where the demands of competitive employment are minimized—as are the wages. Since sheltered employment programs have long been criticized as warehousing solutions that are disrespectful to participants and provide them with no vocational training or prospect for entering the labor force (Block, 1997; Visier, 1998), the most attractive alternative option pro-posed is some form of supported employment. Although not often seen in this light, supported employment is another kind of solution to the balancing problem.

Supported employment is full integration within a competitive work environment, with supports of various sorts funded by state placement agencies. Depending on the kind of disability and the degree of support required, the individual may be supplied with a job coach, who will pro-vide on-site assistance on all aspects of work and the work environment tailored to his or her specific needs; or, for those with fewer needs, the support may take the form of help with transportation, or finding appro-priate assistive technology, or periodic, off-site, specialized job training. These supports are temporary, at least in principle, since the long-term aim is to develop among supervisors and co-workers "natural supports" to slowly integrate the individual with developmental disabilities or men-tal health problems into the job environment. In some cases, groups of people with similar disabilities can be trained and supervised as a group (the "enclave" model) or work as a self-contained business, supervised by a job coach and their services advertised to businesses that can employ them for discrete, subcontracted jobs (the "mobile work crew"). Finally, a group of persons with similar or diverse disabilities can be trained and supported to own and operate their own small business.

The point of all these approaches, and what makes them models of private–public balancing, is that the workplace is not altered fundamen-tally for the supported employees. Rather, the support, including AT and other accommodations, is brought to the workplace and financed by state agencies. The private employer is obliged to provide the same level of pay and all relevant benefits he or she would have provided to any employees, and gets in return some substantial advantages. First of all, the support will last as long as required, and if necessary will last the duration of the employment; in addition, this professional support is available to all employees. The employer also gets the advantage of having highly motivated and well-screened employees. Research indicates that full integration depends on whether the external supports are augmented by internal support from the employer and co-workers but, when that occurs, that the results are very encouraging (Kirsh et al., 2009). The private setting, once again, maintains its characteristic strengths, but these are augmented by the introduction of public-sector supports.

These are all best practices, and there may well be others in the future. In the end, the challenge of finding the right balance, the right mixture, of the private and public sectors depends both on the nature of the policy objective involved and on how amendable the desired outcomes are to the strategies that are most successfully accomplished in one sector rather than another. The vigor and economic growth of the free market is an invaluable policy tool; but, without some measure of regulation or oversight from agencies at the state or federal level, these forces may not work to the short- or long-term advantage of persons with disabilities. At the same time, unless the regulation and oversight is congenial to the private sector, and enhances rather than stifles economic vigor and the growth potential of the free market, the results will benefit no one, private or public.

Should Policy Be Mainstream or Targeted?

The best way to introduce the controversy between the policy strategies of mainstreaming and targeting is to turn to the views of two giants of American disability policy: Irving Kenneth Zola and Harlan Hahn. Each was a strong advocate for disability rights and policy reforms; both were enthusiastic supporters of the ADA and other legislative innovations. However, they diverged on the fundamental policy issue of whether disability policy should be focused on and targeted to people with disabilities as a specific social group, or whether the political advances that this strategy helped to create needed to be replaced in time by a more permanent policy strategy, in which disability as a distinct policy category would slowly disappear.

In several groundbreaking articles in the mid-1980s, seamlessly merging the political and the academic, Harlan Hahn argued for a "sociopolitical" model of disability that would serve the twin, and to his mind utterly intertwined, purposes of structuring academic writing on disability and reformulating disability policy and activism (Hahn, 1985, 1986, 1987). Hahn's version of the social model of disability was crafted to support his "minority group" paradigm, which identified people with disabilities as a distinct social minority group. Basic to this approach was the recognition that "all aspects of the external world—including architecture, communications, and social organization—are shaped by public policy and that policies are a reflection of pervasive cultural values and attitudes" (Hahn, 1987, p. 184). As a minority group, in short, people with disabilities are creations of social attitudes and, given this reality, the only logical policy response had to be targeted to precisely this social group.

In a single, but powerfully argued, thought piece in 1989, sociologist Irving Zola made the case for "universalizing" disability policy (Zola, 1989). Granting that the historical moment demanded a political strategy of correction based on a vision of an oppressed "discrete and insular minority," Zola argued that this special-needs and discrete-minority approach to disability policy is inevitably of only short-run usefulness. His reasoning was both statistical and practical. First, the population of people with disabilities is at any point in time indeterminately large and, from a longitudinal perspective, disability is more or less a universal human phenomenon. But second, it is far more efficient and cost effective to mainstream disability so that policy changes are uniform and consistent across the population. Anti-discrimination law will always be relevant, even though it is fundamentally corrective and reactive to individual complaints. In the long run, however, what is needed is to proactively and systematically change basic features of employment, education, transportation, and the human-built environment so that it is maximally useable by all.

The debate at the political and policy level reflects another, more abstract debate at the level of the theory of social and political equality. One side insists that the state's power must be limited to guaranteeing *equality of opportunity* for all citizens by creating and protecting social institutions that enable people to utilize their inherent talents and strengths to achieve whatever goals they wish. This strategy typically needs to be buttressed by eliminating irrational obstacles to opportunity based on prejudice or mistaken beliefs about the inherent value and capability of identifiable individuals—hence, the need for anti-discrimination law.

On the other side, it is claimed that, however valuable in itself, equality of opportunity is not enough. In practice, given inequality of natural talents and ambitions, a political strategy of equality of opportunity will always yield inequality of social results, with some members of society leading poor, unhealthy, unproductive, and despairing lives, while others enjoy the benefits of their talents and skills. A more robust theory of social and political equality would sanction direct state action to reform social institutions in order to minimize these inequalities of outcome. Equality of opportunity requires negative rights to protect opportunities against private and public assaults; equality of results requires not only this, but positive rights in the form of universal, redistributive, and ongoing state actions designed to ensure *equality of outcomes*.

Theory, as everyone knows, does not translate neatly into practice, and the controversy between targeted and mainstream or universal policy strategies is not at all straightforward. The contrast between mainstream and targeted policy is played out differently in different policy areas. For persons with intellectual impairments, the issue surfaces as the debate between institutionalization—where targeted care is provided in separate, congregate settings   and deinstitutionalization—where individuals are moved to the community and use generic services (Wolfensberger, 1972, 1976). As we have already seen, these individuals may be offered work experience in separate, sheltered workshop settings, or else in supported employment settings. Educational resources for children with disabilities may be offered either in special schools or by means of full integration into regular classrooms. And assistive technology may be tailor-made to target the special needs of individual persons with specific functional difficulties, or else universally designed to be usable by everyone, irrespective of functional capacity.

Universal programs, as a rule, are politically difficult to initiate but, once established, are very difficult to eliminate. Social Security is a good example, where attempts at privatization are usually rebuffed. Targeted policy, especially ad hoc welfare policy, is often more vulnerable (Gilbert, 2002). Disability policy has from its very origins been targeted (which is arguably one of its major limitations), but yet it seems relatively resistant to attack, possibly because of its stigmatizing link to pity, which protects it from social and political assault (Bagenstos, 2009). The most targeted disability policy tool of all, one fully in line with the historical tradition of disability policy and law, is the Americans with Disabilities Act.

Increasingly there have been calls for mainstreaming in disability policy, but not always with a full understanding of the consequences, or indeed of the potential conflict with the historical roots of the disability movement. The most recent Institute of Medicine volume on disability (2007b), for example, focuses many of its recommendations on "mainstreaming technology" as a solution to the increasing need for more and better-designed assistive technology. Relying directly on the philosophy of universal design—a notion that developed out of architecture and product design, but has been used as a philosophical basis for universalism generally (Ostroff, 2011)—the report defines mainstreamed technology as "any technology that is intended for general use rather than for use entirely or primarily by people with disabilities, . . . [including such] disparate items as pens and pencils, personal computers, kitchen gadgets and appliances, cash machines, automobiles, cell phones, alarm clocks, trains, microwave ovens, and elevators" (IOM, 2007a, p. 189).

The case for mainstreaming technology is almost entirely economic, and it has more general application in other areas of policy. As mentioned, an obstacle to the provision of assistive technology for those with mobility and other functional limitations is the dynamics of the private sector, which is the principal source of innovation, production, and distribution of AT. In particular, assistive technologies constitute a quite broad and varied array of products used by a very diverse population of device users, but the overall market is often too small for private firms to make a profit, especially when development costs are high. This is the same difficulty created by so-called orphan drugs for people with rare medical conditions. Although the Assistive Technology Act of 1998 and its successors tried to address this concern, ultimately the best, and possibly the only, long-term solution is to greatly expand the demand side of the equation. And that of course would be accomplished by mainstreaming technology, as the potential market for these products would be the general public.

The controversy over the best policy tool to use for disability policy is complex and diverse, but in no other area has the debate been more fractious, and as potentially destructive, than in education for children with disabilities.

Targeting or Universalism in Education

The abhorrence of "special" schools is a consistent theme in the disability rights movement and included the reaction against segregated schools for deaf and blind children that was so prevalent in the 19th and early 20th centuries until the notion of "normalization" was made popular in service provision for children with intellectual impairments (Wolfensberger, 1972). The call for school integration for African American children in the 1954 Supreme Court decision *Brown v. Board of Education* not only energized the civil rights movement but was taken up by the disability community, which had its own school integration victories in the federal court cases of *PARC v. Commonwealth of Pennsylvania* and *Mills v. Board of Education*, both in 1972. In the Education for All Handicapped Children Act of 1975, amended in 1990 and renamed the Individuals with Disabilities Education Act (IDEA), the governing presumption was that children with disabilities could be educated with children who are not disabled "to the maximum extent appropriate," except in cases where the severity of the disability made it impossible to achieve a satisfactory level of education, even with all supplementary aids and services in place (Weber, 2007). The No Child Left Behind Act, first enacted in 2001, continued the assumption that integration is always better, for educational outcomes and full social participation, when creating provisions designed to set standards for educational quality and accountability.

In their seminal book *The Unexpected Minority: Handicapped Children in America* (1980), educational theorists John Gliedman and William Roth made the political and sociological case for the abolition of segregated "special education." But the underlying argument for inclusive education was not only political, it was also economic. Special schools were never cost-effective since they reached only a very small proportion of the students who were blind or deaf, and ignored the needs of other students with mobility problems or intellectual impairments (OECD, 1999). In a study done in the mid-1990s, it was estimated that the cost of segregated classes was 2.3 times that of mainstream schools (Chaikind et al., 1993). These and other studies, coupled with the momentum of the disability rights movement, led to legislative reforms such as IDEA at the federal level, and similar laws at the state and local levels. The three-part message of these legal reforms was always the same: (1) It makes economic, social, and educational sense to mainstream students with disabilities; (2) "separate but equal" is as wrongheaded a policy in education as it was in race relations several decades before; and (3) segregated education is a basic violation of human rights (Weber, 2007).

The implementation of both IDEA and the No Child Left Behind Act has not been easy, in part because both acts are only partially funded federal mandates to the states, and as such each state is free to interpret the inclusion mandate in ways compatible with its other priorities and funding arrangements (Palley, 2006; Parrish & Wolmar, 1999). The President's Commission on Excellence in Special Education in 2002 highlighted the fact that many school boards have an incentive to misidentify students with learning disabilities, because doing so qualifies them for additional state resources. The "top-down" political message of inclusiveness in some states has been transformed into a strategy for relieving pressure on strained educational budgets.

More fundamentally, though, it remains controversial whether it is either feasible or desirable to mainstream all children with disabilities, and some disability scholars have criticized integration on grounds of both educational effectiveness and the disruption to the child's life that integration may cause. Deaf students and those with learning disabilities often complain that mainstreaming is not always a positive experience for them (e.g., Foster, 1991; Fuchs & Fuchs, 1994), and some disability advocates have made the case that it should be a matter of individual choice whether mainstream or special educational placement best serves the physical, academic, and emotional needs of the child (Norwich, 2002; Pitt & Curtin, 2004).

The most prominent critic of the "integration presumption" has been deaf activist and researcher Ruth Colker, who argued in 2005 that the presumption of full inclusiveness in education is not justified for many children with disabilities. Insisting that it is time "to examine the cold data about the success and failures of full integration for children with disabilities," Colker cited educational research suggesting that teachers in mainstream classrooms are not trained to teach children with intellectual impairments and, even when they are, the teacher-student ratio in mainstream classes is far too high for them to do the extra work required (Colker, 2005a, p. 795). As a result, mainstreamed students with learning disabilities do not progress well and, worse, face stigma and rejection from other students. Colker doubted whether the self-esteem of the child with disabilities was truly enhanced simply by being clustered with children of the same age, or whether teachers would be able to serve the interests of inclusiveness while also respecting individual differences that might require different pedagogical strategies. Colker concluded that perhaps it is time to set aside the politically motivated presumption of mainstreaming in favor of a more case-by-case approach.

Can We Reconcile Targeting With Universalism? Possible Solutions

Lawyer Martha Minow once described a fully inclusive classroom she visited in which the non-deaf students and teacher all learned American Sign Language in order to communicate with the sole deaf student, thereby bridging the gap between mainstreaming and respecting different needs (Minow, 1990). Although perhaps an extreme example, a 1997 OECD report pointed to the state of Colorado, which had achieved an astonishing 99.6% inclusion rate for children with disabilities, and painted a more realistic picture of what is required for successful mainstreaming: a funding model that guarantees educational resources to accommodate all students; a system of individual student assessment to identify needs; curriculum development that integrates all learning styles into the classroom; teacher-to-student ratios low enough to allow teachers to spend time on each student as required; well-trained classroom assistants; integrated support systems, including peer support; a sophisticated special-needs training program built into teacher qualifications; and strong community and parental involvement in school activities and governance (OECD, 1999). A tall order, indeed.

Making educational mainstreaming and universalism in education work is obviously not easy and, at a minimum, requires political will, multisectorial planning and, of course, substantial resources: The mere legal presumption of inclusion is not enough. This is fully recognized in Article 24 of the CRPD, which sets out in detail the state's obligations in order to achieve "reasonable accommodation of the individual's requirements" and the support required to "facilitate their effective education," including training teachers and staff at all levels of the educational system in disability awareness and the use of appropriate augmentative and alternative modes of communication. Educational specialists agree, however, that even the best mainstreaming strategy may have difficulties dealing with the isolation and lack of self-esteem that some students with disabilities experience in fully integrated settings (Hocutt, 1996; Zigmond, 1995).

Are there any lessons here for the general policy controversy of whether to target policy to populations or to strive for universal policy? It is dangerous to generalize but, historically, targeted programs tended to be the product of policy-making done under the assumption that the affected population is small and easily identified (for example, victims of an earthquake), or in reaction to some public outcry or high-profile scandal in which the government of the day responds to pressure and tries to solve the problem as narrowly, and cheaply, as possible. Advocates of universal design and mainstreaming disability policy argue for cost savings in the long run, making the obvious point that impairments are a permanent feature of the human condition and that the prevalence of disability will increase with the aging population. The downside of targeting is segregation and the vulnerability of "special programs" thought to be too costly to maintain. The downside of universal policy, on the other hand, is that it requires considerable planning, cross-sectorial policy coordination, up-front costs, and the political will to stay the course so that the investment in resources in the short term can play out as cost savings in the long term. Clearly, this debate, which extends beyond disability policy, is not over.

Future Policy Issues

It is always dangerous to reduce the complexities of law and policy to a few large themes or debates, or to anticipate what the future may bring. The looming issues in the early 21st century may appear to be historical oddities in a decade or two. But it is easy to predict a few enduring policy issues that will have to be tackled in the near future: the need for a solution to the rapidly escalating, and unsustainable, costs of health care provision; the demographic fact of an aging population and its impact on disability policy; and the potential impact of the United Nations Convention on the Rights of Persons with Disabilities, should it be ratified.

The aging phenomenon deserves special attention, since the international impact on all aspects of social policy of an aging population is well-known (Jacobzone, 2000; OECD, 2001). The reality of increased longevity and decreased birthrate in high-resource countries such as the United States is a recognized public health issue (Kalache et al., 2002), but it also creates burdens on age-related programs such as Social Security, pensions, and long-term care, at the same time that the tax base to fund these programs is shrinking given the proportionately ever-smaller workforce. The fact that aging advocates have steadfastly refused to see age-related health problems as impairments and, from their side, disability advocates have focused their attention on youth and middle adulthood issues, means that both groups have ignored their common cause. This artificial sociological divide between aging issues and disability issues has created an obstacle to effective lobbying for legal and policy changes that could benefit both groups.

As the population ages, of course, the prevalence of moderate to severe impairments—mobility, sensory, and cognitive—will dramatically increase. Inevitably, this will also increase the need for service provision and the gap between the need for and availability of accessible environments. At the same time, as the affected population increases in size, its voice (especially if it is united) will be louder and less easily ignored. The stigma of being different, and the tendency to segregate people with impairments from mainstream society, will be undermined by the blunt fact that what used to be a minority of people is creeping slowing toward becoming the majority. This growth might spur on research and innovation in assistive technology and environmental modifications for accommodation to serve a larger market. Given that the impairments of aging are both predicable and inevitable, proactive policy solutions will be more feasible. In short, the obstacles, hurdles, and dilemmas of disability policy might be resolved by the simple fact of an aging population. The aging phenomenon will dominate the policy agenda for the foreseeable future, and its impact on all aspects of disability policy will be profound.

Issues in Disability Ethics

We turn now from disability policy and law to disability ethics, where more fundamental issues have been debated. Although it might appear that the policy controversies just surveyed are wholly different in nature from the ethical debates we will look at next, in fact, at the conceptual level, they are strongly connected. In many respects, the policy controversies are merely manifestations, in practical policy language, of the deeper issues that dominate disability ethics. Just as an example, the first ethical debate discussed below—the moral value of the impaired life—is certainly the driving force in the never-ending discussion about what disability is; but it is also in the background of the universal versus targeted policy controversy. Other linkages between ethics and policy—between fundamental values and the application of these values in practical policy objectives—will become clear.

As mentioned in Chapter 1, disability scholars objected to mainstream bioethics because of the assumption that the presence of an impairment or chronic disease automatically lowers the quality, and moral value, of the life. Some disability advocates have also suggested that bioethicists either claim, or assume without argument, that poverty, unemployment, low social status, and other disadvantages associated with disability are directly linked to the individual's biological state, rather than to the social environment (e.g., Koch, 2006). Though the first objection was a fair criticism, the second is less so, primarily because only recently have bioethicists turned their attention to wider issues of the fairness of the allocation of resources based on health status, where considerations of the impact of the social environment on people with disabilities would more naturally arise. Bioethicists, in short, are now revising their early naïve views about the nature of disability, although some disability scholars remain skeptical (Amundson & Tresky, 2008). Since disability scholars have been preoccupied with their critiques of bioethics, the agenda for disability ethics has, up until fairly recently, been set by the bioethicists rather than the disability ethicists.

What follows is a quick review of some of the lasting ethical issues and debates that have been the focus of disability ethical scholarship in the last decade or so. As with the policy controversies, this is of necessity a selection rather than an exhaustive list.

Nature and Value of Health: Normality, Impairment, and Quality of Life

Disability researchers opened the debate by challenging what they viewed as a dominant assumption in bioethics: that health and normal functioning are intrinsically valuable, or that assaults on health and functioning intrinsically and invariably devalue human life. What might be called the "disability critique of bioethics" has taken several forms, some more plausible than others. One extreme view is the insistence that impairments—blindness, lower body paralysis, memory loss—are merely neutral "differences" that can and should be detached from any disadvantage that an individual may experience (Hughes & Paterson, 1997; Rock, 2000). This unnecessarily strong rejoinder (what about pain, psychological anguish, and unending fatigue?) is usually tempered by a weaker, and far more plausible, claim that although health and normal functioning are valuable things, they are not the only things in life that make it worth living, and we should not overestimate their significance (Silvers, 2005).

Another facet of this debate is how people with severe impairments evaluate the quality of their own lives. There is some empirical evidence that these individuals judge their lives to be of considerably higher value than might be objectively assumed, and indeed, paradoxically, that the objectively worse the health, the better the subjectively assessed quality of life (Albrecht & Devlieger, 1999). What is more intriguing is that third-party assessments of the quality of life of people with impairments—by either health professionals or the general public—tend to be far lower than self-assessments by people with impairments (Ubel et al., 2003). Recently, Ron Amundson (2010) has compiled evidence from hedonistic psychology to support his claim that third-party assessments are highly distorted, while those of people with impairments are more likely to be valid.

The abstract question of the inherent badness of impairments underlies several concrete bioethical debates in which the disability perspective has been vigorously defended. One such debate is whether deaf parents of children who also have innate or acquired deafness can refuse consent for cochlear implant surgery to restore some hearing capacity, on the grounds that the child should not be deprived of becoming part of the "culture of deafness" for the sake of the "tyranny of the 'normal'" (Lane & Grodin, 1997; Silvers, 1994). Another and more dramatic example of this debate involves "sexually ambiguous" or "intersexed" children who may be subjected, with parental approval, to surgical interventions for normalization (Beh & Diamond, 2000–2001). Besides these specific quality-of-life ethical issues is the far more influential debate about the allocation of health and other resources, which revolves around the cost-effectiveness of using scarce resources to improve the lives of people with pre-existing impairments, rather than to help those without impairments who could use the same resources to greater benefit (Ubel, 2000), an issue to which we return below.

Autonomy: Informed Consent, Compromised Capacity, and Substitute Decision Making

Since bioethics was created out of a reaction against abuses in medical research, the value of autonomy, and in particular the right to decide whether to participate in research or treatment, has always been a core value in bioethics (Beauchamp & Childress, 2001). Autonomy is also a central value in disability ethics, especially for people with intellectual impairments or mental health problems, for whom denial of autonomy and the legal capacity to make decisions for oneself is a prevalent practice

(Dhanda, 2007). Standard bioethical doctrine—and the law on informed consent across U.S. jurisdictions—specifies that consent to treatment or research must be based not only on full information and absence of coercion, but also on the mental competency to understand and appreciate the consequences of the decision. If a person is not competent to consent, then some form of substitute decision maker—next of kin, best friend, or, in the case of a formal declaration of permanent incapacity, an agency of the state acting as a guardian—will make a proxy decision (Buchanan & Brock, 1990). This is standard practice for medical treatment, and increasingly also for decisions to participate in research (Stineman & Musick, 2001).

Disability scholars noticed that bioethicists tended to assume that impairments, either cognitive or communicative, deprive individuals of their ethical status as autonomous agents, and therefore of their legal rights. Recalling a history of "de-personalizing" marginalized groups, including African Americans and women, which involved stripping these individuals of their legal capacity to make decisions about all aspects of their social life, disability advocates have insisted that depriving people with cognitive impairments of this capacity is just more of the same. While the ethical dimension of autonomy has been more or less settled for decades, the successful lobbying effort of advocacy groups for people with mental illness, leading to the insertion of a very strong guarantee of legal capacity in the UN Convention on the Rights of Persons with Disabilities (see Minkowski, 2007; Perlin, 2007), will open the door to a more rigorous ethical debate in the future. In particular, the Convention appears to reject substitute decision making in all or nearly all instances, in favor of supportive decision making, in which the individual is provided the supports needed to express his or her will, and maintain legal capacity.

Beginning-of-Life Issues: Prenatal Testing and Newborns With Impairments

In 1982, a boy was born with Down syndrome and an esophageal blockage. He died six days later of starvation after his parents decided not to treat the blockage on the advice of their physician, who had warned them that a life with Down syndrome was not worth living. This was, at the time, a practice that was common, although not well known. Shortly thereafter, the President's Commission for the Study of Ethical Problems in Medicine and Biomedical and Behavioral Research (1983) explicitly recommended that, in this kind of case, surgery to save the life of the infant should be provided. Thus began the so-called "Baby Doe" legal cases, brought on behalf of newborns with serious impairments whose parents and physicians refused to treat them. The next year, a pro-life federal government supplemented this advice by proposing amendments to the 1984 Child Abuse Act that would make such behavior potentially abusive.

Coincidently, the legal battle took place during a period of intense academic publication and political activism in the disability community focusing on the stigma of impairments and chronic health conditions. Although disability rights advocates wished to distance themselves from the anti-abortion focus of the Baby Doe cases, they also were concerned about the anti-disability arguments found in influential bioethical work defending the practice of letting "defective newborns" die without treatment (Singer & Kuhse, 1985). The Baby Doe era effectively ended with the U.S. Supreme Court's 1986 decision in *Bowen v. American Hospital Association*, in which the Court rejected the claim that such treatment was discriminatory, but the ethical debate continued and soon expanded to a range of other beginning-of-life issues and standard medical practices.

Undoubtedly the most prominent of the related issues, which gave further support for the disability critique of bioethics, was the practice of prenatal screening or genetic testing for impairments. Although no one objected to screening as such, what was seen as ethically objectionable was the fact that when screening information revealed a congenital impairment or genetic propensity to a serious disease, it was used as the grounds, and often the only grounds, for a selective abortion. The disability critique focused on what were argued to be the underlying misconceptions about a life with impairments. While affirming the right of a woman to an abortion, the critique raised what was called the "expressivist" objection—that the practice sent a negative message about the value of disabled people, and in particular the highly destructive message that people with impairments ought not to have been born (Asch & Wasserman, 2005; Parens & Asch, 2000; Silvers, 1994).

The screening debate has matured since the 1980s, as medical developments have greatly increased the reliability of genetic testing, while lowering its cost. The disability critique has been countered in various ways, raising considerations of parental choice, reproductive freedom, and equal access to medical resources (Amundson & Tresky, 2007; Buchanan et al., 2000; Shakespeare, 2005), as well as the somewhat bizarre suggestion that refusing to abort a "defective fetus" is a violation of the right of the unborn child to live with an "open future," unencumbered with disability (Purdy, 1996). Disability ethics has had to tread carefully between the feminist position, which strongly favors the right of the woman to decide whether to carry the child to birth or not, and the objection that abortion on the grounds of impairment merely reinforces stereotypes that devalue persons with precisely those impairments. The battle continues, and whenever reproductive choice is compromised by legal case or public opinion, the disability response has to tread even more carefully (Asch, 2001).

End-of-Life Issues: Euthanasia and Physician-Assisted Suicide

The disability community was also pitted against mainstream bioethics in a case that raised concerns about how life should end. In the 1986 case of *Bouvia v. Superior Court of State of California,* a state appeals court decided that an intelligent young woman by the name of Elizabeth Bouvia had the right to die by starvation as long as it was her informed and uncoerced choice. Since she was fully competent to refuse consent to treatment, the court was bound by clear precedent to grant her the right to do so. Instead of making that decision on the grounds of autonomy alone, however, the unanimous court, arguably unnecessarily, wrote in their judgment that her disabilities made her decision reasonable: "She herself is imprisoned, and must lie physically helpless, subject to the ignominy, embarrassment, humiliation, and dehumanizing aspects created by her helplessness." This gratuitous remark mobilized the disability community. While fully supporting the right of a person with disabilities to make such decisions, many activists felt that it was extremely dangerous to raise the issue of disability as an explanation of why this form of suicide should be allowed (Asch, 2001).

During the mid-1990s, the euthanasia debate revolved around conflicting reports about the existence or potential for abuse in those few jurisdictions in the world that had legalized consensual euthanasia on the grounds of patient autonomy (Weir, 1992). As the *Bouvia* case made clear, if a person was competent to decide and wished to have life-sustaining medical treatment (for example, a respirator) discontinued, and died as a result, the law had nothing to say about it. And ethically, too, it was difficult to make the case that a person should be kept alive against his or her will. Disability scholars were always suspicious of the rationale for allowing consensual euthanasia, but rarely objected to it (but see Battin, Rhodes, & Silvers, 1998).

The ethical response became more complex when the practice of voluntary euthanasia was institutionalized, as it was in the Netherlands in the late 1980s and when the state of Oregon passed the Death with Dignity Act in 1997. In the case of Oregon, terminally ill patients who were mentally competent could ask to self-administer lethal medications that were legally prescribed by a physician. The state is required to keep detailed records of the practice, and the data indicate that only 460 Oregonians had taken advantage of the law between the time of its passage and 2010 (Oregon Department of Human Services, 2010). Since these patients were essentially seeking assisted suicide, the debate altered its focus, as did the disability response. It was at this time that two Supreme Court cases—*Washington v. Glucksberg* and *Vacco v. Quill*—once again brought the issue to the public's attention. In both cases, terminally ill patients requested assistance from physicians to end their lives. Despite some powerfully argued *amicus curae* briefs from prominent bioethicists in favor of allowing physician-assisted suicide, the Court flatly rejected the idea, upholding state bans on the practice on the grounds that the states had an interest in protecting the vulnerable from coercion.

The disability community split in its reaction to the decisions. Some argued that Chief Justice William Rehnquist's reasoning, while correctly acknowledging that people with disabilities face prejudice and negative stereotypes, was in the end both paternalistic in tone and discriminatory in consequence. People with disabilities, as a group, do not need to be protected by the state (Silvers, 1998). Others argued that since banning physician-assisted suicide would flatly violate the autonomy of persons with disabilities—and since surely safeguards could be put into place to protect against abuse—legalization would not be ethically problematic. One of those who so argued is Tom Shakespeare who, perhaps noticing the dangerous ground he is entering, concludes by saying: "It is an important principle that the qualification for assisted suicide is the end stage of incurable disease accompanied by unbearable suffering. Simply being a disabled person is not a reason to be permitted assisted suicide" (Shakespeare, 2006, p. 130).

On the other side, opponents stressed the novel argument that had been made during the hearing—that one should be somewhat skeptical about how uncoerced and wholly voluntary requests for assisted suicide are in practice. Would the decision be the same if people were fully informed of all aspects of their health condition, if they were guaranteed the full range of palliative services, including pain relief, or if they would not have to worry about bankrupting family or friends to pay for these services? Research supports the intuition that the decision to kill oneself is always constrained, if not coerced, by circumstances, including the attitude of the health care provider, and that it is often motivated by patients' legitimate fears that they will not be provided with the services they require, or will receive them only at a tremendous cost to their loved ones (Gill, 2000; Gill & Voss, 2005). Opponents of assisted suicide realize the difficult position they are in, making an argument that sounds either vaguely paternalistic or frankly paranoid (Gill, 2000). Recent discussions focus on the more nuanced ethical concerns about the feasibility of legalization in a manner that safeguards against abuse.

The Schiavo Case

One of the age-old arguments that all opponents of euthanasia resort to at some point is the so-called "slippery slope" concern, namely, that even if fully consensual assisted suicide is ethically unobjectionable, legalizing and institutionalizing the practice will inevitably open the door to other, more objectionable practices, and in particular the practice of involuntary euthanasia. The argument came into its own in the controversy surrounding Terri Schiavo in 2005. Schiavo had lived in a persistent vegetative state in nursing homes, with constant care, being nourished and hydrated through tubes, for 15 years. Although there was some controversy about her condition, the best evidence indicated that Schiavo had no upper brain activity whatsoever, making her utterly incompetent to consent one way or another. Her husband, Michael, as her substitute decision maker (Terri Schiavo left no advance medical directive or living will), requested that her feeding tube be removed so that she could die. This request was not motivated by any desire to make his wife suffer; rather, under the law of Florida, any attempt to directly or indirectly kill his wife would be murder, punishable in that state by death.

Since Terri Schiavo's parents were profoundly religious and strenuously objected to Michael Schiavo's request, the case quickly became a cause célèbre for the "culture of life" community (Annas, 2005). The parents used all legal avenues to prevent the discontinuation of tube feeding, but lost each case. Florida Governor Jeb Bush took up the case and convinced the state legislature to pass "Terri's law," which required the reinsertion of the feeding tube. The constitutionality of the law was successfully challenged, and the U.S. Supreme Court refused to hear an appeal. After more legal attempts, the U.S. Senate adopted a bill to require continued feeding and hydration of Schiavo, which was quickly passed by the House of Representatives. The bill never took effect because a U.S. District Court refused to grant the parents' request for emergency feeding and, after several more unsuccessful legal challenges, Terri Schiavo finally died.

From the disability perspective, the Schiavo case may represent a turning point in the application of the disability critique to bioethics. Although the case was framed by pro-life advocates as a matter of disability rights, and indeed at different junctures in the legal battle many of the prominent disability rights organizations that track bioethical issues actively participated on the side of Schiavo's parents, it was clear that many in the disability community were uncomfortable being aligned with fundamentalist religious groups and like-minded politicians. In retrospect, doubts have been raised about the advisability of moving disability ethics in this extreme direction (Shepherd, 2006). The argument made with enthusiasm by some disability advocates—that a person in a permanent vegetative state is just like any other disabled person—may have rhetorical force, but is mistaken in a way that prejudices the interests and dignity of people with profound intellectual impairments. These individuals have abilities to interact meaningfully with people and their environment; but a person in a permanent vegetative state has—by definition—no such ability at all. Ethical judgments depend on seeing similarities and differences and, in this case, the important differences may have been ignored for political purposes.

Justice: Health Care Allocation and Access to Health Care

In 1995, bioethicist Dan Brock asked the question whether rationing health care in ways that disadvantage persons with severe disabilities is always discriminatory, and in particular a violation of the ADA (Brock, 1995). Brock was writing in the context of an attempt by the state of Oregon to prioritize health care allocations, in light of both professional and public input, into a scheme that would take into account the relative quality of life of potential recipients of care. Although Brock was cautious about answering the question he posed, others argued that any scheme of health care allocation that took into account pre-existing impairments, and the purported lowering of quality of life that resulted, would be discriminatory (Orentlicher, 1996). Again, the disability critique focused not so much on the broader issue of the need to prioritize health care resources, and so to allocate them in some manner or other, but on the too-easy and stereotypical approach that characterized the lives of persons with disability as being, essentially, less valuable and less worthy of resources.

Since some form of rationing health care is a necessity, given the escalating costs of providing health care, the literature on this subject is large and growing. The ethical issues involved in rationing concern the justice of the procedures used to determine who gets what, as well as the justice of the end results, in what is often called the domain of distributive justice (Daniels, 2008). Here the debate broadens to include fundamental issues in political theory, and in particular the question of political equality. Increasingly, disability scholars are entering into this domain, with promising results (Silvers, Wasserman, & Mahowald, 1998; Stein, 2006; Wasserman & Bickenbach, 2005). The pressure of worldwide economic woes will inevitably heighten the importance of the disability ethical input into this crucial area of social policy.

Future Issues in Disability Ethics

As the history of disability policy makes clear, in economic downturns, when politicians look for policies to trim or cut, it is disability policy that suffers the hardest hit. Ultimately, this is an issue of ethics, and debates about justice in allocation, the need for accessibility and accommodation for full participation, and the "burden" of disability will resurface. Recently, too, calls for non-economic indicators to assess policy, and in particular indicators of "well-being" (Nussbaum, 2011; Stiglitz et al., 2009), have raised once again the issue of the impact of impairment on the quality, and value, of a human life (Amundson, 2010). It is certain that the standard bioethical issues involving disability will continue to be debated and, less optimistically, that some bioethicists will continue to misconstrue disability as a wholly medical phenomenon (see Savulescu & Kahane, 2009). At the same time, most of the future disability issues, even if they arise initially within bioethics, will be debated in the intersection between ethics and political philosophy. Disability ethics is clearly an area of ever-increasing interest and academic activity.

References

Acemoglu, D., & Angrist, J. D. (2001). Consequences of employment protection? The case of the Americans with Disabilities Act. *Journal of Political Economy, 10*(5), 915–957.

Agency for Healthcare Research and Quality, U.S. Department of Health and Human Services. (2010). *National healthcare disparities report, 2009.* Rockville, MD: Author.

Albrecht, G. A., & Devlieger, P. J. (1999). The disability paradox: High quality of life against all odds. *Social Science and Medicine, 48*, 977–988.

Altman, B., & Bernstein, A. (2008). *Disability and health in the United States, 2001–2005.* Hyattsville, MD: National Center for Health Statistics.

American Medical Association (AMA). (2007). *Guides to the evaluation of permanent impairment* (6th ed.). Chicago, IL: Author.

Amundson, R. (2010). Quality of life, disability, and hedonic psychology. *Journal for the Theory of Social Behaviour, 40*(4), 374–392.

Amundson, R., & Tresky, S. (2007). On a bioethical challenge to disability rights. *Journal of Medicine and Philosophy, 32*, 541–561.

Amundson, R., & Tresky, S. (2008). Bioethics and disability rights: Conflicting values and perspectives. *Journal of Bioethical Inquiry, 5*, 111–123.

Anderson, C. L. (2009, March 25). *Ideological dissonance, disability backlash, and the ADA Amendments Act.* Retrieved from http://ssrn.com/abstract=1368445

Annas, G. (2005). "Culture of life" politics at the bedside: The case of Terri Schiavo. *New England Journal of Medicine, 352*(16), 1710–1715.

Anspach, R. (1979). From stigma to identity politics: Political activism among the physically disabled and former mental patients. *Social Science and Medicine, 13*, 765–773.

Asch, A. (2001). Disability, bioethics, and human rights. In G. L. Albrecht, K. D. Seelman, & M. Bury (Eds.), *Handbook of disability studies* (pp. 297–326). Thousand Oaks, CA: Sage.

Asch, A., & Wasserman, D. (2005). Where is the sin in synechoche? Prenatal testing and the parent-child relationship. In D. Wasserman, J. E. Bickenbach, & R. Wachbroit (Eds.), *Quality of life and human difference: Genetic testing, health care, and disability* (pp. 172–216). New York, NY: Cambridge University Press.

Bagenstos, S. (2004). The future of disability law. *Yale Law Journal, 114*(1), 1–84.

Bagenstos, S. (2009). *Law and the contradictions of the disability rights movement.* New Haven, CT: Yale University Press.

Baldwin, M. L. (1997). Can the ADA achieve its employment goals? *The Annals of the American Academy of Political and Social Science, 549*, 37–52.

Batavia, A. I. (2002). Consumer direction, consumer choice, and the future of long-term care. *Journal of Disability Policy Studies, 13*(2), 67–74.

Batavia, A. I., & Beaulaurier, R. L. (2001). The financial vulnerability of people with disabilities: Assessing poverty risks. *Journal of Sociology and Social Welfare, 28*(1), 139–162.

Batavia, A. I., De Jong, G., & McKnew, L. B. (1991). Toward a national personal assistance program: The independent living model of long-term care for persons with disabilities. *Journal of Health Politics, Policy, and Law, 16,* 523–545.

Battin, M., Rhodes, R., & Silvers, A. (1998). *Physician assisted suicide: Expanding the debate.* New York, NY: Routledge.

Beauchamp, T., & Childress, J. (2001). *Principles of biomedical ethics* (5th ed.). New York, NY: Oxford University Press.

Beh, H. G., & Diamond, M. (2000–2001). An emerging ethical and medical dilemma: Should physicians perform sex assignment surgery on infants with ambiguous genitalia? *Michigan Journal of Gender and Law, 7*(1), 1–63.

Berkowitz, E. D. (1992). Disabled policy: A personal postscript. *Journal of Disability Policy Studies, 3*(1), 1–16.

Bickenbach, J. (2000). The *ADA v. the Canadian Charter of Rights*: Disability rights and the social model of disability. In L. Francis & A. Silvers (Eds.), *Americans with disabilities: Exploring implications of the law for individuals and institutions* (pp. 342–356). New York, NY: Routledge.

Bickenbach, J. (2001). Disability human rights, law, and policy. In G. L. Albrecht, K. D. Seelman, & M. Bury, (Eds.), *Handbook of disability studies* (pp. 565–584). Thousand Oaks, CA: Sage.

Bickenbach, J. E., Chatterji, S., Badley, E., & Üstün, T. B. (1999). Models of disablement, universalism, and the ICIDH. *Social Science and Medicine, 48*(9), 1173–1187.

Blanck, P., Adya, M., Myhill, W. N., Salmant, D., & Chen, P.-C. (2007). Employment of people with disability: Twenty-five years back and ahead. *Law and Inequality, 25*(2), 232–253.

Blanck, P., Schur, S., Kruse, D., Schwochau, S., & Song, C. (2003). Calibrating the impact of the ADA's employment provisions. *Stanford Law and Policy Review, 14*(2), 267–290.

Blanck, P., & Schwochau, S. (2003). Does the ADA disable the disabled? More comments. *Industrial Relations, 42*(1), 67–77.

Block, S. (1997). Closing the sheltered workshop: Toward competitive employment opportunities for persons with developmental disabilities. *Journal of Vocational Rehabilitation, 9*(3), 267–275.

Brock, D. W. (1995). Justice and the ADA: Does prioritizing and rationing health care discriminate against the disabled? *Social Philosophy and Policy, 12*(2), 159–185.

Buchanan, A., & Brock, D. (1990). *Deciding for others: The ethics of surrogate decision making.* New York, NY: Cambridge University Press.

Buchanan, A., Brock, D. W., Daniels, N., & Wikler, D. (2000). *From chance to choice: Genetics and justice.* New York, NY: Cambridge University Press.

Chaffin, S. (2005). Challenging the United States position on a United Nations convention on disability. *Temple Political and Civil Rights Law Review, 15,* 121–145.

Chaikind, S., Danielson, L. C., & Brauen, M. L. (1993). What do we know about the costs of special education? A selective review. *Journal of Special Education, 26*(4), 344–379.

Charlton, J. (1998). *Nothing about us without us: Disability oppression and empowerment.* Berkeley, CA: University of California Press.

Colker, R. (1999). The Americans with Disabilities Act: A windfall for defendants. *Harvard Civil Rights–Civil Liberties Law Review, 34,* 99–162.

Colker, R. (2001). Winning and losing under the Americans with Disabilities Act. *Ohio State Law Journal, 62*(1), 239–284.

Colker, R. (2005a). The disability integration presumption: Thirty years later. *University of Pennsylvania Law Review, 154,* 789–852.

Colker, R. (2005b). *The disability pendulum: The first decade of the Americans with Disabilities Act.* New York, NY: New York University Press.

Daniels, N. (2008). *Just health.* New York, NY: Cambridge University Press.

DeJong, G. (1979). Independent living: From social movement to analytic paradigm. *Archives of Physical Medicine and Rehabilitation, 60*(10), 435–436.

DeJong, G. (1981). *Environmental accessibility and independent living outcomes: Directions for disability programs and research.* East Lansing, MI: Michigan State University, University Center for International Rehabilitation.

Dhanda, A. (2007). Legal capacity in the disability rights convention. Stranglehold of the past or lodestar for the future? *Syracuse Journal of International Law and Commerce, 34,* 429–462.

Disability Research Institute (DRI). (2005). *Disability claims, review, hearings, and appeals procedures: An anaylsis of administrative best practices.* Retrieved from http://www.dri.illinois.edu/research/p04-03c/default.htm

Driedger, D. (1989). *The last civil rights movement.* London, UK: Hurst.

Drimmer, J. C. (1993). Cripples, overcomers, and civil rights: Tracing the evolution of federal legislation and social policy for people with disabilities. *UCLA Law Review, 40*(5), 1341–1410.

Epstein, R. A. (1992). *Forbidden grounds: The case against employment discrimination laws.* Cambridge, MA: Harvard University Press.

Fineman, M. A. (2008). The vulnerable subject: Anchoring equality in the human condition. *Yale Journal of Law and Feminism, 20*(1), 1–20.

Foster, S. (1991). Mainstreaming the deaf student: A blessing or a curse? *Journal of Disability Policy Studies, 2,* 61–76.

Franks, P., Muennig, P., and Gold, M. (2005). Is expanding Medicare coverage cost-effective? *BMC Health Services Research, 5,* 23–25.

Fuchs, D., & Fuchs, L. S. (1994). Sometimes separate is better (education for learning disabled children). *Educational Leadership, 54*(4), 22–27.

Gilbert, N. (1992). From entitlements to incentives: The changing philosophy of social protection. *International Social Security Review, 45*(3), 5–17.

Gilbert, N. (2002). *Transformation of the welfare state: The silent surrender of public responsibility.* New York, NY: Oxford University Press.

Gill, C. (2000). Health professionals, disability, and assisted suicide: An examination of relevant empirical evidence and reply to Batavia. *Psychology, Public Policy, and Law, 6*, 526–545.

Gill, C., & Voss, L. A. (2005). Views of disabled people regarding legalized assisted suicide before and after a balanced informational presentation. *Journal of Disability Policy Studies, 16*, 6–15.

Gliedman, J., Roth, W., & Carnegie Council on Children. (1980). *The unexpected minority: Handicapped children in America.* New York, NY: Harcourt.

Golden, M., & Zoanni, T. (2010). Killing us softly: The dangers of legalizing assisted suicide. *Disability and Health Journal, 3*, 16–30.

Goodwin, G. L. (2009). A disability by any other name is still a disability: Log Cabin, the disability spectrum, and the ADA(AA). *Seventh Circuit Review, 4*(2), 253–290. Retrieved from http://www.kentlaw.edu/7cr/v4-2/goodwin.pdf

Government Accountability Office (GAO). (1994). *Social Security Disability Insurance: SSA quality assurance improvements can produce more accurate payments.* Report to the Chairman, Committee on Finance, U.S. Senate, Pub. No. GAO/HEHS-94-107. Washington, DC: Author.

Hahn, H. (1985). Towards a politics of disability: Definitions, disciplines, and policies. *Social Science Journal, 22*(4), 87–105.

Hahn, H. (1986). Public support for rehabilitation programs: The analysis of U.S. disability policy. *Disability and Society, 1*, 121–137.

Hahn, H. (1987). Civil rights for disabled Americans: The foundation of a political agenda. In A. Gartner & J. Tom (Eds.), *Images of the disabled, disabling images* (pp. 181–200). New York, NY: Praeger.

Hanson, K. W., Neuman, P., Dutwin, D., & Kasper, J. (2003). Uncovering the health challenges facing people with disabilities: The role of health insurance: Findings from a 2003 national survey of people with disabilities highlight barriers to care among the uninsured and those with gaps in coverage. *Health Affairs.* Retrieved from http://content.healthaffairs.org/content/early/2003/11/19/hlthaff.w3.552.short

Hocutt, A. M. (1996). Effectiveness of special education: Is placement the critical factor? *Special Education for Students With Disabilities, 6*, 77–102.

Hotchkiss, J. (2003). *The labor market experience of workers with disabilities: The ADA and beyond.* Kalamazoo, MI: W. E. Upjohn Institute for Employment Research.

Hughes, B., & Paterson, K. (1997). The social model of disability and the disappearing body: Towards a sociology of impairment. *Disability and Society, 12*(3), 325–340.

Institute of Medicine (IOM). (1991). *Disability in America: Toward a national agenda for prevention.* Washington, DC: National Academies Press.

Institute of Medicine (IOM). (1997). *Enabling America: Assessing the role of rehabilitation science and engineering.* Washington, DC: National Academies Press.

Institute of Medicine (IOM). (2002). *The dynamics of disability: Measuring and monitoring disability for Social Security programs* (G. S. Wunderlich, D. P. Rice, & N. L. Amado, Eds.). Washington, DC: National Academies Press.

Institute of Medicine (IOM). (2007a). *The future of disability in America* (M. J. Field & A. M. Jette, Eds.). Washington, DC: National Academies Press.

Institute of Medicine (IOM). (2007b). *Improving the Social Security disability decision process* (J. D. Stobo, M. McGeary, & D. K. Barnes, Eds.). Washington, DC: National Academies Press.

Interagency Committee on Disability Research (ICDR). (2003). *Federal statutory definitions of disability.* Retrieved from http://www.icdr.us/documents/definitions.htm

Issacharoff, S., & Nelson, J. (2001). Discrimination with a difference: Can employment discrimination law accommodate the ADA? *North Carolina Law Review, 79,* 307–358.

Jacobzone, S. (2000). Coping with aging: International challenges. *Health Affairs (Millwood), 19*(3), 213–225.

Jette, A., & Badley, E. (2000). Conceptual issues in the measurement of work disability. In N. Mathiowetz & G. S. Wunderlich (Eds.), *Survey measurement of work disability: Summary of a workshop* (pp. 183–210). Washington, DC: National Academies Press.

Jones, M., & Marks, L. (2000). A bright new era of equality, independence, and freedom: Casting an Australian gaze on the ADA. In L. Francis & A. Silvers (Eds.), *Americans with disabilities: Exploring implications of the law for individuals and institutions* (pp. 371–386). New York, NY: Routledge.

Jonsson, U. (2003). *Human rights approach to development programming.* New York, NY: UNICEF.

Kalache, A., Aboderin, I., & Hoskins, I. (2002). Compression of morbidity and active ageing: Key priorities for public health policy in the 21st century. *Bulletin of the World Health Organization, 80*(3), 243–250.

Kelman, M. (2000–2001). Market discrimination and groups. *Stanford Law Review, 53*(4), 833–896.

Kennedy, C. (2002). SSA's disability determination of mental impairments: A review toward and agenda for research. In G. S. Wunderlich et al. (Eds.), *The dynamics of disability: Measuring and monitoring disability for Social Security programs* (pp. 241–280). Washington, DC: National Academies Press.

Kirchner, C. (1993). Disability statistics: The politics and science of counting. *Journal of Disability Policy Studies, 4,* 1–7.

Kirsh, B., Stergiou-Kita, M., Gewurtz, R., Dawson, D., Krupa, T., Lysaght, R., & Shaw, L. (2009). From margins to mainstream: What do we know about work integration for persons with brain injury, mental illness, and intellectual disability? *Work, 32*(4), 391–405.

Koch, T. (2006). Bioethics as ideology: Conditional and unconditional values. *Journal of Medicine and Philosophy, 31,* 251–267.

Krieger, L. H. (Ed.). (2003). *Backlash against the ADA: Reinterpreting disability rights.* Ann Arbor, MI: University of Michigan Press.

Lane, H., & Grodin, M. (1997). Ethical issues in cochlear implant surgery: An exploration into disease, disability, and the best interests of the child. *Kennedy Institute of Ethics Journal, 7,* 231–252.

Lord, J., & Brown, R. (2010). *The role of reasonable accommodation in securing substantive equality for persons with disabilities: The UN Convention on the Rights of Persons with Disabilities.* Retrieved from http://papers.ssrn.com/sol3/papers .cfm?abstract_id=1539479

Mashaw, J. L. (1983). *Bureaucratic justice: Managing Social Security disability claims.* New Haven, CT: Yale University Press.

Meyer, J. A., & Zeller, P. J. (1999). *Profiles of disability: Employment and health coverage.* Washington, DC: Kaiser Commission on Medicaid and the Uninsured.

Minkowitz, T. (2007). United Nations Convention on the Rights of Persons with Disabilities and the right to be free from nonconsensual psychiatric interventions. *Syracuse Journal of International Law and Communication, 34*(2), 359–404.

Minow, M. (1990). *Making all the difference: Inclusion, exclusion, and American law.* Ithaca, NY: Cornell University Press.

Mitra, S. (2006). The capability approach and disability. *Journal of Disability Policy Studies, 16*(4), 236–247.

Moon, M. (2006). *Medicare: A policy primer.* Washington, DC: The Urban Institute.

Morris, J. (1992). Personal and political: A feminist perspective on researching physical disability. *Disability, Handicap, and Society, 7*(2), 157–166.

Nagi, S. Z. (1964). A study in the evaluation of disability and rehabilitation potential: Concepts, methods, and procedures. *American Journal of Public Health, 54,* 1568–1579.

Nagi, S. Z. (1969). *Disability and rehabilitation: Legal, clinical, and self-concepts and measurement.* Columbus, OH: Ohio State University Press.

Nagi, S. Z. (1976). An epidemiology of disability among adults in the United States. *Milbank Memorial Fund Quarterly: Health and Society, 54,* 439–467.

Nagi, S. Z. (1979). The concept and measurement of disability. In E. D. Berkowitz (Ed.), *Disability policies and government programs* (pp. 1–15). New York, NY: Praeger.

Nagi, S. Z. (1991). Disability concepts revisited: Implications for prevention. In IOM, *Disability in America: Toward a national agenda for prevention* (pp. 307–327). Washington, DC: National Academies Press.

National Council on Disability (NCD). (2009). *The current state of health care for people with disabilities.* Washington, DC: Author. Retrieved from http://www .ncd.gov/newsroom/publications/2009/HealthCare/HealthCare.html

Norwich, B. (2002). Education, inclusion, and individual differences: Recognising and resolving dilemmas. *British Journal of Educational Studies*, 50(4), 482–502.

Nussbaum, M. (2007). *Frontiers of justice: Disability, nationality, species membership.* Cambridge, MA: Harvard University Press.

Nussbaum, M. (2011). *Creating capabilities: The human development approach.* Cambridge, MA: Harvard University Press.

Oregon Department of Human Services. (2010). *Death with Dignity Act records and reports.* Retrieved from http://www.oregon.gov/DHS/ph/pas/

Orentlicher, D. (1996). Destructuring disability: Rationing of health care and unfair discrimination against the sick. *Harvard Civil Rights-Civil Liberties Law Review, 31*(19), 49–87.

Organisation for Economic Co-operation and Development (OECD). (1999). *Inclusive education at work: Students with disabilities in mainstream schools.* Paris, France: Author.

Organisation for Economic Co-operation and Development (OECD). (2001). *Fiscal implications of ageing: Projections of age-related spending.* Paris, France: OECD Economic Outlook.

Organisation for Economic Co-operation and Development (OECD). (2004). *Transforming disability welfare policies towards work and equal opportunities* (B. Marin, C. Prinz, & M. Queisser, Eds.). Farnham, UK: Ashgate.

Ostroff, E. (2011). Universal design: An evolving paradigm. In W. F. E. Preiser (Ed.), *Universal design handbook* (2nd ed., pp. 1.3–1.8). New York, NY: McGraw-Hill.

Palley, E. (2006). Challenges of rights-based law: Implementing the Least Restrictive Environment mandate. *Journal of Disability Policy Studies, 16*, 229–235.

Parens, F., & Asch, A. (Eds.). (2000). *Prenatal testing and disability rights.* Washington, DC: Georgetown University Press.

Parrish, T. B., & Wolmar, J. (1999). Trends and new developments in special education funding: What the states report. In T. B. Parrish, J. G. Chambers, & C. M. Guarino (Eds.), *Funding special education.* Thousand Oaks, CA: Corwin.

Perlin, M. (2007). International human rights law and comparative mental disability law. *Syracuse Journal of International Law and Communication, 34*(2), 323–332.

Pitt, V., & Curtin, M. (2004). Integration versus segregation. The experiences of a group of disabled students moving from mainstream school into special needs further education. *Disability and Society, 19*(4), 387–401.

Powers, L., Sowers, J., & Singer, G. (2006). A cross-disability analysis of person-directed, long-term services. *Journal of Disability Policy Studies, 17*(2), 66–77.

President's Commission for the Study of Ethical Problems in Medicine and Biomedical and Behavioral Research. (1983). *Deciding to forego life-sustaining treatment: A report on the ethical, medical, and legal issues in treatment decisions.* Washington, DC: Government Printing Office.

President's Commission on Excellence in Special Education. (2002). *A new era: Revitalizing special education for children and their families.* Washington, DC: Government Printing Office.

Purdy, L. (1996). *Genetics and reproductive risk: Can having children be immoral?* Ithaca, NY: Cornell University Press.

Rock, M. (2000). Discounted lives? Weighing disability when measuring health and ruling on "compassionate" murder. *Social Science and Medicine, 51,* 407–417.

Ruger, J. P. (2010). *Health and social justice.* New York, NY: Oxford University Press.

Russell, M. (2000). Backlash, the political economy, and structural exclusion. *Berkeley Journal of Employment and Labor Law, 21*(1), 335–366.

Satz, A. B. (2006). A jurisprudence of dysfunction: On the role of "normal species functioning" in disability analysis. *Yale Journal of Health Policy, Law, and Ethics, 6,* 221–269.

Satz, A. B. (2008a). Disability, vulnerability, and the limits of antidiscrimination. *Washington Law Review, 83,* 513–568.

Satz, A. B. (2008b). Toward solving the health care crisis: The paradoxical case for universal access to high technology. *Yale Journal of Health Policy, Law, and Ethics, 8,* 93–144.

Sauer, M., Wallace, J., Knorr, K., Yoder, D., Moulton, G., Trachtman, L., et al. (2000). Public and private partnerships: The future for assistive technology. *Journal of Technology and Disability, 12,* 29–40.

Savulescu, J., & Kahane, G. (2009). The moral obligation to create children with the best chance of the best life. *Bioethics, 23*(5), 274–290.

Scotch, R. K. (1984). *From good will to civil rights: Transforming federal disability policy* (2nd ed. 2001). Philadelphia, PA: Temple University Press.

Sengupta, I., Reno, V., & Burton, J. F., Jr. (2009). *Workers' compensation: Benefits, coverage, and costs.* Washington, DC: National Academy of Social Insurance.

Shakespeare, T. W. (2005). Disability, genetics, and global justice. *Social Policy and Society, 4*(1), 87–95.

Shakespeare, T. W. (2006). *Disability rights and wrongs.* New York, NY: Routledge.

Shapiro, J. P. (1993). *No pity: People with disabilities forging a new civil rights movement.* New York, NY: Times Books.

Shepherd, L. L. (2006). Terri Schiavo and the disability rights community: A cause for concern. *University of Chicago Legal Forum,* 253–260.

Silvers, A. (1994). "Defective" agents: Equality, difference, and the tyranny of the normal. *Journal of Social Philosophy, 154*(1), 75–90.

Silvers, A. (1998). Protecting the innocent from physician-assisted suicide. In M. Battin, R. Rhodes, & A. Silvers (Eds.), *Physician-assisted suicide: Expanding the debate* (pp. 133–148). New York, NY: Routledge.

Silvers, A. (2005). Predicting genetic disability while commodifying health. In D. Wasserman, J. E. Bickenbach, & R. Wachbroit (Eds.), *Quality of life and human difference: Genetic testing, health care, and disability* (pp. 43–66). Cambridge, UK: Cambridge University Press.

Silvers, A., & Stein, M. A. (2007). Disability and the social contract. *University of Chicago Law Review, 74*, 1615–1640.

Silvers, A., Wasserman, D., & Mahowald, M. (1998). *Disability, difference, discrimination: Perspectives on justice in bioethics and public policy.* New York, NY: Rowman and Littlefield.

Singer, P., & Kuhse, H. (1985). *Should the baby live? The problem of handicapped infants.* New York, NY: Oxford University Press.

Smith, D. M. (2007). Who says you're disabled? The role of medical evidence in the ADA definition of disability. *Tulane Law Review, 82*(1), 1–76.

Social Security Administration (SSA). (1994). *Plan for a new disability claim process* (SSA Pub. No. 01-005). Washington, DC: U.S. Government Printing Office.

Social Security Administration (SSA). (2008). *Disability evaluation blue book.* Retrieved from http://www.ssa.gov/disability/professionals/bluebook/AdultListings.htm

Social Security Advisory Board (SSAB). (2001). *Charting the future of Social Security's disability programs: The need for fundamental change.* Washington, DC: Author. Retrieved from http//: www. ssab.gov/Publications/Disability/disabilitywhitepap.pdf

Stapleton, D. C., & Burkhauser, R. V. (Eds.). (2003). *The decline in employment of people with disabilities: A policy puzzle.* Kalamazoo, MI: W. E. Upjohn Institute for Employment Research.

Stein, M. A. (2003). The law and economics of disability accommodations. *Duke Law Journal, 53*(1), 79–190.

Stein, M. A. (2008). The United Nations Convention on the Rights of Persons with Disabilities as a vehicle for social transformation. *William and Mary Law School Research Paper No. 09-30.* Retrieved from http://papers.ssrn.com/sol3/papers.cfm?abstract_id=1539466

Stein, M. A., & Lord, J. (2010a). Accessing economic, social, and cultural rights: The Convention on the Rights of Persons with Disabilities. *William and Mary Law School Research Paper No. 09-34.* Retrieved from http://papers.ssrn.com/sol3/papers.cfm?abstract_id=1540105

Stein, M. A., & Lord, J. (2010b). *The United Nations Convention on the Rights of Persons with Disabilities: Process, substance, and prospects.* Retrieved from http://papers.ssrn.com/sol3/papers.cfm?abstract_id=1539479

Stein, M. A., & Stein, P. J. S. (2006–2007). Beyond disability civil rights. *Hastings Law Journal, 58*(6), 1203–1240.

Stein, M. S. (2006). *Distributive justice and disability: Utilitarianism against egalitarianism.* New Haven, CT: Yale University Press.

Stiglitz, J., Sen, A., & Fitoussi, J.-P. (2009). *Report by the Commission on the Measurement of Economic Performance and Social Progress.* Paris: French Government.

Stiker, H.-J. (1999). *A history of disability* (W. Sayers, Trans.). Ann Arbor, MI: University of Michigan Press.

Stineman, M., & Musick, D. (2001). Protection of human subjects with disability: Guidelines for research. *Archives of Physical Medicine and Rehabilitation, 82*(Suppl. 2), S9–S14.

Stone, D. A. (1984). *The disabled state.* Philadelphia, PA: Temple University Press.

Tucker, B. (2001). The ADA's revolving door: Inherent flaws in the civil rights paradigm. *Ohio State Law Journal, 62,* 335–389.

Ubel, P. (2000). *Pricing life.* Cambridge, MA: MIT Press.

Ubel, P. A., Loewenstein, G., & Jepson, C. (2003). Whose quality of life? A commentary exploring discrepancies between health state evaluations of patients and the general public. *Quality of Life Research, 12,* 599–607.

UNAIDS (United Nations Global Reference Group on HIV/AIDS and Human Rights). (2004). *What constitutes a rights-based approach? Definitions, methods, and practices.* 4th Meeting. Geneva, Switzerland: Author.

United Nations (UN). (2003). *The human rights based approach to development cooperation towards a common understanding among UN agencies.* New York, NY: Author.

United Nations (UN). (2006). *Convention on the Rights of Persons with Disabilities.* A/RES/61/106. Retrieved from http://www.un.org/disabilities

Visier, L. (1998). Sheltered employment for persons with disabilities. *International Labor Review, 137*(3), 347–365.

Wallace, J. (2003). A policy analysis of the assistive technology alternative financing program in the United States. *Journal of Disability Policy Studies, 14*(2), 74–81.

Wasserman, D., & Bickenbach, J. E. (2005). Justice. In G. L. Albrecht (Ed.), *The Encyclopedia of Disability* (Vol. 2). Thousand Oaks, CA: Sage.

Weber, M. (2007). Inclusive education in the United States and internationally: Challenges and response. *The Review of Disability Studies: An International Journal, 3*(1/2), 19–33. Retrieved from http://papers.ssrn.com/sol3/cf_dev/AbsByAuth.cfm?per_id=83733

Weber, M. C. (2008). Disability rights, disability discrimination, and social insurance. *Georgia State University Law Review, 25,* 575. Retrieved from http://ssrn.com/abstract=1276782

Wegner, J. (1983). The antidiscrimination model reconsidered: Ensuring equal opportunity without respect to handicap under Section 504 of the Rehabilitation Act of 1973. *Cornell Law Review, 69*(3), 401–516.

Weir, R. (1992). The morality of physican-assisted suicide. *Law, Medicine, and Health Care, 20,* 116–126.

Williams, G. (1983). The movement for independent living: An evaluation and critique. *Social Science and Medicine, 17*(15), 1003–1010.

Wolfensberger, W. (1972). *The principle of normalization in human services.* Toronto, ON: National Institute on Mental Retardation.

Wolfensberger, W. (1976). On the origin of our institutional models. In R. Kugel & A. Shearer (Eds.), *Changing patterns in residential services for the mentally retarded* (pp. 35–82). Washington, DC: President's Committee on Mental Retardation.

World Health Organization (WHO). (2000). *The world health report 2000–Health systems: Improving performance.* Geneva, Switzerland: Author.

World Health Organization (WHO). (2001). *The International Classification of Functioning, Disability, and Health.* Geneva, Switzerland: Author.

Zigmond, N. (1995). Models for delivery of special education services to students with learning disabilities in public schools. *Journal of Child Neurology,* *10*(Suppl. 1), S86–S92.

Zola, I. (1989). Toward the necessary universalizing of a disability policy. *The Milbank Quarterly, 67,* 401–428.

Court Cases

Alexander v. Choate, 469 U.S. 287 (1985).

Bouvia v. Superior Court of State of California, 179 Cal. App 3d 1127 (1986).

Bowen v. American Hospital Association, 476 U.S. 610 (1986).

Bragdon v. Abbott, 118 S.Ct. 2196 (1998).

Buck v. Bell, 274 U.S. 200 (1927).

Mills v. Board of Education of the District of Columbia, 348 F. Supp. 866 (D. D.C. 1972).

Olmstead v. L. C., 527 U.S. 581 (1999).

Pennsylvania Association for Retarded Children (PARC) v. Commonwealth of Pennsylvania, 343 F. Supp. 257 (E.D. Pa. 1972).

School Board of Nassau County v. Arline, 480 U.S. 273 (1987).

Southeastern Community College v. Davis, 442 U.S. 397 (1979).

Sutton v. United Air Lines, Inc., 527 U.S. 471 (1999).

Toyota Motor Manufacturing, Kentucky, Inc. v. Williams, 534 U.S. 184 (2002).

Vacco v. Quill, 117 S.Ct. 2293 (1997).

Washington v. Glucksberg, 117 S.Ct. 2258 (1997).

Legislation

Americans with Disabilities Act of 1990, Pub. L. No. 101-336, 104 Stat. 328 (1990).

Americans with Disabilities Act Amendments Act, Pub. L. No. 110-325, 122 Stat. 3553 (2008).

Architectural Barriers Act, 42 U.S.C. § 4151 (1968).

Assistive Technology Act, Pub. L. No. 105-394 (1998).

Assistive Technology for Individuals with Disabilities Act, Pub. L. No. 108-364 (2004).

Civil Rights Act, Pub. L. No. 88-352 (1964).

Developmental Disabilities Assistance and Bill of Rights Act, 42 U.S.C. § 6000 (1986).

Education for All Handicapped Children Act, 20 U.S.C. § 1232 (1975).

Individuals with Disabilities Education Act, Pub. L. No. 108-110 (2004).

No Child Left Behind Act, Pub. L. No. 107-110 (2002).

Patient Protection and Affordable Care Act, Pub. L. No. 111-148 (2010).

Telecommunications Act, Pub. L. No. 104-104, 110 Stat. 56 (1996).

Ticket to Work and Work Incentives Improvement Act, Pub. L. No. 106-170 (1999).

Three

Chronology of Critical Events

I t is controversial precisely when the history of disability policy and law begins. Religious texts proscribing the treatment of people with mental or physical impairments, the early legal definitions of people with sensory and mental impairments in classical Rome, the founding of almshouses and charitable foundations, and the beginning of wardship law in Middle Ages are all early versions of "disability law." Still, it was not until the dawn of the 17th century that disability law and policy existed in forms recognizable today. Although we begin this chronology with the English Poor Law of 1601, this law was actually the last, and most influential, of a series of English statutes, going back at least to 1388, which were essentially regulatory laws for economic policy that distinguished between the "deserving poor," who were incapacitated because of age or impairment and would be allowed to beg, and those "sturdy beggars" who could be diverted to public workhouses.

Disability ethics is another matter. Disability issues appear briefly and without much comment in ethical writings since the ancient Greeks, and there is also the well-known Biblical anti-discrimination injunction in Leviticus 19:14: "Thou shalt not curse the deaf nor put a stumbling block before the blind, nor maketh the blind to wander out of the path." Still, one has to wait until the mid-20th century to find ethicists writing at length about the ethical dimension of disability in society, often in the bioethical context in response to high-profile legal cases.

What follows is a chronology of important events and milestones in disability law, policy, and ethics.

17th Century

1601

The English Poor Law (*Reginae Elizabethae Anno* 43) finalizes the distinction between "worthy poor" and "undeserving poor" and shifts the responsibility for both groups to the Parishes, giving them the power to raise taxes to support the worthy poor.

1620

Bethlem Royal Hospital ("Bedlam") is established in London and becomes the model for other such hospitals in England.

1662

The Poor Law is extended to the English colonies, and the first almshouse organized in light of the principles in the Poor Law is established in Boston.

18th Century

1714

English law authorizes confinement for the "furiously mad."

1751

The Pennsylvania Provincial Assembly establishes the first mental hospital in the American colonies, which is built the following year under the leadership of Benjamin Franklin and physician Thomas Bond.

1773

Virginia establishes the first hospital solely for the treatment of "idiots, lunatics, and other people of unsound mind."

1774

England regulates mental health facilities by passing what becomes essentially the first mental health legislation in Europe.

1776

The Continental Congress decides to grant veterans of the Revolutionary War "disability" or "invalid" pensions for war-related impairments.

1783

Congress cuts back invalidity pensions for veterans of the Revolutionary War, and George Washington steps in to negotiate with a group of officers who, in protest, refuse to disband.

1793

The state of Kentucky passes legislation authorizing payment to families who are too poor to take care of relatives with mental illness or intellectual impairment.

1798

President John Adams signs into law the Marine Hospital Act, which is the first military disability act to provide relief to sick and disabled seamen.

19th Century

1817

The American School for the Deaf and, with Thomas Gallaudet's assistance, the American Asylum for the Education of the Deaf and Dumb, are both founded in Hartford, Connecticut.

1830

The U.S. Census first begins to count deaf and blind people, and by 1840 begins to count people labeled "idiotic" and "insane" as well.

1832

What is later to be called the Perkins School for the Blind, directed by Samuel Gridley Howe, opens in Boston.

1841

Dorothea Dix begins her campaign to improve conditions in mental hospitals in New Jersey and to persuade the state legislature to step up the construction of new institutions. Her efforts lead eventually to the establishment of 32 state-run mental institutions across the country.

1846

Edouard Seguin publishes *The Moral Treatment, Hygiene, and Education of Idiots and Other Backward Children*, the first treatise on "special education."

1850

Samuel Gridley Howe opens the first residential institution for people with mental retardation in Boston.

1855

Dr. Hervey Wilbur opens the Syracuse State School to train "improvable" children with cognitive impairments.

1857

The Columbia Institution for the Instruction of the Deaf, Dumb, and Blind opens in Washington, D.C. It changes its name to Gallaudet University in 1894.

1868

The first wheelchair patent is registered with the U.S. Patent Office.

1880

The National Association of the Deaf, the leading exponent of the "oralist" approach to deaf education, is formed.

1881

The Chicago City Council enacts the first "ugly law," forbidding "any person, who is diseased, maimed, mutilated, or deformed in any way . . . to expose himself to public view." This law remains on the books until 1974.

German Chancellor Otto von Bismarck's legislation to guarantee health and accident insurance for workers and, by 1889, invalidity and old age insurance for workers, marks the origins of the "welfare state."

1882

Congress endorses an immigration policy that excludes "defective" individuals, and the practice of intellectual testing to identify mentally deficient immigrants is instituted at all ports of entry.

1883

Sir Francis Galton coins the term "eugenics" for the science of "improving the stock" of humanity by preventing "undesirables," including in particular people with disabilities, from being born. The eugenics movement takes root in the United States and forms the basis for several state eugenics laws preventing people with disabilities from immigrating, marrying, or having children.

1898

The first workmen's compensation bill is introduced in the New York legislature, but it fails to pass.

20th Century

1902

Maryland passes the first Worker's Compensation Act, and other states quickly follow.

1907

Indiana passes the first law allowing for eugenic sterilization of persons with cognitive and other impairments; eventually 30 states pass such laws.

1908

England establishes an old-age pension system and, with the 1911 passage of the National Insurance Act, provides sickness and unemployment insurance benefits for workers.

Clifford Beer's book *A Mind That Found Itself* helps to initiate the mental health hygiene movement. Beer also establishes the Connecticut Committee of Mental Hygiene, which becomes the National Mental Health Association.

1912

Henry H. Goddard publishes *The Kallikak Family*, a best-seller purporting to link disability with immorality and alleging that both are tied to genetics.

1915

Dr. Harry Haiselden publicly recommends the practice of allowing disabled newborns to die as a way to reduce the disabled population. The 1916 movie *The Black Stork* further advocates this practice.

1917

The Smith-Hughes Act provides vocational education for disabled veterans of World War I.

1918

The Smith-Sears Act provides vocational rehabilitation and return to employment for veterans.

1920

President Woodrow Wilson signs into law the Vocational Rehabilitation Act (Smith-Fess Act), which extends the Smith-Sears Act to civilians.

1921

The American Foundation for the Blind is founded as a nonprofit organization with Helen Keller as a spokesperson.

1927

The U.S. Supreme Court's ruling in *Buck v. Bell* declares forced sterilization of the "feebleminded" to be constitutional and affirms the right of
states to sterilize citizens with disabilities against their will.

1932

President Franklin D. Roosevelt creates the Committee on Economic Security to make recommendations on a comprehensive program concerning
old-age security, unemployment, sickness, and health insurance.

The Tuskegee Syphilis Study begins (and lasts for 40 years), in which
African Americans with syphilis bacteria are purposely not treated nor
informed that they have the disease in order to track the progress of the
disease. The public outcry to this experiment when it becomes known
leads to the institution and regulation of Research Ethics Boards.

1935

The League for the Physically Handicapped is formed in New York City
as one of the first disability activist groups, staging sit ins and other political actions to protest against discrimination by the city.

The first comprehensive federal welfare legislation in the United States,
the Social Security Act, creates a system of old-age benefits, unemployment compensation, aid to "dependent and crippled children" and blind
persons, and insurance to promote maternal and child welfare and public
health.

1936

The Randolph-Sheppard Act allows blind individuals to be licensed to
operate vending stands in federal buildings.

1937

The Fair Housing Act passes and is administered by the newly formed
Federal Housing Administration to fund the cost of public housing for
poor and disabled individuals.

1938

The Fair Labor Standards Act provides training and job opportunities for blind individuals, although the minimum-wage exception is used by states to launch sheltered workshop programs for blind workers.

1940

Lawyer Jacobus tenBroek helps to organize the National Federation for the Blind in Wilkes-Barre, Pennsylvania.

1943

The Vocational Rehabilitation Act (LaFollette-Barden Act) passes and is administered by the Federal Security Agency, led by Mary Switzer, who emphasizes the use of physical rehabilitation and medical services to meet the needs of Americans with physical and mental disabilities.

1950

The Social Security Amendments establish a federal-state program to aid the permanently and totally disabled, which later turns into the Social Security Disability Insurance (SSDI) program.

1952

The President's Committee on Employment of the Physically Handicapped is organized on a permanent footing to report to the president and Congress.

1954

The Vocational Rehabilitation Amendments Act, signed by President Dwight D. Eisenhower, provides funds for state vocational rehabilitation programs and demonstration projects showcasing how rehabilitation addresses the needs of America's disabled population.

The U.S. Supreme Court hands down the landmark *Brown v. Board of Education* decision, beginning an era of school desegregation. The ruling also serves as an inspiration to the emerging disability rights movement, which sees it as a realistic tool for anti-discrimination.

1956

The Social Security Disability Insurance program (SSDI) is enacted, becoming the primary system of old-age and disability benefits from the Social Security Administration.

1958

Congress passes the Social Security Amendments, extending SSDI benefits to the dependents of disabled workers.

1962

Edward V. Roberts becomes the first severely disabled student to gain admission to the University of California at Berkeley and begins to organize the group of student disability activists known as the Rolling Quads.

1963

Congress passes the Mental Retardation Facilities and Community Health Centers Construction Act, authorizing federal grants for the construction of public and private nonprofit community mental health centers.

1964

The Civil Rights Act outlaws discrimination on the basis of race in public accommodations, employment, and federally assisted programs; it is the model for all subsequent disability anti-discrimination legislation. Together with the Voting Rights Act of 1965 and the Civil Rights Act of 1968, the law not only addresses discrimination against African Americans but also establishes a constitutional doctrine granting the federal government power to legislate and enforce protections of civil rights.

1965

The Vocational Rehabilitation Amendments Act is passed, authorizing federal grants for the construction of rehabilitation centers, expanding existing vocational rehabilitation programs, and creating the National Commission on Architectural Barriers to Rehabilitation of the Handicapped.

Following passage of the Economic Opportunity Act, the Office of Economic Opportunity launches the Head Start program to promote school readiness by providing educational, health, nutritional, and social services to low-income children and families.

Passage of the Elementary and Secondary Education Act (ESEA) increases federal funding for education; 1966 amendments to the law establish programs for children with developmental disabilities.

1968

The Architectural Barriers Act mandates that federally constructed buildings and facilities be accessible to people with physical disabilities, and establishes what is now known as the Access Board. This is generally considered to be the first federal disability rights legislation, and it helped to set the stage for the Americans with Disabilities Act.

1970

Ed Roberts and other members of the Rolling Quads, including John Hessler and Hale Zukas, form the Physically Disabled Students Program (PDSP) at the University of California, Berkeley. The program provides for living arrangements, personal assistance services, and political advocacy for disabled students.

After a successful employment discrimination suit against New York's public school system, Judith Heumann founds Disabled in Action to pursue litigation for disability rights and to organize demonstrations (including, two years later, a highly successful sit-in on Madison Avenue to protest President Richard Nixon's veto of the Rehabilitation Act).

Max and Colleen Starkloff of St. Louis found Paraquad for people with spinal cord injury and establish one of the first federally funded independent living centers in the United States.

Originally passed in 1964 as one of President Lyndon Johnson's Great Society programs, the Urban Mass Transportation Assistance Act authorizes federal funding to ensure "that elderly and handicapped persons have the same right as other persons to utilize mass transportation facilities and services." The act lacks enforcement powers, so it has little impact.

1971

The first Center for Independent Living (CIL) is formed by members of the PDSP at the University of California, Berkeley.

The National Center for Law and the Handicapped opens at the University of Notre Dame. An early advocacy center for people with disabilities, it launches the careers of many influential disability lawyers, including Robert Burgdorf Jr.

On March 12, the U.S. District Court for Alabama rules in *Wyatt v. Stickney* that people in residential state schools and institutions have a constitutional right to receive treatment to give them a realistic chance to improve their mental condition, and cannot be put into indefinite "custodial institutions" without treatment or education. This decision is seen as the first victory in the fight for deinstitutionalization.

On October 7, the consent agreement in *Pennsylvania Association for Retarded Children (PARC) v. Commonwealth of Pennsylvania* holds that segregated education for disabled children is unconstitutional, sending the message that educational mainstreaming is the preferred option.

1972

The Social Security Amendments create the Supplemental Security Income (SSI) program. The law relieves families of the financial responsibility of caring for their adult disabled children. It consolidates existing federal programs for people who are disabled but not eligible for Social Security Disability Insurance.

The Rehabilitation Act is proposed, but President Nixon vetoes it, sparking disability rights protests across the country.

The Houston Cooperative Living Residential Project is established in Houston, Texas, by activist Lex Frieden. It becomes, along with the CIL in Berkeley, California, a model for independent living programs across the country.

The Judge David L. Bazelon Center for Mental Health Law is founded in Washington, D.C., to provide legal representation and advocacy for the rights of people with mental illness.

Decided on August 1 by the U.S. District Court for the District of Columbia, *Mills v. Board of Education of D.C.* holds that every child, regardless of the type and severity of his or her disability, is entitled to a free public education. This decision, along with *PARC*, leads to the passage of the Education for All Handicapped Children Act of 1975 (EAHCA).

1973

After twice vetoing similar legislation, President Nixon signs the Rehabilitation Act, including sections 501, 503, and 504. The act for the first time legally prohibits discrimination against "otherwise qualified handicapped individuals" that prevents their participation in, or causes them to be denied the benefits of, any federal program or service. Full implementation of the law, however, requires federal agencies to adopt regulations governing the implementation process, and these do not form part of the act for four more years. Nonetheless, lawsuits arising from Section 504 help to create important legal doctrines, such as "reasonable accommodation," which become the framework for the Americans with Disabilities Act of 1990.

1974

After an inaugural meeting in Victoria, British Columbia, the first convention of People First is held in Salem, Oregon. People First becomes the largest American organization composed of and led by people with cognitive disabilities.

Ronald Mace, one of the developers of the principles of universal design, founds Barrier Free Environments to help create fully accessible buildings and products.

1975

The Education for All Handicapped Children Act (EAHCA) allocates federal money to states for the education of children with disabilities in the "least restrictive environment," and preferably integrated into a public school. The act is renamed the Individuals with Disabilities Education Act (IDEA) in 1990.

After several years of underfunding, the Community Services Act creates the Community Services Administration as a successor to the Economic Opportunity Commission, increases funding for the Head Start program, and establishes the Follow Through program for children with disabilities.

The Developmentally Disabled Assistance and Bill of Rights Act provides federal funding to programs serving children and adults with developmental disabilities and includes a statement of rights for those who are institutionalized, including the availability of protection and advocacy services.

The first trans-disability, consumer-led advocacy group, the American Coalition of Citizens with Disabilities (ACCD), is founded, with Frank Bowe as its first executive director. Its members join in the sit-ins and other actions to protest the government's failure to implement the anti-discrimination provisions of the Rehabilitation Act of 1973. The ACCD grows rapidly until the early 1980s, when its funding base dries up during the Reagan administration, and by 1983 is dissolved.

The highly influential British civil rights organization the Union of Physically Impaired Against Segregation (UPIAS) is formed.

The U.S. Supreme Court rules in *O'Connor v. Donaldson* that states cannot commit to institutions non-dangerous individuals with mental health problems who are capable of living on their own.

1976

An amendment to the Higher Education Act of 1972 provides funding for services to support students with disabilities entering college.

The *Disabled in Action of Pennsylvania, Inc. v. Coleman* case is filed in Philadelphia, arguing that Section 504 of the Rehabilitation Act of 1973 requires the federal government to force states to make public transportation accessible. The *Coleman* case, better known as the "Transbus case," is settled later in 1976 when the Carter administration agrees to pass regulations making federally funded transit wheelchair accessible.

The right-to-die case of Karen Ann Quinlan causes controversy in the disability community. At the age of 21, Quinlan sustained serious brain injuries, leaving her in a persistent vegetative state. Her parents requested that her life-support be removed, but the hospital refused. Following a high-profile legal battle, the New Jersey Supreme Court found in favor of the parents and her ventilator was turned off. Against the odds, she continued to breathe on her own for several years.

1977

The Carter administration organizes the first White House Conference on Handicapped Individuals, bringing together 3,000 disabled people to discuss federal disability policy. The conference focuses on health and other issues and acts as a catalyst for disability rights organizing.

On April 5, demonstrators led by Judy Heumann take over the San Francisco offices of the Health, Education, and Welfare Department to protest Secretary Joseph Califano's refusal to sign regulations to give effect to the anti-discrimination provisions of the Rehabilitation Act of 1973. Disability rights activists in ten other cities stage similar demonstrations. The demonstrators occupy the offices until Califano signs the regulations on April 28, making this the first major direct action victory for the American disability movement.

1978

The National Council on the Handicapped, later renamed the National Council on Disability (NCD), is established as an advisory board within the Department of Education to provide advice and research to promote policies and practices for inclusion, independent living, and equal opportunity for people with disabilities. NCD is made an independent agency in 1984.

The National Institute on Disability and Rehabilitation Research (NIDRR) is established within the Office of Special Education and Rehabilitative Services (OSERS) at the U.S. Department of Education. NIDRR supports research to "improve the abilities of people with disabilities to perform activities of their choice in the community, and also to expand society's capacity to provide full opportunities and accommodations for its citizens with disabilities."

The *Belmont Report*, released by the National Commission for the Protection of Human Subjects of Biomedical and Behavioral Research in the

Department of Health, Education, and Welfare, establishes ethical guidelines for the protection of the rights of human subjects of research.

Title VII of the Rehabilitation Act Amendments establishes the first federal funding for consumer-controlled independent living centers.

1979

The Disability Rights Education and Defense Fund (DREDF) is founded in Berkeley, California, and becomes an important disability rights legal advocacy center, participating in much of the landmark litigation and lobbying efforts of the 1980s and 1990s.

On June 11, the U.S. Supreme Court issues its decision in *Southeastern Community College v. Davis.* By rejecting the argument that reasonable accommodation is required by Section 504 of the Rehabilitation Act of 1973, the ruling is a setback for disability rights litigation

1980

The Civil Rights of Institutionalized Persons Act gives the Department of Justice power to sue state mental hospitals, nursing homes, juvenile justice facilities, and other institutions if they violate the rights of people with disabilities held against their will. Despite its mandate, the department chooses instead to use voluntary conciliation to secure compliance, disappointing mental disability rights advocates.

1981

The United Nations establishes 1981 as the International Year of Disabled Persons with the theme of "full participation and equality." The International Year leads to the World Program of Action Concerning Disabled Persons and the Decade of Disabled Persons, 1983–1992, both of which set the stage for the Convention on the Rights of Persons with Disabilities that is approved in 2006.

The Social Security Act is amended to allow states to provide home and community services for the elderly and those with physical, developmental, and mental disabilities as an alternative to institutionalization.

The Home and Community-Based Services (HCBS) waivers are quickly taken up by states, which appreciate the flexibility they provide.

In the case of *Halderman v. Pennhurst*, the U.S. Supreme Court rules in favor of residents of the Pennhurst State School and Hospital, who complained of poor conditions and lack of treatment at state schools for the "mentally retarded." The case becomes an important precedent for the legal right to community services for people with developmental disabilities.

1982

The Telecommunications for the Disabled Act mandates that all public phones be accessible to the hearing impaired by January 1, 1985, and calls for state subsidies for production and distribution of teletypewriters (TTY) and other telecommunications devices for the deaf (TDD).

The National Council on Independent Living is formed by Max Starkloff and others to advocate on behalf of independent living centers and the independent living movement.

Alan A. Reich founds the National Organization on Disability (NOD) in Washington, D.C., as a follow-up to the United Nations International Year of Disabled Persons. NOD's mission is to expand the participation and contribution of Americans with disabilities in all aspects of life and to close the participation gap by raising disability awareness through programs and information. NOD is an active player in the efforts to gain passage of the Americans with Disabilities Act of 1990.

The President's Commission Report on Bioethics provides hospital guidelines for withholding lifesaving therapies for newborns with impairments, raising concerns among the disability community about so-called "quality of life" decisions that may undermine the respect for and rights of people with disabilities.

The infant labeled "Baby Doe" dies on April 15 after being born a week earlier with Down syndrome and an underdeveloped esophagus. Doctors advised the parents to refuse corrective surgery and to withhold nutrition and fluids so that the child would die, a decision supported by the case of *In re Infant Doe*. As this was the first such case to attract national attention, it quickly led to the adoption of a Health and Human Services regulation of similar situations.

1983

The U.S. Commission on Civil Rights publishes *Accommodating the Spectrum of Individual Abilities,* which debates the issue of whether disability discrimination follows the pattern of race discrimination and requires a legislative response.

Americans with Disabilities for Accessible Public Transportation (ADAPT) is established in Denver, Colorado, and begins a national campaign for accessible public transit for people with disabilities.

Ed Roberts, Judy Heumann, and Joan Leon establish the World Institute on Disability (WID) in Berkeley, California, to spread the independent living approach to communities and nations worldwide.

The National Council on the Handicapped issues a call for Congress to "act forthwith to include persons with disabilities in the Civil Rights Act of 1964 and other civil and voting rights legislation and regulations."

1984

In reaction to the "Baby Doe" cases, the Child Abuse Prevention and Treatment Act Amendments are passed to require states to put into place procedures for reporting medical neglect of children, including withholding medically indicated treatment from infants with disabilities with life-threatening conditions.

The Voting Accessibility for the Elderly and Handicapped Act requires that federal polling places to be accessible and accommodating to people with disabilities and the elderly.

In response to the Reagan administration's attempt to revoke regulations implementing Section 504 of the Rehabilitation Act of 1973 and the Education for All Handicapped Children Act of 1975, Patrisha Wright and Evan Kemp Jr. organize a campaign that generates more than 40,000 cards and letters to President Ronald Reagan in protest.

1985

The Mental Illness Bill of Rights Act requires states to provide protection and advocacy services for people with psychological disabilities.

Helga Kuhse and Peter Singer publish the provocative book *Should the Baby Live? The Problem of Handicapped Infants*, which advocates euthanasia. It provokes a strong response from the disability community.

On January 9, the U.S. Supreme Court rules in *Alexander v. Choate* that Section 504 of the Rehabilitation Act of 1973 does not protect against "disparate impact discrimination," which occurs when neutral legislation without discriminatory motive affects persons with disabilities more adversely than others. The decision is viewed by disability advocates as a setback for anti-discrimination protection.

On July 1, the Supreme Court holds in *City of Cleburne v. Cleburne Living Center* that communities cannot use zoning laws to prohibit a group home for people with developmental disabilities from opening in a residential area solely because its residents are disabled. Disability lawyers view the case as a positive sign of the court beginning to extend its narrow interpretation of the anti-discrimination protections in Section 504 of the Rehabilitation Act of 1973.

1986

The National Council on the Handicapped releases its report *Toward Independence: An Assessment of Federal Laws and Programs Affecting Persons With Disabilities—With Legislative Recommendations*, which makes the case that an effective anti-discrimination law is an essential component of an overall strategy for persons with disabilities. The report marks an important step toward the enactment of the Americans with Disabilities Act of 1990.

The Air Carrier Access Act prohibits airlines from refusing to serve people simply because they are disabled and from charging them more for airfare than non-disabled travelers.

On June 5, the California Court of Appeals overturns a lower court ruling in the case of *Bouvia v. Superior Court*. The decision affirms that Elizabeth

Bouvia, a 26-year-old, mentally competent woman with quadriplegia, has the right to end her life by refusing to take nourishment, arguing that the value of self-determination outweighs the state's legitimate interest in preserving life.

On June 9, the U.S. Supreme Court releases it decision in *Bowen v. American Hospital Association*, in which it rejects the argument that withholding lifesaving medical care from "handicapped infants" qualifies as discrimination under Section 504 of the Rehabilitation Act of 1973. The ruling invalidates the Department of Health and Human Services' "Baby Doe" regulations requiring hospitals to provide such care.

1987

Justin Dart resigns from his position as commissioner of the Rehabilitation Services Administration after saying in testimony before Congress that "an inflexible federal system, like the society it represents, still contains a significant portion of individuals who have not yet overcome obsolete, paternalistic attitudes toward disability."

On March 3, the U.S. Supreme Court releases the most positive Section 504 anti-discrimination decision since the provision was implemented in 1977: *School Board of Nassau County v. Arline*. School teacher Gene Arline had been dismissed because of unsupported fears that her tuberculosis might be contagious. The court affirms that she is a "handicapped individual" within the meaning of the Rehabilitation Act, and that her dismissal was the result of "prejudiced attitudes or ignorance of others" and as such was discriminatory.

1988

The National Council on the Handicapped releases its follow-up report *On the Threshold of Independence*, which contains the first draft of a bill titled the Americans with Disabilities Act of 1988. It is submitted by Senator Tom Harkin and Representative Tony Coelho on April 28.

Amendments to the Civil Rights Act of 1968, called the Fair Housing Amendments Act, require a proportion of new multi-family housing be accessible.

The Technology-Related Assistance for Individuals with Disabilities Act is passed, improving access, availability, and funding for assistive technology through state and federal initiatives.

The Congressional Task Force on the Rights and Empowerment of Americans with Disabilities, designed to create grassroots support for the passage of the Americans with Disabilities Act, is created by Representative Major R. Owens, with Justin Dart and Elizabeth Boggs as co-chairs.

Dr. I. King Jordan becomes the first deaf president of Gallaudet University in Washington, D.C., on March 13. The university's Board of Trustees had appointed a hearing person as president, but it was forced to rescind the decision in the wake of a week-long student demonstration demanding a "Deaf President Now."

1989

The Center for Universal Design, first called the Center for Accessible Housing, is founded by one of the developers of universal design, Ronald Mace, in Raleigh, North Carolina.

On May 9, Senator Tom Harkin introduces the Americans with Disabilities Act—a slightly redrafted version of the bill he and Representative Tony Coelho had sponsored the year before—to the Senate, which then sends the bill to committee.

1990

The newly renamed ADAPT (American Disabled for Attendant Programs Today) brings its "Wheels of Justice" campaign to Washington, D.C., in support of the Americans with Disabilities Act. ADAPT activists occupy the Capitol rotunda and are arrested when they refuse to leave.

The Surgeon General's office publishes *Healthy People 2000*, a national agenda for health promotion that includes new data on inequities in access to both basic and specialized health care needs for persons with disabilities and sets targets to reduce those differences in the next decade.

Following passage in the Senate on July 12 and the House on July 13, the landmark Americans with Disabilities Act is signed into law on July 26 by

President George H. W. Bush. He is joined at the signing ceremony by Justin Dart, the ADA's "founding father," and the original bill's sponsors, Senator Harkin and Congressman Coehlo. The ADA is the most comprehensive civil rights protection for people with disabilities in American history.

The Individuals with Disabilities Education Act (IDEA) requires states receiving federal education funds to provide children with disabilities with a free and appropriate public education designed to meet each child's specific needs. IDEA is based on the Education for all Handicapped Children Act of 1975.

1991

The Institute of Medicine publishes its first major report on disability, *Disability in America: Toward a National Agenda for Prevention*. The report sets out a new, non-medical conception of disability, based on the work of S. Z. Nagi, and introduces the health community to the sociopolitical dimension of disability.

1992

As the Decade of Disabled Persons ends, the International Day of Disabled Persons (December 3) is established by the United Nations to create awareness and understanding.

Amendments to the Rehabilitation Act are adopted that further promote the independent living philosophy by providing funding directly to Statewide Independent Living Councils (SILC), which are given broader responsibilities.

1993

In the *Holland v. Sacramento City Unified School District* case, an early test of the new Individuals with Disabilities Education Act, the U.S. Ninth Circuit Court affirms that children with disabilities have a right to attend public school classes with non-disabled children.

The United Nations passes the Standard Rules on the Equalization of Opportunities for Persons with Disabilities, which reorients the focus of disability rights at the international level from rights to treatment to more broadly defined human rights. Although not legally enforceable, the Standard Rules offer concrete guidelines for countries to follow when developing and implementing disability law and policy.

1994

The 1994 National Health Interview Survey on Disability is released. The largest nationally representative survey on disabilities in 20 years, it reports that nearly 60 million Americans, or 23% of the population, have a long-lasting disability requiring long-term care or access to a work-related or other disability program, or a perceived disability.

1995

The American Association of People with Disabilities (AAPD) is founded by Paul G. Hearne in Washington, D.C., and becomes the largest national, nonprofit, cross-disability organization "dedicated to ensuring economic self-sufficiency and political empowerment for the more than 56 million Americans with disabilities."

The U.S. Court of Appeals rules in *Helen L. v. Snider* that to continue the publicly funded institutionalization of a disabled woman in a nursing home, when not medically necessary, is a violation of her rights under the Americans with Disabilities Act of 1990. This case sets the stage for the powerful *Olmstead* decision later in the 1990s.

1996

Under pressure from a Republican congressional majority, President Bill Clinton signs the Contract with America Advancement Act and the Personal Responsibility and Work Opportunity Reconciliation Act, which are intended to reduce the numbers of successful SSDI and SSI applicants by requiring more stringent medical examinations, preventing people with drug addiction from applying, and terminating benefits for non-citizens.

The Telecommunications Act comprehensively overhauls telecommunication law in the United States. The law contains Section 255, which requires all telecommunications products and services to be accessible to people with disabilities, to the extent that accessibility is "readily achievable."

As a response to increased discussion of rationing health care to people with disabilities, the passage of laws such as Oregon's Death with Dignity Act that decriminalize euthanasia, and the acquittal of Dr. Jack Kevorkian in the assisted suicides of two women with non-terminal disabilities, a group of disability advocates found Not Dead Yet.

1997

The Individuals with Disabilities Education Act (IDEA) is reauthorized to improve education programs and services for children with disabilities, and to strengthen the role of parents in their children's education.

The Institute of Medicine releases its second major report on disability, *Enabling America: Assessing the Role of Rehabilitation Science and Engineering*. The report focuses on the role that assistive technology and other supports play in increasing the participation of persons with disabilities in all areas of social life.

In two unanimous decisions issued on June 26, *Vacco v. Quill* and *Washington v. Glucksberg*, the U.S. Supreme Court upholds the state prohibition on physician-assisted suicide. Chief Justice William Rehnquist draws a sharp distinction between ending life by refusing treatment and ending life by assisted suicide, insisting that the government has a legitimate interest in banning assisted suicide, since failing to do so would undermine the role of the physician as healer, expose the vulnerable to abuse, and initiate a steady slide toward euthanasia.

1998

The Rehabilitation Act of 1973 Amendments Act is signed by President Clinton, expanding Section 508 to require all federally funded electronic and information technology media to be usable by persons with disabilities.

The Assistive Technology Act provides federal funds to states in order to increase research and development of assistive technology to meet the need of individuals with disabilities.

A federal judge rules on January 11 that professional golfer Casey Martin, who has a rare circulatory disorder that severely limits his ability to walk, can use the Americans with Disabilities Act of 1990 to secure the right to use a golf cart, as a "reasonable accommodation," in PGA Tour tournaments.

On June 15, the U.S. Supreme Court unanimously rules in *Pennsylvania Department of Corrections v. Yeskey* that the Americans with Disabilities Act of 1990 extends protections to prison inmates.

Bragdon v. Abbott is decided by the Supreme Court on June 25. The court holds that a woman denied dental services because she was asymptomatic HIV-positive had been discriminated against.

1999

The Ticket to Work and Work Incentives Improvement Act becomes law. SSDI and SSI recipients who qualify and agree to participate receive a "ticket" that can be used to obtain vocational rehabilitation, employment, or other support services from an approved provider to help them go to work. The act also allows states to extend Medicaid coverage to those who are working.

In its May 24 decision in *Carolyn C. Cleveland v. Policy Management Systems Corporation et al.*, the U.S. Supreme Court holds that the receipt of SSDI benefits does not automatically prevent a complaint of discrimination under the Americans with Disabilities Act of 1990, but a court can take that receipt of benefits into account when the complainant argues that she or he is a "qualified person with a disability," that is, someone who can perform the essential functions of her or his job, at least with reasonable accommodation.

Widely viewed as the most successful ADA case, *Olmstead v. L. C. and E. W.* is decided by the U.S. Supreme Court on June 22. The majority holds that unjustified institutionalization is discrimination and that individuals with disabilities must be placed in the community "when the State's treatment professionals have determined that community placement is appropriate, the transfer from institutional care to a less restrictive setting is not opposed by the affected individual, and the placement can be reasonably accommodated, taking into account the resources available to the State and the needs of others with mental disabilities."

Also on June 22, the Supreme Court issues rulings in the "Sutton Trilogy" of cases (*Sutton et al. v. United Air Lines, Inc., Murphy v. United Parcel Service, Inc.*, and *Albertsons, Inc. v. Kirkingburg*). The overall outcome of these complex decisions is to severely restrict the applicability of the definition of "disability" in the ADA, in particular by arguing that "mitigating measures"—i.e., wearing glasses for severe myopia or taking medication for hypertension—disqualify the underlying impairment as one that substantially limits the person's ability to perform a major life activity. These cases and others form the basis of what becomes known as the "judicial backlash" to the ADA and begin the process of lobbying for what will become the ADA Amendments Act of 2008.

The International Disability Alliance, a network of global and regional, trans-disability organizations of persons with disabilities, is created. Initially formed to further the aims of the United Nations' Standard Rules for the Equalization of Opportunities for Persons with Disabilities, in later years the IDA promotes the implementation of the Convention on the Rights of Persons with Disabilities.

21st Century

2000

The National Council on Disability publishes *Promises to Keep: A Decade of Federal Enforcement of the Americans with Disabilities Act*, a detailed account of the challenges in enforcing the ADA and the setbacks caused by recent Supreme Court decisions. The report provides a blueprint for addressing the shortcomings that have hindered ADA compliance and enforcement, including the possibility of amendments to the ADA.

The 2000 Census updates the number of Americans with disabilities: Not counting children under 5, the military, and people in institutional care, 49.7 million Americans, or 19.3% of the U.S. population, have some type of long-lasting health condition or disability.

2001

As a part of the New Freedom Initiative, President George W. Bush issues an Executive Order on Community-Based Alternatives for Individuals with Disabilities that calls upon the federal government to assist states and localities in implementing the *Olmstead* decision.

The No Child Left Behind Act passes with overwhelming bipartisan support in Congress. The act entrenches the view that integration is always better for educational outcomes and social participation for students with disabilities. But because it relies on the mechanism of educational standards and requires states to develop assessment procedures for basic skills for students without providing sufficient funding, the aims of the act are not fully achieved in the following years.

The Commonwealth of Virginia House of Delegates approves a resolution expressing regret for its eugenics practices between 1924 and 1979.

The Social Security Advisory Board issues its report *Charting the Future of Social Security's Disability Programs: The Need for Fundamental Change,* calling for a complete revamping of the SSDI and SSI eligibility process. The SSA asks the Institute of Medicine to report back on possible reforms.

The Ad Hoc Committee on the Comprehensive and Integral Convention on the Protection and Promotion of the Rights and Dignity of Persons with Disabilities is formed in New York to begin the process of drafting a proposed United Nations Convention, which eventually becomes the Convention on the Rights of Persons with Disabilities.

The World Health Organization releases its International Classification of Functioning, Disability, and Health (ICF), which becomes the standard for disability data collection and provides a biopsychosocial conceptualization of disability for health and social policy.

2002

The Institute of Medicine releases its report *The Dynamics of Disability: Measuring and Monitoring Disability for Social Security Programs* in response to the Social Security Administration's request to lower the cost and increase the efficiency of the SSDI and SSI determination process. The report makes it clear that the difficulty lies in the fact that "there is no agreement on the definition and measurement of disability."

The President's Commission on Excellence in Special Education releases its report on the state of the nation's special education system, which notes that the No Child Left Behind Act had unfortunately created new complexities and administrative challenges, including an incentive to misidentify students with learning disabilities to qualify for state resources, and that these challenges were preventing the reforms from working.

The Help America Vote Act is passed and signed into law. Although the act was designed in reaction to the controversy surrounding the 2000 presidential election, it authorizes federal funding to states to make polling areas fully accessible to persons with disabilities.

The U.S. government inter-agency Web portal Disability.gov is launched to provide access to comprehensive information about disability-related programs and services in ten key areas: benefits, civil rights, community life, education, emergency preparedness, employment, health, housing, technology, and transportation.

On January 8, the U.S. Supreme Court rules in the case of *Toyota Motor Manufacturing, Kentucky, Inc. v. Williams* that an impairment such as carpal tunnel syndrome must have a "substantial effect" on an employee's daily life, not just on that person's ability to perform a job. This decision further restricts the applicability of the ADA's anti-discrimination protections in the employment sector.

On June 20, the Supreme Court issues its ruling in *Atkins v. Virginia*, which prohibits, on the grounds of the Constitution's Eighth Amendment ban on cruel and unusual punishment, the execution of prisoners with "mental retardation."

Justin Whitlock Dart Jr., an advocate for persons with disabilities best known for his efforts in getting the Americans with Disabilities Act of 1990 drafted, passed, and signed into law, dies on June 22.

2003

Assistant Secretary of State for International Organization Affairs Kim R. Holmes informs National Council of Disability Chairman Lex Frieden that the United States will not be a party to any proposed United

Nations convention on disability, because "the United States has an outstanding record with regard to the promotion and protection of basic human rights and fundamental freedoms."

2004

The National Council on Disability responds to the judicial backlash against the ADA by starting up its "Righting the ADA" series of reports, which examines each Supreme Court decision point by point, showing how the court's activism contradicts the intentions of Congress. These well-researched reports make a strong case for a legislative overturning of the "Sutton trilogy" and other Supreme Court ADA cases.

The Individuals with Disabilities Education Act is reauthorized, with the aim of bringing this civil rights legislation closer in alignment with the No Child Left Behind Act of 2002, which is primarily concerned with ensuring standards of achievement and accountability. Education advocates argue that the two acts are not as fully complementary as they were hoped to be.

The Assistive Technology for Individuals with Disabilities Act creates the Assistive Technology Act Project, which provides funding to states for the research and development, marketing, distribution, and technical support of AT equipment to persons with disabilities.

The first annual Disability Pride Parade takes place in Chicago, inspired by the actions of ADAPT in the 1980s.

On May 17, the U.S. Supreme Court decides the case of *Tennessee v. Lane*, in which a person with a disability sued the state of Tennessee because it had failed to make courthouses accessible. At issue was whether the federal government could abrogate the sovereign immunity of the state, guaranteed by the Eleventh Amendment, to have citizens sue states under the ADA (which had been successfully argued in the 2001 case of *University of Alabama v. Garrett*). A narrow majority of the court concludes that the Fourteenth Amendment gives the federal government this authority.

2005

The Department of Housing and Urban Development, under the Fair Housing Act, expands its regulations and guidelines for accessible housing, including "visitable" housing to ensure that homes can be visited by people with disabilities.

After several legal actions lasting seven years in Florida, passage of state and federal legislation, and four appeals to the Supreme Court, a Pinellas County judge orders the removal of Terri Schiavo's feeding tube, and she dies a month later. Schiavo collapsed in 1990 from cardiac arrest, sustained massive brain damage from lack of oxygen, and was determined to be in a persistent vegetative state. After eight years of attempts to raise her out of her coma, her husband began legal actions to have her feeding tube removed, which were opposed by her immediate family and by various religious and disability groups. The situation generated political controversy at both the state and federal levels, and it raised public awareness about the ethical issue of involuntary euthanasia in the case of individuals in persistent comas with no identifiable brain activity.

Breaking the record set in 1977 by the Berkeley sit-in, disability rights protesters begin a 75-day sit-in at the office of Tennessee Governor Phil Bredesen, who had asked for substantial cuts in the state's Medicaid program.

2006

The Consortium for Citizens with Disabilities (CCD), a coalition of national disability organizations formed to advocate for national public policy, step up pressure on the federal government for a "restoration" of the Americans with Disabilities Act.

The National Council of Disability releases its final suggestions on how to "restore" the ADA by "addressing the barriers that are preventing full achievement of the overarching goals of the ADA," and officially recommends that Congress adopt the ADA Restoration Act.

The "Road to Freedom" bus tour is launched from Washington, D.C., to travel to all 50 states in the coming year to promote public awareness of the rollback of disability rights protections by the courts.

Gallaudet University's first deaf president, I. King Jordan, resigns and backs the Board of Trustees' choice of successor, who is rejected by many students for being hard of hearing rather than deaf and for not having been raised using American Sign Language. Despite Jordan's support, student protests force the board to rescind the appointment, and it takes four years to find a new president of the university.

On September 29, Representative Jim Sensenbrenner, chair of the House Committee on the Judiciary, and House Minority Leader Steny Hoyer introduce the ADA Restoration Act to "restore the intent of the Americans with Disabilities Act of 1990 to more fully remove the barriers that confront disabled Americans." Based on drafts produced and distributed by the NCD and CCD, the bill dies in committee soon thereafter.

After five years of drafting and debate among international organizations of persons with disabilities and governments around the globe, the Convention on the Rights of Persons with Disabilities (CRPD) is adopted by a consensus vote at the United National General Assembly in New York on December 13.

2007

The Institute of Medicine releases its final report on Social Security, *Improving the Social Security Disability Decision Process*. The expert committee returns to the traditional, and long-discredited, medical or impairment listings approach to eligibility, arguing that in the absence of a better and politically acceptable mechanism, the risk of false positives is worth the benefit of increasing the likelihood that true positives will be expedited.

The Institute of Medicine also releases its report *The Future of Disability in America*, in which it maps out recommendations for monitoring disability data, disability research, access to health care and support services, and professional education. The report has considerable impact within the agencies of the federal government.

On July 26, Senators Thomas Harkin and Arlen Specter, and Representatives Jim Sensenbrenner and Steny Hoyer, introduce companion versions of the Americans with Disabilities Act Restoration Act, which is described as "a bill to amend the Americans with Disabilities Act of 1990 to restore the intent and protections of that Act." It includes provisions on definitions of disability designed to set aside Supreme Court rulings on "mitigating measures" and other restrictions.

A negotiation coalition is formed by the American Association of People with Disabilities, the National Disabilities Rights Network, and the Epilepsy Foundation (representing the disability advocates), and the U.S. Chamber of Commerce, the Society for Human Resource Management, the National Association of Manufacturers, and the Human Resource Policy Association (representing the business community). They formally state that any agreement they mutually reach will be jointly supported and presented to Congress.

2008

The disability advocate and business community coalition negotiating the terms of the "restoration act" reaches agreement, and a new bill is substituted and renamed the Americans with Disabilities Act Amendments Act of 2008. At the last minute, Senators Harkin and Orrin Hatch propose a new definition of "substantially limits" with regard to activities of daily living, but the section is dropped before a vote takes place.

The United Nations Convention on the Rights of Persons with Disabilities, having reached the necessary number of signatories and ratifying countries, enters into force on May 3.

George W. Bush signs the Americans with Disabilities Act Amendments Act into law on September 25 after both houses of Congress pass it with overwhelming majorities. The compromise ADAAA broadens the scope of who is considered disabled under the law by ignoring the impact of mitigating measures and by requiring courts to consider how impairments impact major life activities when determining whether a person is "substantially limited." The act also deletes the finding that "individuals with disabilities are a discrete and insular minority," which had been relied on by the Supreme Court to restrict the application of the ADA to only those with very serious disability or health conditions.

2009

The Matthew Shepard and James Byrd Jr. Hate Crimes Prevention Act, also known as the Matthew Shepard Act, is signed into law by President Barack Obama to extend federal hate-crime law to include crimes motivated by the victims' actual or perceived gender, sexual orientation, or disability.

The National Council on Disability releases its report *The Current State of Health Care for People With Disabilities*, which argues that the changes in health insurance being debated in Congress will improve the employment situation of persons with disabilities more than any other policy change.

On July 30, President Obama directs Susan Rice, his ambassador to the United Nations, to sign the UN Convention on the Rights of Persons with Disabilities, making the United States the 142nd country to do so.

References

This chronology has benefited from a rich collection of existing chronologies of disability, of which three stand out and have been the most helpful:

Chronology. (2005). In G. L. Albrecht (Ed.), *The encyclopedia of disability*. Thousand Oaks, CA: Sage.

Millington, P. (n.d.). *Timeline of disability history*. Council of Disabled People Coventry and Warwickshire. Retrieved from http://www.cdp.org.uk/documents/timeline/timeline06.htm

Pelka, F. (1997). *The ABC-CLIO companion to the disability rights movement*. Santa Barbara, CA: ABC-CLIO.

Also helpful to confirm some of the details in these chronologies were:

Fleischer, D. Z., & Zames, F. (2001). *The disability rights movement*. Philadelphia, PA: Temple University Press.

Museum of disABILITY History. (n.d.). *Timeline*. Retrieved from http://disability historyweek.org/pages/timeline

National Consortium on Leadership and Disability for Youth. (n.d.). *Disability history timeline*. Retrieved from http://www.ncld-youth.info/Downloads/disability_history_timeline.pdf

Parents United Together. (n.d.). *A chronology of the disability rights movements: Timeline*. Retrieved from http://www.parentsunitedtogether.com/RightsMovements.html

U.S. Department of Transportation. (n.d.). *Federal Transit Administration disability rights movement timeline*. Retrieved from http://www.fta.dot.gov/civilrights/ada/civil_rights_4064.html

Four

Biographies of Key Contributors in the Field

M any individuals have made significant contributions to the study and development of disability ethics, law, and policy. The biographical sketches in this chapter, presented in alphabetical order, profile some of those individuals and their contributions.

Adrienne Asch

American bioethicist specializing in issues of reproductive ethics and disability

Adrienne Asch attended Swarthmore College in Pennsylvania, earning a bachelor's degree in philosophy in 1969. During her undergraduate years, she was an active participant in the antiwar and civil rights protests of the era. Asch pursued graduate study at Columbia University, earning a master's degree in social work in 1973. Afterward, she worked for the New York State Division of Human Rights, served on the New Jersey Bioethics Commission, and maintained a private practice as a consultant, trainer, and psychotherapist. Asch returned to Columbia to earn a Ph.D. in social psychology in 1992. Her main area of academic interest is bioethics, and particularly the ethical, political, and social implications of human reproduction and the family.

Asch has held a variety of teaching positions over the years. She taught a course at Barnard College called Disabled Persons in the American Society, for instance, as well as a course in reproductive technology at the University of Oregon and a course in human behavior at Boston University. From 1994 to 2005, she was the Henry R. Luce Professor in Biology, Ethics, and the Politics of Human Reproduction at Wellesley College, where she designed an innovative program of undergraduate study on reproductive issues, including such courses as Multi-disciplinary Approaches to Abortion, Ethical and Social Issues in Reproduction, and Women and Motherhood. She is currently the Edward and Robin Milstein Professor of Bioethics at Yeshiva University in New York, as well as a professor of family and social medicine and a professor of epidemiology and population health in Yeshiva's Albert Einstein College of Medicine.

A frequent focus of Asch's research has been the moral issues raised by new genetic testing technologies. Along with her colleague Erik Parens, Asch coordinated a two-year project for the Hastings Center, a health ethics research facility, in which a panel of experts sought to establish moral guidelines for the use of prenatal testing to uncover genetic disabilities. In 2000, Parens and Asch reported their conclusions in *Prenatal Testing and Disability Rights*. Asch argued that the use of genetic testing and selective abortion to prevent the births of babies with disabilities sends a clear message that devalues people with disabilities: "It is better not to exist than to have a disability. Your birth was a mistake. Your family and the world would be better off without you alive."

Asch has authored numerous journal articles and book chapters, including *After Baby M: The Legal, Ethical, and Social Dimensions of Surrogacy*, with A.R. Schiff. She is also the co-editor of *The Double-Edged Helix: Social Implications of Genetics in a Diverse Society*, published in 2002. A past board member of the Society for Disability Studies and the Ethical, Legal, and Social Implications Planning Group of the National Human Genome Research Institute, Asch currently serves on the boards of the American Society of Bioethics and Humanities, the Society of Jewish Ethics, and the Council for Responsible Genetics. She is the recipient of several honors and awards, including being named Blind Educator of the Year in 1997 by the National Federation of the Blind.

Further Reading

Center for Ethics at Yeshiva University: Director and Staff. (2006). Retrieved from
    http://www.yu.edu/ethics/page.aspx?id=12616
Parens, E., & Asch, A. (Eds.). (2000). *Prenatal testing and disability rights*. Washington,
    DC: Georgetown University Press.

Sam Bagenstos (1970–)

*American civil rights lawyer and policy analyst
specializing in the Americans with Disabilities Act*

Civil rights official and disability scholar Samuel R. Bagenstos was born
in 1970. He earned his bachelor's degree in political science (with highest
honors) from the University of North Carolina in 1990. He earned his law
degree from Harvard Law School in 1993. After graduating from Harvard,
Bagenstos served as a law clerk to a U.S. appeals court judge (1993–1994)
and as an attorney for the Civil Rights Division of the U.S. Department of
Justice (1994–1997). In 1997–1998, he served as a clerk to U.S. Supreme
Court Justice Ruth Bader Ginsberg.

Bagenstos next entered academia, spending five years as an assistant
professor of law at Harvard Law School. In 2004, he became a professor
of law at Washington University, and in 2007–2008, he also served as
Washington's associate dean for research and faculty development. He
spent early 2009 as a visiting professor at UCLA School of Law, and later
that year he accepted a position as professor of law at the University of
Michigan. He took a temporary leave from Michigan, however, to serve
in the administration of President Barack Obama as principal deputy
assistant attorney general in the Civil Rights Division of the U.S.
Department of Justice.

Bagenstos ranks as one of the nation's most prominent experts on civil
rights as they relate to people with disabilities. His research and teaching
focuses include civil rights and constitutional law, with a particular emphasis on the Americans with Disabilities Act. He has testified before Congress
in support of disability rights and disability legislation, such as the Fair Pay
Restoration Act. Bagenstos has also been an active appellate and Supreme
Court litigator in civil rights and federalism cases, including *United States v.
Georgia*, 546 U.S. 151 (2006), in which the U. S. Supreme Court upheld the
constitutionality of Title II of the Americans with Disabilities Act.

Bagenstos has also written numerous papers, articles, and books on disability law and policy, including *Law and the Contradictions of the Disability Rights Movement* (2009), and for many years he maintained a popular blog at http://disabilitylaw.blogspot.com/.

Further Reading

Bagenstos, S. (2009). *Law and the contradictions of the disability rights movement.* New Haven, CT: Yale University Press.

Colin Barnes (1946–)

English disability policy analyst

Colin Barnes is a person with disabilities and a writer who has been closely associated with the disability rights movement throughout his professional career, most of which has been spent at the University of Leeds in England. He is the author of numerous influential books and papers in the field of disability studies, and in 1990, he founded the Disability Research Unit (DRU) within the University of Leeds' School of Sociology and Social Policy as a research unit for the British Council of Disabled People. The DRU, now known as the Centre for Disability Studies (CDS), was formally incorporated into the university in 1994. Barnes is also founder and director of The Disability Press, an independent publishing house that he established as "a testament to the growing recognition of 'disability' as an equal opportunities and human rights issue within the social sciences."

Areas of enduring research interest to Barnes have included institutional discrimination, theories of disability, and social and political barriers to mainstream education, employment, and leisure activities experienced by people with disabilities. Barnes has been a steadfast proponent of anti-discriminatory legislation in Great Britain, and a frequent critic of disability as a distinctive and dynamic form of social oppression. He and frequent collaborator Geof Mercer have asserted that "majority world" discrimination against people with disabilities must be resolutely confronted in the same manner as racism, sexism, and other forms of social oppression.

Further Reading

Barnes, C., & Mercer, G. (1999). *Exploring disability.* Cambridge, UK: Polity Press.
Barnes, C., & Mercer, G. (2006). *Independent futures: Creating user-led disability services in a disabling society.* Cambridge, UK: Polity Press.

Monroe Berkowitz (1919–2009)

American economist on disability issues

Monroe Berkowitz was born on March 19, 1919. A native of Wilkes-Barre, Pennsylvania, Berkowitz earned his undergraduate degree (with high honors) from Ohio University in 1942. After a stint during World War II as a member of the staff of the War Labor Board, he worked for the United Auto Workers before entering Columbia University. Berkowitz earned his Ph.D. in economics from Columbia in 1951. He then joined the Department of Economics at Rutgers University, where he became a mainstay of the department. He remained at Rutgers for the next half-century (though fellowships also took him to India, New Zealand, England, and other parts of the world).

Berkowitz's life work focused on disability issues and their intersections with insurance, public and private rehabilitation, and economic policy. Specifically, he devoted his professional career to research into issues related to disability and workers' compensation, including the administration of such programs. A highly regarded expert on Social Security Disability Insurance (SSDI), he conducted important research into "early intervention" policies designed to provide an alternative to direct enrollment into permanent SSDI or Supplemental Security Income (SSI).

Berkowitz's most important policy contribution in this regard was his "Ticket to Work" program for disability rehabilitation, which President Bill Clinton signed into law in 1999. This program was crafted to address the concern felt by many people with disabilities considering a return to the work force about losing their SSDI health care coverage. The goal of Ticket to Work was to increase opportunities and choices for Social Security disability beneficiaries to obtain employment, vocational rehabilitation (VR), and other support services from public and private providers, employers, and other organizations.

Berkowitz also conducted research in the areas of national disability expenditures, cost-benefit analyses of vocational rehabilitation, and the economic impacts of permanent partial disability. He also worked extensively as a labor arbitrator. In 2006, he received the National Academy of Social Insurance Robert M. Ball Award for outstanding achievements in social insurance. Berkowitz died on November 15, 2009.

Further Reading

Berkowitz, M. (2003). The Ticket to Work program: The complicated evolution of a simple idea. In K. Rupp & S. H. Bell (Eds.), *Paying for results in vocational rehabilitation: Will provider incentives work for Ticket to Work?* Washington, DC: Urban Institute Press.
Berkowitz, M., & Hill, A. (1986). *Disability and the labor market.* Ithaca, NY: ILR Press.

Peter Blanck (1957–)

American disability policy analyst and lawyer

Peter David Blanck was born on August 27, 1957, in Elmont, New York. A 1979 graduate (in psychology) of New York's University of Rochester, Blanck earned his Ph.D. in social psychology from Harvard University in 1982. Three years later, he received his law degree from Stanford University, where he also served as a president of the *Stanford Law Review.*

Blanck spent the next several years working in private law practice and clerking for U.S. Appeals Court Judge Carl McGowan (D.C. Circuit). In 1993, he went to the University of Iowa, where he became a professor of law and professor of psychology. Blanck spent the next 13 years at Iowa as a professor in its College of Medicine, Department of Preventive Medicine and Environmental Health (1997–2006); College of Public Health, Department of Occupational Medicine (1999–2006); and College of Law (2002–2006). He also served as director of the College of Law's Law, Health Policy and Disability Center from 2000 to 2006.

Since 2005, Blanck has been at Syracuse University, with appointments as a professor in the College of Law, College of Human Services and Health Professions, College of Arts and Sciences, School of Education, and the Maxwell School of Citizenship and Public Affairs. The year 2005 also marked the beginning of his tenure as chairman of the Burton Blatt Institute's Centers of Innovation on Disability.

Blanck's multi-faceted law career has focused in particular on the Americans with Disabilities Act (ADA), ADA amendments, and other laws and policies intended to guarantee the rights of individuals with mental and/or physical disabilities in institutional and community settings. In conjunction with his ADA work, Blanck has received grants to study disability law and policy, represented clients before the U.S. Supreme Court in ADA cases, and testified before Congress. Blanck has also written widely on the ADA and related laws (Blanck is co-editor of the Cambridge University Press series *Disability Law and Policy*).

Other areas of interest for Blanck have included international disability and human rights law, law and ethics in behavioral sciences, the social and political history of disability policy, and social science experimental and field research methodologies. A former board member of the National Organization on Disability (NOD), the Disability Rights Law Center (DRLC), and Disability Rights Advocates (DRA), Blanck is a trustee of YAI/National Institute for People with Disabilities Network, a fellow at Princeton University's Woodrow Wilson School, a senior fellow of the Annenberg Washington Program, and chairman of the Global Universal Design Commission (GUDC), a nonprofit organization dedicated to advancing sustainable and usable design practices in the building industry.

Further Reading

Blanck, P. (1998). *The Americans with Disabilities Act and the emerging workforce: Employment of people with mental retardation*. Washington, DC: American Association on Mental Retardation.

Burton Blatt (1927–1985)

American advocate for people with developmental disabilities

Burton Blatt was born in New York City on May 23, 1927. His parents were Abraham and Jennie Starr Blatt. Blatt served with the U.S. Navy during World War II, then returned to his hometown after the war, earning a bachelor of science degree from New York University in 1949. One year later, he received a master's degree from Teacher's College, Columbia University. From 1950 to 1955, he taught children with developmental disabilities in New York City. In 1955, he was awarded both a graduate scholarship and a teaching assistantship to Pennsylvania State University, from which he earned his doctorate in 1956.

After leaving Penn State, Blatt became an associate professor of special education at New Haven State Teachers College (later Southern Connecticut State College, now Southern Connecticut State University). In 1957, he and Yale University's Seymour Sarason collaborated to establish the first of three psycho-educational clinics (other clinics were later established at Boston University and Syracuse University). In 1959, he was promoted to professor and chair of the college's newly minted Special Education Department. In 1961, Blatt joined Boston University's School of Education as professor and chair of its Special Education Department.

By this time, Blatt was already well-known for his expertise on mental health issues, as well as his passionate advocacy for the rights of people with developmental disabilities. Much in demand as a lecturer on these subjects, he also frequently served as a consultant to a wide array of state and federal agencies, philanthropic organizations, universities, and associations for citizens with disabilities on cognitive impairment policy issues. In 1966, though, Blatt became known far beyond the circles of academia and government with his groundbreaking book *Christmas in Purgatory*, an explosive and haunting exposé of what he termed "cruel and inhuman" living conditions in American mental institutions. The book, published with photographer Fred Kaplan, became a rallying cry for institutional reformers, who took aim at facilities charged with caring for children and adults with cognitive impairments across the United States. In 1967, Blatt and Kaplan published a version of the exposé in *Look Magazine*, "The Tragedy and Hope of Retarded Children."

In 1969, Blatt moved on to Syracuse University, where he accepted a position as professor of education and director of the school's Division of Special Education and Rehabilitation. In 1971, he helped founded the Center on Human Policy, a research institution dedicated to advocacy on behalf of people with disabilities. Blatt was appointed dean of the Syracuse University School of Education and Rehabilitation in 1976. Three years later, he published a sequel to his groundbreaking *Christmas in Purgatory* titled *The Family Papers: A Return to Purgatory*, in which he reiterated his calls for deinstitutionalization and his support for community living programs, family support services, and education programs for children and adults with severe cognitive disabilities. Blatt died on January 20, 1985, but his work lives on through Syracuse University's Burton Blatt Institute, a leading advocacy organization for the advancement of civic, economic, and social rights of persons with disabilities.

Further Reading

Blatt, B. (1970). *Exodus from pandemonium: Human abuse and a reformation of public policy.* Boston, MA: Allyn & Bacon.

Blatt, B. (1999). *In search of the promised land: The collected papers of Burton Blatt.* Washington, DC: American Association on Mental Retardation.

Frank Bowe (1947–2007)

American scholar and advocate for people with disabilities

Frank G. Bowe was born on March 29, 1947, in Danville, Pennsylvania. He contracted measles as a toddler and eventually lost his hearing as a result (his treatment with the then-new antibiotic streptomycin has also been discussed as a possible factor in his hearing loss). Bowe received his bachelor's degree from Western Maryland College in 1969. Two years later he received his master's degree from Washington D.C.'s Gallaudet University, an institution for deaf students that finally gave Bowe the opportunity to become fluent in American Sign Language (ASL). Bowe earned his Ph.D. in 1976 from New York University. It was at NYU that he met his wife, Phyllis Schwartz, with whom he eventually had two children.

Bowe's emergence as one of America's most prominent and effective advocates for people with disabilities began in the late 1970s. In 1976, Bowe became the first executive director of the American Coalition of Citizens with Disabilities (ACCD). The following year, he helped organize major demonstrations in cities across the United States to publicize the routine discrimination that disabled people endured on a daily basis and to pressure the Carter administration to begin enforcing Section 504 of the 1973 Rehabilitation Act, which prohibits discrimination on the basis of disability in programs conducted or funded by federal agencies, in federal employment, and in the employment practices of federal contractors. These protests were later cited as a contributing factor in the 1990 passage of the Americans with Disabilities Act, which outlawed discrimination against people with disabilities in the private sector. In 1978, Bowe published *Handicapping America,* an influential investigation of social policy as it related to citizens with disabilities.

In 1981, Bowe left ACCD for public service. His efforts on behalf of people with disabilities during the 1980s included positions of leadership within the U.S. Congressional Office of Technology Assessment, the Task

Force on the Rights and Empowerment of Americans with Disabilities, and the Department of Education's Rehabilitation Services Administration. From 1984 to 1986 Bowe was the chairman of the U.S. Congress Commission on Education of the Deaf.

In 1989, Bowe became a professor at Hofstra University on Long Island, New York, where he taught and conducted research in special education, disability rehabilitation, and counseling. He also helped craft sections of the 1996 Telecommunications Act that enhanced Internet access for people with disabilities. In 1992, he received the Distinguished Service Award from President George H. W. Bush in recognition of his lifetime achievements. He remained an outspoken voice for the rights of disabled Americans throughout his tenure at Hofstra. He died of cancer in Melville, New York, on August 21, 2007.

Further Reading

Bowe, F. (1986). *Changing the rules.* Silver Spring, MD: TJ Publishers.
McMahon, B. T. (2000). Frank Bowe. In B. T. McMahon & L. R. Shaw (Eds.), *Enabling lives: Biographies of six prominent Americans with disabilities.* Boca Raton, FL: CRC Press.

Marca Bristo

*American activist, policy developer, and president
of the Access Living disability advocacy organization*

Marca Bristo's career as an advocate and policy analyst for people with disabilities began in 1977, when she became paralyzed from the chest down at the age of 23 after a diving accident in Lake Michigan. The accident, which occurred three years after Bristo had graduated from Wisconsin's Beloit College with a bachelor's degree in sociology (she also earned a bachelor's degree in nursing from Chicago's Rush College of Nursing), quickly led her into the disability rights movement.

Angered and dismayed by societal attitudes toward people with disabilities—as well as the many ways in which public and private institutions made it difficult for people with disabilities to fully engage with their wider communities—Bristo in 1979 helped found Access Living, a Chicago-based advocacy organization with the self-proclaimed mission of "promoting the empowerment, independence, and inclusion of people with all types of disabilities in every aspect of community life." Under Bristo's leadership, Access Living flowered from a modest local operation into a nationally recognized organization with an annual budget of $3.7 million that provides housing, in-home assistance, and other services and programs for more than 1,000 people a year.

Access Living also played an integral role in pressuring Chicago authorities to address longstanding architectural barriers to full equality in the city. The success of Chicago's disability movement in securing wheelchair-accessible sidewalks and outfitting public buses with hydraulic lifts became a model for other advocacy organizations around the country, as well as an inspiration to countless individuals with disabilities. As Bristo related in a 1999 commencement address at Beloit, "A young girl came to my office in Chicago one day and said, 'Before I met you and before I came to Access Living, I thought my wheelchair was too wide for the bathroom doors. Now I know the bathroom doors are too narrow for my wheelchair.' It is that paradigm shift, that change in world view, that gave the disability-rights community its power."

Access Living vaulted Bristo to national prominence in disability policy circles. She participated in the development of the Americans with Disabilities Act of 1990, and in 1994 President Bill Clinton appointed her chairperson of the National Council on Disability, a post she held for eight years (Bristo was the first person with a disability to hold the position). In 1998, Bristo was appointed to the Presidential Task Force on Employment for Adults With Disabilities. She has also served on the boards of numerous organizations, including the Rehabilitation Institute of Chicago, the United States Council on International Disability, and the Disability Funders Network. In addition, Bristo participated in the negotiation sessions for the United Nations Convention on the Rights of Persons with Disabilities, which the UN adopted in 2006.

Bristo has received numerous honors and awards over her career, including the Distinguished Service Award of the President of the United States; the Americans with Disabilities Act Award for her role in the creation and passage of the law; the Distinguished Service Award from the National Council on Independent Living; and the prestigious Henry B. Betts Laureate. *Chicago Magazine* named Bristo one of its "Chicagoans of the Year" for 2007. Bristo lives in Chicago with her husband, Bob Kettlewell, and their two children.

Further Reading

Bristo, M. (2000). ADA at a crossroads. In P. D. Blanck (Ed.), *Employment, disability, and the Americans with Disabilities Act.* Evanston, IL: Northwestern University Press.

Trice, D. T. (2010, June 7). An anniversary for Access Living: Disability-rights activists celebrate 30 years of opening eyes—and doors. *Chicago Tribune.* Retrieved from http://articles.chicagotribune.com/2010-06-07/health/ct -met-trice-accessliving-0607-20100607_1_access-living-disabilities-act -marca-bristo

Robert Burgdorf (1948–)

American disability policy expert and lawyer

Robert L. Burgdorf Jr. was born on July 27, 1948, in Evansville, Indiana, and contracted polio in August 1949. He earned his bachelor's degree and law degree from the University of Notre Dame in 1970 and 1973, respectively. Exhibiting an interest in disability law from the outset of his career, Burgdorf co-authored *Accommodating the Spectrum of Individual Abilities* (1983), the first major report on discrimination against people with disabilities published by the U.S. Commission on Civil Rights. He also served as the principal researcher and author of *Toward Independence*, a landmark 1986 report from the National Council on the Handicapped (now the National Council on Disability).

Burgdorf's work on *Toward Independence* equipped him to draft what became the basic template for the Americans with Disabilities Act (ADA) of 1990. His original version, penned in 1987, was introduced in the 100th Congress in 1988. A heavily revised version that was nonetheless recognizably based on Burgdorf's work ultimately was signed into law in 1990.

In 1989, Burgdorf joined the faculty of the University of the District of Columbia's School of Law. In 1991, he and colleague David A. Clarke (for whom the law school was later named after Clarke's death) founded the law school's Legislation Clinic. Four years later, Burgdorf published an influential legal treatise on the rights of people with disabilities in the workplace, *Disability Discrimination in Employment Law* (1995).

Since the late 1990s, Burgdorf has emerged as a prominent critic of legal rulings that have narrowed ADA protections. He served as general editor and principal contributing legal analyst for *Promises to Keep: A Decade of Federal Enforcement of the Americans with Disabilities Act* (2000), a critical report of the National Council on Disability on federal enforcement of the Americans with Disabilities Act (ADA). As both a lawyer and an author, Burgdorf has actively pushed for legislative measures that would "restore" the ADA. In addition to various policy analysis papers, he wrote *Righting the ADA*, which was published by the National Council on Disability in 2004. He has also testified before Congress in support of various ADA restoration bills.

Further Reading

Burgdorf, R. L., Jr. (2008, January 29). *Testimony to the Committee on Education and Labor, U.S. House of Representatives.* Hearing on H.R. 3195, ADA Restoration Act of 2007. Retrieved from http://edlabor.house.gov/testimony/2008-01-29-RobertBurgdorf.pdf

Shapiro, J. P. (1993). *No pity: People with disabilities forging a new civil rights movement.* New York, NY: Random House.

Richard V. Burkhauser (1945–)

American economist specializing in poverty policy as it relates to disability and old age

Richard Valentine Burkhauser was born on December 27, 1945, in Trenton, New Jersey. He earned his bachelor's degree in economics from St. Vincent College in Latrobe, Pennsylvania, in 1967. He earned his master's degree in economics from Rutgers University two years later. After a two-year stint in the Peace Corps (1970–1972), during which time he worked as a teacher in Jamiaca, Burkhauser received his Ph.D. in economics from the University of Chicago in 1976.

In 1979, Burkhauser joined the faculty of Vanderbilt University, where he has engaged in a wide range of scholarly research on U.S. economic policy, with a growing emphasis on policy issues affecting people with disabilities, the poor, elderly individuals, and other vulnerable citizens. He continued in these realms of research after moving on to a professorial position with the Department of Economics at the Maxwell School, University of Syracuse, in 1990. In 1998, he joined the Department of Policy Analysis and Management (PAM) at Cornell University in Ithaca, New York.

In addition to his ongoing teaching work, Burkhauser is co-principal investigator of the Department of Education RRT Center for Economic Research on Employment Policy for Persons with Disabilities, which is exploring linkages between state and federal anti-discrimination and workers' compensation laws related to people with disabilities and the accommodation practices of existing and potential employers. He is also co-principal Investigator on the RRT Center on Disability Demographics and Statistics and a member of the RAND Financial Planning Research Consortium (Social Security Administration).

Burkhauser, who has criticized many federal disability policies as well-intentioned but counterproductive in terms of their impact on the economic independence of people with disabilities, also maintains affiliations with the Cato Institute, the American Enterprise Institute, and other research institutions dedicated to free market and limited government principles. In 2010, he became president of the Association for Public Policy Analysis and Management (APPAM).

Further Reading

Burkhauser, R. V., & Haveman, R. H. (1982). *Disability and work: The economics of American policy.* Baltimore, MD: Johns Hopkins University Press.
A card-carrying capitalist tackles poverty: Richard Burkhauser's research on nearly every aspect of U.S. poverty policy—income inequality, minimum wage, welfare reform, health care, and social security—has turned up some surprising facts. (2009, Fall). *Human Ecology, 37*(2). Retrieved from http://www.human.cornell.edu/che/Outreach/upload/HEMAGweb.pdf

Justin Dart (1930–2002)

American disability rights advocate

Justin Dart Jr. was born in Chicago, Illinois, on August 29, 1930. The son of wealthy parents (his mother was an heir to the Walgreen's pharmacy fortune and his father, Justin Whitlock Dart, founded Dart Industries), Justin contracted polio at age 18. He used a wheelchair for the rest of his life. In 1951, he enrolled as a student at the University of Houston, and one year later, he founded the first organization dedicated to promoting racial integration of the segregated campus. He left the University of Houston in 1954, after earning bachelor's degrees in political science and history. The University of Houston is now home to the Justin Dart Jr. Center for Students with Disabilities, a facility designed for students who have any type of temporary or permanent health impairment, physical limitation, psychiatric disorder, or learning disability. Dart then briefly attended law school at the University of Texas before entering the business world. He spent the next several years running businesses in the United States, Mexico, and Japan. During this period he met Yoshiko Saji, whom he married in 1968 (Dart was married twice before), and who eventually became a partner in Dart's disability activism.

Dart's years abroad were tremendously influential. Guided in part by his longstanding interest in the social justice teachings of Gandhi, Dart implemented business policies designed to help women and people with disabilities obtain employment. He also began to study the status of disabled persons in Asia and other parts of the world, and he was profoundly shaken by the squalid conditions he witnessed at a children's "polio rehabilitation center" in Vietnam. This grim experience accelerated Dart's evolution into an international advocate for disability rights.

In 1974, Dart and Yoshiko returned to Texas, where they became prominent grassroots activists for disability rights. Dart served on a variety of state and federal commissions devoted to studying disability issues as well, and in the early 1980s he became a commissioner of rehabilitation services in the U.S. Department of Education. In 1986, Dart was appointed to head the Rehabilitation Services Administration, an agency within the Department of Education that oversees programs for people with disabilities. One year later, Dart's mounting frustration with the Education Department's resistance to his proposed reforms led him to openly criticize the department in congressional testimony. He resigned under political pressure, but in 1988 he and parents' advocate Elizabeth Boggs were tapped to chair the Congressional Task Force on the Rights and Empowerment of Americans with Disabilities. One year later, he joined the George H. W. Bush administration as chairman of the Committee on Employment of People with Disabilities.

Throughout these years, Dart worked tirelessly for passage of the Americans with Disabilities Act (ADA). He undertook a self financed public relations blitz across the country to drum up support for the ADA, which he described as the "civil rights act of the future," and he also catalogued numerous incidents of discrimination against people with disabilities. When the ADA was finally signed into law in 1990, Dart was widely credited as one of its key champions. In 1993, Dart helped found the organization Justice For All to defend the ADA and other civil rights laws for people with disabilities against efforts to weaken them. In 1998, Dart received the Presidential Medal of Freedom in recognition of his years of advocacy work for the disabled community in the United States and around the world. Dart died on June 22, 2002, in Washington, D.C., of congestive heart failure related to complications of post-polio syndrome.

Further Reading

Fleischer, D. J., & Zames, F. (2001). *The disability rights movement: From charity to confrontation.* Philadelphia, PA: Temple University Press.

Reid, C. (2000). Justin Dart Jr. In B. T. McMahon & L. R. Shaw (Eds.), *Enabling lives: Biographies of six prominent Americans with disabilities.* Boca Raton, FL: CRC Press.

Gunnar Dybwad (1909–2001)

*German-born American scholar and advocate
for people with developmental disabilities*

The son of a Norwegian architect, Gunnar Dybwad was born in Leipzig, Germany, on July 12, 1909. He earned a doctorate in law from the University of Halle in 1934 before fleeing Nazi Germany to join his wife Rosemary (an American exchange student who had returned home in 1933) in the United States. Dybwad spent the next several years working with juvenile delinquents in Indiana, New Jersey, and New York. In 1939, he graduated from the New York School of Social Work, and from 1943 to 1951, he served as director of Michigan's Child Welfare Program.

In 1951, Dybwad took the executive directorship of a parents' education organization called the Child Study Association of America. He remained in that position until 1957, when he began a six-year tenure as executive director of the National Association for Retarded Children (now known as the Arc of the United States), where he further burnished his reputation as an authority on cognitive impairments, autism, cerebral palsy, and other developmental disabilities.

During the 1950s and 1960s, Dybwad and his wife were also leaders of the International League of Societies for Persons With Mental Handicaps (now Inclusion International), an organization dedicated to championing the civil, economic, and societal rights of people with mental disabilities, as well as their families. In 1964, Gunnar and Rosemary Dybwad accepted co-directorships of the Mental Retardation Project of the International Union for Child Welfare in Geneva, Switzerland. Under this three-year project, the couple traveled to 34 different countries to foster parental involvement and grassroots political advocacy among parents of children with developmental disabilities.

In 1967, Dybwad began teaching at Brandeis University, where he was professor of human development and founding director of the Starr Center for Mental Retardation at Brandeis's Florence Heller Graduate School. Dybwad's continuing advocacy work during this time is widely credited with advancing reformers' conviction that mental disability was a civil rights issue. He was an early proponent of using litigation as a tool to help children with mental disabilities gain equal access to public education institutions and to aid disabled persons in their quests for inclusion in the wider communities in which they lived.

The Dybwads also wrote numerous books, papers, and essays explaining their bedrock convictions about the untapped potential of people with developmental disabilities to meaningfully contribute to their communities and their own life paths, and they served as consultants on disability issues to organizations and governmental agencies in the United States and around the world throughout the 1970s. In 1978, Gunnar Dybwad assumed the presidency of Inclusion International, a position he held until 1982. Rosemary Dybwad died in 1992, and Gunnar Dybwad died on September 13, 2001, in Needham, Massachusetts.

Further Reading

Dybwad, G. (1999). *Ahead of his time: Selected speeches of Gunnar Dybwad* (M. A. Allard, Ed.). Washington, DC: American Association on Mental Retardation.
Spudich, H., & Eigner, W. (n.d.). *Gunnar Dybwad, 1909–2001, untiring advocate of persons with special needs.* Retrieved from http://www.gunnardybwad.net

Vic Finkelstein (1938–)

South African–born British disability activist and leading promoter of the social model of disability

Vic Finkelstein was born in Johannesburg, South Africa, in January 1938. He became reliant on a wheelchair in 1954 after suffering a spinal injury in a pole vaulting accident. He took architecture classes at the University of Natal Durban before relocating to Pietermaritzburg to study psychology and rehabilitation. By the time he earned his bachelor's degree in 1963, Finkelstein had become a member of the Congress of Democrats, an organization of white South Africans opposed to the nation's apartheid policies.

Finkelstein pursued a master's degree in psychology at the University of the Witwatersrand in Johannesburg. In April 1966, however, a relentless government crackdown on protest activity (which had resulted in the 1964 arrest and imprisonment of Nelson Mandela, leader of the anti-apartheid African National Congress) ensnared Finkelstein. Arrested and charged with being an enemy of the state, he was subjected to brutal interrogation and served a 10-month prison sentence. After his release, he completed his master's degree, and in 1968, he immigrated to England.

Finkelstein continued to support the ANC as an exile, but after striking up a friendship with disability activists Paul and Judy Hunt, who pointed out the similarities between apartheid and England's unofficial segregation of people with disabilities, Finkelstein focused much of his energy on the disabled people's movement. He was a founding member of the Union of the Physically Impaired Against Segregation (UPIAS) in 1972, and in 1981, Finkelstein became the first chair of the British Council of Organizations of Disabled People (BCODP). He also represented the United Kingdom at the first world council of Disabled Peoples' International (DPI). In 1975, Finkelstein became a professor of disability studies at Open University.

Finkelstein became best known during this period for his collaboration with Paul Hunt in creating what came to be known as the "social model of disability." Finkelstein and Hunt asserted that disability was in fact no more than social repression from Western industrialized cultures that take little or no account of people with impairments because of their allegedly diminished economic value. This revolutionary call for transformative change in perceptions of disability invigorated the disability movement, which became increasingly radicalized in its condemnations of businesses, public transport systems, and other elements of society that paid no heed to the special needs of people with disabilities. Finkelstein continues his activities in the disability movement, and he remains one of the best-known promoters of the social model of disability.

Further Reading

Finkelstein, V. (1980). *Attitudes and disabled people.* New York, NY: World Rehabilitation Fund.

Finkelstein, V. (2001). *A personal journey into disability politics.* Independent Living Institute. Retrieved from http://www.independentliving.org/docs3/finkelstein 01a.html

Lex Frieden (1949–)

American disability advocate and policy developer

Lex Frieden was born in 1949 in Alva, Oklahoma. He broke his neck in a car accident in November 1968, during his freshman year at Oklahoma State University in Stillwater. Frieden spent three months at The Institute for Rehabilitation and Research (TIRR) in Houston, where he received valuable assistance in coming to terms with his sudden quadriplegic status, then he attempted to return to school. Despite a sparking academic record, however, he was rebuffed by Oral Roberts University, which explicitly rejected him on the grounds of his disability. He ultimately ended up at the University of Tulsa, where he earned a bachelor's degree in psychology in 1971. During this same time, Frieden became involved with Win Independence Now (WIN), a local organization of disabled people campaigning to make the Tulsa community more open and accessible to people with disabilities.

Frieden attended graduate school at the University of Houston, where he earned a master's degree in social and environmental psychology, on a teaching fellowship. While at Houston, he participated in an experimental TIRR "independent living" program for former patients. The success of this experience became a foundational event in Frieden's advocacy of independent living programs for people with disabilities, and it eventually led to his directorship of TIRR's Independent Living Research Utilization Program.

Frieden became a recognized leader of the independent living movement in the late 1970s and 1980s, during which time he served as a consultant to the U.S. House of Representatives' Committee on Science and Technology (1976–1978) and to the 1977 White House Conference on Handicapped Individuals. In 1984, he was named executive director of the National Council on the Handicapped (now the National Council on Disability), and during his four-year term at the helm of this organization, he helped lay the groundwork for the 1990 Americans with Disabilities Act (ADA). In 1989–1990, he represented the United States on a disability and employment panel at the Organisation for Economic Co-operation and Development (OECD) in Paris, France, and he later served an eight-year term as a member of the UN Panel of Experts on the Standard Rules for Disability. Frieden has also served as president of Rehabilitation International, a global organization dedicated to the rights and inclusion of people with disabilities; and from 2002 to 2006, he was chairman of the National Council on Disability.

A recognized authority on—and leader of—the independent living movement, Frieden is currently a professor of health informatics and professor of physical medicine and rehabilitation at the University of Texas Health Science Center in Houston. He is also an adjunct professor with the Physical Medicine and Rehabilitation Department of the Baylor College of Medicine and serves as senior vice president at TIRR Memorial Hermann Hospital. He has received numerous honors and awards for his work in the field of disability.

Further Reading

Lex Frieden Homepage. Retrieved from http://www.lexfrieden.com

National Council on Disability. (n.d.). *One man's loss . . . humanity's gain*. Retrieved from http://www.ncd.gov/newsroom/inthenews/frieden_tu.htm

Hugh Gallagher (1932–2004)

American disability policy advocate and author

Hugh Gregory Gallagher was born on October 17, 1932, in Palo Alto, California. His father, Hubert R. Gallagher, was a government policy analyst and teacher of political science. In 1952, while he was a 19-year-old student at Haverford College, Gallagher contracted polio and was paralyzed from the chest down. He spent several months at a polio rehabilitation center in Warm Springs, Georgia, that President Franklin D. Roosevelt had established in 1927, following his own bout with polio. In addition to helping Gallagher deal with the physical and psychological effects of his disability, his experience at the center contributed to a life-long fascination with Roosevelt.

Gallagher graduated from Claremont McKenna College in California in 1956, then attended Oxford University in England on a Marshall Scholarship, earning the equivalent of a master's degree in political science, economics, and philosophy. Oxford made few accommodations for Gallagher and other students with disabilities at that time. He often had trouble negotiating the cobblestone streets in his wheelchair, for instance, and the closest accessible bathroom was located more than a block from his living quarters.

Upon returning to the United States, Gallagher focused his efforts on gaining federal legislation to address some of the practical implications of living with a disability, including accessibility, medical costs, and end-of-life care. During the 1960s, while working as a Congressional aide, he drafted what eventually became the Architectural Barriers Act of 1968, which mandated that all buildings constructed with federal funds be made accessible to people with disabilities. The law put disability rights on the national agenda for the first time and paved the way for such landmark legislation as the Americans with Disabilities Act (ADA).

During the 1970s, Gallagher took a job with British Petroleum, launching a 25-year career as a lobbyist and policy consultant for the oil industry. His work involved a great deal of travel, which prompted him to become involved in efforts to make airports and other transportation facilities accessible to people with disabilities.

Gallagher was also a prolific writer of opinion pieces for newspapers as well as nonfiction books on a variety of topics, from the inner workings of Congress in *Advise and Obstruct: The Role of the United States Senate in Foreign Policy Decisions* (1969) to indigenous peoples' struggle for land rights in Alaska in *Etok: An Eskimo Story* (1974). He is best known for his 1985 biography of Roosevelt, titled *FDR's Splendid Deception: The Moving Story of Roosevelt's Massive Disability—and the Intense Efforts to Conceal It From the Public.* Unlike previous biographies, which largely ignored the president's struggles with the effects of polio, Gallagher's work looked at Roosevelt's life from a disability studies perspective.

In 1998, Gallagher published a memoir, *Black Bird Fly Away: Disabled in an Able-Bodied World,* about his personal struggles with disability and depression. He received a number of honors over the course of his career, including the 1995 Henry B. Betts Award for lifetime service on behalf of people with disabilities. In 2001, Gallagher played an important role in the successful effort to add a statue of the president in a wheelchair to the Roosevelt Memorial on the National Mall in Washington, D.C. Gallagher died of cancer on July 13, 2004.

Further Reading

Bernstein, A. (2004, July 16). Hugh Gallagher dies; Crusaded for the disabled. *Washington Post.* Retrieved from http://www.compassionandchoices.org/documents/20040716_HughGallagherDies_38.pdf

Gallagher, H. (1998). *Black bird fly away: Disabled in an able-bodied world.* St. Petersburg, FL: Vandamere Press.

Carol Gill (1949–)

American disability ethicist and social psychologist

Carol Gill was born in Chicago, Illinois, in 1949. She has used a wheelchair for mobility since contracting polio at the age of five. Gill attended Chicago's Spalding High School, a school specifically set aside for "crippled children." Gill's awareness of mainstream society's prejudicial attitudes toward people with disabilities greatly increased during this period, as did her strong sense of community with other disabled people. In 1966, she entered Chicago's Saint Xavier College, where she earned a bachelor's degree in 1970. She then went on to the University of Illinois, Champaign, where she achieved a master's degree (1973) and Ph.D. (1979) in psychology. In 1979, she married Larry Voss.

Gill's professional career began in the late 1970s in California, where she worked as a rehabilitation psychologist and therapist to clients with disabilities. She briefly taught at the University of Southern California in the school's disability studies program. In 1990, she returned to Chicago, where she founded the Chicago Institute of Disability Research and joined the faculty of the University of Illinois at Chicago in the Department of Disability and Human Development (she currently serves as the school's director of graduate studies in disabilities). In 1998, she became the executive officer of the Society for Disability Studies.

Gill has conducted wide-ranging research on disability issues in all of these professional capacities, and she is known as one of the country's foremost disability ethicists. A frequent writer on such subjects as disability culture and identity, women's disability issues, and disabilities studies curriculum development, Gill is also an outspoken critic of physician-assisted suicide who has frequently worked with Not Dead Yet, a national disability rights group that opposes the legalization of assisted suicide and euthanasia.

Further Reading

Gill, C. (1999). The false autonomy of forced choice: Rationalizing suicide for persons with disabilities. In J. L. Werth (Ed.), *Contemporary perspectives on rational suicide*. Philadelphia, PA: Psychology Press.

Gill, C. (2002). Disability Rights and Independent Living Movement Oral History Project [interview with Kathy Cowan]. *Calisphere*. Retrieved from http://content

John Gliedman (1942–2010)

American writer; co-author of The Unexpected Minority:
Handicapped Children in America

John Lowell Gliedman was born on May 5, 1942, in El Paso, Texas. The son
of Dr. Lester H. Gliedman, a psychiatrist, and Gertrude Gliedman, he was
raised in Lutherville, Maryland. After completing his early education at
the Park School, near Baltimore, he went on to graduate *magna cum laude*
with a bachelor's degree in English from Harvard University. He later
earned a doctoral degree at the Massachusetts Institute of Technology in
experimental psychology and linguistics. Gliedman's first marriage ended
in divorce, and he married radio journalist and author Margot Adler in
1988. The couple raised one son, Alexander Gliedman-Adler.

Gliedman is best known for the 1980 study *The Unexpected Minority:
Handicapped Children in America*, which he co-authored with William Roth.
Part of a series of reports commissioned by the Carnegie Council on
Children, *The Unexpected Minority* proved to be a highly influential work
that helped focus attention on the social implications of disability. The
book offered a detailed analysis of the challenges faced by young people
with disabilities and also noted that these conditions often extended into
adulthood. The authors' overriding contention was that individuals with
physical and mental disabilities were in fact a persecuted minority.
Moreover, Gliedman and Roth held that the social attitudes and reactions
directed toward disabled people were often more harmful than whatever
physical or mental impairments the individuals were faced with.

The authors aimed special criticism at the "medical model" that had
become the preeminent method of treating people with disabilities. They
argued that the underlying theory of such treatment—that the patient
would "get well"—did not apply to those with permanent disabilities,
and that such a focus ignored the issue of how these individuals fit into
the larger society. With its emphasis on the unfair treatment faced by the
disabled, *The Unexpected Minority* was part of the growing dialog about
the way in which members of the disabled community were regarded in
the nation's laws and public discourse.

An author with a wide range of interests, Gliedman also published
books concerning the Vietnam War and computer technology as well as

articles on physics, evolutionary biology, and the environment. At the time of his death, on February 2, 2010, he was at work on a revised edition of *The Unexpected Minority*.

Further Reading

Gliedman, J., & Roth, W. (1980). *The unexpected minority: Handicapped children in America.* New York, NY: Harcourt Brace Jovanovich.

Harlan Hahn (1939–2008)

American educator and disability rights activist

Harlan Dean Hahn was born in Osage, Iowa, on July 9, 1939, the son of Harold Hahn and Ada (Tollefson) Hahn. At age six, he contracted polio, which would force him to use crutches or a wheelchair for most of his life. Frequently hospitalized during his early youth, he did not enroll in school until age 11, but since both of his parents worked as educators, they were able to assist him with home studies. Hahn went on to graduate *magna cum laude* from St. Olaf College in 1960. He then enrolled at Harvard University, earning a master's degree in 1963 and a doctorate in 1964. He later earned two additional master's degrees, one from California State University, Los Angeles, in 1982 and another in public health from the University of California, Los Angeles, in 2004. He was the father of one daughter, Emily Hahn.

Hahn's work as a professor of political science began in 1964 at the University of Michigan. Three years later, he joined the faculty at the University of California, Riverside, and in 1972, he moved to the University of Southern California, where he worked for the next 35 years. His teaching duties at USC initially focused on American and urban politics, but in the early 1980s, he helped develop the Program in Disability and Society, which was one of the first programs of its kind in the country. He ultimately held an appointment as a professor of psychiatry and behavioral science in the university's Keck School of Medicine.

A pioneering figure in the area of disability rights, Hahn forcefully promoted the idea that individuals with disabilities were a minority group whose civil rights were being violated. He was a prominent supporter of the Rehabilitation Act of 1973 as well as the more comprehensive Americans with Disabilities Act of 1990.

Hahn's views on the barriers faced by individuals with disabilities played a role in the highly publicized 1983 court case involving Elizabeth Bouvia, a quadriplegic with cerebral palsy who sought to starve herself to death while committed to a California hospital. Giving voice to a widely held view in the disabled community, Hahn filed a legal brief arguing that Bouvia should not be allowed to die and contending that expanded services for the disabled could allow her and other people with disabilities to lead more productive and fulfilling lives. Hahn was also outspoken about the need for accessible facilities. He sued USC in 1998 over the difficulties he faced entering certain buildings, which prompted the university to undertake a comprehensive initiative to eliminate obstacles throughout the campus.

Hahn expressed his views on disability and health issues in articles that appeared in numerous journals and newspaper editorials. He published *The Issue of Equality: European Perceptions of Employment for Disabled Persons* in 1984 and collaborated with others to write the 1988 study *Disabled Persons and Earthquake Hazards*. In addition, he was a respected voice in the field of political science, co-authoring books that included *Ghetto Revolts: The Politics of Violence In American Cities*, which was nominated for a Pulitzer Prize. Hahn retired from USC in 2007 and passed away on April 23, 2008, after suffering a heart attack at his home in his Santa Monica, California.

Further Reading

Johnson, P. J. (2008, May 5). In memoriam: Harlan Hahn, 68. *USC News*. Retrieved from http://www.usc.edu/uscnews/stories/15214.html

Woo, E. (2008, May 10). USC professor advocated civil rights, access for disabled. *Los Angeles Times*. Retrieved from http://articles.latimes.com/2008/may/10/local/me-hahn10

Judy Heumann (1947–)

Disability policy developer and advocate for people with disabilities

Born in 1947, Judith Heumann contracted polio in 1949, at 18 months of age. She was homeschooled during her first few years of education because the local public school in Brooklyn, New York, called the wheelchair-using Heumann a fire hazard and refused to admit her. But Heumann's mother took the school to court, and Judy finally began taking classes at the school in the fourth grade. She went on to earn a bachelor's degree from Long Island University in 1969, but when she applied for a teaching position in the New York City public school system, the school board denied her a teaching license, claiming that she would be unable to care for herself or her students in case of a building fire. Heumann promptly sued the board of education, and when the school board backed down (heeding the advice of the presiding judge), she became the first wheelchair user to teach in the New York City public school system.

In 1970, Heumann and several friends with disabilities founded Disabled in Action, an organization devoted to securing and protecting equal rights for disabled people. Over the next few years, she served as a legislative assistant in the office of Senator Harrison Williams (D-NJ), where she helped develop legislation that became the Education for All Handicapped Children Act (EAHCA) and Section 504 of the Rehabilitation Act of 1973. One year later, Heumann helped craft the Individuals with Disabilities Education Act (IDEA), a successor to EAHCA that regulated how states and public agencies managed the early intervention and special education services provided to schoolchildren with disabilities. In 1975, she received a master's degree in public health from the University of California, Berkeley.

Heumann stayed in Berkeley to become deputy director of disability advocate Ed Roberts' Center for Independent Living, a major institution in the emerging independent living movement. In 1977, she helped organize sit-ins at the U.S. Department of Health, Education, and Welfare (HEW) offices in San Francisco and other U.S. cities. This protest action has been credited with convincing HEW Secretary Joseph Califano to sign the 1973 Rehabilitation Act's vital Section 504 regulations, which prohibited organizations or employers receiving federal monies from discriminating against qualified people with disabilities on the basis of disability.

In 1983, Heumann and Roberts co-founded the World Institute on Disability, and she served as a co-director of that organization until 1993, when she began an eight-year stint as an administrator in the U.S. Department of Education's Office of Special Education and Rehabilitation Services. In 2002, she became the World Bank Group's first official advisor on disability issues, a post she held for four years. She then served as director of the Department of Disability Services for the District of Columbia until 2010, when she was appointed a special advisor on disability rights for the U.S. State Department. Throughout these years of public service, Heumann has also remained active with Disabled People International, Rehabilitation International, the World Institute on Disability, and many other advocacy groups for people with disabilities.

Further Reading

Bennett, L. (2001). Wheels of justice. In M. Fleming (Ed.), *A place at the table: Struggles for equality in America.* New York, NY: Oxford University Press.

Shaw, L. R. (2000). Judy Heumann. In B. T. McMahon & L. R. Shaw (Eds.), *Enabling lives: Biographies of six prominent Americans with disabilities.* Boca Raton, FL: CRC Press.

Arlene S. Kanter

American attorney and educator specializing in disability law

Arlene Susan Kanter was born in Boston, Massachusetts, to Yale Kanter and Faith M. (Block) Kanter. She began her undergraduate education at Amherst College and went on to attain her bachelor's degree from Trinity College in 1976. After completing postgraduate studies in the Social Work Program at Columbia University in 1978, she earned a doctor of jurisprudence degree from New York University in 1981 and a master of law degree from the Georgetown University Law Center in 1983. Kanter married Steven D. Kepnes in 1985, and she is the mother of two children.

Kanter gained early experience in representing disabled litigants while working as a consultant for the Mental Health Law Project in Washington, D.C., from 1984 to 1988. In that capacity, she served as a counsel before the U.S. Supreme Court in *City of Cleburne, Texas v. Cleburne Living Center.* The Court handed down a unanimous decision that said that the city's refusal to grant a building permit for a home for individuals with cognitive impairments amounted to discrimination on the basis of disability. Kanter was involved in another Supreme Court case in 1983 while a graduate fellow at Georgetown.

In 1988, Kanter joined the faculty at the Syracuse University College of Law in Syracuse, New York, where she has continued to focus on disability law, becoming an internationally recognized expert on the subject. She has been a driving force behind two innovative initiatives based at the university, serving as the founder and director of the

Disability Law and Policy Program and as the co-director of the Center on Human Policy, Law, and Disability Studies. In 2005, she received the Laura J. and L. Douglas Meredith Award for Excellence in Teaching, the university's highest teaching honor.

Kanter's work has placed special emphasis on addressing the discrimination suffered by individuals with disabilities, and she has adopted a global perspective on the subject, noting that disabled people face similar prejudices and problems around the world. Because of her expertise in the subject, she was invited to participate in the drafting of the United Nations Convention on the Rights of Persons with Disabilities, which took place from 2001 to 2006. More recently, she was a Fulbright Senior Scholar in Israel in 2009 and 2010, assisting Tel Aviv University in establishing that country's first academic program in disability studies. She has also been invited to work with governments and non-governmental organizations in countries such as India, Jordan, Turkey, and Vietnam in regard to their domestic disability laws.

A frequent contributor to journals, books, and reports in the areas of law, disability, and human rights, Kanter is also the author of *Current Issues in Mental Health Law* and collaborated on such publications as *Foreign Policy and Disability: Legislative Strategies and Civil Rights Protections to Ensure Inclusion of People With Disabilities* and *Behind Closed Doors: Human Rights Abuses in the Psychiatric Facilities, Orphanages and Rehabilitation Centers of Turkey*. In addition, she is founder and co-editor of the Social Science Research Network *Journal on Disability Law*.

Further Reading

Eglash, R. (2010, May 20). A world of rights. *The Jerusalem Post*. Retrieved from http://law.syr.edu/faculty/facultymember.aspx?fac=72

Edward Kennedy (1932–2009)

American politician and supporter of
disability rights legislation

Edward M. "Ted" Kennedy was born on February 22, 1932, in Boston, Massachusetts. The son of Joseph Patrick Kennedy, a businessperson and diplomat, and Rose (Fitzgerald) Kennedy, he hailed from a powerful political family. He graduated from Harvard University in 1956 and attended the International Law School in The Hague, the Netherlands, in 1958 before attaining his law degree from the University of Virginia the following year. He married Virginia Joan Bennet on November 29, 1958, and the couple raised three children before divorcing in 1981. Kennedy married Victoria Reggie in 1992.

Ted Kennedy was thrust into politics at an early age, helping manage his brother John F. Kennedy's senatorial and presidential campaigns in the late 1950s and early 1960s. After a brief tenure as the district attorney of Suffolk County in Massachusetts, he was elected to the U.S. Senate in November 1962. He would spend the next 47 years in Congress, becoming one of the nation's most powerful senators. He was also viewed as a viable presidential candidate, but his chances of gaining the White House were harmed by the Chappaquiddick scandal of 1969, when he was involved in an automobile accident that claimed the life of a female passenger in his car. Kennedy ended up entering just one presidential campaign, unsuccessfully seeking the Democratic nomination in 1980.

During his senatorial career, Kennedy was especially effective in championing legislation to benefit Americans with disabilities. His actions were partly inspired by his experiences with family members: His sister Rosemary was institutionalized for most of her life; his son Edward had his leg amputated during childhood; and another son, Patrick, struggled with bipolar disorder. A supporter of the civil rights bills that became law in the 1960s, Kennedy later worked to broaden the scope of those protections to encompass disabled citizens and played a central role in passing laws that helped achieve important objectives of the disability rights movement.

Kennedy's early accomplishments included co-sponsoring the Education for All Handicapped Children Act in 1975, which mandated that free and appropriate public education (FAPE) be made available to all children with disabilities. The following decade, he championed the Fair Housing Act Amendments of 1988, which extended the provisions of the 1968 housing legislation to apply to the disabled. In one of the crowning achievements of his career, Kennedy guided the landmark Americans with Disabilities Act through the Senate in 1990, and his leadership helped bring about overwhelming support for the bill in that chamber.

A series of other disability-related bills became law with Kennedy's assistance. These included the Family and Medical Leave Act of 1993, which provided more options for caregivers; the Help America Vote Act (2002), which required equal access for disabled voters at polling places; and the Family Opportunity Act (2006), which made Medicaid coverage available to a greater number of families with disabled children. During his final year in Congress, the senator helped win passage of the Genetic Information Nondiscrimination Act to prevent health care providers and employers from using an individual's genetic information in making employment and health coverage decisions.

In addition to these successes, Kennedy sought comprehensive health care reform for more than four decades, though he did not live to see that goal realized. He was diagnosed with brain cancer in 2008 and passed away on August 25, 2009, in Hyannis Port, Massachusetts.

Further Reading

Hersh, B. (2010). *Edward Kennedy: An intimate biography*. Berkeley, CA: Counterpoint.
Kennedy, E. (2009, July 18). The cause of my life. *Newsweek*. Retrieved from http://www.newsweek.com/2009/07/17/the-cause-of-my-life.html

Eva Feder Kittay (1946–)

*American educator and author specializing
in disability ethics and philosophy*

Eva Feder Kittay was born in Malmo, Sweden, on August 13, 1946, the daughter of Leo and Sara (Golembioski) Feder. After moving to the United States in 1953, she became a naturalized citizen in 1958. Her undergraduate studies took place at Sarah Lawrence College, where she earned a bachelor's degree in philosophy in 1967. She went on to attend the City University of New York, earning a master's degree in 1977 and a Ph.D. in 1978. She married Jeffrey Kittay in 1967 and is the mother of two children.

After completing her doctoral degree, Kittay became a visiting assistant professor at the University of Maryland in 1978. The following year, she joined the faculty at the State University of New York at Stony Brook as an assistant professor in the Department of Philosophy. She was promoted to associate professor in 1986, to professor in 1993, and to distinguished professor in 2009. She is also a senior fellow in the university's Center for Medical Humanities, Compassionate Care, and Bioethics, and an associate in the area of Women's Studies.

Kittay has specialized in a range of areas, including feminist philosophy and ethics, social and political theory, and the philosophy of language. Since the mid-1990s, she has also turned her attention to disability studies, with her interest in the subject growing out of her own experiences with her daughter, Sesha, who has a cognitive disability. Kittay's book *Love's Labor: Essays on Women, Equality and Dependency*, published in 1999, discusses her life with Sesha and considers the philosophical implications of caring for others. She argues that Western culture's emphasis on rational, autonomous individualism prevents both individuals with disabilities and those who care for them from fully participating in society, and she makes a case for changing law and public policy so that care-giving can become more of a community-based effort.

Kittay's contributions to the field of disability studies have also included serving as co-editor of the books *Cognitive Disability and Its Challenge to Moral Philosophy* and *The Subject of Care: Feminist Perspectives on Dependency*. She is also the author of *Metaphor: Its Cognitive Force and Linguistic Structure* and has edited a number of works on feminism, philosophy, and language.

Further Reading

Kittay, E. F. (1999). *Love's labor: Essays on women, equality and dependency*. New York, NY: Routledge.

Kittay, E. F. (2010). The personal is philosophical is political: A philosopher and mother of cognitively disabled person sends notes from the battlefield. In E. F. Kittay & L. Carlson (Eds.), *Cognitive disability and its challenge to moral philosophy*. Malden, MA: Wiley-Blackwell.

Paul Longmore (1946–2010)

American historian and disability ethicist

Paul K. Longmore was born in 1946 in New Jersey. The son of a Baptist minister, he grew up in various cities on the West Coast of the United States. Longmore contracted polio at the age of seven and spent more than a year in the hospital. He never recovered the use of his arms, and he used a ventilator to aid his breathing for part of each day. Determined to live independently, Longmore studied history and political science at Occidental College, earning a bachelor's degree in 1968 and a master's degree in 1971. He went on to earn a Ph.D. in history from Claremont Graduate School in 1984.

After being rejected for teaching positions at numerous colleges because of his disability, Longmore finally landed at Stanford University on a fellowship. It was there that he first applied his expertise in history to the emerging field of disability studies to pioneer the new discipline of disability history. In 1988, Longmore published his first book, a scholarly biography titled *The Invention of George Washington*. He made news across the country when he burned a copy of the book on the steps of the federal building in Los Angeles to protest government disincentives that prevented many people with disabilities from working. Longmore pointed out that if he earned royalties from his book, he stood to lose state Medicaid funding that paid for his ventilator and home health care assistant. The Social Security Administration later changed its rules on royalties through what became known as the Longmore Amendment.

Longmore went on to teach at California Polytechnic University at Pomona and at the University of Southern California, where he also served as administrator of the Program in Disability and Society. In 1992, he joined the faculty at San Francisco State University. In addition to teaching popular courses in early American history and disability history, Longmore helped establish and served as director of the university's Institute on Disability, a multidisciplinary research, curriculum development, and community service program. The recipient of numerous grants and fellowships, Longmore wrote many articles for scholarly journals and opinion pieces for newspapers. He was also the co-editor of *The New Disability History: American Perspectives,* published in 2001.

In 2003, Longmore published *Why I Burned My Book and Other Essays on Disability History,* a collection of essays that challenged popular views and stereotypes of people with disabilities. Longmore strove to redefine disability as a problem that resides in society rather than in individuals. "The truth is that the major obstacles we must overcome are pervasive social prejudice, systematic segregation, and institutionalized discrimination," he wrote. In 2005, he was honored with the Henry B. Betts Award from the American Association of People with Disabilities for his work in improving the lives of people with disabilities. Longmore died suddenly of natural causes on August 9, 2010. He is remembered as a leading voice in the disability rights movement and in the opposition to legalized assisted suicide.

Further Reading

Longmore, P. (2003). *Why I burned my book and other essays on disability history.* Philadelphia, PA: Temple University Press.

Shapiro, J. (2010, Aug. 11). *Paul Longmore, historian and advocate for the disabled, dies.* NPR. Retrieved from http://www.npr.org/blogs/health/2010/08/11/129127432/paul-longmore-historian-and-advocate-for-disabled-dies

Theodore Marmor

American disability policy analyst and economist

Theodore R. "Ted" Marmor is a leading expert on health care policy in North America. Marmor earned a bachelor's degree in American studies and politics from Harvard University in 1960. After studying at the University of California at Berkeley and Oxford University, he returned to Harvard to complete his Ph.D. in 1966. Marmor launched his career in public policy by serving as a special assistant to Wilbur Cohen, the U.S. Secretary of Health, Education, and Welfare (HEW), in the late 1960s.

Following stints at the University of Minnesota and the University of Chicago, Marmor began his long association with Yale University in 1979. He taught courses as a professor of politics, management, and law in the School of Management, served as director of the Center for Health Studies, and eventually became a professor emeritus. In 2005, Marmor began teaching part-time as an adjunct professor of public policy in the executive education program at Harvard University's Kennedy School of Government.

Marmor has also worked as a health care policy consultant and served as an expert witness in litigation related to health care coverage. His main areas of expertise include fraud cases involving prescription pricing, asbestos defense cases involving public knowledge of the risks of exposure, and disability rights cases involving Medicare coverage of wheelchairs.

Marmor also provides expert commentary on issues involving health care reform, Social Security reform, and welfare policies for a variety of media outlets. During the debate over President Barack Obama's health care reform bill in 2010, he was frequently called upon to analyze the impact of the legislation and compare it to programs enacted in other countries. "One of the most striking features of the American health care debate is how little attention was paid to the subject of justice," he noted. "The idea of fundamental fairness, questions about solidarity and what it requires in the way of patient cost sharing, and the importance of equal access: all were central components of the public conversation about health care in Canada and Britain and democracies elsewhere."

Marmor has written or edited 13 books in the areas of health care and public policy, including his classic case study *The Politics of Medicare* (1973, updated and republished in 2000). Other books include *Social Security: Beyond the Rhetoric of Crisis* (1988), *America's Misunderstood Welfare State* (1992), *Understanding Health Care Reform* (1994), and *Fads, Fallacies, and*

Foolishness in Medical Care Management and Policy (2007). A former editor and frequent contributor to the *Journal of Health Politics, Policy, and Law,* Marmor has published more than 100 articles in scholarly journals, including the award-winning "Rethinking National Health Insurance." He is a member of the National Academy of Social Insurance and the Institute of Medicine.

Further Reading

Theodore R. Marmor. Yale School of Management. Retrieved from http://mba.yale
.edu/faculty/profiles/marmor.shtml

Jerry L. Mashaw (1941–)

*American educator and author specializing
in social welfare and disability policy*

Jerry L. Mashaw was born in Shreveport, Louisiana, in 1941. He earned a bachelor's degree in philosophy from Tulane University in 1962 and remained at the university to study law, graduating first in his class in 1964. From 1964 to 1966, he was a Marshall Scholar at the University of Edinburgh Law School, and he received a Ph.D. in European governmental studies from that institution in 1969. He is married to Anne MacClintock and is the father of two children.

Mashaw's career as an educator began in 1966, when he became an assistant professor at the Tulane University Law School. He moved to the University of Virginia Law School in 1968 and joined the faculty at the Yale University Law School in 1976. During his years at Yale, he has held the positions of William Nelson Cromwell Professor of Law and Gordon Bradford Tweedy Professor of Law and Organization. Since 1994, he has been the Sterling Professor of Law and Management at the Yale Institute for Social and Policy Studies.

One of Mashaw's main areas of interest is social welfare policy, and he has frequently written on the subject of disability benefits. Taking issue with those who claim the U.S. social insurance system is in crisis and unsustainable, he has advocated a moderate approach to reforming Social Security and other programs, defending them as essential to the nation's economic well-being. In seeking to make the system more effective and financially sound, he and his co-authors have considered methods by which disability assistance could be restructured to allow more citizens with disabilities to become productive members of the workforce. These have included innovations such as disabled worker tax credits and return-to-work vouchers. Mashaw and his collaborators believe such approaches can result in greater employment among those with impairments while maintaining the basic framework of disability assistance.

Among the more than 20 books to which Mashaw has contributed are *America's Misunderstood Welfare State: Persistent Myths, Enduring Realities* (1990), *Balancing Security and Opportunity: The Challenge of Disability Income Policy* (1996), *The Environment of Disability Policy: Programs, People, History, and Context* (1996), *Restructuring the SSI Disability Program for Children and Adolescents* (1996), and *True Security: Rethinking American Social Insurance* (1999). In addition, he is a founder of the National Academy of Social Insurance and has served as its president and as a member of its board of trustees.

Further Reading

Jerry L. Mashaw. Retrieved from http://www.law.yale.edu/faculty/JMashaw.htm

Reno, V. P., Mashaw, J. L., & Gradison, B. (1997). *Disability: Challenges for social insurance, health care financing, and labor market policy.* Washington, DC: National Academy for Social Insurance.

Arlene B. Mayerson

American attorney specializing in disability rights

Arlene B. Mayerson completed her undergraduate studies at Boston University, where she earned a bachelor of science degree. She went on to attain two legal degrees, a J.D. from the University of California, Berkeley, School of Law (Boalt Hall), and a master of laws degree from the Georgetown University Law Center.

From the beginning of her legal career, Mayerson has focused on disability rights, and she has been the directing attorney of the Disability Rights Education and Defense Fund since 1981. Her work as a counsel has included a number of cases that established legal precedents related to important disability legislation of the late 1980s, including the Handicapped Children's Protection Act (1986) and the Fair Housing Amendments Act (1988). She also served as an advisor to members of Congress and to disability activists as laws were drafted and debated, and she has frequently filed amicus briefs in Supreme Court cases related to disability.

Mayerson played an especially prominent role in the formulation of the Americans with Disabilities Act of 1990 (ADA), testifying before congressional committees and filing comments on behalf of hundreds of disability rights organizations. She is considered one of the foremost authorities on the ADA and is the author of two books on the law that were published in 1994: *Explanation of the Contents of the Americans with Disabilities Act of 1990* and the three-volume *Americans with Disabilities Act Annotated: Legislative History, Regulations, and Commentary.*

From 1995 to 2001, Mayerson was a member of the Civil Rights Reviewing Authority of the U.S. Department of Education, the board responsible for reviewing civil rights decisions made by the department. She has also taught classes on disability law at her alma mater, the University of California, Berkeley, School of Law. Her work has been recognized with honors such as the Spirit of Independence Leading Advocate Award, which she received from the Center for Independent Living in 1993, and the American Diabetes Association Public Policy Award, which she received in 1997.

Further Reading

Arlene B. Mayerson. Retrieved from http://www.dredf.org/about/staff/mayerson .shtml

Martha Minow (1954–)

American lawyer, educator, and author

Martha Minow was born on December 6, 1954, in Highland Park, Illinois. Her parents were Newton Minow, a lawyer and former chairman of the Federal Communications Commission (FCC), and Josephine Baskin Minow. She completed her undergraduate studies at the University of Michigan, attaining a bachelor's degree in 1975, and went on to earn a master's degree in education from Harvard University in 1976 and a law degree from Yale University in 1979. She married Joe Singer in 1986 and is the mother of one child.

Minow began her career by serving as a law clerk for Judge David L. Bazelon of the U.S. Court of Appeals for the District of Columbia in 1979 and 1980. She then held the same position for Justice Thurgood Marshall of the U.S. Supreme Court in 1980 and 1981. A member of the faculty at Harvard Law School since 1981, she was named the William Henry Bloomberg Professor of Law in 2003 and the Jeremiah Smith Jr. Professor of Law in 2005. She became the dean of Harvard Law School in 2009.

In her research and writing, Minow has studied the legal implications of a range of issues, including equality, pluralism, and education. Her work has frequently considered the subject of disability, and she offered a detailed examination of the topic as part of her book *Making All the Difference: Inclusion, Exclusion, and American Law* (1990). A central feature of her analysis is the concept of "difference," and more specifically the interactions between members of the population who are defined as "different" and those who are defined as "normal." In regard to individuals with disabilities, she probes the dilemma of balancing equality against the specialized needs of those with impairments and studies how that dilemma has shaped the laws that govern schools and other social institutions.

Minow served as the co-editor of *Just Schools: Pursuing Equality in Societies of Difference* (2008), and she collaborated with the U.S. Department of Education and the Center for Applied Special Technology on a five-year project to provide students with disabilities with increased access to curricular materials. Her interest in disability issues is also reflected in her book *In Brown's Wake* (2010). This study considers the legacy of the Supreme Court ruling in *Brown v. Board of Education*, including the way in which it influenced the trend toward "mainstreaming" students with impairments in the nation's public schools.

Minow has also published works on the legal aspects of topics such as multiculturalism, privatization, genocide, and human rights. She served on the Independent International Commission on Kosovo and has been involved in the Imagine Co-existence program of the United Nations High Commissioner for Refugees. She is vice chair of the Legal Services Corporation, having been nominated to that post by President Barack Obama in 2009. Minow was also on the short list of candidates the president considered in nominating a new Supreme Court justice in 2010, though that appointment ultimately went to Elena Kagan.

Further Reading

Martha Minow named dean of Harvard Law School (2009, June 11). *Harvard Gazette*. Retrieved from http://news.harvard.edu/gazette/story/2009/06/martha-minow-named-dean-of-harvard-law-school

Martha Nussbaum (1947–)

American philosopher, ethicist, and political theorist

Martha Craven Nussbaum was born on May 6, 1947, in New York City to George Craven, an attorney, and Betty Craven, a homemaker. She grew up in Bryn Mawr, Pennsylvania, and attended Wellesley College from 1964 to 1966 before graduating from New York University with a bachelor's degree in 1969. After enrolling at Harvard University for her graduate studies, she earned a master's degree in 1971 and a Ph.D. in 1975. She married Alan Jeffrey Nussbaum in 1969, and the couple became the parents of one daughter, Rachel Emily, before divorcing in 1987.

Initially specializing in philosophy, the classics, and comparative literature, Nussbaum taught at Harvard University from 1975 to 1983 and then served as a visiting professor at Wellesley College in 1983 and 1984. A member of the faculty at Brown University from 1984 to 1995, she was named David Benedict Professor of Classics in 1987 and 1988. She moved to the University of Chicago in 1995, where she is the Freund Distinguished Service Professor of Law and Ethics, appointed in the Philosophy Department and the Law and Divinity Schools. She also served as a research advisor for the World Institute for Development Economics Research from 1986 to 1993.

An author who has written on a wide range of topics, from ancient Greek civilization to contemporary political, ethical, and philosophical issues, Nussbaum has become especially well known for her central role in the development of the "capabilities approach" to understanding human well-being, first enunciated by Nobel Prize-winning economist Amartya Sen. She has applied this theory to the subject of disability in a number of her works, most notably in *Frontiers of Justice: Disability, Nationality, Species Membership*. In that book, she identifies the inequality experienced by people with physical and mental impairments as one of the three most urgent problems of social justice. Further, she argues that the social contract theory of justice, in which people organize themselves under a set of laws for mutual advantage, is unable to solve this problem because of the differences in power between disabled individuals and the non-disabled population. A far better standard of justice, she argues, is to weigh the degree to which those with impairments are able to access 10 essential capabilities, which include the ability to live a life of normal length, the ability to have good bodily health, and the ability to move freely from place to place.

Nussbaum has also used the capabilities approach to measure economic development and to assess gender inequality and other issues. Some of her better known books include *Cultivating Humanity: A Classical Defense of Reform in Liberal Education* (1997), *Sex & Social Justice* (1999), *Women and Human Development: The Capabilities Approach* (2000), and *Hiding from Humanity: Disgust, Shame, and the Law* (2004).

Further Reading

Boynton, R. (1999, November 21). Who needs philosophy? A profile of Martha Nussbaum. *New York Times Magazine*. Retrieved from http://www.robert boynton.com/articleDisplay.php?article_id=55

Nussbaum, M., & Kreisler, K. (2006, September 14). *Women's rights, religious freedom, and liberal education: Conversation with Martha Nussbaum*. Conversations with History, Institute of International Studies, University of California, Berkeley. Retrieved from http://globetrotter.berkeley.edu/people6/Nussbaum/nussbaum-con0.html

Michael Oliver (1945–)

British disability activist and social theorist

Michael Oliver was born into a working-class family in Great Britain in 1945. He was paralyzed at age 17 as a result of a spinal injury he suffered while diving into a swimming pool. In the years that followed, he was a patient at Stoke Mandeville Hospital in England and became involved in sports competitions for the disabled. After finding work as a clerk and lecturer at a prison facility, he undertook university studies in 1972, earning an undergraduate degree and a doctorate in sociology. He went on to teach as a professor of disability studies at the University of Greenwich in London until his retirement.

During his years as a graduate student in the 1970s, Oliver became increasingly interested in the political implications of disability. He was greatly influenced by *Fundamental Principles of Disability*, a publication produced by the Union of the Physically Impaired Against Segregation (UPIAS), a British activist group. Expanding on the ideas presented in the publication, Oliver helped develop the "social model" of disability, which counters the so-called medical model and its emphasis on an individual's medical state and possible treatments for his or her condition.

The social model draws a distinction between *impairment* (the actual physical or mental condition experienced by the individual) and *disability* (the social limitations that are placed on those with impairments). As a consequence, the social model emphasizes that individuals with impairments are victims of discrimination because society fails to accommodate their needs, and it stresses the need for new policies to help alleviate that injustice. "It is not individual limitations, of whatever kind, which are the cause of the problem," Oliver notes in his paper "The Individual and Social Models of Disability," "but society's failure to provide appropriate services and adequately ensure the needs of disabled people are fully taken into account in its social organisation." Along the same lines, Oliver also criticizes the "personal tragedy" view of disability that focuses on the unfortunate circumstances experienced by those dealing with impairments rather than on actions that might be taken to alleviate the discrimination they experience and to allow them participate more fully in the world around them.

Oliver's views provided some of the sociological underpinning for the disability rights movement in Great Britain, and he has been involved in organizations such as the Spinal Injuries Association and the British Council of Disabled People. His published works include *The Politics of Disablement: A Sociological Approach* (1990) and *Understanding Disability: From Theory to Practice* (1996), and he is also the co-author of *Social Work With Disabled People* (2006).

Further Reading

Campbell, J., & Oliver, M. (1996). *Disability politics: Understanding our past, changing our future.* London, UK: Routledge.

Oliver, M. (1996). *Understanding disability: From theory to practice.* London, UK: Macmillan.

Carol Padden (1955–)

American linguist focusing on deaf languages and culture

Carol A. Padden was born in 1955 in Washington, D.C. She is deaf, and her parents, who are also deaf, were on the faculty of Gallaudet University. Padden went to the Kendall School for the Deaf at Gallaudet for several years, then transferred to a public school. She has said that the experience of moving between the worlds of deaf and non-deaf language and culture sparked her interest in language. Padden received her bachelor's degree in linguistics from Georgetown University in 1978 and her Ph.D. in linguistics from the University of California, San Diego, in 1983. She is married to Tom Humphries, who has collaborated with her on several books.

In 1983, Padden joined the faculty at the University of California, San Diego, where she is a professor in the Department of Communication and Center for Research in Language, and also an associate dean in the Division of Social Sciences. Her research is focused on language and communication, specifically the structure and evolution of sign languages, the social implications of signed communication, and the interrelationship of linguistic structures in signed and spoken languages.

Padden and her colleagues have conducted a study of Al-Sayyid Bedouin Sign Language, which developed approximately 75 years ago in a village in the Negev Desert in Israel. Through their study, they have made groundbreaking insights into the complexity and adaptability of emerging languages. Padden has published several major works on deafness and deaf culture, including *Deaf in America: Voices From a Culture* and *Inside Deaf Culture*, both co-authored with Humphries, and two textbooks on American Sign Language. In addition, Padden has published numerous professional papers and has directed several major research projects funded by federal grants from the National Institutes of Health, the National Science Foundation, the U.S. Department of Education, and the Spencer Foundation. She has also served on the board of directors of Deaf Community Services of San Diego, the board of trustees of Gallaudet University, and the board of directors of Deaf West Theater in Los Angeles.

Padden has received numerous awards, including a Guggenhiem Fellowship and a Laurent Clerc Cultural Award for distinguished contributions to the field of deafness. In 2010, she was named a MacArthur Fellow by the John D. and Catherine T. MacArthur Foundation for work that "demystifies sign language and opens windows of understanding regarding how languages evolve over time and the role of language in building and maintaining communities."

Further Reading

Boswell, S. (2006). Signs from the desert: New language sheds light on linguistic evolution. *ASHA Leader, 11*(1), 12–14.

2010 MacArthur Fellows: Carol Padden. Retrieved from http://www.macfound
    .org/site/c.lkLXJ8MQKrH/b.6241263/k.7598/Carol_Padden.htm

Gerard Quinn (1958–)

*Irish attorney and specialist in
international disability rights*

Gerard Quinn received his bachelor's degree from the National University
of Ireland, Galway, and his bachelor of laws degree from King's Inn. He
has also earned three law degrees, an LL.B. from the National University of
Ireland, and a master's in law (LL.M.) and a doctorate in law (S.J.D.) from
Harvard University.

Quinn is currently the director of the Centre for Disability Law and
Policy at the National University of Ireland School of Law. His area of spe-
cialization is international disability law and policy. He has served on
many national and international commissions examining these areas. He
is a member of the Irish Human Rights Commission, helped coordinate
the National Human Rights Institutions on disability issues, and has held
the post of director of research for the Irish Government's Law Reform
Commission. Quinn has also served as vice president of the European
Committee of Social Rights for the Council of Europe and on commissions
of the European Union in the area of discrimination. He is the former
director of the European Commission's Network of European Legal
Experts on Discrimination Law in the Field of Disability and also led the
Rehabilitation International delegation for the Working Group on the
United Nations Convention on Rights of Persons with Disabilities.

Quinn has also served on several major boards that examine disability
policy on the international level, including SOROS-OSI, headquartered in
Washington, D.C.; the Disability Rights Fund, in Boston; the European
Centre Consortium on Disability, in Brussels; and the European Coalition
for Community Living, in London.

Quinn is the author of many key books and professional publications
in his field, including several with disability specialist Theresia Degener.
These works trace the recent change in society's policies and approaches
toward people with disabilities, from one motivated by charity to one
based on human rights. He has examined the links between disability and
poverty and social exclusion around the world and helped to create viable
human rights instruments to allow people with disabilities access to the
same rights as all people.

Further Reading

Quinn G. (2007). Disability discrimination law in the European Union. In H. Meenan, (Ed.), *Equality law in an enlarged European Union: Understanding the Article 13 Directives*. Cambridge, UK: Cambridge University Press.

Quinn, G., & Degener, T. (Eds.). (2002). *Human rights and disability: The current use and future potential of United Nations human rights instruments in the context of disability*. Geneva, Switzerland: Office of the United Nations Commissioner for Human Rights.

Ed Roberts (1939–1995)

*American activist and founder of
the disability rights movement*

Edward Verne Roberts was born on January 23, 1939, in San Mateo, California. His parents were Verne and Zona Roberts. At the age of 14, Ed contracted polio. His life as an activist began soon thereafter. When he started college at the University of California at Berkeley in the 1960s, he was the first student with severe disabilities to attend the school. However, he faced discrimination from his first day on campus. Roberts brought the iron lung he needed with him to Berkeley, but he could not find campus housing that would accommodate him. He was offered a room in the hospital that housed the student health center, and soon he and several other severely disabled students were living there.

Calling themselves the Rolling Quads, Roberts and his fellow students began to work for change on the Berkeley campus, demanding accommodation and support services for disabled students, including barrier removal and personal attendant services, so that students with disabilities could live independently. Their efforts resulted in the Physically Disabled Student Program, the first organization of its kind in the nation.

Roberts received his bachelor's degree in political science from Berkeley in 1964 and his master's degree in 1966. He was a member of the faculty at the university for several years, while continuing to work on such key issues as accessibility, inclusion, and equality for people with disabilities. He founded the Center for Independent Living in 1972, and it became a model for similar programs for people with disabilities worldwide. In 1975, Governor Jerry Brown made Roberts director of the Department of Rehabilitation for California. In 1983, Roberts co-founded the World Institute on Disability, which became a forum for research and the dissemination of programs in education, transportation, housing, health, independent living, and other key areas for people with disabilities.

In all his work as an activist, Roberts stressed that it was important for people with disabilities to lead self-directed lives. He encouraged disabled people to challenge the perceptions held by the able-bodied community, and to see themselves not as passive objects of pity, but as self-actualizing people able to articulate their goals and to demand civil rights.

Ed Roberts died after a stroke on March 14, 1995. In August 2010, his life and work on behalf of people with disabilities was commemorated by Governor Arnold Schwarzenegger, who signed a bill declaring that January 23 (Roberts's birthday) would now be celebrated as "Ed Roberts Day" in California. The bill encourages educational programs to promote awareness of disability issues. At the University of California at Berkeley, an Ed Roberts Campus is being built that will include several organizations offering services and programs to people with disabilities.

Further Reading

Burris, M. (2010, August 2). Day to honor local disability rights activist. *The Daily Californian.*

Ed Roberts. Retrieved from http://www.ilusa.com/links/022301ed_roberts.htm

Franklin D. Roosevelt (1882–1945)

American president and advocate for disability policies

Franklin Delano Roosevelt was born on January 30, 1882, in Hyde Park, New York. He was the son of James Roosevelt, a successful businessman and lawyer, and Sara Delano Roosevelt. He received his bachelor's degree from Harvard University in 1904 and went on to study law at Columbia University. In 1905, he married Eleanor Roosevelt, a distant cousin. They had six children, five of whom lived to be adults: Anna, James, Elliott, Franklin, and John.

Roosevelt entered politics in 1910, when he was elected to the New York State Senate. He served until 1913, when he was chosen to be Assistant Secretary of the Navy, a position he held for seven years. In 1920, he ran unsuccessfully for the vice presidential nomination of the Democratic Party. In 1921, at the age of 39, Roosevelt contracted polio, and his legs became paralyzed. He learned to walk with braces and canes, and he also worked to regain the use of his legs through exercise, especially swimming in the mineral waters of Warm Springs, Georgia. After completing his rehabilitation program, Roosevelt continued his political career, serving as governor of New York from 1928 to 1930.

In 1932, during the early years of the Great Depression, Roosevelt was elected president of the United States. He went on to become the only president ever elected to serve four terms in office. During his election campaign and throughout his 12 years in the White House, Roosevelt used a wheelchair every day. Yet he did not allow himself to be photographed in his wheelchair, which is difficult for many people in the modern disability rights movement to accept. Most historians believe that Roosevelt made the decision for political reasons, knowing that American society at the time would not accept a disabled president. Instead, he made every effort to appear physically vigorous and capable as he led the nation through the challenges of the Great Depression and World War II.

Despite his efforts to conceal his own disability, Roosevelt was a staunch supporter of programs for people with disabilities. In the 1920s, he purchased land in Georgia and formed the Warm Springs Foundation, which treated polio patients for decades. Also, as part of his New Deal policies, he helped develop the Social Security Administration and its disability policies. During World War II, Roosevelt signed legislation that provided vocational rehabilitation and secured pension benefits for disabled veterans.

In 1995, on the 50th anniversary of the founding of the United Nations, the Franklin and Eleanor Roosevelt Institute and the World Committee on Disability established the Franklin Delano Roosevelt International Disability Award. The honor was created to recognize progress by individual nations and non-governmental groups toward the realization of the goals of the UN's World Programme of Action Concerning Disabled Persons, which seeks to expand the participation of people with disabilities in all aspects of life and work.

Further Reading

Bibliography. The Franklin D. Roosevelt Library and Museum. Retrieved from http://www.fdrlibrary.marist.edu/archives/resources/bibfdr.html

The Franklin and Eleanor Roosevelt Institute. Retrieved from http://www .rooseveltinstitute.org/search/node/Franklin%20D.%20Roosevelt

Kate Seelman (1938–)

*American academic focusing on
rehabilitation technology to advance
independence in people with disabilities*

Katherine D. Seelman was born on May 26, 1938. After receiving her bachelor's degree in history and political science from Hunter College in 1964, she pursued graduate studies at New York University, earning her master's degree in public policy in 1970 and her doctoral degree in science, technology, and public policy in 1982.

Seelman began her career as a community organizer in the 1960s, working in New York City and Little Rock, Arkansas. In 1986, Seelman, who is hard of hearing, became the director of public education for the Massachusetts Commission for the Deaf and Hard of Hearing. In 1989, she became a research specialist for the National Council on Disability, and in 1993, was named the director of program development for the Administration of Developmental Disabilities, part of the U.S. Department of Health and Human Services. The following year, she joined the National Institute on Disability and Rehabilitation Research, where she served as director until 2001.

In 2001, Seelman joined the faculty of the University of Pittsburgh, where she is associate dean and professor of rehabilitation science and technology at the School of Health and Rehabilitation Sciences, which is part of the Quality of Life Technology Center, a National Science Foundation Engineering Research Center run jointly by the University of Pittsburgh and Carnegie Mellon University. She also serves as an adjunct professor at Xian Jiaton University in China.

Seelman's research focuses on the development of science, technology, and public policy programs to create supports needed by people with disabilities and older adults to attain independence and community integration. She has shared her research as a representative of the United States in several international venues, including Japan and China, and also organized and directed a panel of disability specialists at the 2000 Rehabilitation International Meeting in Rio de Janeiro. Seelman currently serves on the international World Health Organization editorial committee, which is developing the first world report on disability.

Seelman has published many professional papers and books in the area of health and technology for persons with disabilities and aging adults. She is a contributor to *Handbook of Smart Technology for Aging* and *Disability and Independence: Computing and Engineering Design and Application,* and co-editor of *Handbook of Disability Studies.* She is the recipient of many awards, including the Gold Key Award from the American Congress of Rehabilitation Medicine, the Distinguished Public Service Award from the American Academy of Physical Medicine and Rehabilitation, and a Switzer Fellowship.

Further Reading

Linkov, F., LaPorte, R., & Seelman, K. D. (2010). Cancer, disability and public health service providers: Better education through informatics and the Supercourse. *International Journal of Public Policy, 6*(3/4), 247–257.

Seelman, K. D., Collins, D. M., Bharucha, J. A., & Osborn, J. (2007). Giving meaning to quality of life through technology: Cutting-edge research on aging-in-place technologies at Carnegie Mellon University/University of Pittsburgh. *Nursing Homes, 56*(10) 40–42.

Tom Shakespeare (1966–)

British academic, writer, and disability advocate who focuses on bioethics and the cultural and social issues of disability

Thomas William Shakespeare was born on May 11, 1966, in Norwich, England. His parents were Sir William Geoffrey Shakespeare, a physician, and Susan Raffel Shakespeare. Like his father, Shakespeare has achondroplasia (dwarfism), and it has become central to his study of disability and society. Shakespeare received his master's degree in sociology from Pembroke College, Cambridge, and his doctoral degree in sociology from King's College, Cambridge.

Shakespeare became involved with the disability movement in 1986, when he co-founded Disability Action North East and the Northern Disability Arts Forum. He was a lecturer in sociology at the University of Sunderland from 1993 to 1999, a research fellow in sociology at the University of Leeds from 1996 to 1999, and director of outreach for the Policy, Ethics, and Life Sciences Research Centre at the University of Newcastle from 1999 to 2005. Always fascinated by the intersection of science and the arts, Shakespeare has also served as a fellow for NESTA (the National Endowment for Science, Technology and the Arts), working on writing and performance art in the area of disability and genetics. He has been a member of the Arts Council of England since 2004.

Shakespeare has published several books on issues in disability, including *The Sexual Politics of Disability, Exploring Disability,* and *Genetic Politics: From Eugenics to Genome.* In his book *Disability Rights and Wrongs,* he takes issue with the "social model" of disability, which says that "disability" is a construct of nondisabled society and that people with disabilities are oppressed by societal barriers. Shakespeare argues instead that individuals with disabilities, as well as those who care for them and write about them, must deal directly and realistically with the range of impairments they face.

Shakespeare is a consultant to the World Health Organization on disability and rehabilitation, and he is a regular contributor to Ouch! a Web site run by the BBC on disability issues. In addition to his prolific writings on disability, he is also a speaker and broadcaster on the topic. In 2003, RADAR awarded him the U.K. People of the Year Award for his work on human rights for disabled people.

In 2008, Shakespeare lost the use of his legs and became a paraplegic. He is now writing about his experiences with the rehabilitation aspects of disability.

Further Reading

Koch, T. (2008). Is Tom Shakespeare disabled? *Journal of Medical Ethics, 34,* 18–20.
Tom Shakespeare. Retrieved from http://www.bbc.co.uk/ouch/writers/tom shakespeare.shtml

Eunice Kennedy Shriver (1921–2009)

American activist and founder of the Special Olympics

Eunice Mary Kennedy Shriver was born on July 10, 1921, in Brookline, Massachusetts, to Joseph and Rose Kennedy. She was part of a power political family that included a brother, John, who became president of the United States, and two brothers, Robert and Edward, who became U.S. senators. Another sibling, Rosemary, was born with mild cognitive impairments that worsened after she underwent brain surgery. It was the inspiration of Rosemary that led Shriver to later found the Special Olympics.

Shriver attended Stanford University, where she was active in sports and received her bachelor's degree in sociology in 1942. After graduation, she worked for the U.S. State Department's Special War Problems Division. In 1950, she spent a year working in a women's prison in West Virginia, then moved to Chicago, where she worked for a Catholic social services organization. In 1953, Eunice Kennedy married Sargent Shriver, a career public servant, who served over the years as the first director of the Peace Corps and helped inaugurate Head Start, Vista, and many other government programs. They had five children.

In 1957, Eunice Kennedy Shriver helped establish the Joseph P. Kennedy Jr. Foundation, created to honor the memory of her eldest brother, Joseph, who died during World War II. Its mission was to prevent intellectual disabilities by finding the causes of cognitive impairments and to improve the lives and opportunities of those born with these impairments. When John F. Kennedy became president in 1961, Shriver worked with him to develop the Presidential Committee on Mental Retardation and establish the National Institute for Child Health and Human Development.

In 1968, Shriver established the organization for which she is best known, the Special Olympics. Inspired in part by her brother's Presidential Fitness Award, Shriver developed a similar training program and Olympic competition for disabled people. The first Special Olympics took place in Chicago in 1968, with 1,000 athletes from 26 states, who competed in swimming, track and field, and hockey. Shriver inspired the athletes with the Special Olympian's oath: "Let me win. But if I cannot win, let me be brave in the attempt." The participants, in turn, inspired Shriver. "Special Olympians and their families are challenging the common wisdom that says that only intellectual achievement is the measure of human life," she declared. "They have proved that the common wisdom is wrong. Special Olympians and their families are proof that the value of human life should be measured in many ways."

Today, more than three million athletes in 175 countries take part in the Special Olympics. With Shriver as their champion, these Special Olympians and their achievements have helped to change the attitudes of millions of people around the world about what people with intellectual and physical disabilities can do.

Shriver received many honorary degrees for her work on the Special Olympics, as well as the Presidential Medal of Freedom, the highest civilian honor in the country. *Sports Illustrated* named her its first Sportsman of the Year Legacy Award recipient in 2008, recognizing her as the founder of the Special Olympics and calling her "the single most important person to have advanced the rights and enriched the lives of people with intellectual disabilities." Eunice Kennedy Shriver died on August 11, 2009, in Hyannis Port, Massachusetts.

Further Reading

Eunice Kennedy Shriver. Retrieved from http://www.eunicekennedyshriver.org/bios/eks

Sandomir, R. (2009, August). The mother of the Special Olympics. *New York Times, 158,* B9.

Anita Silvers (1940–)

American academic and disability rights advocate

Anita Silvers was born in New York on November 1, 1940. She contracted polio at the age of nine and has used a wheelchair since that time. Silvers received her bachelor's degree from Sarah Lawrence College in 1962 and her doctoral degree in philosophy from Johns Hopkins University in 1967.

Silvers joined the faculty at San Francisco State University in 1967, where she is professor and chair of the Department of Philosophy and a nationally prominent advocate for disability rights. The focus of her research in disability studies includes ethics, bioethics, law, and public policy. Her research and writings have contributed to legal interpretations in cases involving the rights and ethical treatment of people with disabilities. One of her best-known works, *Disability. Difference. Discrimination: Formal Justice*, published in 1998, has been cited in court proceedings, and her work has also contributed to interpreting the Americans with Disabilities Act (ADA).

Silvers has also dealt with such current and controversial topics as physician-assisted suicide and genomic testing, and she has explored the concept of "normality" and the intolerance and social stigmas that people with disabilities confront in society and its institutions, including the legal and medical systems. One of Silvers's recent book projects addresses social contract theory for "outliers" and establishes inclusiveness as the primary value of justice.

Silvers has also published widely in other areas of philosophy, including aesthetics, social philosophy, and feminism. She was appointed by President Jimmy Carter to the National Council for the Humanities in 1980 and served as trustee of the American Society for Aesthetics. Silvers is also credited with advocating and developing critical thinking as an undergraduate subject, for promoting a high level of education in philosophy in non-doctoral institutions, and for consistently working to make the field of philosophy more welcoming to women, minorities, and people with disabilities. In addition to her academic research, Silvers has worked to make the campuses of California colleges more accessible to students with disabilities.

Silvers has received numerous awards for her scholarship and contributions to disability studies. She is a recipient of California's Distinguished Humanities Scholar Award, and in 1989 she received the first California Faculty Association's Equal Rights Award for her work in making higher education accessible to people with disabilities. In 2010, the American Philosophical Association awarded her the Quinn Prize, honoring her lifetime achievement in the field of philosophy.

Further Reading

Silvers, A., & Francis, L. (Eds.). (2000). *Americans with disabilities: Exploring implications of the law for individuals and institutions.* London, UK: Routledge. Retrieved from http://www.sfsu.edu/~phlsphr/?page=anita_silvers - articles

Silvers, A., & Stein, M. A. (2003). From *Plessy* (1896) and *Goesart* (1948) to *Cleburne* (1986) and *Garrett* (2001): A chill wind from the past blows equal protection away. In L. Krieger (Ed.), *Backlash against the ADA: Reinterpreting disability rights.* Ann Arbor, MI: University of Michigan Press.

Peter Singer (1946–)

Australian philosopher focusing on theoretical ethics with controversial views on the rights of people with disabilities

Peter Albert David Singer was born on July 6, 1946, in Melbourne, Australia. His parents were Cora and Ernest Singer, who had immigrated to Australia from Austria in 1938; Cora was a physician, and Ernest was an importer. Peter attended the University of Melbourne, earning his bachelor's degree in 1967 and his master's degree in 1969. He went on to earn his bachelor of philosophy degree from Oxford University in 1971.

Singer began his academic career at Oxford, where he was Radcliffe Lecturer at University College from 1971 to 1973. After serving as a visiting professor at New York University and La Trobe University, he joined the faculty at Monash University in 1977, where he held a variety of appointments, including professor and chair of the Department of Philosophy and co-director of the Institute for Ethics and Public Policy. In 1999, he became the Ira W. DeCamp Professor of Bioethics at Princeton University's Center for Human Values.

Singer is widely acknowledged to be one of the most brilliant—and controversial—philosophers of the modern era. He first came to the attention of the general public in 1975 with the publication of *Animal Liberation*, a book that is credited with launching the animal rights movement. Singer famously argued that the exploitive treatment of animals, in factory farms or for research, amounts to "speciesism" (prejudice in favor of the human species) and is indefensible.

Singer is also the author of several books on the issues of bioethics and the treatment of people with disabilities that have made him one of the most contentious figures in the disability studies community. In works like *Should the Baby Live? The Problem of Handicapped Infants* and *Rethinking Life and Death*, he insists that it is necessary to "recognize that the worth of human life varies." He claims that neither severely disabled infants nor cognitively disabled adults are "persons," because they lack self-awareness and rationality. Further, he believes that parents have the right to euthanize severely disabled infants, and he also supports the euthanization of people with lifelong cognitive disabilities and those who acquire severe cognitive disabilities.

Disability rights advocates representing groups as diverse as Not Dead Yet and the Disability Rights Education and Defense Fund have condemned Singer's work. Activists have protested his appointment at Princeton and his speeches in the United States and abroad, and they have critiqued his philosophy both in print and in person. Perhaps the best-known rejoinder to his work appeared in the *New York Times Magazine* in 2003, in a piece titled "Unspeakable Conversations" by the late disability activist Harriet McBryde Johnson, who debated Singer publicly and wrote about her experience for the magazine. Singer remains a highly influential and widely controversial figure in the disability studies community.

Further Reading

Borchert, D. (Ed.). (2006). Peter Singer. In *Encyclopedia of philosophy*. Farmington Hills, MI: Gale/Cengage Learning.

Schaler, J. A. (Ed.). (2009). *Peter Singer under fire: The moral iconoclast faces his critics*. Chicago, IL: Open Court.

Michael Stein (1963–)

American scholar, lawyer, and disability advocate

Michael Ashley Stein was born in 1963. He received his bachelor's degree in political science from New York University in 1985, his law degree from Harvard Law School in 1988, and his doctoral degree from Cambridge University in 1998.

After finishing law school, Stein worked as an attorney with the law firm of Sullivan & Cromwell in New York. He also served as president of the National Disabled Bar Association, as pro bono counsel for the Legal Aid Society's Juvenile Rights Division, and as counsel to the Environmental Division of the U.S. Department of Justice. Stein next worked a law clerk for U.S. Supreme Court Justice Samuel A. Alito Jr., when the judge sat on the Third Circuit Court of Appeals.

Stein is currently co-founder and executive director of the Harvard Law School Project on Disability, as well as the Cabell Professor at William & Mary Law School. According to its mission statement, the Harvard Law School Project on Disability "supports the development of disability civil society, informs innovative legislative and policy development, provides legal advice and human rights training to persons with disabilities, their representative organizations, non-governmental organizations, National Human Rights Institutions, and governments." Stein serves the project in various roles, as a teacher, researcher, policy maker, and advocate for people with disabilities.

Stein is recognized around the world for his work on behalf of disability rights. He helped to draft the United Nations Convention on the Rights of Persons with Disabilities, and he continues to serve as an advisor to UN organizations, such as UNICEF. He has worked as a consultant with international governments on disability laws and policies; serves on the board of the American Bar Association Commission on Mental and Physical Disability Law; and is a legal advisor to Rehabilitation International, Disabled Peoples' International, and the Special Olympics.

A prolific author, Stein has published professional papers in legal and disability journals and books. He has also received many fellowships and grants for his work on disability policy, including an American Council of Learned Societies' Andrew W. Mellon Faculty Fellowship, a Mark DeWolfe Howe Fund Grant, a National Endowment for the Humanities Summer Stipend, and a National Institute on Disability and Rehabilitation Research Merit Fellowship.

Further Reading

Stein, M. A. (2004). Same struggle, different difference: ADA accommodations as antidiscrimination. *University of Pennsylvania Law Review, 579.*

Stein, M. A., & Quinn, G. (2010). *The United Nations Convention on the Rights of Persons with Disabilities: A commentary.* Cambridge, UK: Cambridge University Press.

Henri-Jacques Stiker

French disability historian

Henri-Jacques Stiker's academic background is in philosophy and anthropology, disciplines he brings to bear in his groundbreaking work on the history of disability. Stiker is currently the director of research and a member of the faculty in the Department of the History and Civilization of Western Societies, University of Paris VII. He has published 12 volumes on various aspects of disabilities throughout history, examining the representations of disabilities in culture and in art, as well as the development of public policy and theories of disability. He is best known for his book *A History of Disability*, a much-praised volume that marked the first attempt to chronicle the history of disability from ancient Greece to the present day, encompassing cultures worldwide.

Stiker has said that he was motivated to explore disability history by meeting an individual with disabilities, and also by reading a book by the French theorist Michel Foucault on madness. That experience prompted him to explore the depiction of disability in the history and mythology of the Greeks, in the Bible, in the Christian art of the Middle Ages, and in the present era. Stiker examines the concepts of equality and sameness in history, and shows how those concepts gave rise to intolerance of people with disabilities because of their inherent "difference." He further explores how societal mores are revealed in the treatment of people with disabilities.

Stiker has continued his examination of historical perspectives on disability through studies of disability, poverty, and exclusion in 19th-century France, as well as the influence of politics, psychology, and public policy on attitudes toward people with disabilities as they have evolved in the modern era.

Further Reading

Interview with Henri-Jacques Stiker. (2008, Fall). *Disability History Newsletter.* Retrieved from http://www.dishist.org/news/fall08/DHA_Newsletter_V4I1.doc

Stiker, H.-J. (1999). *A history of disability* (W. Sayers, Trans.). Ann Arbor, MI: University of Michigan Press. (Original work published 1982)

Deborah Stone

American policy analyst, author, and advocate
for a "compassionate government"

Deborah Anne Stone decided to go into medicine at age 12, as she recalled in her book *The Samaritan's Dilemma*, because it seemed "the surest way to help people." She first attended the University of Michigan with that goal in mind. While there, however, she discovered a passion for democracy and government and decided that she could do even greater good by following that path. She received a bachelor's degree in Russian studies from Michigan in 1969, then moved on to the Massachusetts Institute of Technology (MIT), where she completed her Ph.D. in political science in 1976.

Stone began her academic career as an assistant professor at Duke University before joining the faculty at MIT in 1977 as an assistant professor of political science. From 1980 to 1986, she served as director of MIT's Public Policy Forum. In 1984, she published *The Disabled State*, a seminal work in which she compellingly identified gaps and contradictions in government policies toward, and even definitions of, disabilities. This book is still frequently cited in academic books and articles and is considered a classic in the field of disability policy. Having established herself as an expert in policy analysis, she joined the faculty of Brandeis University, where she held the position of David R. Pokross Chair in Law and Social Policy from 1986 to 1999.

In 1990, Stone was one of the founding editors of the *The American Prospect* magazine, and she also serves on the editorial board of the *Journal of Health Politics, Policy, and Law*. In 1997, she published the book for which she is best known in the policy analysis community, *Policy Paradox: The Art of Political Decision Making*. It has been translated into five languages and is used in classrooms worldwide. In 2002, it was recognized by the American Political Science Association with the Aaron Wildavsky Award for an enduring contribution to policy studies.

Stone is currently an independent scholar and a research professor with Dartmouth University's Department of Government. She is an internationally recognized authority in the field of government and social policy analysis and has written numerous articles and essays in the areas of health care and disability policy. In 1999, she was recognized by the

Robert Wood Johnson Foundation with an Investigator Award in Health Policy Research for Care, Work, and Citizenship.

In her most recent book, *The Samaritan's Dilemma*, published in 2008, Stone argues that policy makers in the United States have increasingly placed self-interest ahead of the moral value of helping people in need. Her call for a "compassionate government" that plays an active role in helping people received attention nationwide and led one reviewer to state that "Deborah Stone could be appointed our first Secretary of Compassion."

Further Reading

Deborah A. Stone. Retrieved from http://www.dartmouth.edu/~govt/faculty/stone.html

Stone, D. A. (1984). *The disabled state*. Philadelphia, PA: Temple University Press.

Stone, D. A. (2008). *The Samaritan's dilemma: Should government help your neighbor?* New York, NY: Nation Books.

Jacobus tenBroek (1911–1968)

American legal scholar and advocate for the blind

Jacobus tenBroek was born in 1911 in Alberta, Canada. At age 7, he was blinded in one eye by a bow-and-arrow accident. By age 14, he had lost the sight in his other eye and was completely blind. His family moved to Berkeley, California, so that Jacobus could enroll in the California School for the Blind. He also became involved with a local organization for the blind, which gave him a springboard for the activist life that he led from that point forward. He married Hazel Feldheym in 1937, and they had three children, Jacobus Zivnuska, Anna Carlotta, and Nicolaas Perry.

tenBroek attended the University of California, Berkeley, graduating with a bachelor's degree in history in 1934. He then went on to attend the university's prestigious Boalt Hall of Law, completing a master's degree in political science and a doctorate in law by 1940. During his college years, he and a group of friends formed the California Council of the Blind. In 1940, this organization became the National Federation of the Blind (NFB), which tenBroek served as president until 1961. tenBroek continued his academic career by attending Harvard Law School on a Brandeis Fellowship and then spending two years on the faculty of the

Chicago Law School. He returned to Berkeley in 1942, and by 1953, he was a full professor.

While tenBroek is primarily remembered for his work on behalf of blind people, he was a legal scholar who helped expand legal protection for people with disabilities of any kind, as well as people from racial and ethnic minority groups. His writings on the Fourteenth Amendment—especially his book *The Antislavery Origins of the Fourteenth Amendment*, published in 1951 (with a revised edition published in 1965 under the title *Equal Under Law*)—argued for inclusion of blind and disabled people under the Citizenship and Equal Protection clauses. His arguments were also cited frequently by the burgeoning civil rights movement of the 1950s, including by Thurgood Marshall when he successfully argued the *Brown v. Board of Education* case before the U.S. Supreme Court in 1954.

tenBroek was a prolific writer with several other books and dozens of articles and monographs to his credit. In 1950, he was assigned to the California State Board of Social Welfare by Governor Earl Warren, and he served as its chairman from 1960 to 1963. tenBroek was re-elected to his position as president of the NFB in 1966, and he remained there until he died of cancer on March 27, 1968. Under his leadership, the NFB became the foremost organization of blind people in the United States. In 2008, the NFB honored tenBroek's legacy by initiating the Jacobus tenBroek Disability Law Symposium, an annual conference that gathers key figures from around the country to assess the state of disability law in the United States.

Further Reading

Blake, L. A. (2006, May). Who was Jacobus tenBroek? *Braille Monitor, 49*(5). Retrieved from http://www.nfb.org/Images/nfb/Publications/bm/bm06/bm0605/bm060503.htm

Matson, F. W. (2005). *Blind justice: Jacobus tenBroek and the vision of equality*. Washington, DC: Library of Congress.

Wolf Wolfensberger (1934–)

*American academic who developed the theory
of social role valorization for people with disabilities*

Wolf Wolfensberger was born in 1934 in Mannheim, Germany, and immigrated to the United States in 1950. He earned his bachelor's degree from Siena College, his master's degree in clinical psychology from St. Louis University, and his doctoral degree in psychology, specializing in developmental disabilities and special education, from Peabody College.

In 1964, Wolfensberger joined the University of Nebraska Medical School's Nebraska Psychiatric Institute, where he worked as a research scientist in cognitive disabilities for seven years. In 1971, he was a visiting scholar at the National Institute on Mental Retardation in Toronto, Canada. Two years later, he joined the faculty of Syracuse University's Special Education Department, where he established the Training Institute on Human Services Planning, Leadership, and Change Agentry, which provides training to individuals who wish to be agents of change in human services. He is now a professor emeritus at Syracuse University and continues to direct the Training Institute.

Wolfensberger's research focuses on the ideologies, structures, and patterns of human service systems, particularly as they affect people with intellectual and developmental disabilities and their families. In the 1970s, he became an outspoken advocate for "normalization," or the idea that people with disabilities should be given access to educational and living conditions that were as close as possible to those of people without disabilities. In the 1990s, Wolfensberger developed the theory of social role valorization, which addresses the social devaluation of impaired and other vulnerable people in society, and seeks to increase the value, respect, and dignity accorded to people with disabilities. Wolfensberger's theories have proven to be of international importance, as governments outside of the United States adopted his ideas in their development of human service systems for people with disabilities.

Wolfensberger's scholarship includes more than 40 books as author or co-author, as well as more than 250 book chapters and professional papers. Among his books are *Changing Patterns in Residential Services for the Mentally Retarded* and *The Principle of Normalization*, both of which are considered primary texts in the field. His research is considered so significant that Syracuse University received a grant from the Annie E. Casey Foundation to organize his archives and books, which will eventually become a part of the University Library's Special Collections. In 1999, Wolfensberger was honored with the Century Award in Mental Retardation, which was presented by a consortium of organizations to 36 individuals who made the most significant impact in the fields of developmental disabilities and mental retardation in the 20th century.

Further Reading

Dr. Wolf Wolfensberger. Retrieved from http://www.srvip.org/about_wolfens berger.php

Sherrill, C. (2003, Summer). Normalization or valorization: Which should be our aim? *Palaestra, 19*(3), 56–58.

Irving Zola (1935–1994)

American sociologist, educator, author, and activist for disability rights

Irving Kenneth Zola was born on January 24, 1935, in Boston, Massachusetts, to Bernard and Betty Zola. At age 16, he contracted polio, and four years later, he was involved in an automobile accident. The combination of these two events left him permanently disabled, requiring braces on his leg and back. It also gave him a lifelong commitment to disability rights and a desire to redefine and better understand what it means to be "disabled."

Zola attended Harvard University, earning a bachelor's degree in 1956 and a Ph.D. in 1962. He stayed in the Boston area throughout his professional life. Zola started his career as a researcher at Boston State Hospital and Harvard in 1956, became a member of the counseling staff at Massachusetts General Hospital in 1959, and joined the faculty of Brandeis University in 1963. By 1971, he was a full professor at Brandeis and served as chair of the Department of Sociology from 1972 to 1974. He maintained his association with Brandeis for the rest of his life.

In 1972, Zola spent a week in the Het Dorp village for the disabled in the Netherlands. He returned as an outspoken advocate for disability rights with a new vision of how best to help the cause of people with disabilities. In 1976, he helped establish the Boston Self Help Center and served as its first executive director. In 1982, he was a founding member and first president of the Society for Disability Studies (SDS). He also became editor of the *Disability and Chronic Disease Newsletter* (renamed the *Disability Studies Quarterly* in 1986).

Zola wrote and contributed to a number of books and published many articles in professional journals. His best-known work is *Missing Pieces*, published in 1982, in which he recounts his personal experience at the Het Dorp village and how it impacted his life and thinking. The book offers a stark reminder that nearly all people will have to deal with chronic disability of some sort during their lifetimes. Zola passionately argues for an understanding of how attitudes in society and in the medical community toward disability—and even the words used to describe disabilities—serve to negatively impact the place of people with disabilities in their communities.

Zola died of a heart attack on December 1, 1994. The SDS recognized his lifetime contributions through its annual Irving K. Zola Award for Emerging Scholars in Disability Studies. A collection of his writings is maintained in the Samuel Gridley Howe Library in Waltham, Massachusetts.

Further Reading

Williams, G. (1996). Irving Kenneth Zola, (1935–1994): An appreciation. *Sociology of Health & Illness, 18*(1), 107–125.

Zola, I. K. (1982). *Missing pieces: A chronicle of living with a disability.* Philadelphia, PA: Temple University Press.

Five

Annotated Data, Statistics, Tables, and Graphs

Bruno Trezzini and Jerome Bickenbach

n this chapter, we collect statistics about disability relevant to disability ethics, law, and policy. The most important number for disability policy is *prevalence:* how many people with disabilities there are in the United States at any given moment. Prevalence is a crucial number for policy makers, who have to make two kinds of decisions about the needs and resources of sub-populations. Macro-allocation decisions are about the targeted population and the size of the overall budget required to cover needs. Micro-allocation decisions are about distributing this overall budget across the population for specified programs and policies. Obviously, micro-allocations depend on the prior macro-allocation, and this decision depends in turn on prevalence. Making allocation decisions, however, depends on yet another number, namely, *incidence:* the number of people who in the future will acquire disabilities, for example, through aging. Incidence depends on information about past and future trends (or longitudinal comparisons) and, of course, is difficult to be confident about.

Prevalence and incidence data are the basic epidemiological numbers, without which disability policy planning would be pure guesswork. These data are traditionally disaggregated by age, gender, race, and type of disability. The other kind of disability data we present here is information about people with disabilities as a socio-demographic group: education and employment rates, income levels, and poverty status. These data are presented in comparison with persons without disabilities (cross-sectional comparisons). We also present some of the available data on the application of the Americans with Disabilities Act of 1990 (ADA) as well as data on the two major Social Security programs, Supplemental Security Income (SSI) and Social Security Disability Insurance (SSDI). Although comparisons between the United States and other countries of the world, for both kinds of data, would be insightful, because of wide differences in how disability data are collected, these comparisons are extremely difficult to make with any confidence and are not presented here.

Before discussing these statistics, we need to say a word about the most important authoritative sources of disability data in the United States and introduce the reader to online sources that provide convenient access to disability data. Along the way we mention two challenges in collecting and interpreting such data. As is discussed in considerable detail in Chapter 2, these challenges have to do with the definition of disability.

Data Sources

Public surveys and administrative records are the two primary means for collecting disability-related data. Public surveys are either (a) large-scale surveys undertaken by federal agencies (e.g., decennial censuses) or (b) privately sponsored small-scale surveys with a topical focus. The former tend to be more comprehensive, but disability is not usually their main concern. Topical surveys, on the other hand, tend to be of limited sample size, and thus their estimates are less reliable and analyses at the state level, or for demographic subgroups, are not always possible. Yet, since they focus on disability, these smaller-scale surveys can include a more detailed array of relevant questions.

Data based on administrative records (e.g., SSDI records) are routinely collected in the course of running state and federal programs. Systematic data coverage can extend over long time periods, providing relatively complete longitudinal comparisons. However, since these data are based on specific eligibility criteria, the group of beneficiaries is usually not a perfect representation of the national population of persons with disabilities.

Disability Definition

The first major challenge in collecting, interpreting, and comparing data on disability lies in the fact that definitions of disability vary enormously, across survey instruments, in program eligibility criteria, and from one point in time to another. Depending on the disability definition and the actual wording of the questions used, surveys can come to different conclusions about prevalence, incidence, and the socio-demographic profile of disabled persons. Changing disability definitions also undermine longitudinal comparisons.

In recent years, though, there has been a convergence in how disability is understood and defined for survey purposes. There has been an awareness that the epidemiological numbers—prevalence and incidence—should be based on a very broad definition of disability, whereas the more restricted socio-demographic comparisons can use what we described in Chapter 2 as narrower, "fit for purpose" definitions. The statistician's requirements of validity (that the definition actually captures what you want to capture) and reliability (that two people using the same definition will come up with the same number) are challenges when definitions vary.

Reference Population

When a sub-population is surveyed, not every member of it can actually be contacted. Ensuring that the sampling strategy one uses is representative is a challenge, but one with which demographers are used to dealing. The other concern, though, is what population makes up the reference population, namely, the group of individuals who represent all persons in the group. Until very recently, all major federal surveys covered only the civilian, non-institutionalized population living in the United States. This reference group was thought to be sufficient, but recently, based on data collected as part of a federal survey in 2006, Brault (2008b) has argued that the characteristics of the institutionalized population of persons with disabilities is such that including them would have a substantial impact on our prevalence estimates. Also, Stapleton and She (2009) have criticized the neglect of institutionalized populations and have offered results based on the same underlying survey data as Brault. By the same token, most federal surveys use the working-age population—roughly 16 or 18 to 64— as their reference population. This, too, very likely underestimates overall population prevalence. Anyone interpreting or comparing published disability statistics should be aware of these standard limitations.

In what follows, we briefly describe the most important data sources for disability statistics in the United States (which are the sources of most of the statistics collected here in this chapter).

Federal Surveys

The four federal household surveys relevant to disability are administered by the U.S. Census Bureau (2010f): (a) the American Community Survey (ACS); (b) the Current Population Survey (CPS); (c) the Censuses 2000 and 2010; and (d) the Survey of Income and Program Participation (SIPP) (for further information about the surveys, see Cornell University, 2010a; U.S. Census Bureau, 2010e). Stapleton et al. (2009) give a more detailed overview of what they call the "national disability data system." The ACS and the CPS, because of their relative frequency and coverage, have become particularly popular as sources for disability-related statistics.

American Community Survey

The ACS is conducted every year and is designed to collect data similar to that in the decennial censuses but on a more frequent basis (U.S. Census Bureau, 2011). All age groups are covered, and in 2006 the ACS began to include people living in institutional and non-institutional group quarters as well. The sample size is about 2.9 million housing units and 200,000 people living in group quarters. Despite this, the sample sizes for group quarters are too small in many states to serve as reliable estimates. In order to increase the validity and reliability of the data collected on disabilities, the 2008 ACS changed the wording of its disability question, which made it impossible to compare prevalence numbers from previous years. The current disability definition includes the following six disability categories: hearing, visual, cognitive, ambulatory, self-care, and independent living (see Cornell University, 2010c; U.S. Census Bureau, 2010a). The "2008 Disability Status Report: United States" by Erickson et al. (2010), an important source of basic information, relies on the 2008 ACS data.

Current Population Survey

The CPS is conducted on a monthly basis and focuses on labor force and employment issues (U.S. Census Bureau, 2010c; U.S. Department of

Labor, 2010). Residents of 60,000 households are interviewed face-to-face or by telephone. The survey coverage includes the civilian non-institutional population of age 16 and older. Disability data are not available by state. Disability-related questions were originally collected only once a year in the CPS March Supplement. Since June 2008, similar questions to the ones used in the ACS were added to identify persons with a disability more reliably and on a monthly basis. This makes comparisons with previous years inadvisable. The inclusion of these new questions was also intended to provide an alternative to the question on employment limitations ("Item 62b—Does . . . have a health problem or a disability which prevents work or which limits the kind or amount of work?" U.S. Census Bureau, March 2010), which in the past has been popular with many researchers because it allows longitudinal comparisons due to its long-lasting inclusion in the CPS questionnaires. Arguably, though, the use of this question as a proxy for disability status leads to biases and questionable results, in particular with regard to the employment rate trend for disabled persons (see the employment data below). The Bureau of Labor Statistics publishes data from the CPS in the form of news releases and bulletins (U.S. Department of Labor, 2010).

Census 2000

Due to its universal coverage, the Census 2000 (U.S. Census Bureau, 2000) allows for geographically fine-grained analyses, even at the county level. Because of the large intervals between decennial censuses, however, the information becomes quickly dated. Two survey questions focused on disability, the first one asking respondents about vision, hearing, and ambulatory impairments, and the second one about learning, self-care, independent living, and employment limitations. Insights on disability based on the Census 2000 data were published in two official studies: "Disability Status: 2000" (Waldrop & Stern, 2003) and "Disability and American Families: 2000" (Wang, 2005).

Survey of Income and Program Participation

The SIPP (U.S. Census Bureau, 2009) does not usually include disability-related questions, except for those to establish whether a respondent is receiving payments from disability insurance programs. However, as part of the fifth wave of the 2004 SIPP panel, broader functional limitations and "activities of daily living" questions were asked. Based on these data, the Census Bureau published the "Americans With Disabilities: 2005" report (Brault, 2008a).

Social Security Administration Records

The Social Security Disability Insurance program (SSDI) was enacted in 1956 and has since paid cash benefits to eligible disabled persons (for detailed eligibility requirements, see U.S. Social Security Administration, 2009a). Drawn from the SSA's administrative records, extensive program and socio-demographic information about the recipients of such benefits is published in the Annual Statistical Report on the Social Security Disability Insurance Program (U.S. Social Security Administration, 2011b). Additional information on SSDI beneficiaries and payments can be found in the Annual Statistical Supplement to the Social Security Bulletin (U.S. Social Security Administration, 2011a). Some data on beneficiaries can also be retrieved online (U.S. Social Security Administration, 2009b).

Non-Governmental Topical Surveys

One of the better-known non-governmental surveys focusing on the lived experience of people with disabilities in the United States is the Harris Poll. Since 1986, when it was first commissioned by the Kessler Foundation and the National Organization on Disability, Harris Interactive has been tracking, at varying time intervals, ten key indicators of socioeconomic achievement and participation: (1) employment, (2) poverty, (3) education, (4) health care, (5) transportation, (6) socializing, (7) going to restaurants, (8) attendance at religious services, (9) political participation, and (10) satisfaction with life. In 2010, three additional items were included: (1) access to mental health services, (2) technology, (3) and financial situation. We present a summary of their findings below. Additional surveys focusing on employers were conducted in 1995 and 2010 (Harris Interactive, 2010b).

Online Data Retrieval

Official statistics are no longer disseminated only as hefty hard-copy reports. Electronic copies of these publications are increasingly available online. In addition, the underlying raw data files can often be downloaded from the Internet or accessed directly through online databases with convenient user interfaces. While online databases make it easy to search for and download data, however, they also have limitations in that they do not allow full flexibility in selecting data points and producing customized tabulations. More flexibility comes with raw data files. Yet, these require considerable experience in how to use them and so are of limited practical utility to non-experts. In this section, we present three online sources that facilitate retrieval of disability-related data: American FactFinder, DataFerrett, and the Employment and Disability Institute at Cornell University. Most of the data presented in this chapter can be retrieved using these tools.

American FactFinder

American FactFinder is the U.S. Census Bureau's most popular data access tool for the general public (U.S. Census Bureau, 2010b). Data from ACS and the Census 2000 can be conveniently accessed by searching through predefined tables and geographical maps (more specifically, disability data can be found in Census 2000 Summary File 3 [SF 3]–Sample Data, and Census 2000 Summary File 4 [SF 4]–Sample Data). A new and improved version of FactFinder became available in January 2011 (see http://factfinder2.census.gov).

DataFerrett

DataFerrett (U.S. Census Bureau, 2010d) is a data mining and extraction tool that provides convenient access to ACS, CPS, Census 2000, and SIPP data. Allowing data manipulations and the production of customized tables, it is somewhat more complex than American FactFinder. At the time of writing, DataFerrett is available only in beta version.

Employment and Disability Institute, Cornell University

One of the most user-friendly and comprehensive online databases currently available is maintained by the Employment and Disability Institute at Cornell University (Cornell University, 2010b). It allows access to ACS, CPS, and Census 2000 data. One inconvenience, however, is that longitudinal comparisons between persons with and without disabilities cannot be directly generated. Fortunately, such longitudinal comparative data can be found in a number of publications by the institute (see Bjelland et al., 2009; Houtenville et al., 2009).

FTP Download Sites

As mentioned above, access to raw data affords the user more liberty in defining the proper unit of analysis and the structure of tabulations, but it also requires more familiarity with data files management and statistical procedures such as survey weighting. There exist FTP download sites for all four federal surveys:

- ACS and Census 2000: http://www2.census.gov
- CPS: http://www.bls.census.gov/cps_ftp.html
- SIPP: http://www.sipp.census.gov/sipp_ftp.html#sipp

In what follows, we begin with the data relevant for estimates of the prevalence of disability before looking at data on dimensions of socio-demographic profiles. We then move on to data relevant to the application of the ADA and statistics on the two SSA disability programs, SSDI and SSI.

Prevalence of Disability

The prevalence of disability varies across different dimensions, such as geography, time, gender, age, and race. More importantly, disability is not at all a homogeneous category, in the sense that some impairments are more widespread than others, and as a result, some disabilities are more common than others. Since the actual impact on a person's life of a disability depends on the kind of impairments (mobility, sensory, and so on), on the degree or extent of the disability, and lastly on the environment in which the person lives, changes in prevalence numbers do not tell the whole story.

In general, the notion of the "prevalence of disability" is at the best of times a very rough indicator of actual need and resources. Indeed, both prevalence and incidence numbers are very rough indicators for this reason, so that anticipated demographic trends, such as an increasingly older population, may have a more profound policy impact than the changes in the "bottom line" numbers of prevalence and incidence might suggest. In real terms, as already mentioned, since prevalence is based on data from non-institutionalized populations, and since the institutional populations—for example, those in long-term care facilities—would have a very high prevalence rate, the estimates that follow are very much on the low side. The problem has been that institutionalized populations, when they are surveyed at all, are surveyed in terms of their needs, which can be very rough proxies for disability. What is urgently needed is a technical solution for bridging general population data with the differently collected and analyzed institutional data.

Prevalence Across States

The disability prevalence for the United States as a whole was estimated to be 12.1% in 2008. Puerto Rico, West Virginia, and Arkansas had the highest prevalence rates: 21.2%, 19.2%, and 17.6%, respectively. The lowest rates were registered in Utah (8.9%), Colorado (9.4%), and Minnesota (9.5%) (see Figure 1 and Table 1).

Figure 1   Disability Prevalence Rate Across States, All Ages, 2008 (in percent)

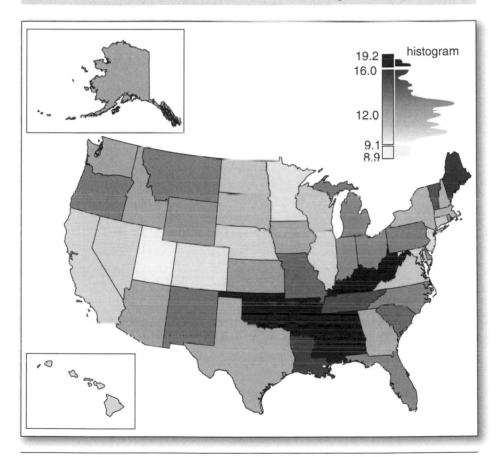

Source: Based on data in Erickson, W., Lee, C., & von Schrader, S. (2010, March 17). *Disability statistics from the 2008 American Community Survey (ACS).* Ithaca, NY: Cornell University Rehabilitation Research and Training Center on Disability Demographics and Statistics (StatsRRTC). Retrieved from http://www.disabilitystatistics.org

Note: Puerto Rico (21.2%) not included in map. The definition of disability used is based on six questions regarding serious hearing, visual, cognitive, ambulatory, self-care, or independent living difficulties. A person is coded as having a disability if he or she or a proxy respondent answers affirmatively for one or more of these six categories.

Table 1   The Percentage of People in the United States Who Reported a
Disability, 2008

Location	Estimate (%)	90% MOE	Location	Estimate (%)	90% MOE
United States	12.1	± 0.05	Montana	13.2	± 0.80
Alabama	16.1	± 0.39	Nebraska	10.3	± 0.53
Alaska	12.0	± 0.84	Nevada	10.1	± 0.43
Arizona	12.0	± 0.29	New Hampshire	11.3	± 0.64
Arkansas	17.6	± 0.52	New Jersey	9.8	± 0.23
California	10.2	± 0.11	New Mexico	13.6	± 0.56
Colorado	9.4	± 0.30	New York	11.2	± 0.16
Connecticut	10.4	± 0.38	North Carolina	13.0	± 0.26
Delaware	12.8	± 0.82	North Dakota	10.9	± 0.90
Dist. of Columbia	10.9	± 0.93	Ohio	13.1	± 0.23
Florida	12.8	± 0.18	Oklahoma	16.5	± 0.45
Georgia	11.7	± 0.24	Oregon	13.3	± 0.40
Hawaii	10.1	± 0.61	Pennsylvania	13.4	± 0.22
Idaho	12.0	± 0.61	Rhode Island	12.7	± 0.75
Illinois	10.3	± 0.20	South Carolina	13.9	± 0.38
Indiana	12.7	± 0.30	South Dakota	11.0	± 0.81
Iowa	11.8	± 0.40	Tennessee	14.8	± 0.33
Kansas	12.3	± 0.45	Texas	11.6	± 0.15

Location	Estimate (%)	90% MOE	Location	Estimate (%)	90% MOE
Kentucky	17.0	± 0.42	Utah	8.9	± 0.40
Louisiana	14.9	± 0.39	Vermont	14.4	± 0.95
Maine	15.7	± 0.73	Virginia	10.7	± 0.26
Maryland	10.2	± 0.29	Washington	12.0	± 0.29
Massachusetts	11.3	± 0.29	West Virginia	19.2	± 0.63
Michigan	13.2	± 0.25	Wisconsin	10.7	± 0.30
Minnesota	9.5	± 0.30	Wyoming	12.7	± 0.98
Mississippi	16.7	± 0.50	Puerto Rico	21.2	± 0.44
Missouri	14.1	± 0.33			

Source: Erickson, W., et al. (2010, March 17). *Disability statistics from the 2008 American Community Survey (ACS).* Ithaca, NY: Cornell University Rehabilitation Research and Training Center on Disability Demographics and Statistics (StatsRRTC). Retrieved from http://www .disabilitystatistics.org

Note: Survey population includes non-institutionalized, male or female, all ages, all races, regardless of ethnicity, with all education levels. Base population and sample size for United States: 299,852,800 and 2,949,415 respectively. MOE = margin of error. The definition of disability is based on six questions regarding serious hearing, visual, cognitive, ambulatory, self-care, or independent living difficulties. A person is coded as having a disability if he or she or a proxy respondent answers affirmatively for one or more of these six categories.

Prevalence Across Time

The prevalence rate showed only a very slight upward trend between 1981 and 2009, hovering around 8%. In 1989, it reached its lowest level of 7.3%, and it last reached its highest level of 8.4% in 2009. Note the difference between the generally lower prevalence levels in Figure 2 and Table 2 as compared to the national average in Table 1. The discrepancy is due to differences in the reference populations in terms of age and in the survey questions used to determine whether a respondent has a disability.

Figure 2   Disability Prevalence Rate, 1981–2009 (in percent)

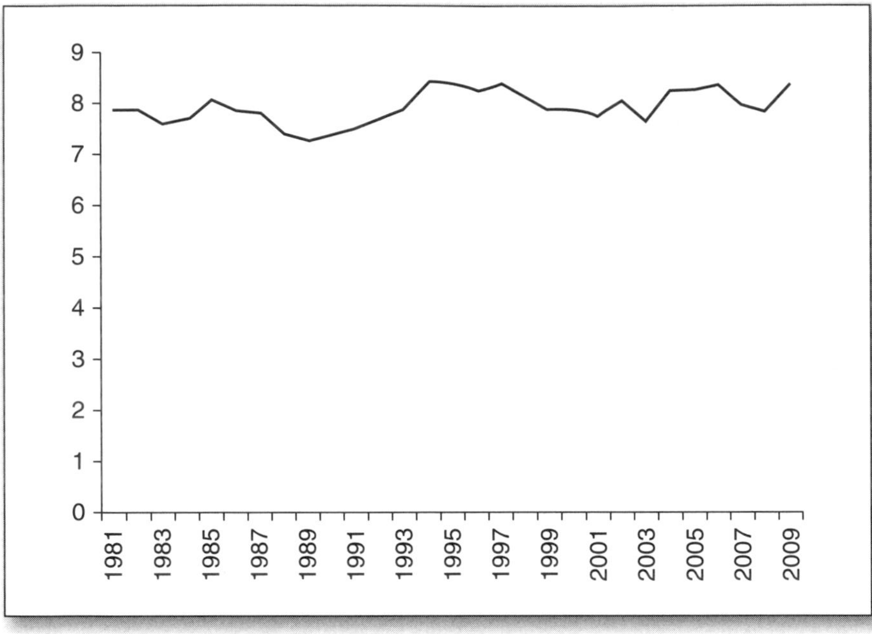

Source: Bjelland, M. J., Burkhauser, R. V., von Schrader, S., & Houtenville, A. J. (2009). *2009 progress report on the economic well-being of working-age people with disabilities* (p. 3). Ithaca, NY: Rehabilitation Research and Training Center on Employment Policy for Persons with Disabilities, Cornell University. Based on data from the 1981–2009 Annual Social and Economic Supplement to the Current Population Survey.

Note: The population with disabilities is identified using the work limitation question: "Does anyone in this household have a health problem or disability which prevents them from working or which limits the kind or amount of work they can do? [If so,] who is that? Anyone else?"

Table 2   Prevalence Rate, Standard Error, and Sample Size, by Disability Status and Year, 1981–2009 (in percent)

Year	Prevalence Rate	Standard Error	Sample Size
1981	7.9	0.11	98,196
1982	7.9	0.12	88,593

Year	Prevalence Rate	Standard Error	Sample Size
1983	7.6	0.11	89,277
1984	7.7	0.11	89,048
1985	8.1	0.11	89,656
1986	7.9	0.11	87,819
1987	7.8	0.11	86,783
1988	7.4	0.11	87,005
1989	7.3	0.12	80,683
1990	7.4	0.11	88,505
1991	7.5	0.11	88,658
1992	7.7	0.11	87,562
1993	7.9	0.11	86,835
1994	8.4	0.11	83,984
1995	8.4	0.11	83,606
1996	8.3	0.12	72,573
1997	8.4	0.12	73,606
1998	8.2	0.12	73,807
1999	7.9	0.12	74,400
2000	7.9	0.12	75,515
2001	7.8	0.08	73,029
2002	8.1	0.09	119,812
2003	7.7	0.08	119,994
2004	8.3	0.08	118,462

(Continued)

Table 2 (Continued)

Year	Prevalence Rate	Standard Error	Sample Size
2005	8.3	0.12	116,889
2006	8.4	0.12	116,219
2007	8.0	0.11	115,477
2008	7.9	0.11	115,617
2009	8.4	0.12	116,497

Source: Bjelland et al. (2009). *2009 progress report on the economic well-being of working-age people with disabilities* (p. 3). Ithaca, NY: Rehabilitation Research and Training Center on Employment Policy for Persons with Disabilities, Cornell University. Based on data from the 1981–2009 Annual Social and Economic Supplement to the Current Population Survey.

Note: The population with disabilities is identified using the work limitation question: "Does anyone in this household have a health problem or disability which prevents them from working or which limits the kind or amount of work they can do? [If so,] who is that? Anyone else?"

Prevalence Across Gender and Age

Across all ages, women show a slightly higher disability prevalence rate than men, 12.4% and 11.7%, respectively (see Figure 3 and Table 3). Overall, the prevalence pattern across age groups is similar for both genders. Not surprisingly, the prevalence rate increases drastically with age.

Prevalence Across Race

In 2008, the two groups Black or African American (14.3%) and Native American or Alaska Native (18.8%) showed prevalence rates that were higher than the national average of 12.1% (see Table 1 and Table 4). The Asian group (4.6%) had by far the lowest prevalence rate.

Prevalence Specified by Type of Disability

At 6.9%, ambulatory disability—serious difficulties in walking or climbing stairs—is the most prevalent disability in 2008, followed by independent living (5.5%) and cognitive (4.8%) disability (see Table 5).

Figure 3   Prevalence of Disability Among Non-Institutionalized People by Gender and Age Group in the United States, 2008 (in percent)

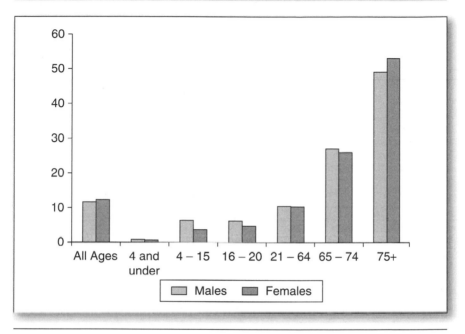

Source: Erickson, W., Lee, C., & von Schrader, S. (2010). *2008 disability status report: United States* (p. 26). Ithaca, NY: Cornell University Rehabilitation Research and Training Center on Disability Demographics and Statistics.

Note: Children aged 0 to 4 were asked only about visual and hearing disabilities, children aged 5 to 15 were not asked the "Independent Living Disability" question. 2008 ACS disability definition.

Table 3   Prevalence of Disability Among Non-Institutionalized People by Gender and Age Group in the United States, 2008

	%	MOE	Number	MOE	Base Pop.	Sample Size
Males						
All Ages	11.7	0.07	17,182,300	112,030	147,192,100	1,422,424
4 and under	0.8	3.29	88,800	8,290	10,702,800	91,486
4–15	6.4	0.14	1,454,400	33,480	22,658,100	218,391

(Continued)

Table 3 (Continued)

	%	MOE	Number	MOE	Base Pop.	Sample Size
16–20	6.3	0.20	712,200	23,450	11,297,600	102,575
21–64	10.5	0.09	9,100,900	82,680	86,569,500	813,909
65–74	27.1	0.41	2,486,200	43,690	9,157,800	113,020
75+	49.1	0.53	3,339,800	50,570	6,806,200	83,043
Females						
All Ages	12.4	0.07	18,986,900	117,400	152,660,700	1,526,991
4 and under	0.7	3.29	67,400	7,220	10,173,700	87,608
4–15	3.7	0.11	811,400	25,030	21,641,800	208,756
16–20	4.8	0.18	521,500	20,080	10,810,200	97,542
21–64	10.4	0.09	9,212,000	83,160	88,798,700	879,766
65–74	26.1	0.37	2,801,100	46,350	10,744,200	130,867
75+	53.1	0.43	5,573,500	65,080	10,492,300	122,452

Source: Erickson et al. (2010). *2008 disability status report: United States* (p. 26). Ithaca, NY: Cornell University Rehabilitation Research and Training Center on Disability Demographics and Statistics.

Note: Children aged 0 to 4 were asked only about visual and hearing disabilities, children aged 5 to 15 were not asked the "Independent Living Disability" question. 2008 ACS disability definition. MOE = margin of error.

Table 4   Prevalence of Disability Among Non-Institutionalized Working-Age People (Ages 21 to 64) by Race in the United States, 2008

Race	%	MOE	Number	MOE	Base Pop.	Sample Size
White	10.2	0.07	13,555,900	100,140	133,078,900	1,345,915
Black/African American	14.3	0.21	2,968,400	47,710	20,797,800	160,618
Native American or Alaska Native	18.8	0.92	260,900	14,210	1,386,100	14,552

Race	%	MOE	Number	MOE	Base Pop.	Sample Size
Asian	4.6	0.20	395,700	17,490	8,578,100	80,849
Some other race(s)	9.8	0.24	1,132,000	29,550	11,527,300	91,741

Source: Erickson et al. (2010). *2008 disability status report: United States* (p. 31). Ithaca, NY: Cornell University Rehabilitation Research and Training Center on Disability Demographics and Statistics.

Table 5   Prevalence of Disability Among Non-Institutionalized People of All Ages in the United States, 2008

Disability Type	%	MOE	Number	MOE	Base Pop.	Sample Size
Any disability	12.1	0.05	36,169,200	157,070	299,852,800	2,949,415
Visual	2.3	0.02	6,826,400	71,880	299,852,800	2,949,415
Hearing	3.5	0.03	10,393,100	88,160	299,852,800	2,949,415
Ambulatory	6.9	0.04	19,203,700	118,020	278,976,400	2,770,321
Cognitive	4.8	0.04	13,462,900	99,810	278,976,400	2,770,321
Self-care	2.6	0.03	7,195,600	73,750	278,976,400	2,770,321
Independent living	5.5	0.04	13,179,300	98,800	238,826,000	2,384,789

Source: Erickson et al. (2010). *2008 disability status report: United States* (p. 11). Ithaca, NY: Cornell University Rehabilitation Research and Training Center on Disability Demographics and Statistics.

Note: Children under the age of 5 were asked only about vision and hearing disabilities. The independent living disability question was asked only of persons aged 16 years and older. MOE = margin of error.

Socio-Demographic Profiles and Gaps

Socio-demographic profiles of people with disabilities are more instructive for policy purposes when they contrast the situation for people with disabilities with that of people without disabilities, as well as present that information longitudinally across time. A cross-sectional approach makes it possible to pinpoint the gaps that need to be filled and, with longitudinal comparisons, determine whether those gaps have been widening or clos-ing over time. This sort of information is essential for monitoring the implementation of policy initiatives: Has the policy worked or not? And if so, by how much? With good information about the effectiveness, or lack of effectiveness, of policy, it is possible to further refine the policy objec-tives, or to look for better policy mechanisms to achieve the objectives, or both. Without these data, it is mostly guesswork.

For examples of the kind of socio-demographic profile data that are use-ful for policy analysis, we look at the major areas of participation for which data is standardly collected, for persons with disabilities and the general population, namely, education, employment, income, and poverty rates.

Education

Figure 4 and Table 6 provide some fairly current educational attain-ment data in which it is possible to compare persons with disabilities with the general population. We can see that far fewer persons with dis-abilities obtained a bachelor's degree or higher (14%) as compared to nondisabled persons (32%), and conversely that many more persons with disabilities (26% versus 11%) did not obtain a high school diploma. However, these data, by themselves, do not allow one to make infer-ences about cause and effect (e.g., whether persons with disabilities are less likely to attain higher education or whether persons with low edu-cation are more likely to sustain a disability).

It might be thought that, since all respondents in this set of data were aged 25 years and over, the gaps in education might partly be due to the fact that older people are over-represented in the group of persons with disabilities and that older generations tend to have a lower educational attainment than younger ones. Data for 2005 in Haugen (2009, p. 267) based only on the age group 18 to 34 suggests that this effect, although present, does not make a big difference in the overall picture.

Employment

In 2009, the employment rate of men with disabilities aged 16 to 64 was much lower than that for men without disabilities, namely, 31.7% as com-pared to 75.2% (see Table 7). For women of the same age group the propor-tions were similar: 27.7% and 66.3%, respectively. The gap in unemployment rates was less pronounced between persons with and without a disability. The rate for men with disabilities aged 16 to 64 was 16.4% and for women

Figure 4   Educational Attainment of the Civilian Non-Institutionalized
Population 25 Years and Over by Disability Status, 2009 Annual
Average

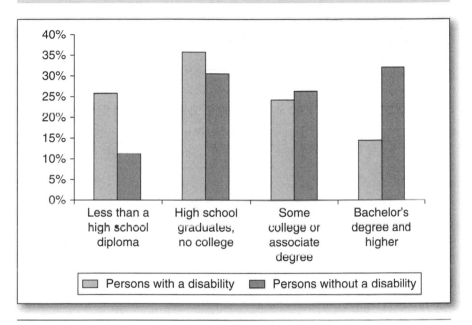

Source: U.S. Department of Labor, Bureau of Labor Statistics. (2010). *Economic news release.*
Retrieved from http://www.bls.gov/news.release/disabl.t01.htm

Table 6   Educational Attainment of the Civilian Non-Institutionalized
Population 25 Years and Over by Disability Status, 2009 Annual
Average (numbers in thousands)

Educational Attainment	Persons With a Disability		Persons Without a Disability	
Total, 25 years and over	25,591	100%	172,642	100%
Less than a high school diploma	6,558	26%	19,571	11%
High school graduates, no college (1)	9,160	36%	52,309	30%

(Continued)

Table 6 (Continued)

Educational Attainment	Persons With a Disability		Persons Without a Disability	
Some college or associate degree	6,174	24%	45,552	26%
Bachelor's degree and higher (2)	3,700	14%	55,210	32%

Source: U.S. Department of Labor, Bureau of Labor Statistics. (2010). *Economic news release.* Retrieved from http://www.bls.gov/news.release/disabl.t01.htm

Notes: (1) Includes persons with a high school diploma or equivalent. (2) Includes persons with bachelor's, master's, professional, and doctoral degrees.

14.7%. The figures for men and women without disabilities were 10.2% and 7.9%, respectively. The most likely explanation for this is that persons with disabilities who are out of the labor force entirely (who, for example, have given up looking for suitable and accessible employment, or who are eligible for SSDI or other state programming and have left the labor force) are not counted as unemployed or seeking work. This is the standard approach for collecting this sort of data, and it applies to people without disabilities as well. The approach has long been objected to because of the distortion it causes, but it is unlikely to change.

Table 7   Employment Status of the Civilian Population by Sex, Age, and Disability Status, Annual Average, 2009 (numbers in thousands)

Employment Status, Sex, and Age	Persons With a Disability	Persons With No Disability
Total, 16 years and over		
Civilian non-institutional population	26,981	208,820
Civilian labor force	6,050	148,092
Participation rate (%)	*22.4*	*70.9*
Employed	5,174	134,703

Employment Status, Sex, and Age	Persons With a Disability	Persons With No Disability
Employment-population ratio (%)	19.2	64.5
Unemployed	876	13,389
Unemployment rate (%)	14.5	9.0
Not in labor force	20,931	60,728
Men, 16 to 64 years		
Civilian labor force	2,745	75,781
Participation rate (%)	37.9	83.7
Employed	2,294	68,018
Employment-population ratio (%)	31.7	75.2
Unemployed	451	7,762
Unemployment rate (%)	16.4	10.2
Not in labor force	4,489	14,707
Women, 16 to 64 years		
Civilian labor force	2,475	66,607
Participation rate (%)	32.5	72.0
Employed	2,112	61,340
Employment-population ratio (%)	27.7	66.3
Unemployed	364	5,267
Unemployment rate (%)	14.7	7.9
Not in labor force	5,136	25,863
Both sexes, 65 years and over		
Civilian labor force	830	5,705
Participation rate (%)	6.8	22.1

(Continued)

Table 7 (Continued)

Employment Status, Sex, and Age	Persons With a Disability	Persons With No Disability
Employed	768	5,345
Employment-population ratio (%)	6.3	20.7
Unemployed	61	359
Unemployment rate (%)	7.4	6.3
Not in labor force	11,306	20,158

Source: U.S. Department of Labor, Bureau of Labor Statistics. (2010). *Data retrieval: Labor force statistics (CPS).* Retrieved from http://www.bls.gov/webapps/legacy/cpsatab6.htm

Note: For the Bureau of Labor Statistics, a person with a disability is defined as someone with at least one of the following conditions: deafness or serious difficulty hearing; blind or serious difficulty seeing, even when wearing glasses; serious difficulty concentrating, remembering, or making decisions because of a physical, mental, or emotional condition; serious difficulty walking or climbing stairs; difficulty dressing or bathing; or difficulty doing errands alone, such as visiting a doctor's office or shopping, because of a physical, mental, or emotional condition.

Figure 5 and Table 8 show how the employment rate of persons with disabilities has been declining since its peak in 1989, when it reached 28.8%. Until that year, and even up to 1993, the rates for disabled and nondisabled persons were moving more or less in tandem. However, the already large gap between the two groups started widening due to the divergent increase of the employment rate for nondisabled persons.

The validity of the CPS data has been questioned due to the less-than-perfect determination of who is disabled. Hale (2001, p. 39), for instance, states that "neither the work limitation nor the income questions were designed to identify the population with disabilities, nor were they tested to determine if they do so." However, Bjelland et al. (2009) argue that while the employment levels might be too low, the trends are still valid. With the recent introduction of six questions aimed at directly identifying respondents with specific disabilities, validity might become less of an issue, although it will not permit comparisons with previous years.

As we discuss in Chapter 2, the impact of the Americans with Disabilities Act of 1990 on the employment of persons with disabilities has remained an

Figure 5   Employment Rate, by Disability Status and Year, March 1981–2009 (in percent)

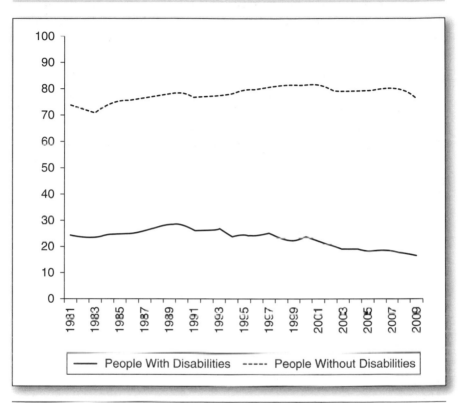

Source: Calculations by the Employment Policy Rehabilitation Research and Training Center (EP-RRTC) using the March Current Population Survey, 1981–2009; based on 1981–2009 Annual Social and Economic Supplement to the Current Population Survey. Bjelland et al. (2009). *2009 progress report on the economic well being of working-age people with disabilities* (p. 5). Ithaca, NY: Rehabilitation Research and Training Center on Employment Policy for Persons with Disabilities, Cornell University.

Note: The population with disabilities is identified using the work limitation question: "Does anyone in this household have a health problem or disability which prevents them from working or which limits the kind or amount of work they can do? [If so,] who is that? Anyone else?"

ongoing, contentious issue (see Bagenstos, 2004; Stapleton & Burkhauser, 2003). Whether the act has had a negative, positive, or no effect at all on employment of persons with disabilities has been hotly debated. What evidence there is seems to suggest that the ADA has had an inconsequential, rather than a negative effect and that the decreasing rate of employment of people with disabilities is more likely due to the 1990 economic recession and the ensuing expansion of the SSDI (Bagenstos, 2004, p. 22; Goodman & Waidmann, 2003). Yet, the question remains difficult, if not impossible, to resolve since it would require a detailed study not only of employer behavior but also of employer intention, because there need be no overt evidence of the tendency of employers to avoid hiring people with disabilities on the grounds of, for example, fear of legal actions based on discrimination if the workplace is not accessible. Although a majority of employers when asked state that the ADA had no positive or negative effect on their company (Harris Interactive, 2010b, p. 12), still, potential employers might be inclined to give "politically correct" responses to questions to hide their true feelings.

Table 8   Employment Rate, Standard Error, and Sample Size, by Disability Status and Year, March 1981–2009

Year	People With Disabilities			People Without Disabilities		
	Employment Rate	Standard Error	Sample Size	Employment Rate	Standard Error	Sample Size
1981	24.4	0.62	7,708	73.9	0.19	90,488
1982	23.8	0.65	7,005	72.5	0.20	81,588
1983	23.5	0.65	6,835	71.3	0.20	82,442
1984	24.8	0.66	6,825	74.0	0.19	82,223
1985	25.1	0.64	6,990	75.3	0.19	82,666
1986	25.3	0.64	6,680	75.5	0.19	81,139
1987	26.3	0.65	6,526	76.5	0.18	80,257
1988	27.9	0.68	6,300	77.2	0.18	80,705
1989	28.8	0.74	5,858	78.2	0.19	74,825
1990	28.4	0.70	6,448	78.4	0.18	82,057
1991	26.6	0.68	6,463	77.1	0.18	82,195
1992	26.5	0.66	6,577	77.2	0.18	80,985

	People With Disabilities			People Without Disabilities		
Year	Employment Rate	Standard Error	Sample Size	Employment Rate	Standard Error	Sample Size
1993	27.2	0.65	6,684	77.4	0.18	80,151
1994	23.9	0.60	6,775	78.3	0.18	77,209
1995	24.6	0.61	6,755	79.6	0.17	76,851
1996	24.4	0.67	5,892	79.7	0.19	66,681
1997	25.4	0.67	6,082	80.7	0.18	67,524
1998	23.3	0.65	5,929	81.3	0.18	67,878
1999	22.3	0.65	5,772	81.4	0.18	68,628
2000	24.1	0.66	5,934	81.7	0.17	69,581
2001	22.1	0.47	5,691	81.6	0.13	67,338
2002	20.8	0.44	9,070	79.9	0.13	110,742
2003	19.3	0.44	8,971	79.1	0.13	111,023
2004	19.2	0.42	9,334	79.1	0.13	109,128
2005	18.6	0.57	9,194	79.5	0.18	107,695
2006	18.9	0.57	9,193	80.1	0.18	107,026
2007	18.7	0.58	8,649	80.3	0.17	106,828
2008	17.7	0.57	8,662	79.7	0.18	106,955
2009	16.8	0.54	9,106	76.5	0.18	107,391

Source: Calculations by the Employment Policy Rehabilitation Research and Training Center (EP-RRTC) using the March Current Population Survey, 1981–2006; based on 1981–2009 Annual Social and Economic Supplement to the Current Population Survey. Bjelland et al. (2009). *2009 progress report on the economic well-being of working-age people with disabilities* (p. 5). Ithaca, NY: Rehabilitation Research and Training Center on Employment Policy for Persons with Disabilities, Cornell University.

Note: The population with disabilities is identified using the work limitation question: "Does anyone in this household have a health problem or disability which prevents them from working or which limits the kind or amount of work they can do? [If so,] who is that? Anyone else?"

Income Level

While in real terms the median household income of disabled people has stayed virtually unchanged between 1980 ($31,991) and 2008 ($32,161), the income for households without people with disabilities has grown markedly from $52,281 to $60,946 (see Figure 6 and Table 9).

Figure 6   Median Household Income, by Disability Status and Year, 1980–2008 (in constant 2008 dollars)

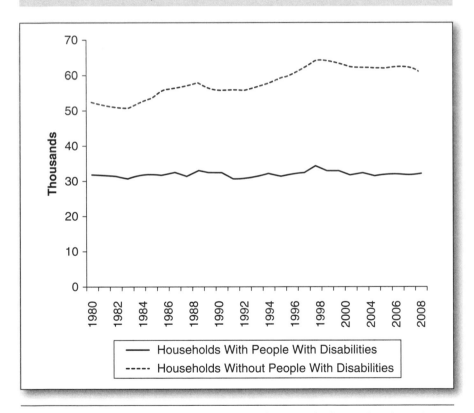

Source: 1981–2009 Annual Social and Economic Supplement to the Current Population Survey. Bjelland et al. (2009). *2009 progress report on the economic well-being of working-age people with disabilities* (p. 11). Ithaca, NY: Rehabilitation Research and Training Center on Employment Policy for Persons with Disabilities, Cornell University.

Note: The population with disabilities is identified using the work limitation question: "Does anyone in this household have a health problem or disability which prevents them from working or which limits the kind or amount of work they can do? [If so,] who is that? Anyone else?"

Table 9   Median Household Income, Standard Error, and Sample Size, by Disability Status and Year, 1980–2008 (in constant 2008 dollars)

Year	Households With People With Disabilities			Households Without People With Disabilities		
	Median Household Income	Standard Error	Sample Size	Median Household Income	Standard Error	Sample Size
1980	31,911	319	7,354	52,281	137	47,707
1981	31,606	319	6,645	51,471	148	42,973
1982	31,491	322	6,515	50,898	146	43,046
1983	30,919	320	6,507	50,820	149	43,095
1984	31,535	319	6,655	52,345	153	43,444
1985	32,097	336	6,337	53,458	155	42,854
1986	31,766	336	6,222	55,964	159	42,456
1987	32,664	349	6,016	56,388	161	43,041
1988	31,480	368	5,615	56,951	174	40,187
1989	33,028	371	6,146	57,986	168	43,682
1990	32,418	349	6,171	56,213	163	43,712
1991	32,422	335	6,213	55,820	163	42,943
1992	30,676	333	6,358	56,005	165	42,455
1993	30,813	300	6,429	55,807	169	40,799
1994	31,376	327	6,431	56,854	170	40,776
1995	32,188	358	5,554	57,804	186	35,645
1996	31,429	354	5,697	59,236	188	36,031
1997	32,102	375	5,589	60,190	193	36,462
1998	32,485	385	5,422	62,290	198	36,886
1999	34,455	391	5,607	64,369	205	37,010

(Continued)

Table 9 (Continued)

Year	Households With People With Disabilities			Households Without People With Disabilities		
	Median Household Income	Standard Error	Sample Size	Median Household Income	Standard Error	Sample Size
2000	33,065	278	5,327	64,035	146	36,177
2001	33,094	270	8,480	63,258	146	59,182
2002	31,803	265	8,372	62,324	143	59,371
2003	32,362	264	8,636	62,141	147	58,095
2004	31,560	355	8,564	62,009	202	57,361
2005	31,971	345	8,588	61,801	202	56,983
2006	32,061	367	8,158	62,544	205	56,939
2007	31,783	370	8,114	62,315	204	57,360
2008	32,161	338	8,517	60,946	199	57,125

Source: 1981–2009 Annual Social and Economic Supplement to the Current Population Survey. Bjelland et al. (2009). *2009 progress report on the economic well-being of working-age people with disabilities* (p. 11). Ithaca, NY: Rehabilitation Research and Training Center on Employment Policy for Persons with Disabilities, Cornell University.

Note: The population with disabilities is identified using the work limitation question: "Does anyone in this household have a health problem or disability which prevents them from working or which limits the kind or amount of work they can do? [If so,] who is that? Anyone else?"

Poverty Rate

The poverty rate for people without disabilities saw a slight decrease between 1980 (8.6%) and 2000 (7.4%), but then started to rise again and reached 9.4% in 2008 (see Figure 7 and Table 10). People with disabilities, on the other hand, showed a roughly three times higher poverty rate in 1980 (24.8%), which increased in the early 1990s, reaching its highest level of 30.1% in 1993. It then fell back to mid-1980s levels by 1999 (26.4%), only to rise again to 28.2% in 2008.

Figure 7   Poverty Rate by Disability Status and Year, 1980–2008 (in percent)

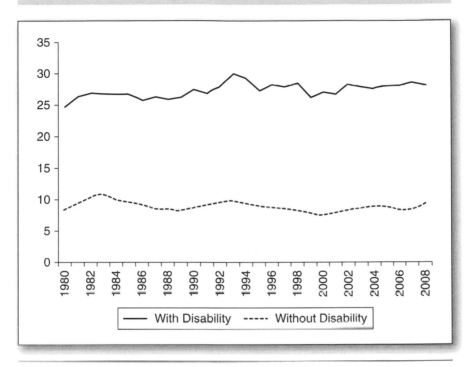

Source: 1981–2009 Annual Social and Economic Supplement to the Current Population Survey. Bjelland et al. (2009). *2009 progress report on the economic well-being of working-age people with disabilities* (p. 9). Ithaca, NY: Rehabilitation Research and Training Center on Employment Policy for Persons with Disabilities, Cornell University.

Note: The population with disabilities is identified using the work limitation question: "Does anyone in this household have a health problem or disability which prevents them from working or which limits the kind or amount of work they can do? [If so,] who is that? Anyone else?"

Trends and Gaps From the Harris Interactive Data

Harris Interactive uses 13 indicators for a variety of life domains of people with disabilities, including employment (see Table 11). Based on the data collected, the declining number of respondents who have not graduated from high school is the most lasting improvement. Levels of other forms of social participation have stayed relatively constant, and general life satisfaction has remained stable over the years as well. The

Table 10   Poverty Rate, Standard Error, and Sample Size, by Disability Status and Year, 1980–2008

Year	People With Disabilities			People Without Disabilities		
	Poverty Rate	Standard Error	Sample Size	Poverty Rate	Standard Error	Sample Size
1980	24.8	0.62	7,951	8.6	0.12	88,544
1981	26.3	0.66	7,270	9.5	0.13	79,760
1982	27.0	0.67	7,053	10.6	0.14	80,779
1983	26.8	0.66	7,079	10.9	0.14	80,621
1984	26.8	0.64	7,259	10.1	0.13	81,224
1985	26.8	0.64	6,901	9.7	0.13	79,859
1986	25.8	0.64	6,780	9.3	0.13	79,202
1987	26.2	0.65	6,518	8.7	0.12	79,731
1988	25.9	0.71	6,074	8.6	0.13	74,016
1989	26.2	0.67	6,673	8.3	0.12	81,121
1990	27.5	0.67	6,673	8.8	0.12	81,172
1991	27.0	0.66	6,748	9.3	0.13	79,963
1992	28.1	0.65	6,873	9.6	0.13	79,191
1993	30.1	0.64	6,999	10.0	0.13	76,328
1994	29.4	0.63	6,977	9.5	0.13	76,048
1995	27.3	0.68	6,049	9.1	0.13	66,013
1996	28.3	0.68	6,227	9.0	0.13	66,731
1997	27.9	0.69	6,056	8.6	0.13	67,181
1998	28.5	0.70	5,891	8.3	0.13	67,723
1999	26.4	0.67	6,091	7.8	0.12	68,763
2000	27.2	0.50	5,811	7.4	0.09	66,581

	People With Disabilities			People Without Disabilities		
Year	Poverty Rate	Standard Error	Sample Size	Poverty Rate	Standard Error	Sample Size
2001	26.8	0.48	9,281	7.9	0.09	109,400
2002	28.3	0.50	9,144	8.4	0.09	109,676
2003	28.0	0.47	9,524	8.7	0.09	107,857
2004	27.7	0.65	9,400	9.0	0.13	106,483
2005	28.0	0.65	9,413	8.8	0.13	105,780
2006	28.0	0.66	8,870	8.5	0.12	105,685
2007	28.6	0.67	8,866	8.6	0.12	105,977
2008	28.2	0.64	9,334	9.4	0.13	106,443

Source: 1981–2009 Annual Social and Economic Supplement to the Current Population Survey. Bjelland et al. (2009). *2009 progress report on the economic well-being of working-age people with disabilities* (p. 9). Ithaca, NY: Rehabilitation Research and Training Center on Employment Policy for Persons with Disabilities, Cornell University.

Note: The population with disabilities is identified using the work limitation question: "Does anyone in this household have a health problem or disability which prevents them from working or which limits the kind or amount of work they can do? [If so,] who is that? Anyone else?"

most prominent deterioration between 2004 and 2010 is found in the percentage of respondents who were working either full- or part-time, which dropped from 35% to 21%.

It is useful to look at the gaps between persons with disabilities and those without and at how they have changed over time. While the largest gap still exists in employment, according to the Harris Interactive data, the spread has narrowed somewhat over the years (see Table 12). In 1998, the difference in employment rates was 50 percentage points; in 2010, it fell to 38. In 2010, large gaps remain in the domains of household income, transportation, restaurant visits, and life satisfaction. Of the three newly introduced indicators in 2010, Internet access shows the largest gap, pointing to an existing "digital divide." However, age is an important confounding factor here. The data also show that a much larger proportion of people with disabilities are struggling to get by.

Table 11 Trends in Key "Indicators" for People With Disabilities, 1986–2010 (in percent)

	2010	2004	2000	1998	1994	1986
Works either full- or part-time (18-64)	21	35	32	29	31	34
Annual household income $15,000 or less*	34	26	29	34	40	51
Has not graduated from high school*	17	21	22	20	24	39
Did not get needed care on at least one occasion in past year*	19	18	19	21	18	n/a
Inadequate transportation considered a problem*	34	30	30	30	n/a	n/a
Socializes with close friends, relatives, or neighbors at least twice a month	79	79	81	82	81	n/a
Goes to a restaurant at least twice a month	48	56	56	51	50	48
Goes to church, synagogue, or any other place of worship at least once a month	50	49	47	54	48	55
Voter turnout in the presidential election**	59 (2008)	52	41	33 (1996)	45 (1992)	n/a
Very satisfied with life in general	34	34	33	33	35	39

	2010	2004	2000	1998	1994	1986
Did not get help from mental health professional on at least one occasion in past year *	7	n/a	n/a	n/a	n/a	n/a
Uses a computer/electronic device to access the Internet	54	n/a	n/a	n/a	n/a	n/a
Struggling to get by or living paycheck to paycheck *	58	n/a	n/a	n/a	n/a	n/a
Sample size	1,001	1,267	997	989	1003	981

Source: Harris Interactive. (2010a). *The Kessler Foundation/National Organization on Disability 2010 survey of Americans with disabilities* (p. 21). New York, NY: Kessler Foundation and National Organization on Disability.

Note: *These variables are "negative" in that a higher score indicates more of a disadvantage. **2008 Harris Poll, selected presidential election years. (Some data inconsistencies in the table corrected based on information on pp. 109 and 155; n/a = not available.)

Table 12   Trends in Gaps Between People With and Without a Disability for "Indicator" Measures, 1986–2010 (percentage points)

	2010	2004	2000	1998	1994	1986
Works either full- or part-time (age 18–64)	38	43	49	50	n/a	n/a
Annual household income $15,000 or less	19	17	19	22	22	22
Has not graduated from high school	6	10	13	11	12	24

(Continued)

Table 12 (Continued)

	2010	2004	2000	1998	1994	1986
Did not get needed care on at least one occasion in past year	9	11	13	10	5	n/a
Inadequate transportation considered a problem	18	17	20	13	n/a	n/a
Socializes with close friends, relatives, or neighbors at least twice a month	11	10	11	n/a	n/a	n/a
Goes to a restaurant at least twice a month	27	16	25	n/a	n/a	25
Goes to church, synagogue, or any other place of worship at least once a month	7	8	18	3	10	11
Voter turnout in the presidential election*	0 (2008)	4	11	17 (1996)	11 (1992)	n/a
Very satisfied with life in general	27	27	34	28	20	11
Did not get help from mental health professional on at least one occasion in past year	4	n/a	n/a	n/a	n/a	n/a

	2010	2004	2000	1998	1994	1986
Uses a computer/ electronic device to access the Internet	31	n/a	n/a	n/a	n/a	n/a
Struggling to get by or living paycheck to paycheck	24	n/a	n/a	n/a	n/a	n/a

Source: Harris Interactive. (2010a). *The Kessler Foundation/National Organization on Disability 2010 survey of Americans with disabilities* (p. 24). New York, NY: Kessler Foundation and National Organization on Disability.

Note: *Harris Poll, selected presidential election years. (n/a = not available.)

Statistics Related to the ADA

The prominent role of the Americans with Disabilities Act of 1990 and the ADA Amendments Act of 2008 in U.S. disability law has been discussed at length in previous chapters. Here we focus on administrative and legal outcomes of workplace discrimination complaints grounded in the ADA, as well as results of a survey about the perceived importance of the ADA for people with disabilities.

Equal Employment Opportunity Commission Charges

The Equal Employment Opportunity Commission (EEOC) enforces laws against workplace discrimination in Title I of the ADA. The EEOC was set up in 1965 under the Civil Rights Act of 1964, and its mandate was extended first to the Rehabilitation Act of 1973 and then to the ADA and finally to the ADA Amendments Act. The commission has the authority to investigate charges of discrimination in employment under the seven federal acts that prohibit discrimination on various grounds. If the commission finds that discrimination has occurred, it is required first to try to settle the complaint, and only if it fails to do so does it have the authority to file a lawsuit in its name. The commission also has the influential, although often controversial, mandate to issue interpretations of the law as guidance for courts. Throughout the judicial "backlash" period (see Chapter 2) when courts, from the Supreme Court down, were substantially restricting the scope of the ADA, the EEOC vigorously objected to these judicial pronouncements. These efforts were unsuccessful and ultimately the ADA Amendments Act of 2008 was required.

Figure 8 Americans with Disabilities Act of 1990 Charges, Fiscal Year 1992–Fiscal Year 2009

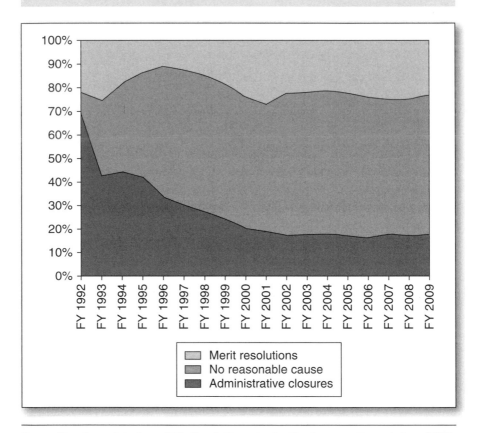

Source: Based on data from U.S. Equal Opportunity Employment Commission. (2010). *Americans with Disabilities Act of 1990 (ADA) charges FY 1997–FY 2010,* retrieved from http:// www.eeoc.gov/eeoc/statistics/enforcement/ada-charges.cfm, and *Americans with Disabilities Act of 1990 (ADA) charges FY 1992–FY 1996,* retrieved from http://www.eeoc.gov/eeoc/statistics/enforcement/ada-charges-a.cfm

Note: These statistics include cases of charges under the ADA as well as those concurrently charged under Title VII of the Civil Rights Act, the Age Discrimination in Employment Act, and the Equal Pay Act.

The EEOC charges are divided into three categories: those that merited resolutions, those for which no reasonable cause of discrimination was found, and those that were closed for administrative reasons. Figure 8 shows their relative shares between 1992 and 2009.

Employment Discrimination
Legal Decisions Under the ADA

According to statistics collated regularly by the American Bar Association from the EEOC database, the percentage of employer wins against disabled complainants in employment decisions under the ADA has stayed consistently high between 1992 and 2009, never falling below 92% (see Table 13). There also seems to be a relatively high uniformity across circuit courts, with the Second Circuit Court being the only one never to rule 100% in favor of employers in any year during the period covered. These data are the source of the argument by disability scholar Ruth Colker that the ADA was essentially "a windfall for defendants" (Colker, 1999; 2001; 2005). In the years 2005 and 2007, however, the First Circuit showed further drops in the proportion of employer wins, to 63.6% and 76.5% respectively.

ADA Appellate Outcomes

Colker (2001) argues, also based on EEOC data, that the American Bar Association's methodology may involve some double counting, with the result of producing more pro-defendant outcomes due to the high incidence of summary judgments at the district court level. However, while the proportions of pro-defendant wins at the appellate level were indeed somewhat lower, the numbers are nonetheless not encouraging (see Table 14).

Perceived ADA Impact

The general perception of the value of the Americans with Disabilities Act by people with disabilities is mixed. Harris Interactive (2010a) asked a sample of 1,101 people with disabilities whether or not the ADA made a difference in their lives. The results (see Figure 9) indicated that 23% of the respondents felt that their lives had improved due to the ADA, but slightly more than two-thirds stated either that they had never heard of

Table 13 Percentage of Employer Wins, 1992–2009

Circuit	2009	2008	2007	2006	2005	2004	2003	2002	2001	2000	1999	1998	1992–97
First	100	94.4	76.5	100	63.6	100	100	92.3	96.0	88.9	83.3	94.4	93.1
Second	98.6	95.2	96.7	94.7	93.0	96.3	97.4	96.2	97.8	98	95.6	93.0	91.8
Third	97.6	100	100	92.3	97.1	100	100	95.8	94.7	97.1	100	100	93.0
Fourth	100	82.4	93.8	100	100	100	100	100	95.5	94.4	100	83.3	98.0
Fifth	90.0	100	94.4	100	92.3	100	93.8	84.6	92.3	90.6	94.9	96.6	98.1
Sixth	97.5	100	100	100	94.3	100	93.3	97.1	88.9	100	100	96.3	88.3
Seventh	95.8	100	95.3	100	100	97.5	100	98.3	98.3	96.4	96.5	92.3	93.4
Eighth	96.6	97.6	91.9	100	100	100	91.4	85.4	95.0	91.3	95.0	100	96.3
Ninth	95.0	100	100	96.2	91.7	88.9	100	93.8	93.8	100	87.5	93.8	83.3
Tenth	100	100	94.4	87.5	88.9	93.3	100	90.5	96.9	97.6	94.9	89.3	84.0
Eleventh	100	96.6	96.4	100	100	91.7	100	100	100	100	100	100	92.8
DC	100	100	100	100	100	100	50.0	100	100	100	100	0	87.5
US Sup. Ct.	*	*	*	*	0	*	0	100	100	*	100	0	0
Total	97.4	97.8	95.5	97.2	93.8	97	98	94.5	95.7	96.4	95.7	94.3	92.1

Source: Allbright, A. L. (2010). 2009 employment decisions under the ADA Title I—Survey update. *Mental and Physical Disability Law Reporter, 34*(3), 339–343.

Notes: *No cases. In 2009, the actual numbers of adjudicated cases were as follows: 454 cases, of which 339 were employer wins, 9 employee wins, and 106 without final resolution (Allbright, 2010, p. 339).

Table 14   ADA Appellate Outcomes, 1994–1999

Year	Frequency of Pro-Defendant Results	Percentage
1994	5 of 6	83
1995	35 of 42	83
1996	96 of 114	84
1997	158 of 178	89
1998	189 of 219	86
1999	140 of 161	87
Total	623 of 720	87

Source: Adapted from Colker, R. (2001). Winning and losing under the Americans with Disabilities Act. *Ohio State Law Journal, 62,* p. 13; and Colker, R. (2005). *The disability pendulum: The first decade of the Americans with Disabilities Act.* New York, NY: New York University Press, p. 86.

the ADA (7%) or that it had made no difference to them (61%). It remains to be seen whether the ADA Amendments Act of 2008 will have more of an impact on the lives of people with disabilities.

Statistics Related to the SSDI and the SSI Programs

Administered by the Social Security Administration, the Supplemental Security Income (SSI) and Social Security Disability Income (SSDI) programs are the two most important federal assistance schemes for persons with disabilities. As an insurance scheme, the SSDI requires the fulfillment of eligibility criteria to qualify for its benefits. SSI disability payments are based on financial need and so require means testing. In this section, we present longitudinal statistics on the number of people receiving payments from these programs and the administrative outcomes—either denial or allowance of benefits—of disability benefit applications.

Figure 9   Perceived Impact of the ADA, 2010

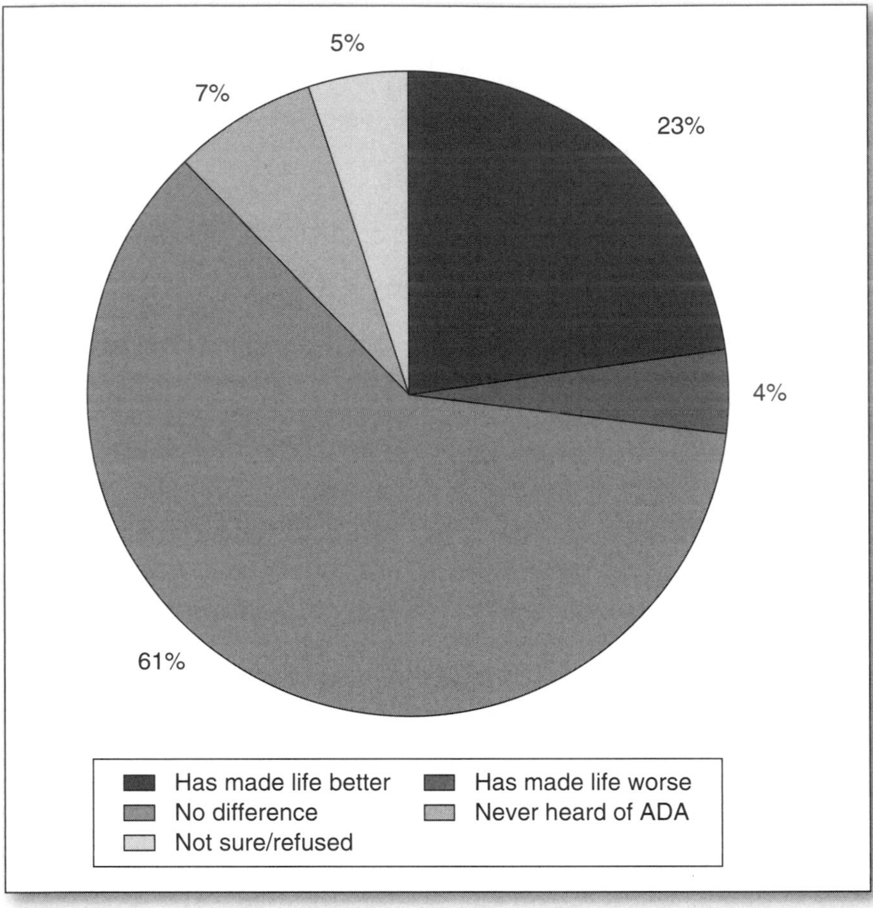

Source: Harris Interactive. (2010a). *The Kessler Foundation/National Organization on Disability 2010 survey of Americans with disabilities* (p. 144). New York, NY: Kessler Foundation and National Organization on Disability.

Note: People with disabilities (*n* = 1,001) were asked the following question: "Do you think that the Americans with Disabilities Act has made your life better, worse, or made no difference?"

Disabled Beneficiaries Receiving Social Security, SSI, or Both

Between 1996 and 2009 the total number of beneficiaries receiving SSDI, SSI, or both increased by almost 50% from 7,689,664 to 11,451,980 (see Figure 10 and Table 15). The increase was mostly due to SSDI-only recipients. In 1996, 53.6% received SSI only, 33.3% SSDI only, and 13.1% both. In 2009, the proportions were 61.1%, 27.4%, and 11.5%, respectively.

Disabled Beneficiaries in Current-Payment Status

The number of all beneficiaries of SSDI in current-payment status (i.e., those people actually receiving some form of SSDI case benefit) underwent an almost 16-fold increase between 1960 and 2009, rising

Figure 10   Disabled Beneficiaries Receiving SSDI, SSI, or Both, December 1996–2009 (aged 18–64)

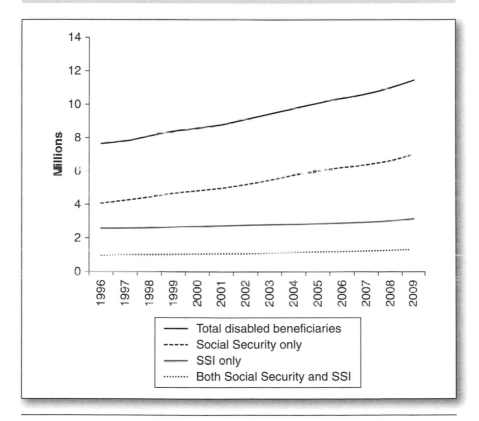

Source: Based on data in U.S. Social Security Administration, Office of Retirement and Disability Policy. (2009). *Annual statistical report on the Social Security Disability Insurance program: Disabled beneficiaries receiving Social Security, SSI, or both (Table 65).* Retrieved from http://www.ssa.gov/policy/docs/statcomps/di_asr/2009/sect05.html#table65

Table 15 Disabled Beneficiaries Receiving SSDI, SSI, or Both, December 1996–2009 (aged 18–64)

Year	Total	SSDI Only				SSI Only	Both SSDI and SSI			
		Total	Workers	Widow(er)s	Adult Children		Total	Workers	Widow(er)s	Adult Children
1996	7,689,664	4,122,152	–	–	–	2,559,750	1,007,762	–	–	–
1997	7,811,748	4,250,155	–	–	–	2,550,105	1,011,488	–	–	–
1998	8,086,259	4,440,264	–	–	–	2,618,615	1,027,380	–	–	–
1999	8,399,309	4,703,774	–	–	–	2,650,586	1,044,949	–	–	–
2000	8,599,465	4,850,835	–	–	–	2,690,446	1,058,184	–	–	–
2001	8,791,338	4,979,844	4,495,477	87,833	396,534	2,732,020	1,079,474	772,562	35,222	271,690
2002	9,106,014	5,228,262	4,738,246	87,900	402,116	2,768,782	1,108,970	801,351	34,671	272,948
2003	9,445,573	5,492,325	4,997,137	87,203	407,985	2,811,647	1,141,601	833,269	34,101	274,231
2004	9,773,201	5,756,093	5,257,314	89,874	408,905	2,850,815	1,166,293	858,850	33,072	274,371
2005	10,081,625	5,998,755	5,491,980	86,422	420,353	2,880,931	1,201,939	893,437	32,302	276,200
2006	10,362,419	6,210,289	5,698,494	85,259	426,536	2,928,034	1,224,096	915,832	31,443	276,821
2007	10,627,905	6,405,985	5,888,133	83,481	434,371	2,956,648	1,255,272	942,011	30,876	282,385
2008	10,974,914	6,641,818	6,115,214	82,100	444,504	3,040,764	1,292,332	971,455	30,608	290,269
2009	11,451,980	7,000,692	6,462,635	82,167	455,890	3,138,143	1,313,145	989,094	29,991	294,060

Source: U.S. Social Security Administration, Office of Retirement and Disability Policy. (2009). *Annual statistical report on the Social Security Disability Insurance program: Disabled beneficiaries receiving Social Security, SSI, or both (Table 65).* Retrieved from http://www.ssa.gov/policy/docs/ statcomps/di_asr/'2009/sect05.html#table65

from 559,425 to 8,945,376 (see Figure 11). The year 1980 marked a local maximum of 3,436,429 recipients. The numbers dropped in each of the following three years, but by 1984 the total number of recipients began to rise slightly again and it has been rising ever since, with an accelerated rate from 1990 onward. Although the slowdown started somewhat earlier, the dip in the 1980s has commonly been attributed to measures introduced by the Reagan administration to purge the Social Security rolls of those benefit recipients who were still able to work (Stone, 1984, p. 12).

More general factors influencing the number of recipients of disability benefits include population growth, the age structure and general health of the population, and the prevalence of disability, as well as changes in program coverage and eligibility criteria. From Figure 11 it is clear that the workers group, being by far the largest of the three beneficiary groups

Figure 11   All Disabled Beneficiaries in Current-Payment Status (SSDI), 1960–2009

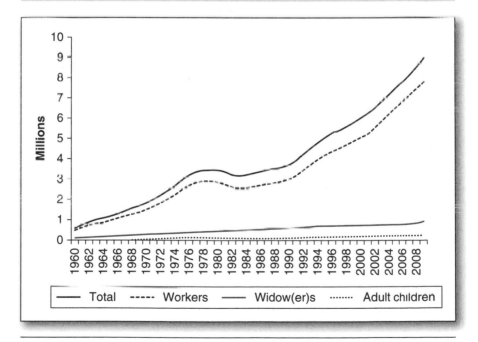

Source: Based on data in U.S. Social Security Administration, Office of Retirement and Disability Policy. (2009). *Annual statistical report on the Social Security Disability Insurance program: Beneficiaries in Current-Payment Status (Table 3)*. Retrieved from http://www.ssa.gov/policy/docs/statcomps/di_asr/2009/sect01.html#table3

shown, has driven the overall growth pattern. It is not immediately clear what to make of the fact that the numbers of widow(er)s and adult children grew at a much steadier and more moderate pace, but it could be an indication that the accelerated increase of beneficiaries among the workers group was indeed not due to medical factors alone, and that more contentious socioeconomic factors and program changes may have played a role as well.

Outcomes of Applications for Federal Disability Benefits

The total number of yearly applications for disability benefits declined between 1993 (1,384,501) and 1998 (1,138,101), but then sharply increased until 2004 (2,145,633) (see Figure 12). After a short-lived dip, the highest number of applications for the entire period was recorded in 2008 (2,196,906). Both the sharp increase in the early 2000s and the dip after 2004 are closely paralleled by the number of technical denials (e.g., insufficient recent work credits).

After reaching its highest level of 54.8% in 1999 and 2000, the final award rate of applications for disability benefits has been dropping steadily and markedly, reaching its (provisional) lowest point of 34.2% in 2009. (The final award rate is determined by the disability adjudication process, which involves four stages: reconsideration, hearing before an administrative law judge, appeals council review, and district court case. For detailed data and a discussion of the disability determination process, see Social Security Advisory Board, 2006.) However, this observation, taken on its own, is potentially misleading for two reasons. First, comparisons across years are problematic because of the enormous number of cases pending final decision for more recent years (pending cases are subtracted from the denominator when calculating the award rate).

For the period from 1992 to 2001, for which no pending cases are left, the award rate was above 50% for most years, with a slightly increasing trend. Looking only at the upper bounds of the final award rates for the years 2002 to 2009, we still find a slight downward trend since 2000. (To arrive at the upper bound for 2008, for example, we assume that all of the 320,266 pending decisions refer to cases submitted in that year and that all resolutions will eventually lead to an allowance verdict. The respective values for the years 2002 to 2008 are: 51.32%, 46.79%, 41.3%, 42.47%, 40.85%, 42.27%, and 43.75%.)

Second, the total number of applications has grown rapidly since its trough in 1999, when there were 1,167,650 applications. From 2000 onward, an increasing proportion of all applications have failed for nonmedical reasons, and the "allowance rate"—the medical allowances as a proportion of all medical decisions—has remained relatively constant. The falling award rate, then, is not an unequivocal indication of tougher medical eligibility requirements or stricter policy implementation, but could as well be a reflection of ever more ineligible people knocking at SSA's door.

Figure 12 Outcomes of Disabled-Worker Applications for Disability Benefits at All Adjudicative Levels, by Year of Application, 1992–2008

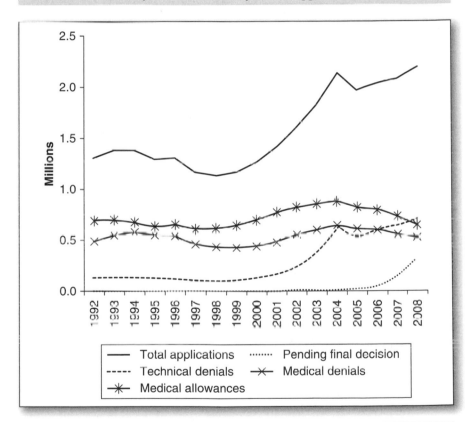

Source: Based on data in U.S. Social Security Administration, Office of Retirement and Disability Policy. (2009). *Annual statistical report on the Social Security Disability Insurance program: Outcomes of applications for disability benefits (Table 59).* Retrieved from http://www.ssa.gov/policy/docs/statcomps/di_asr/2009/sect04.html#table59

Note: Data include decisions for SSDI-only applications and applications for both SSI and SSDI; SSI-only applications are not included. For each year, medical allowances include a small number (fewer than 3,000) of applications that were denied for nonmedical reasons after a decision was made that the applicant met the medical severity criteria for disability benefits.

References

Allbright, A. L. (2010). 2009 employment decisions under the ADA Title I—Survey update. *Mental and Physical Law Reporter, 34*(3), 339–343.

Bagenstos, S. R. (2004). The future of disability law. *Yale Law Journal, 114*(1), 1–83.

Bjelland, M. J., Burkhauser, R. V., von Schrader, S., & Houtenville, A. J. (2009). *2009 progress report on the economic well-being of working-age people with disabilities.* Ithaca, NY: Rehabilitation Research and Training Center on Employment Policy for Persons with Disabilities, Cornell University.

Brault, M. W. (2008a). *Americans with disabilities: 2005.* Washington, DC: U.S. Census Bureau.

Brault, M. W. (2008b). *Disability status and the characteristics of people in group quarters: A brief analysis of disability prevalence among the civilian noninstitutionalized and total populations in the American Community Survey.* Washington, DC: U.S. Census Bureau.

Colker, Ruth. (1999). The Americans with Disabilities Act: A windfall for defendants. *Harvard Civil Rights-Civil Liberties Law Review, 34,* 99–162.

Colker, R. (2001). Winning and losing under the American with Disabilities Act. *Ohio State Law Journal, 62,* 1–32.

Colker, R. (2005). *The disability pendulum: The first decade of the Americans with Disabilities Act.* New York, NY: New York University Press.

Cornell University, Online Resource for U.S. Disability Statistics. (2010a). *Data sources.* Retrieved from http://www.ilr.cornell.edu/edi/disabilitystatistics/sources.cfm

Cornell University, Online Resource for U.S. Disability Statistics. (2010b). *Find disability statistics.* Retrieved from http://www.ilr.cornell.edu/edi/disabilitystatistics

Cornell University, Online Resource for U.S. Disability Statistics. (2010c). *Glossary.* Retrieved from http://www.ilr.cornell.edu/edi/disabilitystatistics/glossary.cfm?g_id=286&view=true

Erickson, W., Lee, C., & von Schrader, S. (2010). *2008 disability status report: United States.* Ithaca, NY: Cornell University Rehabilitation Research and Training Center on Disability Demographics and Statistics.

Goodman, N., & Waidmann, T. (2003). Social Security Disability Insurance and the recent decline in the employment rate of people with disabilities. In D. C. Stapleton & R. V. Burkhauser (Eds.), *The decline in employment of people with disabilities: A policy puzzle* (pp. 339–368). Kalamazoo, MI: W. E. Upjohn Institute for Employment Research.

Hale, T. W. (2001). The lack of a disability measure in today's Current Population Survey. *Monthly Labor Review, 124*(6), 38–40.

Harris Interactive. (2010a). *The Kessler Foundation/National Organization on Disability 2010 survey of Americans with disabilities.* New York, NY: Kessler Foundation and National Organization on Disability.

Harris Interactive. (2010b). *Kessler Foundation/National Organization on Disability 2010 survey of employment of Americans with disabilities*. New York, NY: Kessler Foundation and National Organization on Disability.

Haugen, D. M. (2009). *Rights of the disabled*. New York, NY: Facts On File.

Houtenville, A. J., Stapleton, D. C., Weathers, II, R. R., & Burkhauser, R. V. (Eds.). (2009). *Counting working-age people with disabilities: What current data tell us and options for improvement*. Kalamazoo, MI: W. E. Upjohn Institute for Employment Research.

Stapleton, D. C., & Burkhauser, R. V. (Eds.). (2003). *The decline in employment of people with disabilities: A policy puzzle*. Kalamazoo, MI: W. E. Upjohn Institute for Employment Research.

Stapleton, D. C., Houtenville, A. J., Weathers, II, R. R., & Burkhauser, R. V. (2009). Purpose, overview, and key conclusions. In A. J. Houtenville, D. C. Stapleton, R. R. Weathers II , & R. V. Burkhauser (Eds.), *Counting working-age people with disabilities: What current data tell us and options for improvement* (pp. 1–26). Kalamanzoo, MI: W. E. Upjohn Institute for Employment Research.

Stapleton, D. C., & She, P. (2009). The group quarter population. In A. J. Houtenville, D. C. Stapleton, R. R. Weathers II, & R. V. Burkhauser (Eds.), *Counting working-age people with disabilities: What current data tell us and options for improvement* (pp. 353–379). Kalamazoo, MI: W. E. Upjohn Institute for Employment Research.

Stone, D. A. (1984). *The disabled state*. Philadelphia, PA: Temple University Press.

U.S. Census Bureau. (2000). *United States Census 2000*. Retrieved from http://www.census.gov/main/www/cen2000.html

U.S. Census Bureau. (2009). *Survey of Income and Program Participation (SIPP)*. Retrieved from http://www.census.gov/sipp

U.S. Census Bureau. (2010a). *The American Community Survey* (p. 9, questions 17–19). Retrieved from http://www.census.gov/acs/www/Downloads/questionnaires/2010/Quest10.pdf

U.S. Census Bureau. (2010b). *American FactFinder*. Retrieved from http://factfinder.census.gov

U.S. Census Bureau. (2010c). *Current Population Survey (CPS)*. Retrieved from http://www.census.gov/cps

U.S. Census Bureau. (2010d). *DataFerrett*. Retrieved from http://dataferrett.census.gov

U.S. Census Bureau, Housing and Household Economic Statistics Division. (2010e). *Disability tables*. Retrieved from http://www.census.gov/hhes/www/disability/disabtables.html

U.S. Census Bureau, Housing and Household Economic Statistics Division. (2010f). *How disability data is collected*. Retrieved from http://www.census.gov/hhes/www/disability/datacollection.html

U.S. Census Bureau. (2010, March). *Annual Social and Economic (ASEC) supplement data dictionary*. Retrieved from http://smpbff2.dsd.census.gov/pub/cps/march/cpsmar10dd.txt

U.S. Census Bureau. (2011). *American Community Survey.* Retrieved from http://www.census.gov/acs/www

U.S. Department of Labor, Bureau of Labor Statistics. (2010). *Labor force statistics from the Current Population Survey: Disability.* Retrieved from http://www.bls.gov/cps/demographics.htm#disability

U.S. Social Security Administration, Office of Retirement and Disability Policy. (2009a). *Annual statistical report on the Social Security Disability Insurance program: Background.* Retrieved from http://www.ssa.gov/policy/docs/statcomps/di_asr/2009/background.html

U.S. Social Security Administration. (2009b). *Beneficiary data.* Retrieved from http://www.ssa.gov/OACT/ProgData/beniesQuery.html

U.S. Social Security Administration, Research, Statistics, and Policy Analysis. (2011a). *Annual statistical supplement, 2010.* Retrieved from http://www.ssa.gov/policy/docs/statcomps/supplement

U.S. Social Security Administration, Research, Statistics, and Policy Analysis. (2011b). *Statistical compilations.* Retrieved from http://www.ssa.gov/policy/docs/statcomps

U.S. Social Security Advisory Board. (2006). *Disability decision making: Data and materials.* Washington, DC: Author.

Waldrop, J., & Stern, S. M. (2003). *Disability status: 2000.* Washington, DC: U.S. Census Bureau.

Wang, Q. (2005). *Disability and American families: 2000.* Washington, DC: U.S. Census Bureau.

Six

Annotated List of Organizations and Associations

*Nandini Devi, Nicole Emmenegger,
and Barbara Phillips*

This chapter provides an annotated listing of agencies and associations (both governmental and non-governmental) involved in legal and ethical aspects of disability policy in the United States. Listings are arranged by (1) federal government agencies; (2) disability advocacy, rights, and legal organizations; and (3) disability special interest groups.

1. Federal Government Agencies

Center for Mental Health Services
Protection and Advocacy for Mentally Ill Individuals
Substance Abuse and Mental Health Services Administration
1 Choke Cherry Road
Rockville, MD 20857
Telephone: (240) 276-1310

Fax: (240) 276-1320

Web site: http://www.samhsa.gov/about/cmhs.aspx

The Center for Mental Health Services (CMHS) coordinates independent agencies in each state to provide technical assistance, information, and referrals on the Americans with Disabilities Act (ADA) and other disability laws. Primary recipients of CMHS services are individuals with mental illnesses and serious emotional disturbances who reside in treatment facilities and are among the groups most vulnerable to potential neglect and abuse. CMHS funds and oversees the Protection and Advocacy for Individuals with Mental Illness Program (PAIMI) that advocates for individuals with mental illnesses. Protection and advocacy services include general information and referrals; investigation of alleged abuse, neglect, and rights violations in facilities; and use of legal, legislative, systemic, and other remedies to correct verified incidents.

Disability.gov

U.S. Department of Labor

Office of Disability Employment Policy (ODEP)

Frances Perkins Building

200 Constitution Avenue, NW

Washington, DC 20210

E-mail: disability@dol.gov

Web site: http://www.disability.gov

Disability.gov is a Web-based resource covering all U.S. programs, services, laws, and regulations of relevance to people with disabilities, including benefits, civil rights, community life, education, emergency preparedness, employment, housing, technology, and transportation. Its mission is "to connect people with disabilities, their family members, veterans, caregivers, employers, service providers, and others with the resources they need to ensure that people with disabilities can fully participate in the workplace and in their communities." Disability.gov is managed by the U.S. Department of Labor's Office of Disability Employment Policy in partnership with numerous other federal agencies. The Web site also links to all state agencies of relevance to persons with disabilities.

National Council on Disability (NCD)

1331 F Street, NW, Suite 850

Washington, DC 20004

Telephone: (202) 272-2004; (202) 272-2074 (TTY)

Fax: (202) 272-2022

Web site: http://www.ncd.gov

This independent federal agency was created in 1978 "to promote policies, programs, practices, and procedures that guarantee equal opportunity for all individuals with disabilities, and that empower individuals with disabilities to achieve economic self-sufficiency, independent living, and inclusion and integration into all aspects of society." NCD is currently working on housing issues, technology issues, and implementation and evaluation of the Developmental Disabilities Assistance and Bill of Rights Act.

National Institute on Disability and Rehabilitation Research (NIDRR)
U.S. Department of Education
400 Maryland Avenue, SW
Mailstop PCP-6058
Washington, DC 20202-2572
Telephone: (202) 245-7640 (V/TTY)
Fax: (202) 245-7323
Web site: http://www2.ed.gov/about/offices/list/osers/nidrr/index.html
NIDRR was created in 1978 as a component of the Office of Special Education and Rehabilitative Services at the Department of Education. Its self-described mission is to "generate new knowledge and promote its effective use to improve the abilities of people with disabilities to perform activities of their choice in the community, and also to expand society's capacity to provide full opportunities and accommodations for its citizens with disabilities." NIDRR funds scientific and consumer activities relevant to disability policy and scientific research for rehabilitation and disability research. Funding priorities have included research funding in disability and employment, health and function, technology for access and function, independent living and community integration, and other associated disability research areas. It helps to integrate disability research into our nation's policies in such areas as science and technology, health care, and economics.

National Rehabilitation Information Center (NARIC)
8201 Corporate Drive, Suite 600
Landover, MD 20785
Telephone: (800) 346-2742; (301) 459-5984 (TTY)
Fax: (301) 459-4263
Web site: http://www.naric.com
NARIC describes itself as an "online gateway to an abundance of disability- and rehabilitation-oriented information organized in a variety of formats designed to make it easy for users to find and use." NARIC is funded by the National Institute on Disability and Rehabilitation Research (NIDRR). For over a quarter of a century, their mission has been to provide information services and document delivery—including important documents relevant to disability law and policy—to the disability and rehabilitation communities across the United States. NARIC moved online in 1992 with a small Web site featuring static pages and directories. NARIC.com became fully interactive in 1995.

Office of Disability Employment Policy (ODEP)
U.S. Department of Labor
200 Constitution Avenue, NW
Room S-1303
Washington, DC 20210
Telephone: (866) 633-7365; (877) 889-5627 (TTY)
Fax: (202) 693-7888
Web site: http://www.dol.gov/odep
ODEP was authorized in 2001 by Congress, which recognized the need for a national policy to ensure that people with disabilities are fully integrated into the 21st century workforce. ODEP is a sub-cabinet level policy agency in the Department of Labor that is under the direct charge of the assistant secretary for disability employment policy. The office provides national leadership on disability employment policy by developing and influencing the use of evidence-based disability employment policies and practices, building collaborative partnerships, and delivering authoritative and credible data on employment of people with disabilities.

U.S. Access Board
1331 F Street, NW, Suite 1000
Washington, DC 20004-1111
Telephone: (202) 272-0080; (800) 872-2253; (202) 272-0082 (TTY); (800) 993-2822 (TTY)
Fax: (202) 272-0081
E-mail: info@access-board.gov
Web site: http://www.access-board.gov
The Access Board is an independent federal agency devoted to accessibility policy implementation for people with disabilities. Created in 1973 to ensure access to federally funded facilities, the board is now a leading source of information on accessible design. The board develops and maintains design criteria for the built environment, transit vehicles, telecommunications equipment, and electronic and information technology. It also provides technical assistance and training on these requirements and on accessible design in general and continues to enforce accessibility standards that cover federally funded facilities.

U.S. Dept. of Justice, Civil Rights Division
Disability Rights Section
950 Pennsylvania Avenue, NW
Washington, DC 20530
Telephone: (202) 514-0301; (800) 514-0301; (800) 514-0383 (TTY)
Fax: (202) 307-1198
Web site: http://www.usdoj.gov/crt
This branch of the Department of Justice promulgates regulations and enforces the antidiscrimination provisions of the Americans with Disabilities Act, specifically those under Title II

involving public services and under Title III involving public accommodations. To this end, the agency provides technical assistance on compliance with ADA Titles II and III. It also enforces employment provisions under Title II of the ADA affecting state and local government entities.

2. Disability Advocacy, Rights, and Legal Organizations

American Association of People with Disabilities (AAPD)
1629 K Street NW, Suite 503
Washington, DC 20006
Telephone: (202) 457-0046 (TTY); (800) 840-8844 (TTY)
Fax: (202) 457-0473
E-mail: aapd@aol.com
Web site: http://www.aapd.com
The AAPD is a nonprofit, nonpartisan, cross-disability organization that promotes partnerships with national, state, and local disability advocacy organizations, and reaches out to the broader civil rights community for coalition building. AAPD supports leadership development and employment opportunities for all people with disabilities, especially young adults and people from diverse backgrounds.

American Association on Intellectual and Developmental Disabilities (AAIDD)
501 3rd Street, NW, Suite 200
Washington, DC 20001
Telephone: (800) 424-3688
Fax: (202) 387-2193
E-mail: anam@aaidd.org
Web site: http://www.aaidd.org
Since 1876 the AAIDD has been a worldwide leader in policy in the field of mental retardation. It represents a powerful community of leaders with a strong voice and an important mission. AAIDD, formerly known as AAMR—American Association of Mental Retardation—is the nation's oldest and largest interdisciplinary organization of professionals and citizens concerned about intellectual and developmental disabilities.

Bazelon Center for Mental Health Law
1101 15th Street, NW, Suite 1212
Washington, DC 20005
Telephone: (202) 467-5730
Fax: (202) 223-0409
Web site: http://www.bazelon.org

The mission of the Judge David L. Bazelon Center for Mental Health Law is to protect and advance the rights of adults and children who have mental disabilities. The center envisions an America where people who have mental illnesses or developmental disabilities exercise their own life choices and have access to the resources that enable them to participate fully in their communities. The center's advocacy work is based on the principle that every individual is entitled to choice, respect, and dignity. For many people with mental disabilities, this means something as basic as having a decent place to live, supportive services, and equality of opportunity. The Bazelon Center for Mental Health Law uses a coordinated approach of litigation, policy analysis, coalition building, public information, and technical support for local advocates.

Center for Independent Living (CIL)
2539 Telegraph Avenue
Berkeley, CA 94704
Telephone: (510) 841-4776; (510) 848-3101 (TTY)
Fax: (510) 841-6168
Web site: http://www.cilberkeley.org

CIL, the world's first organization of its kind, was founded in Berkeley, California, in 1972, and remains a national leader in supporting disabled people in their efforts to lead independent lives. An organization founded by people with disabilities, CIL seeks to achieve immediate and long-term independent living solutions, be it assistance with finding housing or a job, equipping a home with assistive technologies, or enhancing independent living skills. CIL's underlying philosophy and goals are based on the realization that people with disabilities know best how to meet the needs of others with disabilities—and that the strongest and most vibrant communities are those that include and embrace all people.

Commission on Mental and Physical Disability Law
American Bar Association (ABA)
740 15th Street, NW, 9th Floor
Washington, DC 20005
Telephone: (202) 662-1570
Fax: (202) 442-3439
E-mail: cmpdl@abanet.org
Web site: http://www.abanet.org/disability

The commission's mission is "to promote the ABA's commitment to justice and the rule of law for persons with mental, physical, and sensory disabilities and to promote their full and equal participation in the legal profession." Originally the ABA's Commission on the Mentally Disabled was established in 1973 to respond to the advocacy needs of persons with mental disabilities. After the passage of the Americans with Disabilities Act of 1990, the ABA broadened the commission's mission to serve all persons with disabilities and changed its name to the Commission on Mental and Physical Disability Law. Today, the commission carries out an array of projects and activities addressing disability-related public policy, disability law, and the professional needs of lawyers and law students with disabilities.

Consortium for Citizens with Disabilities (CCD)

1660 L Street, NW, Suite 700
Washington, DC 20036
Telephone: (202) 783-2229
Fax: (202) 783-8250
E-mail: Info@c-c-d.org
Web site: http://www.c-c-d.org

The CCD is a coalition of approximately 100 national disability organizations working together to advocate for national public policy that ensures the self-determination, independence, empowerment, integration, and inclusion of children and adults with disabilities in all aspects of society. The CCD also works to enhance the civil rights and quality of life of all people with disabilities and their families, and to reflect the values of the Americans with Disabilities Act.

Disability Rights Advocates (DRA)

2001 Center Street, Fourth Floor
Berkeley, CA 94704-1204
Telephone: (510) 665-8644; (510) 665-8716 (TTY)
Fax: (510) 665-8511
Web site: http://www.dralegal.org

DRA is a nonprofit legal center whose mission is to ensure dignity, equality, and opportunity for people with all types of disabilities throughout the United States and worldwide. Its national advocacy work includes high-impact class-action litigation on behalf of people with all types of disabilities, including mobility, hearing, vision, learning, and psychological disabilities. Through negotiation and litigation, DRA has made thousands of facilities throughout the country accessible for people with disabilities. It also has enforced access rights for millions of people with disabilities in many key areas of life, including access to technology, education, employment, transportation, and health care. DRA also engages in non-litigation advocacy throughout the country, including research and education projects focused on opening up access to schools, the professions, and health care.

Disability Rights Education and Defense Fund (DREDF)

1730 M Street, NW, Suite 801
Washington, DC 20036
Telephone: (202) 986-0375
Fax: (202) 833-2116

E-mail: dredf@dredf.org

Web site: http://www.dredf.org

Founded in 1979, DREDF is a national law and policy center directed by individuals with disabilities and parents who have children with disabilities. The organization's mission is to advance the civil and human rights of people with disabilities through legislation, litigation, advocacy, technical assistance, and education and training of attorneys, advocates, persons with disabilities, and parents of children with disabilities. The vision of DREDF is a just world where all people—those with and without disabilities—live full and independent lives free of discrimination.

Disability Rights Fund (DRF)

89 South Street, Suite 203

Boston, MA 02111-2670

Telephone: (617) 261-4593

Fax: (617) 261.1977

E-mail: info@disabilityrightsfund.org

Web site: http://www.disabilityrightsfund.org

DRF is a collaboration between donors and the disability community to advance the UN Convention on the Rights of Persons with Disabilities (CRPD). It focuses its grant making on building the capacity of DPOs (disabled persons organizations) to be full and equal participants in the quest to achieve full and equal civil rights for people with disabilities.

Disability Rights International (DRI)

1156 15th Street, NW, Suite 1001

Washington, DC 20005 USA

Telephone: (202) 296-0800

Fax: (202) 728-3053

Web site: http://www.disabilityrightsintl.org

This Washington, D.C.-based organization was originally established in 1993 by attorney Eric Rosenthal as Mental Disability Rights International (MDRI). Today, DRI documents conditions of mental institutions, publishes reports on human rights enforcement, and promotes international oversight of the rights of people with mental disabilities. Drawing on the skills and experience of rights attorneys, mental health professionals, human rights advocates, people with mental disabilities, and their family members, DRI trains and supports advocates seeking legal and service system reform and helps governments develop laws and policies to promote community integration and human rights enforcement for people with mental disabilities. The organization is forging new alliances throughout the world to challenge the discrimination and abuse faced by people with mental disabilities, as well as working with locally based advocates to create new advocacy projects and to promote citizen participation and human rights for children and adults. MDRI is dedicated to promoting the human rights and full participation in society of people with mental disabilities worldwide.

Disability Rights Promotion International (DRPI)

York University, 5021 T.E.L. Building
4700 Keele Street
Toronto, Ontario, M3J 1P3, Canada
Telephone: (416) 736-2100 ext. 20883
Fax: (416) 736-5986
E-mail: drpi_can@yorku.ca
Web site: http://www.yorku.ca/drpi

DRPI is a Canadian-based collaborative project of activists who work together to (1) establish a monitoring system to address disability discrimination globally, and (2) track international compliance with the UN Convention on the Rights of Persons with Disabilities.

Independent Living Institute (ILI)

Arenavägen 63, 121 77
Stockholm-Johanneshov, Sweden
Telephone: +46-8-506 22 181
E-mail: admin@independentliving.org www.independentliving.org
Web site: http://www.independentliving.org/indexen.html

The ILI is a policy development center specializing in consumer-driven policies for disabled peoples' self-determination, self-respect, and dignity. Founded and managed by people with disabilities, ILI states that its "ultimate goal is to promote disabled people's personal and political power. Toward this end we provide information, training materials, and develop solutions for services for persons with extensive disabilities."

National Disability Rights Network (NDRN)

900 Second Street, NE, Suite 211
Washington, DC 20002
Telephone: (202) 408-9514; (202) 408-9521 (TTY)
Fax: (202) 408-9520
E-mail: info@ndm.org
Web site: http://www.napas.org

NDRN is the nonprofit membership organization for the federally mandated Protection and Advocacy (P&A) Systems and Client Assistance Programs (CAP) for individuals with disabilities. Collectively, the P&A/CAP network is the largest provider of legally based advocacy services to people with disabilities in the United States. NDRN represents federally funded protection and advocacy agencies and provides materials on the Americans with Disabilities Act to state programs. Every state has such a program that, among other services, provides legal representation on a selective basis to people with disabilities.

U.S. International Council on Disability (USICD)
51 Monroe Street, Suite 805
Rockville, MD 20850
Telephone: (301) 309-8269
Fax: (301) 309-9486
E-mail: usicd-hq@usicd.org
Web site: http://www.usicd.org
An umbrella organization representing 25 other disability law and advocacy groups, USICD acts as a conduit for the exchange of information among its members and other members of Disabled People's International and Rehabilitation International, as well as among other organizations and individuals seeking to find or share information on various aspects of disability, rehabilitation, and inclusion in the United States and abroad. The organization was formerly known as the United States Council for International Rehabilitation (USCIR).

3. Disability Special Interest Groups

American Disabled for Attendant Programs Today (ADAPT)
ADAPT in Denver
201 S. Cherokee
Denver, CO 80223
Telephone: (303) 733-9324

ADAPT of Texas
1640-A E. 2nd Street, Suite 100
Austin, TX 78702
Telephone: (512) 442-0252
E-mail: adapt@Adapt.org
Web site: http://www.adapt.org
ADAPT is a national grassroots community organization with chapters in 30 states that organizes disability rights activists to engage in non-violent direct action, including civil disobedience, to assure the civil and human rights of people with disabilities to live in freedom. ADAPT is known as part of the radical wing of the disability rights movement because of its program of non-violent direct action from its inception in 1983. The organization was founded in Denver, Colorado, by the Reverend Wade Blank, a former nursing home recreational director who assisted several residents to move out and start their own community. The name originally stood for "Americans Disabled for Accessible Public Transit," because its initial issue involved getting wheelchair-accessible lifts on buses. ADAPT's current areas of emphasis include legislative policy advocacy and grassroots education and mobilization. ADAPT has most recently focused on the Community

Choice Act—a community-based alternative to nursing homes and institutions for people with disabilities—and the Money Follows the Person program at the state level. ADAPT also is working on Access Across America, a campaign to ensure safe, affordable, accessible, integrated housing for people with disabilities.

Arc of the United States (The Arc)

1660 L Street, NW, Suite 301
Washington, DC 20036
Telephone: (202) 534-3700; (800) 433-5255
Fax: (202) 534-3731
E-mail: info@thearc.org
Web site: http://www.thearc.org
The Arc is a national organization of and for people with mental retardation and related developmental disabilities and their families. The Arc advocates to enhance the dignity, expand the opportunities, and protect the rights of persons with mental retardation and related developmental disabilities.

Association of University Centers of Disabilities (AUCD)

1010 Wayne Avenue, Suite 920
Silver Spring, MD 20910
Telephone: (301) 588-8252
Fax: (301) 588-2842
E-mail: aucdinfo@aucd.org
Web site: http://www.aucd.org
AUCD is a network of interdisciplinary centers advancing policy and practice for and with individuals with developmental and other disabilities, their families, and communities. It supports members through a wide range of research, education, and service activities.

Association on Higher Education and Disability (AHEAD)

P.O. Box 540666
Waltham, MA 02454
Telephone: (781) 788-0003
Fax: (781) 788-0033
E-mail: AHEAD@ahead.org
Web site: http://www.ahead.org
AHEAD is an international organization of professionals committed to the full participation of individuals with disabilities in higher education. The association provides programs, workshops, publications, and conferences that promote "excellence through education, communication and training."

AUTCOM Autism National Committee

3 Bedford Green
South Burlington, VT 05403
Web site: http://www.autcom.org

AUTCOM is an autism advocacy organization dedicated to "Social Justice for All Citizens with Autism." AUTCOM was founded in 1990 to protect and advance the human rights and civil rights of all persons with autism, pervasive developmental disorder, and related differences of communication and behavior. AUTCOM states that "in the face of social policies of devaluation, which are expressed in the practices of segregation, medicalization, and aversive conditioning, we assert that all individuals are created equal and endowed with certain inalienable rights, and that among these are life, liberty, and the pursuit of happiness."

Center for the Human Rights of Users and Survivors of Psychiatry (CHRUSP)

44 Palmer Pond Road
Chestertown, NY 12817 USA
Telephone: (518) 494-0174
Web site: http://www.chrusp.org

CHRUSP was conceived during the negotiations for the United Nations Convention on the Rights of Persons with Disabilities and sees its role as complementary to organizations such as the World Network of Users and Survivors of Psychiatry. By working collaboratively with other organizations in the user/survivor movement, disability rights movement, and human rights community, CHRUSP works for full human rights and legal capacity for all. It advocates for an end to forced drugging, electroshock, and psychiatric incarceration, and supports policies and programs that respect individual integrity and free will.

Council of Parent Attorneys and Advocates (COPAA)

P.O. Box 6767
Towson, MD 21285
Telephone: (410) 372-0208
Web site: http://www.copaa.net

COPAA is a national, nonprofit membership organization dedicated to enhancing the availability and quality of legal representation for parents of children and youth with disabilities, particularly in the field of special education.

Disabled American Veterans (DAV)

P.O. Box 14301
Cincinnati, OH 45250
Telephone: (877) 426-2838 (V/TTY)

Fax: (859) 441-7300

E-mail: feedback@davmail.org

Web site: http://www.dav.org

*DAV advises veterans of their rights—and employers of their obligations—under the Reha-
bilitation Act, the Americans with Disabilities Act, and other legislation governing the
employment and training of Vietnam-era veterans with disabilities. It provides information
on recruiting sources for veterans with disabilities, removing architectural barriers, providing reasonable accommodations, and locating assistive devices. DAV makes referrals to providers of qualified readers, interpreters, and personal assistants.*

Handicap International (HI)

6930 Carroll Avenue, Suite 240

Takoma Park, MD 20912-4468

Telephone: (301) 891-2138

Fax: (301) 891-9193

E mail: info@handicap-international.us

Web site: http://www.handicap-international.us

*Handicap International works to improve the living conditions of people living in dis-
abling situations in post-conflict and low-income countries around the world. HI works
with local partners to develop programs in health and rehabilitation and social and economic integration. Internationally, HI works with local authorities to clear landmines and
other war debris and to prevent mine-related accidents through education. HI responds
quickly and effectively to natural and civil disasters in order to limit serious and permanent injuries and to assist survivors' recovery and reintegration. It advocates for the universal recognition of the rights of the disabled through national planning and advocacy.*

International Disability Alliance (IDA)

IDA Secretariat Headquarters

25 East 21st Street, 4th Floor

New York, NY 10009

Telephone: (212) 420-1500

Fax: (212) 505-0871

E-mail: stromel@fundaciononce.es

Web site: http://www.internationaldisabilityalliance.org

*Established in 1999, the IDA is a network of global and regional organizations of persons
with disabilities that promotes the effective implementation of the UN Convention on the
Rights of Persons with Disabilities. IDA currently comprises eight global and three
regional DPOs (disabled persons' organizations), with two other regional DPOs having
observer status. With member organizations around the world, IDA represents all people worldwide who are living with a disability. IDA was instrumental in establishing*

the International Disability Caucus, the network of global, regional, and national organizations of persons with disabilities and allied NGOs (non-governmental organizations) that was a key player in the negotiation of the Convention on the Rights of Persons with Disabilities.

Mobility International USA (MIUSA)

132 E. Broadway, Suite 343

Eugene, OR 97401

Telephone: (541) 343-1284 (V/TTY)

Fax: (541) 343-6812

Web site: http://www.miusa.org

Since 1995, MIUSA has served as the National Clearinghouse on Disability and Exchange (NCDE), a project sponsored by the Bureau of Educational and Cultural Affairs of the U.S. Department of State. The purpose of MIUSA is to educate people with disabilities and related organizations about international exchange opportunities; increase the participation of people with disabilities in the full range of international volunteer, study, work, and research programs; advise international exchange organizations about the Americans with Disabilities Act; and facilitate partnerships between people with disabilities, disability-related organizations, and international exchange organizations.

National Association of the Deaf (NAD)

8630 Fenton Street, Suite 820

Silver Spring, MD 20910

Telephone: (301) 587-1788; (301) 587-1789 (TTY)

Fax: (301) 587-1791

Web site: http://www.nad.org

NAD is the premier civil rights organization of, by, and for deaf and hard of hearing individuals in the United States. Established in 1880, the NAD was shaped by deaf leaders who believed in the right of the American deaf community to use sign language, to congregate on issues important to them, and to have their interests represented at the national level. These beliefs remain true to this day, with American Sign Language as a core value. The mission of the National Association of the Deaf is to promote, protect, and preserve the civil, human, and linguistic rights of deaf and hard of hearing people in the United States.

Support Coalition International (SCI)

P.O. Box 11284

Eugene, OR 97440-3484

Telephone: (541) 345-9106

Fax: (541) 345-3737

E-mail: office@MindFreedom.org
Web site: http://www.mindfreedom.org
In 2001, SCI became the first psychiatric survivor-run human rights group to be granted official Non-Governmental Organization status from the United Nations. SCI is active in supporting the UN Convention on the Rights of Persons with Disabilities and supports and promotes organizations working for the rights of people labeled with mental disabilities. SCI includes more than 100 grassroots groups, each functioning independently while sharing resources and benefiting from the exchange of experience, ideas, and energy.

Treatment Advocacy Center

200 N. Glebe Road, Suite 730
Arlington, VA 22203
Telephone: (703) 294-6001; (703) 294-6002
Fax: (703) 294-6010
E-mail: info@treatmentadvocacycenter.org
Web site: http://www.treatmentadvocacycenter.org
The Treatment Advocacy Center is a national nonprofit organization dedicated to eliminating barriers to the timely and effective treatment of severe mental illnesses. The Center promotes laws, policies, and practices for the delivery of psychiatric care and supports the development of innovative treatments for—and research into the causes of—severe and persistent psychiatric illnesses such as schizophrenia and bipolar disorder.

United Nations Enable

Secretariat for the Convention on the Rights of Persons with Disabilities
Two United Nations Plaza, DC2-1382
New York, NY 10017
Fax: (212) 963-0111
E-mail: enable@un.org
Web site: http://www.un.org/disabilities
This is the official UN Web site for all disability-related matters. Maintained by the Secretariat for the Convention on the Rights of Persons with Disabilities, the Web site combines the resources of the UN Department of Economic and Social Affairs and the Office of the High Commissioner for Human Rights. It contains extensive information about the Convention and international and national disability human rights legislation and policy.

World Institute on Disability (WID)

3075 Adeline Street, Suite 280
Berkeley, CA 94703
Telephone: (510) 225-6400; (510) 225-4778 (TTY)
Fax: (510) 225-4777

E-mail: wid@wid.org

Web site: http://www.wid.org

WID is a nonprofit public policy center dedicated to promoting independence and the full societal inclusion of people with disabilities. WID works internationally on a number of fronts to achieve these goals, and it maintains programs focused on adaptive technology, education, rehabilitation, vocational training, and information referral. Organized by and for people with disabilities, WID brings a diverse disability perspective to public policy on health care, technology, and employment.

Seven

Selected Print and Electronic Resources

Nandini Devi, Nicole Emmenegger,
and Barbara Phillips

This chapter provides a list of selected print and electronic resources relevant to topics in disability ethics, law, and policy. The print resources are presented in three categories: (1) History and Conceptualization of Disability Law and Policy; (2) Disability Ethics and Ethical Issues; and (3) Analysis and Description of Disability Law. These print resources are either the "classics" in disability ethics, law, and policy, or else valuable contributions to these areas that are worth noting. These resources are briefly described for the reader's convenience.

For legal cases and legislation, at federal and state levels, and for governmental and non-governmental agencies and groups that provide resources for disability ethics, law, and policy, the easiest way to access these materials is electronically. In the last section, therefore, we provide some examples of the vast range of electronic resources that are available, including the official government sites for legal decisions and legislation, federal and state.

Print Resources

History and Conceptualization of Disability Law and Policy

Albrecht, G. L. (1992). *The disability business: Rehabilitation in America*. Newbury Park, CA: Sage.

Albrecht explores the "big business" of rehabilitation, health care, and insurance companies that has developed around the disabled population, exposing some of the ethical and social inequities that this business perpetuates. He considers some policy options that may help to ensure that quality rehabilitation services are equally available to all.

Albrecht, G. L., Seelman, K. D., & Bury, M. (Eds.). (2001). *Handbook of disability studies*. Thousand Oaks, CA: Sage.

The Handbook *is an interdisciplinary and international collection of essays covering all of the ethical, policy, and legal issues discussed in this book. An invaluable collection for the emerging area of scholarship called "disability studies," it serves as both an introduction and an ongoing resource for advanced research.*

Anspach, R. (1979). From stigma to identity politics: Political activism among the physically disabled and former mental patients. *Social Science and Medicine, 13*, 765–773.

This article provides one of the first sociological discussions of the impact of disability advocacy and activism on U.S. law and policy.

Batavia, A. I., & Beaulaurier, R. L. (2001). The financial vulnerability of people with disabilities: Assessing poverty risks. *Journal of Sociology and Social Welfare, 28*(1), 139–162.

This article offers a theoretical model for understanding and a call for empirical research into the major disability social policy challenge: Why is there a persistent link between disability and poverty, which threatens the health and lives of people with disabilities, despite decades of legal and policy efforts to address this association?

Batavia, A. I., De Jong, G., & McKnew, L. B. (1991). Toward a national personal assistance program: The independent living model of long-term care for persons with disabilities. *Journal of Health Politics, Policy, and Law, 16*(3), 523–545.

Using the independent living model (see Roberts, 1989), the authors explore federal and state policy solutions to the provision of personal assistants in the disabled person's home to satisfy the needs for long-term care outside of institutions.

Berkowitz, M. (1989). *Disabled policy: America's programs for the handicapped*. New York, NY: Cambridge University Press.
Berkowitz's book is a classic economic study of the contradictions in America's disability social policy, focusing on the unstated but implicit tactic of removing people with disabilities from the mainstream of the labor market and other major areas of life into some form of institution or "special" social status.

Bickenbach, J. E. (1993). *Physical disability and social policy*. Toronto, ON: University of Toronto Press.
This book offers an interdisciplinary and philosophical approach to the persistent controversy about the definition of disability in policy and law, in terms of broad streams of social and political thought that have, often in contradictory ways, shaped and distorted disability law and policy.

Blanck, P. D. (2000). *Employment, disability, and the Americans with Disabilities Act: Issues in law, public policy, and research*. Evanston, IL: Northwestern University Press.
Blanck's book offers a major response—based on empirical research in law, health policy, and government—to the challenge raised by statistical trends that suggest the Americans with Disabilities Act has either been ineffective in helping people with disabilities enter and remain in the workforce or has actually stood in the way of these goals.

Bowe, F. (1978). *Handicapping America: Barriers to disabled people*. New York, NY: Harper and Row.
Bowe's book is a classic treatment of the social and political consequences of misperceptions, stigma, and well-intended but destructive stereotypes about the nature of disability and the potential of people with disabilities to live in the social mainstream.

Burkhauser, R. V., & Daly, M. C. (1996). Employment and economic well-being following the onset of a disability. In J. L. Mashaw, V. P. Reno, R. V. Burkhauser, & M. Berkowitz (Eds.), *Disability, work, and cash benefits* (pp. 59–101). Kalamazoo, MI: W. E. Upjohn Institute for Employment Research.
Burkhauser and Daly present an empirical study of the importance of accommodation strategies for persons who acquire impairments while working and wish to remain at or return to work. It includes a discussion of ways to meet workers' needs to transition out of and back into the labor market.

Burkhauser, R. V., & Haveman, R. T. (1982). *Disability and work: The economics of American public policy*. Baltimore, MD: Johns Hopkins University Press.
This book provides an early economic discussion of the contradictions, disincentives, and other anomalies that undermine the effectiveness of policies designed to improve access to meaningful work for persons with disabilities.

DeJong, G., & Batavia, A. (1990). The Americans with Disabilities Act and the current state of U.S. disability policy. *Journal of Disability Policy Studies*, 1(3), 65–75.
One of the first discussions of the potential policy consequences of the newly passed Americans with Disabilities Act, this article reviews six policy changes that the act should bring about.

Driedger, D. (1989). *The last civil rights movement*. London, UK: Hurst.
Driedger's book is a classic treatment of the history of the disability rights movement, from an international political and sociological perspective.

Fine, M., & Asch, A. (Eds.). (1988). *Women with disabilities: Essays in psychology, culture, and politics*. Philadelphia, PA: Temple University Press.
This collection of essays draws attention to the importance of cross-cutting gender issues as they impact all aspects of disability law, policy, and ethics, especially the abortion debate.

Gliedman, J., & Roth, W. (1980). *The unexpected minority: Handicapped children in America*. New York, NY: Harcourt Brace.
Gliedman and Roth provide a classic treatment of the impact of the "social pathology" approach and the medicalization of developmental problems facing children with intellectual impairments. The book, for the first time, highlighted the need to adopt a policy analysis to special education that is grounded in the view that these children are an oppressed social group.

Hahn, H. (1985). Towards a politics of disability: Definitions, disciplines, and policies. *Social Science Journal*, 22(4), 87–105.
Hahn, H. (1986). Public support for rehabilitation programs: The analysis of U.S. disability policy. *Disability and Society*, 1, 121–137.
These two seminal articles were written by the influential American disability scholar who created and utilized to great benefit the so-called "minority group approach" to conceptualizing disability for political, legal, and policy purposes. Hahn brings standard theoretical and empirical political science methods to disability policy analysis.

Imrie, R. (1996). *Disability and the city: International perspectives*. London, UK: Paul Chapman.
Imrie provides an extensive review of the city planning and policy applications in the United States and United Kingdom of the realization that features of the built environment—in the home, the community, the city, and beyond—are the primary causes of the marginalization and ostracism that people with disabilities experience in their lives.

Institute of Medicine, Committee on Disability in America, Field, M. J., & Jette, A. M. (Eds.). (2007). *The future of disability in America*. Washington, DC: National Academies Press.
The most recent report of the Institute of Medicine on disability science, practice, and policy describes the state of the art on all aspects of the development and implementation of disability policy, including assistive technology and the removal of environmental barriers, access to health and social care, aging and secondary health problems, and health financing.

Issacharoff, S., & Nelson, J. (2001). Discrimination with a difference: Can employment discrimination law accommodate the Americans with Disabilities Act? *North Carolina Law Review, 79*, 307–314.
This article discusses the "redistributive" impact of anti-discrimination laws and the concern that these laws may have perverse effects on employment rates for persons with disabilities.

Johnson, M. (2003). *Make them go away: Clint Eastwood, Christopher Reeve, and the case against disability rights*. Louisville, KY: Avocado Press.
Johnson's book is an intriguing discussion of the extent to which high-profile individuals, often unintentionally, become enemies of disability rights and how disability advocates need to respond to this threat.

Kavka, G. (2000). Disability and the right to work. In L. P. Frances & A. Silvers (Eds.), *Americans with disabilities: Exploring the implications for individuals and institutions* (pp. 174–192). New York, NY: Routledge.
Kavka provides a classic statement of the right to work and examines the social and policy obstacles that stand in the way of persons with disabilities enjoying that right equally with others.

Morris, J. (1992). Personal and political: A feminist perspective on researching physical disability. *Disability, Handicap, and Society, 7*(2), 157–166.
Morris calls for the application of feminist theory and methodology in social policy research conducted by, and for the benefit of, people with disabilities.

Nagi, S. Z. (1969). *Disability and rehabilitation: Legal, clinical, and self-concepts and measurement*. Columbus, OH: Ohio State University Press.
Nagi offers a highly influential account of the epidemiological nature of disability that has shaped U.S. disability policy for decades, primarily by creating a model of disability that is used in policy development and data collection.

O'Brien, R. (2001). *Crippled justice: The history of modern disability policy in the workplace*. Chicago, IL: University of Chicago Press.

This book is a historical treatment of disability policy from the perspective of government officials and "experts" who, often inadvertently or through ignorance of disability, undermined the effectiveness of legislative advances.

Oliver, M. (1990). *The politics of disablement*. London, UK: Macmillan Press.
This statement of the U.K. version of the social model of disability, and its impact on law and policy, comes from one of the most influential British disability rights theoreticians.

Roberts, E. V. (1989). A history of the independent living movement: A founder's perspective. In B. W. Heller, L. S. Zegans, & L. M. Flohr (Eds.), *Psychosocial interventions with physically disabled persons* (pp. 231–252). New Brunswick, NJ: Rutgers University Press.
The inventor and founder of the influential notion of independent living provides a history of how it became a consumer and political movement that helped to shape America's disability policy.

Scotch, R. K. (2001). *From good will to civil rights: Transforming federal disability policy* (2nd ed.). Philadelphia, PA: Temple University Press.
This landmark contribution to disability studies traces the changes in federal disability policy at a crucial point in the history of its development.

Shakespeare, T. W. (2006). *Disability rights and wrongs*. New York, NY: Routledge.
Disability Rights and Wrongs is an iconoclastic treatment of disability policy and politics from one of Britain's most prolific and influential disability scholars.

Shapiro, J. P. (1993). *No pity: People with disabilities forging a new civil rights movement*. New York, NY: Times Books.
This history of the disability rights movement in the United States, drawn from 2,000 interviews, surveys all the major advocacy and political developments up to the passage of the Americans with Disabilities Act in 1990.

Silvers, A., Wasserman, D., & Mahowald, M. R. (1998). *Disability, difference, discrimination: Perspectives on justice in bioethics and public policy*. Lanham, MD: Rowman & Littlefield.
This book provides a philosophical debate over fundamental notions that form the foundations of disability policy and politics and that raise questions about the meaning and consequences of equality as a political and legal notion.

Stiker, H. (1999). *A history of disability* (W. Sayers, Trans.). Ann Arbor, MI: University of Michigan Press.
This sweeping historical account, by one of France's leading disability scholars, traces the underlying currents of disability policy that persist to this day.

Stone, D. A. (1984). *The disabled state.* Philadelphia, PA: Temple University Press.
Stone puts the disability policy agenda into the context of the American welfare state, not only raising issues about the role of administrative definitions of disability, but also exposing contradictions in the underlying rationale for all aspects of modern disability policy.

U.S. Commission on Civil Rights. (1983). *Accommodating the spectrum of individual abilities.* Washington, DC: Author.
This is an important document in the early development of the conception of disability policy that argues for a universalistic perspective rather than one based on the then-prominent minority rights model.

Wolfensberger, W. (1975). *The origin and nature of our institutional models* (Rev. ed.). Syracuse, NY: Human Policy Press.
The author of the influential principle of "normalization" traces the history of institutionalization for persons with developmental, intellectual impairments and mental health problems.

Zola, I. (1989). Toward the necessary universalizing of a disability policy. *Milbank Quarterly, 67,* 401–428.
America's leading sociologist of disability raises the prospect of moving beyond the minority group and individual rights perspective, which he argues was an essential step toward equality for persons with disabilities, toward a wider universalist approach to disability policy.

Disability Ethics and Ethical Issues

Annas, G. (2005). "Culture of life" politics at the bedside: The case of Terri Schiavo. *New England Journal of Medicine, 352*(16), 1710–1715.
One of America's most prominent bioethicists weighs in on the euthanasia debate as it played out with Terri Schiavo, and explains how, in his view, that debate was co-opted by religious fundamentalists and disability advocates.

Asch, A. (1998). Distracted by disability: The difference of disability in the medical setting. *Cambridge Quarterly of Healthcare Ethics, 7*(1), 77–87.
Asch discusses the impact of medical professionals on the social status of persons with disabilities and their failure to be "normal."

Asch, A. (2001). Critical race theory, feminism, and disability: Reflections on social justice and personal identity. *Ohio State Law Journal, 62*(1), 391–425.
America's most prominent disability ethicist reviews the methods and principles found in race and gender research in light of the need for methods in disability studies and the ethical issues of concern to people with disabilities.

Brock, D. W. (1995). Justice and the ADA: Does prioritizing and rationing health care discriminate against the disabled? *Social Philosophy and Policy, 12*(2), 159–185.
This article offers one of the first philosophical treatments, by a leading bioethicist, of the ethical issues involved in health resource allocation decisions that are made in terms of the value of the "disabled life."

Buchanan, A. E., & Brock, D. W. (1989). *Deciding for others: The ethics of surrogate decision making.* New York, NY: Cambridge University Press.
This resource provides a bioethical review of surrogate or proxy decision making for health treatment and its impact on autonomy and respect for people with disabilities.

Buchanan, A. E., Brock, D. W., Daniels, N., & Wikler, D. (2000). *From choice to chance: Genetics and justice.* New York, NY: Cambridge University Press.
The authors provide an extensive, multidisciplinary discussion of the ethics and politics of genetic screening and selective abortion in general, and in light of objections from the disability community that such practices undermine the value of the lives of people with disabilities.

Lane, H., & Grodin, M. (1997). Ethical issues in cochlear implant surgery: An exploration into disease, disability, and the best interests of the child. *Kennedy Institute of Ethics Journal, 7,* 231–252.
Lane and Grodin offer a useful historical, sociological, and ethical discussion of a surgical technique that "cures" deafness and its impact on the deaf community.

McLean, S., & Williamson, L. (2007). *Impairment and disability law and ethics at the beginning and end of life.* New York, NY: Routledge.
This valuable resource reviews the ethical questions raised by issues such as abortion, genetic screening, and in vitro fertilization at the beginning of life, and euthanasia, assisted suicide, and palliative care at the end of life, from the perspective of disability ethics and legal responses.

Orentlicher, D. (1996). Destructuring disability: Rationing of health care and unfair discrimination against the sick. *Harvard Civil Rights-Civil Liberties Law Review, 31,* 49–87.
Orentlicher offers an important discussion of the ethical and legal impact of health care rationing that takes into account the value of life when one has pre-existing health problems or disabilities.

Parens, E., & Asch, A. (Eds.). (2000). *Prenatal testing and disability rights.* Washington, DC: Georgetown University Press.
This collection of essays looks at the practices of prenatal testing and selective abortion both as a matter of equal access to medical resources and in terms of ethical objections raised by the disability rights community.

Reilly, P. R. (1991). *The surgical solution: A history of involuntary sterilization in the United States*. Baltimore, MD: Johns Hopkins University Press.
Reilly presents a historical and ethical examination, in light of empirical research and theoretical discussions, of the American practice of involuntary sterilization of "mental defectives."

Reinders, H. (2000). *The future of the disabled in liberal society: An ethical analysis*. South Bend, IN: University of Notre Dame Press.
A Dutch philosopher considers ethical questions about disability, and bioethical debates on selective abortion and euthanasia, in light of fundamental contradictions in western liberal political thought.

Shakespeare, T. (1998). Choices and rights: Eugenics, genetics, and disability equality. *Disability and Society, 13*, 665–681.
A leading British disability scholar sets out the debate between disability rights and the practice of choosing characteristics of one's children in light of the spectre of eugenics.

Silvers, A. (1994). "Defective" agents: Equality, difference, and the tyranny of the normal. *Journal of Social Philosophy, 25*(Suppl. 1), 154–175.
An American philosopher surveys the impact of ethical and political debates on the contrast between "normality" and disability and the undermining of autonomy.

Singer, P., & Kuhse, H. (1985). *Should the baby live? The problem of handicapped infants*. New York, NY: Oxford University Press.
This key controversial document presents the argument that selective abortion of "defective" fetuses was a socially acceptable practice that should be encouraged on utilitarian grounds. The book made Singer the primary target of attacks from disability advocates.

Stein, M. (2006). *Distributive justice and disability*. New Haven, CT: Yale University Press.
A philosopher and disability advocate, Stein argues that the conceptual and philosophical basis for resolving many of the ongoing bioethical debates, especially concerning resource allocation, should be utilitarianism.

Tooley, M. (1983). *Abortion and infanticide*. New York, NY: Oxford University Press.
Tooley's influential discussion of the abortion issue sets the stage for much of the debate by arguing that human fetuses, and indeed young infants, are not moral persons and as such do not have a right to life.

Veatch, R. M. (1986). *The foundations of justice: Why the retarded and the rest of us have claims to equality*. New York, NY: Oxford University Press.
Veatch presents a classic argument that people with severe disabilities have a right to health care and other resources based on ethical and political theoretical principles that are at the foundations of our conception of social justice.

Wasserman, D., Bickenbach, J. E., & Wachbroit, R. (Eds.). (2005). *Quality of life and human difference*. New York, NY: Cambridge University Press.
This collection of essays by prominent bioethicists and disability rights scholars surveys the arguments and evidence on a variety of bioethical issues that impact people with disabilities, focusing on the issue of whether impairments, on their own, lower the value of the lives of persons with disabilities.

Analysis and Description of Disability Law

Acemoglu, D., & Angrist, J. D. (2001). Consequences of employment protection? The case of the Americans with Disabilities Act. *Journal of Political Economy*, *109*(5), 915–957.
This article offers an economic treatment of the perceived failure of the Americans with Disabilities Act to improve the employment rates of persons with disabilities.

Bagenstos, S. R. (2009). *Law and the contradictions of the disability rights movement*. New Haven, CT: Yale University Press.
Bagenstos's recent book is a treatise on the potential of the Americans with Disabilities Act to fulfil the expectations of the disability community, and an argument that these expectations cannot be met without augmenting antidiscrimination law with powerful and enforceable protections of social welfare policy of the sort that the American disability community have traditionally been wary of advocating.

Blanck, P., Hill, E., Siegal, C. D., & Waterstone, M. (Eds.). (2006). *Disability civil rights law and policy*. St. Paul, MN: West.
This standard legal textbook on all aspects of disability law and policy, though technical, is also accessible to non-lawyers. Everything worth knowing about disability law and policy in the United States can be found in this book.

Burgdorf, R. L. (Ed.). (1980). *The legal rights of handicapped persons: Cases, materials, and text*. Baltimore, MD: Paul H. Brookes.
This book was the first compilation of legal and policy materials on disability and, though somewhat dated, it is still very useful as a resource.

Drimmer, J. C. (1993). Cripples, overcomers, and civil rights: Tracing the evolution of federal legislation and social policy for people with disabilities. *UCLA Law Review*, *40*(5), 1341–1410.
Drimmer provides an exhaustive review of theoretical and historical issues in the relationship between social conceptions and images of disability and the development of laws and policy concerning disability, arguing that only when changes in social perception occur can the law change.

Engel, D. M., & Munger, F. W. (2003). *Rights of inclusion law and identity in the life stories of Americans with disabilities.* Chicago, IL: University of Chicago Press.
This book offers a unique perspective on the development of laws and policy in America, in terms of the impact of laws on the ordinary lives of persons with disabilities. The authors argue that the actual impact on people's lives in the end determines whether laws are effective or not.

Francis, L. P., & Silvers, A. (Eds.). (2000). *Americans with disabilities: Exploring the implications for individuals and institutions.* New York, NY: Routledge.
This collection of essays surveys all aspects of the implementation and impact of the Americans with Disabilities Act since its passage, focusing on employment and health care, with discussions of judicial interpretation and the underlying principles of the act, and comparison to similar legislation in other countries.

Hahn, H. (1987). Civil rights for disabled Americans: The foundation of a political agenda. In A. Gartner & T. Joe (Eds.), *Images of the disabled, disabling images* (pp. 181–201). New York, NY: Praeger.
Hahn offers an early discussion of the importance of using the law, especially human rights law, to further the aims of the disability rights movement.

Hahn, H. (2000). Accommodations and the ADA: Unreasonable bias or biased reasoning? *Berkeley Journal of Employment and Labor Law,* 21(1), 166 193.
This discussion, from the perspective of employment, of the impact of the "reasonable accommodation" provision of the Americans with Disabilities Act looks primarily at judicial interpretations of the scope of that provision.

Jones, M., & Marks, L. A. (Eds.). (1999). *Disability, divers-ability, and legal change.* The Hague, Netherlands: Martinus Nijhoff.
This international collection of essays on a range of legal topics and approaches focuses on the question of the impact of human rights laws on the lives of persons with disabilities, and in particular on the importance of respecting difference in the context of law and political equality.

Krieger, L. H. (Ed.). (2003). *Backlash against the ADA: Reinterpreting disability rights.* Ann Arbor, MI: University of Michigan Press.
This important collection of essays by disability legal scholars focuses on the need to update and extend the Americans with Disabilities Act in light of a conspicuous effort on the part of unsympathetic courts to water down the provisions of this and other human rights legislation and to ignore the spirit of the law.

Kruse, D., & Schur, L. (2003). Employment of people with disabilities following the ADA. *Industrial Relations,* 42(1), 31–66.
Kruse and Schur offer a detailed review of the impact of the Americans with Disabilities Act on the employment rates of persons with disabilities, with an attempt to

explain the apparent discrepancy between the aspirations of the act and the resulting poor improvement in employment rates.

Liachowitz, C. H. (1988). *Disability as a social construct: Legislative roots.* Philadelphia, PA: University of Pennsylvania Press.
This important book attempts to link the "social constructivist" approach to disability conceptualization to the evolution of legislation in the United States with regard to disability. It is a good sourcebook for pre-Americans with Disabilities Act approaches to disability.

McCluskey, M. T. (1988). Rethinking equality and difference: Disability discrimination in public transportation. *Yale Law Journal, 97*(5), 863–880.
McCluskey makes an early argument for a concerted legal response to discrimination in the area of public transportation and suggestions about what form that response might take.

Minow, M. (1990). *Making all the difference: Inclusion, exclusion, and American law.* Ithaca, NY: Cornell University Press.
This seminal book discusses how the U.S. legal system deals with people on the basis of race, gender, age, ethnicity, religion, and disability—revealing conceptual features of disability that explain certain prevalent but contradictory legal strategies, in some contexts emphasizing and in others ignoring the "difference" that disability makes in attempts to secure equality.

National Council on Disability. (1997). *Equality of opportunity: The making of the Americans with Disabilities Act.* Washington, DC: Author.
National Council on Disability. (2000). *Promises to keep: A decade of federal enforcement of the Americans with Disabilities Act.* Washington, DC: Author.
National Council on Disability. (2004). *Righting the ADA. Implementation of the Americans with Disabilities Act: Challenges, best practices, and new opportunities for success.* Washington, DC: Author.
These three reports survey the operation of the Americans with Disabilities Act over the years and trace trends in judicial interpretation, the lack of enforcement and attention the act received from various administrations, and the need, seen as early as 2004, for amendments to the act that would make it more useful in securing equality, especially in the areas of employment and access to services. The documents were prepared by the principal federal disability advocacy watchdog of the operation of the act and reveal the sense of frustration and disappointment that many members of the disability community felt about the failed promise of the act.

Samaha, A. (2007). What good is the social model of disability? *University of Chicago Law Review, 74,* 1251–1308.

Samaha discusses the problems for legal theory and practice that a single-minded reliance on the social model of disability has created, and the need for an expanded normative theory of equality.

Stein, M. (2003). The law and economics of disability accommodations. *Duke Law Journal, 53*, 1–114.
Stein provides a comprehensive treatment of the controversial issue of whether workplace accommodations, as mandated by the Americans with Disabilities Act, are economically burdensome to business. After reviewing extensive evidence, the article argues that there is no solid evidence to support this conclusion as a general matter.

Stein, M. (2007). Disability human rights. *California Law Review, 95*, 75–121.
This article rethinks, in light of international human rights, the underlying philosophical foundations of disability human rights, arguing that disability might be better understood, in a legal context, as a universal human experience rather than as an aberration that characterizes a small minority of individuals.

tenBroek, J. (1966). The right to live in the world: The disabled in the law of torts. *California Law Review, 54*, 841–919.
This article is perhaps the first legal discussion of disability human rights and the need for legislation by an early leader in the area.

Waterstone, M. (2003). Constitutional and statutory voting rights for people with disabilities. *Stanford Law and Policy Review, 14*, 353–388.
Waterstone discusses the legal mechanisms that can be used to secure and protect the voting rights of persons with disabilities in the face of environmental and other barriers.

Electronic Resources

Governmental and Non-Governmental Disability Resources

ADA: The Americans with Disabilities Act. Retrieved from http://guides.library.fullerton.edu/disabilities
This clearinghouse for ADA information is maintained by the Pollak Library at California State University at Fullerton.

Cornell University, IRL School, Employment and Disability Institute. Retrieved from http://www.ilr.cornell.edu/edi/p-eprrtc.cfm
This is a national institute on disability and rehabilitation research called the Rehabilitation Research and Training Center on Employment Policy for Persons with Disabilities. It

contains useful links, not only to its own research, but to other documents concerning employment policy and practice.

Disability and Business Technical Assistance Center (DBTAC) Southwest ADA Center. Retrieved from http://www.swdbtac.org/html/publications/dlh/index.html
The center is funded by the National Institute on Disability and Rehabilitation Research of the U.S. Department of Education. It maintains the very helpful Disability Law Handbook.

Disability Rights Education and Defense Fund. Retrieved from http://www.dredf.org
This organization of lawyers founded in 1979, with a stated mission "to advance the civil and human rights of people with disabilities through legal advocacy, training, education and public policy and legislative development," is a valuable resource for up-to-date news on disability law and policy in the United States.

Disability Rights Promotion International (DRPI). Retrieved from http://www.yorku.ca/drpi
This Canadian-based collaborative project links many international sites together with the common aim of establishing a monitoring system to address disability discrimination globally, and to track compliance with the UN Convention on the Rights of Persons with Disabilities.

Disability.Gov. Retrieved from http://www.disability.gov
This is the federal government's primary Web site for comprehensive disability-related information and resources. Most of the links involve practical information about job finding, disability benefits, disability law, scholarships, housing, assistive technology, starting a business, health care, government grants, and so on. In addition, there are countless links to essential information about all aspects of disability law and policy at the federal and state levels.

Equal Employment Opportunities Commission (EEOC). Retrieved from http://www.eeoc.gov/policy/laws.html
The EEOC is the agency responsible for the implementation and enforcement of all employment rights-related federal laws, including anti-discrimination legislation covering disability. The commission also provides regulations and policy guidance.

Harvard Law School Project on Disability (HPOD). Retrieved from http://www.hpod.org
This Web site provides access to all of the work done in the project, focusing on the human rights of people with disabilities worldwide, and specifically the UN Convention on the Rights of Persons with Disabilities, to develop fully equitable societies. HPOD supports the development of disability civil society, informs innovative

*legislative and policy development, and provides legal advice and human rights train-
ing to persons with disabilities, their representative organizations, non-governmental
organizations, national human rights institutions, and governments.*

Independent Living Institute (ILI). Retrieved from http://www.independentliving
.org/indexen.html
*The ILI is a policy development center specializing in consumer-driven policies for
disabled peoples' self-determination, self-respect, and dignity. The site has a virtual
library and interactive services to help people with disabilities design and implement
direct payment schemes for personal assistance services, mainstream taxi, and assistive technology.*

MacArthur Research Network on Mental Health and the Law. Retrieved from
http://www.macarthur.virginia.edu/mentalhome.html
*This is one of the best sources for information about mental health law, including
judicial decisions, legislative initiatives, legal professional standards and guidelines,
and general research. The network has two mandates: "to develop new knowledge
about the relationships between mental health and the law, and to turn that understanding into improved tools and criteria for evaluating individuals and making decisions that affect their lives."*

National Council on Disability. Retrieved from http://www.ncd.gov
*This is an independent federal agency that was created "to promote policies, pro-
grams, practices, and procedures that guarantee equal opportunity for all individuals
with disabilities, and that empower individuals with disabilities to achieve economic
self-sufficiency, independent living, and inclusion and integration into all aspects of
society." The Web site contains useful and up-to-date information about the implementation of disability legislation, including the Americans with Disabilities Act.*

National Network of ADA Centers. Retrieved from http://www.adata.org/
index.html
*The ADA National Network includes 10 regional ADA Centers that provide the most
complete and experienced sources for up-to-date information, referrals, resources, and
training on the ADA to businesses, employers, government entities, and individuals
with disabilities, as well as media outlets and news reporters.*

Syracuse University College of Law International and Comparative Disability
Law Web Resources. Retrieved from http://www.law.syr.edu/lawlibrary/
electronic/humanrights.aspx
*This Web site is organized by international disability laws, regional disability laws,
and individual countries' disability laws, which are subdivided into annotations, primary documents, and links to sites where additional resources may be found.*

United Nations Enable. Retrieved from http://www.un.org/disabilities

This is the official UN Web site for all disability-related matters, maintained by the Secretariat for the Convention on the Rights of Persons with Disabilities, which combines the resources of the UN Department of Economic and Social Affairs and the Office of the High Commissioner for Human Rights. The Web site contains extensive information about the Convention and international and national disability human rights legislation and policy.

Official Resources for Legal Cases, Legislation, and the United Nations Convention

Legal Cases

United States Supreme Court decisions (full-text). Retrieved from http://www
.supremecourt.gov/ or http://supreme.justia.com/index.html

These are Supreme Court decisions that are denoted by "U.S." in their citations—as in Bragdon v. Abbott, 524 U.S. 624 (1998), *where 524 identifies the number of the bound volume, and 624 the page number in that volume. The bound volumes are official and are usually published three to four years after a decision is released. The so-called "slip opinions" are the preliminary, unofficial versions that are posted on this Web site almost immediately after the case has been decided. Both of these Web sites are easy to navigate, with good search engines, and contain a wealth of information about upcoming cases (Docket Oral Arguments), submitted arguments (Merit Briefs), and much other background information. All state court decisions are also available online with the same full-text service. For example, cases from the California Supreme Court can be retrieved from http://www.courtinfo.ca.gov/courts/supreme, New York Supreme Court Appellate Division cases can be retrieved from http:// www.courts.state.ny.us/ad3, and so on.*

Legislation

U.S. federal legislation (laws and regulations) resources. Retrieved from http://
www.usa.gov/Topics/Reference_Shelf/Laws.shtml

This is a vast resource pool of information, including all of the constitutional documents, federal regulations, codes, executive orders, and other historical documents. The Web site also contains all of the legal cases for all of the federal courts, as well as a selection of Supreme Court cases. Many of the specific pieces of federal legislation that involve disability have their own Web sites linked to the department or agency that is responsible for the law's implementation. For example, the ADA's Web site from the Department of Justice can be retrieved from http://www.ada.gov. This site is a source for all "information and technical assistance on the Americans with Disabilities Act." Additional material on the ADA is also found at the Web site of the Equal

Employment Opportunity Commission, which can be retrieved from http://www
.eeoc.gov/laws/statutes/ada.cfm. State legislation (laws and regulations) can be
retrieved from Web sites set up by each state government. For example, all California
laws can be retrieved from http://www.leginfo.ca.gov and New York laws from http://
public.leginfo.state.ny.us

United Nations Convention

United Nations "Enable." Retrieved from http://www.un.org/disabilities
   The United Nations "Enable" Web site provides access to all work on disability
   rights across the United Nations system, including treaties, conventions, and all
   official documents relating to disability. It is regularly updated and provides access
   to a huge body of international literature on disability human rights and the interna-
   tional community.

Glossary of Key Terms

ADA *See* Americans with Disabilities Act of 1990

ADAAA *See* Americans with Disabilities Act Amendments Act of 2008

Alexander v. Choate This 1984 U.S. Supreme Court decision created a legal distinction between reasonable accommodation, which is designed to remove present barriers, and affirmative action, which is designed to compensate for past unfairness.

Americans with Disabilities Act Amendments Act of 2008 (ADAAA) Passed in response to judicial interpretations that narrowed the scope of the ADA, this law reestablished the broad range of impairments that qualify as a disability and confirmed that mitigating measures should not be considered in determining whether a person's impairment qualifies as a disability.

Americans with Disabilities Act of 1990 (ADA) This sweeping civil rights law prohibited discrimination against people with disabilities in employment, public transportation, public accommodations, and telecommunications. Under Title I of this law, individuals are considered to have a disability if they have a "physical or mental impairment that substantially limits one or more major life activities" or are "regarded as having such an impairment."

Anti-Discrimination Strategy An approach to disability policy that views individuals with disabilities as an oppressed minority group that faces discriminatory actions or behaviors and is entitled to compensatory remedies for that discrimination.

Architectural Barriers Act of 1968   This federal law mandated equal physical access to public buildings and established what is now know as the Access Board, which remains the primary source of U.S. accessibility standards.

Assistive Technology (AT)   A term used to describe a variety of devices used to increase the independence and community participation of people with disabilities by aiding them with seating and mobility, communication, access, environmental control, or activities of daily living.

Assistive Technology Act Project (ATAP)   Established under the Assistive Technology for Individuals with Disabilities Act, this program provides funding to states for the research and development, marketing, distribution, and technical support of AT equipment to persons with disabilities.

AT   *See* Assistive Technology

ATAP   *See* Assistive Technology Act Project

"Baby Doe" Cases   A series of legal cases brought in the early 1980s on behalf of newborns with serious impairments whose parents and physicians refused to treat them.

Baremas System   A method for assessing an individual's work capacity that assigns percentage values to various parts of the body to determine the extent of disability.

Belmont Report   Formally titled *Ethical Principles and Guidelines for the Protection of Human Subjects of Research*, this 1978 report by the U.S. Department of Health, Education, and Welfare listed three ethical principles to govern research on human subjects: respect for persons and their autonomy, beneficence, and justice.

Bioethics   Also known as health care ethics, this field of study deals with life and death issues involving basic values like autonomy, dignity, and respect for persons; it informs the analysis of moral issues that involve the concept of disability, as well as the lives, rights, and interests of persons with disabilities.

Bouvia v. Superior Court of State of California   In this 1986 right-to-die case, the California Court of Appeals ruled that a mentally competent woman with quadriplegia had the right to end her life by refusing to take nourishment; the court found that the value of an individual's self-determination outweighed the state's legitimate interest in preserving life.

Bowen v. American Hospital Association   In this 1986 ruling, the U.S. Supreme Court rejected the argument that withholding lifesaving medical care from "handicapped infants" qualified as discrimination under Section 504 of the Rehabilitation Act of 1973.

Bragdon v. Abbott   In this 1998 case, the U.S. Supreme Court ruled that a woman who had been denied dental services because she was asymptomatic HIV-positive had been discriminated against.

Buck v. Bell   This 1927 U.S. Supreme Court decision declared forced sterilization of the "feebleminded" to be constitutional and affirmed the right of states to sterilize citizens with disabilities against their will.

Capability Theory   A broad theory of human good developed by Nobel Prize–winning economist Amartya Sen, and applied to disability by philosopher Martha Nussbaum and others, in which disability is analyzed in terms of limitations on an individual's freedom to achieve his or her life goals.

Civil Rights Act of 1964   This landmark legislation outlawed discrimination in public accommodation and facilities on grounds of race, religion, gender, or ethnicity, and banned discrimination on these grounds by any government agencies that received federal funding.

Civil Rights Act of 1968   Also known as the Fair Housing Act, this bill prohibited discrimination in the sale, rental, or financing of housing on the basis of race, religion, or national origin; it was later expanded to cover disability.

Civil Rights Approach   An approach to disability policy and law that views persons with disabilities as members of a minority group who are entitled to equal citizenship.

CLASS   *See* Community Living Assistance Services and Supports

Community Living Assistance Services and Supports (CLASS)   Established under the Patient Protection and Affordable Care Act, this voluntary national long-term care insurance program provides individuals with a cash benefit if they have functional limitations or disability.

Convention on the Rights of Persons with Disabilities (CRPD)   Adopted by the United Nations General Assembly in 2006, this international human rights treaty asserts that persons with disabilities have the same human rights as everyone else in all areas of life and, in particular, that they have the right to be active and fully participating members of society and to be full and equal persons in the eyes of the law.

CRPD   *See* Convention on the Rights of Persons with Disabilities

Dilemma of Difference   A dilemma facing individuals and groups advocating for the rights of a minority or oppressed social group, such as persons with disabilities, in which the advocates feel pressure to de-emphasize features of the group that mark them as different in an effort to gain acceptance and equality, while at the same time seeing the need to highlight these same differences while seeking accommodations and accessibility in order to gain equality.

Disability   A highly contested term that might best be analyzed in terms of the complex interaction between physical and mental impairments that are intrinsic features of a person's body and mind and that restrict mobility, vision, communication, or other body functions, and the physical, human-built, social and attitudinal environment. The environment may facilitate the performance of activities and social roles, in the form of assistive devices or accommodations, or may worsen the performance of activities and social roles, by acting as barriers.

Education for All Handicapped Children Act of 1975   This was the first federal law ensuring educational opportunity for children with special needs. It contained six mandated rights for qualifying students with disabilities, including the prohibition on excluding a child because of disabilities, shared decision making with parents, non-discriminatory testing and classification, and individualized educational programming in the least restrictive environment.

EEOC   *See* Equal Employment Opportunity Commission

English Poor Law of 1601   The first clear example of a law about disability in the English-speaking world, this legislation created three categories of the poor: those who could not work and were provided for in almshouses, the able-bodied poor who were sent to work in workhouses, and the idle poor (and vagrants) who were sent to houses of correction.

Equal Employment Opportunity Commission (EEOC)   This U.S. federal government agency is responsible for enforcing and interpreting several pieces of anti-discrimination legislation in the employment sector, including the Americans with Disabilities Act.

Ethics   A branch of philosophy concerned with the systemic and analytic treatment of moral issues.

Fair Housing Amendments Act of 1988   Legislation that provided individuals with disabilities with protection against discrimination in housing, the right to make reasonable modifications to rental housing, and the right to accommodations in housing rules, policies, and practices.

Federal Security Agency (FSA)   A U.S. government agency that administered Social Security, public health programs, and federal education funding from 1939 to 1953, when it was abolished and most of its responsibilities transferred to the Department of Health, Education, and Welfare.

FSA   *See* Federal Security Agency

Functioning   The normal physiological action or activity of a body part, organ, or system during human activity and involvement in life situations.

HCBS   *See* Home and Community-Based Services

Home and Community-Based Services (HCBS)   A consumer-directed Medicaid program that offers people with disabilities such services as home modification, case management, pre-vocational and educational habilitation, and supported employment in order to help them avoid institutionalization.

Human Rights Approach   This approach to disability law and policy, which is reflected in the 2006 United Nations Convention on the Rights of

Persons with Disabilities, creates governmental accountabilities, not merely to protect specific rights, but also to support all areas of policy that need to be taken into account to successfully implement these rights.

ICF *See* International Classification of Functioning, Disability, and Health

IDEA *See* Individuals with Disabilities Education Act of 1990

IL *See* Independent Living Movement

Impairment A biomedical, underlying functional condition, intrinsic to the person, that constitutes the health component of disability; impairments may be sensory (difficulty in hearing or visual impairment), physical (difficulties in moving or standing up), or psychological (difficulty in coping with stress, depression, or memory loss).

Independent Living Movement (IL) A worldwide initiative undertaken by people with disabilities to promote self-determination, de-institutionalization, and equal opportunity.

Individuals with Disabilities Education Act of 1990 (IDEA) This legislation required states to provide children with disabilities with a free and appropriate public education designed to meet each child's specific needs; it also established the definition of disability used in special education law.

International Classification of Functioning, Disability, and Health (ICF) Released in 2001 by the World Health Organization (WHO), this international classification system is built on a conceptual model of functioning and disability that integrates the medical and social models so as to view functioning and disability as outcomes of the interactions between health conditions and environmental and personal factors.

Intersectionality The recognition that people with disabilities hold multiple social identities (i.e., there are people who are both disabled and women, disabled and elderly, and so on), and that these potentially influential group affiliations pose a challenge for disability policy and law.

Listings of Impairments   Detailed guidelines published by the Social Security Administration for the medical step in the process of determining eligibility for benefits. The categories are defined by medical signs, symptoms, and laboratory findings that describe the level of severity required for each impairment to meet the administrative threshold for "work disability."

Medical Model of Disability   A conceptual model that focuses on diseases, injuries, and conditions that impair the physiological or cognitive functioning of an individual; it defines disability as a condition or deficit that resides within the individual and can be cured or ameliorated, or its progression stopped, through a particular treatment or intervention.

Minority Group Approach   An approach to disability policy and law based on the principle that people with disabilities neither need nor want charity, pity, or government handouts, but only require the impact of ignorance, stigma, and discrimination to be removed in order to be self-sufficient and independent.

Model of Disability   A general theory or conceptual model that embodies a fundamental perspective of what disability is and, therefore, generates one or more operational definitions of disability.

Morality   Ethical beliefs and customs of particular cultures that can be empirically discovered.

NCLB   *See* No Child Left Behind Act of 2001

No Child Left Behind Act of 2001 (NCLB)   Sweeping education legislation that established accountability measures, academic standards, and high-stakes testing designed to ensure that all students gain the skills needed to succeed in college and the workforce. Under NCLB, schools are required to report to the state educational authority (SEA) and demonstrate adequate yearly progress (AYP) toward a goal of 100% proficiency of all tested students by 2014.

Olmstead v. L. C.   In this 1999 case, the U.S. Supreme Court upheld the provision in the Americans with Disabilities Act that required states, where appropriate, to place individuals with mental health problems in community facilities rather than isolating institutions.

Oregon Death with Dignity Act of 1997   A state law allowing mentally competent, terminally ill patients to request permission to self-administer lethal medications that were legally prescribed by a physician.

PAS   *See* Personal Assistance Services

Patient Protection and Affordable Care Act of 2010 (PPACA)   Sweeping health care reform legislation that required that all Americans have health insurance; barred health insurance companies from discriminating based on pre-existing medical conditions, health status, or gender; prohibited lifetime limits on coverage; prohibited rescission (dropping) of customers by insurers; created insurance exchanges; required employers with 50 workers or more to offer health insurance benefits or pay a fee; expanded Medicaid and provided premium assistance; and created temporary insurance pools for consumers with pre-existing conditions until insurance exchanges open in 2014.

Pennsylvania Association for Retarded Children (PARC) v. Commonwealth of Pennsylvania   The consent decree in this 1972 case affirmed that all children with intellectual disabilities are entitled to a free and appropriate public education and that educating students with disabilities in a general education classroom is preferable to doing so in a segregated setting.

Persistent Vegetative State (PVS)   A condition in which a person who has experienced a severe brain injury loses perception and cognition but may retain certain autonomic or involuntary, spontaneous physical behaviors such as breathing, blinking, and smiling.

Personal Assistance Services (PAS)   A method of providing long-term care for people with disabilities within the home or community, rather than in an institution, by offering such services as home health care and assistance with personal care, activities of daily living, and housekeeping chores.

Policy   All of the actions (and inactions) of the state addressed to governance, regulation, and organization for the public good, including the creation and implementation of laws, regulations, entitlements and prohibitions, income generation programs, and taxation strategies and spending priorities.

Policy Analysis   A process for determining the effectiveness of state actions that involves interpreting and clarifying policy goals, exploring the relationship or connection between these goals and proposed objectives, evaluating the effectiveness of policy mechanisms, describing the policy tools involved, and monitoring the outcomes.

PPACA   *See* Patient Protection and Affordable Care Act of 2010

PVS   *See* Persistent Vegetative State

Rehabilitation Act of 1973   This law prohibited discrimination on the basis of disability in federal agencies, programs, and employment, as well as in state and private programs that receive federal funding.

Section 504   A provision of the Rehabilitation Act of 1973 that stated that no qualified individuals with disabilities can be excluded from, denied the benefits of, or subjected to discrimination under any programs receiving federal financial assistance. Section 504 required that school districts provide a free and appropriate public education to qualified students in their jurisdictions who have a physical or mental impairment that substantially limits one or more major life activities.

Sheltered Employment   A form of employment in which individuals with disabilities are effectively removed from the general labor force and put into "protective environments" where the demands of competitive employment are minimized; such programs have long been criticized as warehousing solutions that are disrespectful to participants and provide them with no vocational training or prospect for entering the general labor force.

Smith-Hughes Act of 1917   This law provided vocational education for disabled veterans of the World War I.

Smith-Sears Act of 1918   This law promoted vocational rehabilitation and return to employment of disabled individuals discharged from the armed forces.

Social Ethics   A branch of ethics devoted to issues involved in social organization and relationships between people in communities.

Social Model of Disability   A conceptual model that focuses on the social barriers individuals with impairments face in their environment that create disadvantages or disabilities; disability, in this model, is a disadvantage caused exclusively by forces outside the individual, such as social exclusion, stigma, stereotyping and negative attitudes, and practices and policy that act as barriers to the full participation of persons with impairments.

Social Security Act of 1935   This landmark social welfare legislation created a system of old-age benefits, unemployment compensation, aid to "dependent and crippled children" and blind persons, and insurance to promote maternal and child welfare and public health.

Social Security Disability Insurance (SSDI)   A federal government program that provides wage replacement income for individuals who have worked and paid Social Security taxes and become disabled according to Social Security criteria; its benefits are paid to disabled workers, their widows, widowers, and children, and eligible adults disabled since childhood.

Southeastern Community College v. Davis   In this 1979 decision, which was considered a setback for disability rights, the U.S. Supreme Court held that the school's refusal to accommodate a hearing-impaired student did not constitute discrimination under Section 504 of the Rehabilitation Act of 1973.

SSDI   *See* Social Security Disability Insurance

SSI   *See* Supplemental Security Income

Supplemental Security Income (SSI)   A federal government income supplement program that is designed to help low-income people who are elderly, blind, or disabled meet their basic needs for food, clothing, and shelter.

Supported Employment   A form of employment in which individuals with disabilities are fully integrated within a competitive work environment, with supports of various sorts (i.e., a job coach, specialized training, transportation, or assistive technology) funded by state placement agencies.

Sutton v. United Air Lines   In this 1999 case, the U.S. Supreme Court dramatically restricted the class of persons who could bring complaints for employment discrimination under the Americans with Disabilities Act by ruling that the law did not apply to those whose impairments could be mitigated by corrective measures.

Targeted Policy   A policy that focuses on the needs and objectives of a defined sub-population, and is often created in response to historical inequalities of treatment or abuse.

Ticket to Work and Work Incentives Improvement Act of 1999 (TWWIIA)
A federal government program intended to help create avenues to employment for people with disabilities by providing SSI and SSDI beneficiaries with resources to purchase vocational rehabilitation, employment preparation, and other support services; it also allowed people with disabilities to maintain Medicare eligibility for four additional years.

Toyota Motor Manufacturing, Kentucky, Inc. v. Williams   In this 2002 ruling, the U.S. Supreme Court restricted the applicability of the Americans with Disabilities Act's anti-discrimination protections in the employment sector by narrowing the definition of a "major life activity" to include only those activities of "central importance" to most people's daily lives.

TWWIIA   See Ticket to Work and Work Incentives Improvement Act of 1999

Universal Policy   A policy designed to fulfill objectives fairly and equally for everyone, rather than only for certain sub-populations.

Vocational Rehabilitation Act Amendments of 1954   This legislation allocated more funds for state vocational rehabilitation programs and provided grants for special demonstration projects, research, and training to showcase rehabilitation as the primary response to the needs of America's disabled population.

Vocational Rehabilitation Act of 1920   This legislation extended the coverage of the Smith-Sears Act of 1918, which had been designed to provide vocational rehabilitation and return to employment of disabled individuals discharged from the armed forces.

Vocational Rehabilitation Act of 1943   This legislation initiated a new approach to rehabilitation by expanding coverage to include rehabilitation for people with mental illness and intellectual impairments and by providing funding to support research to reduce, prevent, and eliminate disabilities.

Voting Rights Act of 1965   This landmark civil rights legislation guaranteed equal access to political participation by outlawing various discriminatory state voting requirements.

Wyatt v. Stickney   This 1971 federal court ruling established minimum standards for appropriate treatment of persons with disabilities in institutional settings, including the right to receive treatment designed to improve their condition, and the right to education.

Index